Introductory Mathematical Methods in Economics

Second edition

Introductory Mathematical Methods in Economics

Second edition

Mik Wisniewski

Director
Management Development Unit
University of Stirling

McGRAW-HILL BOOK COMPANY

London · New York · St Louis · San Francisco · Auckland · Bogotá · Caracas · Lisbon
Madrid · Mexico · Milan · Montreal · New Delhi · Panama · Paris · San Juan
São Paulo · Singapore · Sydney · Tokyo · Toronto

Published by

McGRAW-HILL Book Company Europe

Shoppenhangers Road, Maidenhead, Berkshire SL6 2QL, England
Telephone 01628 23432
Fax 01628 770224

British Library Cataloguing in publication data
Wisniewski, Mik
  Introductory Mathematical Methods in
  Economics. – 2Rev.ed
  I. Title
  330.0151

  ISBN 0-07-709109-4

Library of Congress Cataloging-in-Publication Data
Wisniewski, Mik.
  Introductory mathematical methods in economics / Mik Wisniewski.
  – 2nd ed.
      p.   cm.
  Includes bibliographical references and index.
  ISBN 0-07-709109-4 (pbk. : alk. paper)
  1. Economics, Mathematical.   I. Title.
HB135.W57   1996
330′.01′51–dc20   95-50710
                                                                    CIP

McGraw-Hill

A Division of The McGraw·Hill Companies

    3 4 5 CUP 2 1 0 9

Typeset by Keyword Typesetting Services Ltd
and printed and bound in Great Britain at the University Press, Cambridge
Printed on permanent paper in compliance with ISO Standard 9706.

*Dedicated to
my parents
whose sacrifices made
many things possible*

Contents

1 Introduction

We begin this text with a definitive statement: in order to develop a comprehensive understanding of both economic theory and economic analysis it is necessary to have a detailed understanding of key mathematical principles and of the role that mathematics can play in the study of economics. A good many students of economics will have opened this text not quite sure what to expect but, for the most part, with a degree of trepidation and concern. As part of your study of economics you may well have been dismayed to realize that it is necessary to undertake a formal course in mathematical economics (often disguised under the name of applied economics, quantitative economics or the like) and that the use of mathematics is more widespread than you realized. It may also be the case that the prospect of having to recollect and use key mathematical principles and skills from some dim and distant part of your previous education is not one that fills you with undue enthusiasm. Mathematics in general has a particularly poor reputation with many students (a reputation often well deserved).

However, it is an inescapable feature of the serious study of modern economics that a student needs to be familiar with mathematical methods and has to develop the skills necessary to apply such methods to the economic models that they will gradually build and explore. However, it is important to stress from the very beginning that this text is *not* a text on mathematical economics *per se* but rather on the *use* of mathematics in economics. You may be forgiven at this stage in your studies for wondering what the difference is and whether it really matters. We are primarily concerned in this text with:

- Examining the typical and widespread uses of mathematics in the study of economics
- Developing your own skills in using such mathematics
- Improving the level of your own numerical confidence
- Developing your awareness of the widespread and typical uses of mathematics in economics.

By the end of the text you should be in a position to recognize that mathematics need not be viewed as a discipline separate from economics but rather one that can be used as a tool to help develop economic models and economic theory. We stress at this stage, however, that the purpose of this text is not to turn you into a mathematician but rather to allow you to develop the mathematical skills and knowledge that you will inevitably require as an economist.

1.1 Who the text is for

This text is written specifically for the student who has a serious commitment to studying economics at something more than the introductory level but whose knowledge and understanding of mathematics is somewhat limited at present. Such a student will typically recognize the need to develop such skills if they are to pursue a successful career in economics (or at least realize the need for such skills if they are to pass their exams!). This text will gradually introduce the student to a range of mathematical concepts and techniques used in economics and will focus upon understanding both the mathematics of the technique and its applicability to the study of economics. At the same time the text will also prove useful to the student who already has a set of reasonable mathematical skills but who wishes to develop an understanding of the ways in which these skills can be applied to different areas of economics. Naturally, the way in which the two groups approach and use this text will differ, but both will find the text a useful part of their learning.

1.2 The structure of the text

The structure of this text is a simple one. We begin by introducing some of the elementary but essential mathematical concepts and skills that immediately allow us to consider specific applications of mathematics in economics. Students with adequate mathematical skills will be able to move through this material quickly and concentrate on the economic application of these techniques. Those whose grasp of such concepts is limited to begin with will naturally have to move at a more suitable pace to ensure that they develop an adequate understanding of this material before proceeding. However, these introductory chapters all follow a structure that is repeated for the rest of the text and is worth examining in more detail. In each section of the text we begin by outlining the reasons why we need to develop a particular mathematical concept or technique. We shall illustrate our need for such skills with reference to specific examples from the study of economics. Thus, it is hoped, you will appreciate from the very beginning why we are examining a specific technique as *economists* and *not* as mathematicians. We shall then consider in detail the key principles underpinning each mathematical topic—again using a number of illustrative examples from economics—and at a pace to which students can adapt their own level of understanding. Naturally, this pace may be relatively leisurely at the beginning but will quickly gather speed as we progress and develop a cumulative set of skills and knowledge. Finally, we shall return to consider the application of the mathematical techniques we have developed in the context of economics. A number of examples will be drawn from different areas of economics to illustrate the extensive potential application.

Throughout the text we shall use detailed examples and, wherever relevant, graphical development of key concepts. In addition, two further features are of note. The first of these relates to the *student activities* highlighted throughout each chapter. As you will soon begin to appreciate, the development of suitable mathematical skills for economics students is a cumulative process; that is, the skills developed in the early chapters will be assumed in later chapters as we introduce more complex topics. It is essential, therefore, that before you leave a specific chapter you really do understand what has been covered and that you are able to apply the mathematical skills and appreciate the mathematical concepts that have been introduced. We appreciate that it is often tempting to skip over some topic which is proving particularly difficult and obtuse. The student rationalizes this by saying 'I can't understand this at the moment but I'll come back to it later on when I have the time (and patience), and when the exam is closer!'

All too often, however, this return does not take place and students find themselves at a later date in the position of being unable to understand a topic that builds upon the one that was omitted. To try to encourage you to make sure you do understand the material as it progresses, student-based activities appear throughout each chapter. The intention is that each such activity tests your understanding/skills of the material presented thus far. You are strongly encouraged to stop at that point and to complete the activity before proceeding. Solutions to these activities appear either immediately after the activity or in Appendix 1.

The second feature worth noting relates to the exercises at the end of each chapter. These are more detailed and thorough tests of your skills, knowledge and abilities and as such serve a number of purposes. They introduce larger-scale problems than we might have examined in the chapter itself. Naturally, such exercises will also help to reinforce the key points covered in the chapter and encourage you to develop your skills in both mathematical analysis and calculation and in terms of mathematical logic. One final function of the exercises is that they will frequently raise questions and issues that we will address in subsequent chapters, hence encouraging you to consider and evaluate critically what we have covered thus far. For these reasons you are strongly encouraged to undertake as many of these exercises as possible before proceeding to the next chapter. Failure to do so may mean that you are unable to follow the discussions that follow in subsequent chapters.

A last point relates to the use of supporting computer software. If you have been introduced to computing facilities as part of your studies you may well find it useful to support your progress through this text with the use of relevant computer software. Spreadsheets such as Lotus, Excel or SuperCalc, for example, offer a ready method of performing tedious calculations and of generating detailed and high-quality graphics in support of these calculations. If you can, you should begin to use such software as soon as possible (which you will be able to do when we start Chapter 2). If you are unable to access such packages you will not be severely disadvantaged but you must be prepared to spend time on some of the more routine manual calculations, particularly in the early stages of the text.

1.3 The contents of the text

The text begins by reviewing some of the key mathematical principles that we can immediately put to use in the study of economics and which we shall rapidly build upon as we progress. We begin by introducing the general concept of a function and examine its use in economics. We move on quickly to examine how both equations and graphs can provide a precise description of some functional relationships. We examine in detail the principles of linear functions since these are particularly common in economic models (especially at an introductory level). Through such linear functions we examine the mathematical principles underpinning the economic concept of equilibrium. We then move on to the area of matrix algebra. Given that economic models are frequently concerned with large sets of equations we clearly need some straightforward method of dealing with and manipulating such equation systems. Matrix algebra provides this. We then consider the important concept of optimization in economics and examine a number of approaches to the subject. This leads on to an examination of calculus as a general method for dealing with non-linear economic relationships. We examine principles of unconstrained and constrained optimization and the use of integral calculus in economics. Finally, we turn to an examination of dynamic economic models, introducing techniques involving difference equations.

1.4 The need for mathematics in economics

It will probably be apparent to you, even at such an early stage in your economics career, that both to understand many of the more complex (and hence interesting and useful) economics topics and to pursue an active career as an economist it is increasingly necessary to have fundamental mathematical skills. (If you are not convinced of this by now you should peruse any of the leading economic journals available in your college library.) We have already indicated that this is not a text in mathematical economics *per se*. A consideration of what mathematics and economics have in common will go some way to illustrating the need for an adequate grasp of mathematics in the study of economics. There are a number of reasons why the use of mathematics in economics has steadily increased over the years. Probably the most relevant cause of such a growth is the fact that mathematics is a useful tool in the study of economics. It has to be admitted that it is possible to undertake economic analysis and debate without much, if any, use of mathematics. However, appropriate use of mathematical notation and solution methods can make life much easier.

Consider the following. We might hypothesize that the quantity demanded of some product will depend on a variety of factors: the price charged for the product, the price of products that are direct substitutes, the price of products for which the product under examination is a complementary good, the level of consumer income and so on. However, a much more elegant, concise and unambiguous way of summarizing such a relationship is readily provided through simple mathematical notation:

$$Q_x = \alpha + \beta_1 P_x + \beta_2 P_s + \beta_3 P_c + \beta_4 Y \tag{1.1}$$

where

$$Q_x = \text{quantity of product X demanded}$$
$$P_x = \text{price of product X}$$
$$P_s = \text{price of substitute goods}$$
$$P_c = \text{price of complementary goods}$$
$$Y = \text{level of consumer income}$$

and the symbols α, β_1, β_2, β_3, β_4 represent the parameters of the equations (frequently the specific numerical values that are appropriate to this particular economic relationship). Although, depending on your existing level of mathematical skills, it may not be obvious at the moment such a mathematical presentation does offer a number of considerable advantages to the economic analyst. First of all, the use of mathematical notation to define and describe such economic relationships provides a definitive and unambiguous statement of the relationship—at least to those who understand the mathematical symbolism used. A purely verbal exposition of some economic relationships is far more prone to misinterpretation and confusion than a mathematical one. It is for this reason that relationships such as this are usually expressed in mathematical terms. However, not only can we use mathematics to describe such a relationship but we can also apply mathematical reasoning and logic. Mathematics is a particularly powerful tool in enabling us to make logical deductions about economic behaviour patterns based on some set of limiting assumptions. In the above example an economist with the appropriate mathematical understanding can readily deduce the effect of, say, a change in consumer income on the quantity demanded of the product under the critical assumption that the other factors in the equation remain unchanged (this is the common *ceteris paribus* assumption used throughout economics). As we shall see, such deductions are frequently only possible through the use of relevant mathematics.

An important point to note at this stage, and one that is reflected in much of the material covered in the text, is that the above relationship expressed mathematically contains no numbers. This is a common misunderstanding of the role of mathematics in economics. Of course, there are frequent occasions when we wish to use specific numerical values in such an equation.

A business organization, for example, would wish to derive precise predictions of quantity demanded given specific values for the other variables in the equation. From the viewpoint of studying economic principles and theory, however, such number values are frequently irrelevant. We are generally concerned with establishing key principles of economic behaviour—independently of whatever numbers happen to be appropriate. We might wish to deduce, for example, the general principles of consumer behaviour if income changes. We are not specifically interested in exact numerical values for income and the levels of demand. Accordingly, in the text we shall frequently be using general mathematical notation to establish general deductions of behaviour. Of course, we shall also be illustrating such important deductions with specific numerical values although these are generally used primarily as an aid to understanding.

1.5 Economic theory, economic models and mathematics

This leads us to another important area: the link between economic theory, economic models and mathematics. Much discussion and debate has taken place on the process of developing economic theory and economic models and model building. It is not our intention to enter this debate as the interested reader will find appropriate references in the bibliography in the Postscript. Rather, it will be useful as we progress through the text for the reader to have a reasonable understanding of the role of economic theory, its relation to economic models and the use of both mathematics and econometrics in the process linking theory to model building. Typically in economics we begin by observing some economic phenomena. Let us remain with the illustrative example we used earlier. We might observe that a particular quantity of some product is purchased. The economist will ask the question, 'Why?' Why was this product purchased and why this quantity of the product? Typically we will then try to develop some theoretical explanation of this observed economic behaviour (which is what we provided in the earlier equation). Such a theoretical explanation will generally involve the construction of an economic model (again as we have provided in Eq. (1.1)). There is, in principle, no overpowering reason why such a model has to be mathematical or why the underpinning theory needs to be expressed in mathematical terms (and indeed much early economic thinking did not make use of mathematics as such). However, as we have seen, there are factors that may strongly encourage us to make use of mathematics in the model-building process. In addition, if the model is mathematical, then it will involve an equation (or equations) linking certain economic variables together. Typically, we will then wish to examine the model in a mathematical manner. This will involve:

- Specifying the assumptions on which the model is built
- Based on these assumptions examining the logical deductions to be derived from the model
- Reaching conclusions about predicted economic behaviour
- Comparing our conclusions with actual economic behaviour.

Naturally such a process is not usually as simple as at first appears. The whole process, in fact, will be iterative: we specify key assumptions, make deductions, reach conclusions and then may find the conclusions derived from the model are inconsistent with observed economic behaviour. We then have to return to the model for further development and refinement until we are satisfied that the model provides a reasonable explanation of the observed economic phenomenon (or until we abandon this model because of its repeated failure to provide such an explanation). Mathematics in economics, therefore, is primarily concerned with the application of mathematical principles and logic to the theoretical aspects of economic analysis. Frequently, the next stage is a rigorous empirical investigation of the theory that has been developed thus far. At this stage, econometrics comes into play. Econometrics is primarily concerned with the measurement of economic data and economic relationships. Using both mathematics and the principles of statistical inference, econometrics seeks empirically to evaluate some theoretical economic model. In this text we are not concerned with econometrics nor indeed with empirical evaluation of economic models as such, although we do need to be aware of its critical role in the process of economic analysis. Figure 1.1 illustrates the process.

We must remember, however, that any economic model—whether mathematical or not—is a simplified representation of a far more complex real-world situation. The purpose of models in this context is to reduce these real-world complexities to a level that can be understood and analysed. By definition, a model restricts its attention to what are seen to be the key features of the situation under investigation. Thus, in the context of our earlier example, there will be numerous factors influencing the quantity of some good that is purchased. An economic model will, however, focus on only a few of these factors—naturally, the ones thought to be most important in the context of the analysis.

1.6 Summary

We are now in a position to begin our investigation into the uses of mathematics in the study of economics. By now you should appreciate what we intend doing through the text and, equally important, *why* we are doing it. Mathematics plays a critical role in providing economists with

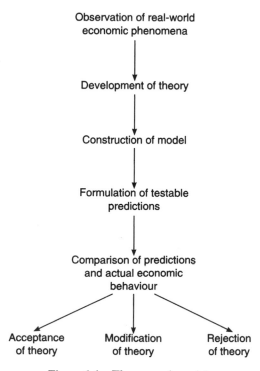

Figure 1.1 Theory and models

the logical and analytical tools needed to develop and investigate economic theories which are at the heart of economics and the study of economic behaviour. Without an adequate understanding of mathematics and its role in economics your career in this subject area will be severely curtailed. You are strongly encouraged to persevere with the material that the text introduces even if, as is likely, you may find certain aspects difficult at first reading. By the time you reach the end of this text your knowledge and appreciation of the usefulness of mathematics to the economist will have undergone a fundamental change.

Exercises

1.1 Return to the equation that we introduced earlier (Eq. (1.1)), where we linked the quantity demanded of some product to a series of other variables. Taking each of the parameters in turn consider whether each would be expected to take a positive or a negative value. Justify your choice in terms of economic logic.

1.2 How do you think such numerical values could be obtained in practice?

1.3 Consider the other side of the picture: the quantity of the good supplied by the individual firm. What variables do you think we would wish to link with the quantity supplied? What numerical values do you think each of these would take?

1.4 Consider a variable, C, which represents the annual expenditure (consumption) of an individual. Derive a set of variables that you think would influence consumption and assess whether you would expect each variable to have a positive or a negative influence.

1.5 Consider an individual's consumption of a particular good—coffee. Deduce a set of variables that you feel would influence such consumption and develop a simple model for determining such consumption. Consider the assumptions you are making—explicitly and implicitly—in your model.

1.6 In the context of Exercise 1.5 consider the annual national import of coffee. What variables do you think would influence imports of this good? How does your list of variables compare with that of Exercise 1.5 and how do you explain the differences?

2 Economic relationships and mathematics

In this chapter we begin our formal investigation into how mathematics helps our understanding of economics by introducing the relevant terminology that we shall require from now on and then introducing a number of key mathematical concepts. We shall be examining the idea of economic relationships, which can be expressed—and understood—in mathematical terms. We shall introduce equations as a means of mathematically describing some relationships and we shall see how a suitable graph can be derived from the relevant equation. As we progress we shall also ensure that you have the necessary mathematical skills for further study of the topics we shall be introducing throughout the text.

Learning objectives

By the time you have completed this chapter you should be able to:

- Construct and use graphs
- Understand what is meant by a function
- Use functional notation
- Use linear functions
- Construct and use common non-linear functions
- Understand functions involving more than one independent variable

2.1 Economic relationships

As we began to see in the previous chapter, economics—in terms of theory, models and analysis—is frequently concerned with the relationship that exists—or is thought to exist—between sets of variables. Examples of such relationships are widespread: the price of a product and the quantity sold, the price of a product and the quantity produced, personal income and spending, imports and the exchange rate, production levels and costs and so on. Typically we may wish to examine such relationships in three—related—ways:

- Through a graph
- Through a function
- Through an equation.

As we shall see, these are effectively alternative ways of looking at the same relationship, but we need to be proficient at each of them. We should also note that we may not use all three approaches every time. We may simply examine a graphical representation, we may introduce some mathematical function or we may investigate an equation.

Let us consider Table 2.1. We can imagine that a firm has carefully monitored the demand for its product by consumers over the last 4 months. On the one hand, we have the price charged per unit (which we can see has altered over this period). On the other, we also have the quantity demanded (which has also varied). Clearly our interest, given our current knowledge of economics, would be to examine the relationship between these two economic variables—that is, to see how the two variables have reacted to each other over this period. From the table it is difficult to draw detailed conclusions although we do see that quantity demanded has fallen steadily over time while the price charged has steadily risen.

The first task is to simplify the relationship by using simplifying symbols for each of the variables. We shall denote price as P and quantity demanded as Q. The second step is to identify what we refer to as the *dependent* variable and the *independent* variable. Logically, from our understanding of economics we would specify P as the independent variable and Q as the dependent variable. Effectively we are indicating that Q depends on P; that is, the quantity demanded of a product will depend on the price charged per unit. As a first step we may now wish to show this relationship visually in the form of a graph.

2.2 Graphical representation of economic relationships

There are a number of reasons why we often want to show some economic relationship in the form of a diagram—as a graph. Graphs provide a quick and easy way of showing some economic situation under analysis. We can readily see the principal features of some economic relationship when it is shown in the form of a graph and, more importantly, it is usually quite easy to assess what effect a specific change in the economic relationship might have. We shall illustrate the ideas behind a graph with the data in Table 2.1 first. Later we shall see how graphs are drawn from equations.

Consider Fig. 2.1 which shows two straight lines known as the *axes* (pronounced *ax ees*) of the graph. The horizontal line is conventionally referred to as the x axis and is used to show the independent variable while the vertical line is known as the y axis and shows the dependent variable. The point where the two axes meet is usually referred to as the *origin* and at this point both variables take a zero value. On the x axis as we move from the origin to the right the independent variable takes increasingly higher, positive values. The same happens for the dependent variable as we move upwards from the origin along the y axis. The two axes—and the numerical scales that we will shortly impose on them—allow us to locate any specific point on the graph.

Consider Fig. 2.2. This shows a point C which takes some numerical value of a for the x variable and a value of b for the y variable. These numerical values for point C enable us to plot the point in terms of its *coordinates* and we would actually denote point C as C(a, b) where the

TABLE 2.1 Prices and quantities over a 4-month period

	Month 1	Month 2	Month 3	Month 4
Price per unit (£)	5	7	9	10
Quantity demanded (daily average 000s)	75	65	55	50

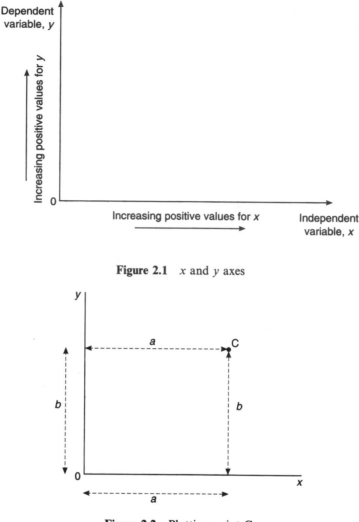

Figure 2.1 x and y axes

Figure 2.2 Plotting point C

first coordinate a shows the numerical value on the x axis and the second coordinate b shows the numerical value on the y axis.

> ***Student activity 2.1***
> Return to Table 2.1 showing prices and quantities.
>
> (i) Which variable would we show on the x axis and which on the y axis?
> (ii) For the four combinations of price and quantity shown in the table, write each point using the coordinate notation.

In the case of Table 2.1 we have already indicated that Q_d is the dependent variable so this would be shown on the y axis while the independent variable, P, would be shown on the x axis. The four points would then be:

M_1 (5,75)
M_2 (7,65)
M_3 (9,55)
M_4 (10,50)

To locate these four points on the graph we clearly need appropriate numerical scales for both the x and y axes. In the case of the x axis (P) a scale from zero (the origin) to 10 seems sensible while for y (Q_d) a scale from 0 to 75 is required (although we might round the 75 to 80 to make calculations slightly easier).

The numerical scales would then be drawn as shown in Fig. 2.3 where the four points are also plotted. It will be evident on careful inspection of Fig. 2.3 that these four points appear to fall on a straight line: that is, we could join these points together with a straight line as shown in Fig. 2.4. Note that we can extend the line joining the four points if we wish. The line has been extended both on the right (beyond $P = 10$) and to the left (below $P = 5$). To do so is an example of *extrapolation*—suggesting a pattern of economic behaviour that goes beyond that which we have observed directly. In this case we have observed consumer behaviour between a price of £5 per unit and of £10 per unit. We have not directly observed consumer behaviour at prices outside this range. We might hypothesize, however, that consumer behaviour would continue to be as it has been in the price range £5 to £10. Conversely, deducing a combination of P and Q_d which occurs within the range of previously observed behaviour is known as *interpolation*. Note that the line we have drawn now shows us all the P, Q combinations between $P = 2$ and $P = 14$. The graph can now be used to deduce P, Q_d combinations even if they have not been directly observed.

> *Student activity 2.2*
> From Fig. 2.4 what quantity will be demanded at the following prices?
>
> - £6
> - £3
>
> If the quantity demanded is 40 what must the price be? (Solution on p. 321.)

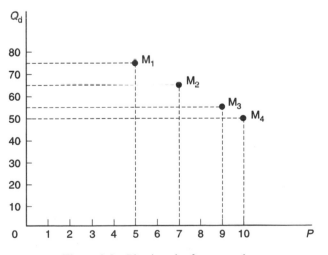

Figure 2.3 Plotting the four months

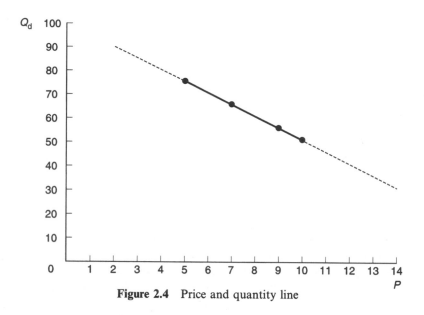

Figure 2.4   Price and quantity line

In this example, the coordinates of both variables that we need to plot have all been positive. We need to be aware that a graph could be drawn using some, or all, of the four *quadrants* as shown in Fig. 2.5. Each quadrant shows different combinations of numerical values for the x and y variables. The x axis to the right of the origin shows positive values as before. The x axis to the *left* of the origin shows negative x values (with these values becoming increasingly negative as we move further to the left). The y axis above the origin shows positive y values but the y axis *below* the origin shows negative values (again with the negative values increasing in size as we move further away from the origin).

The four possible combinations of positive and negative values for the x and y variables thus form the four quadrants. Inspection of Fig. 2.5 reveals that, in terms of much economic analysis,

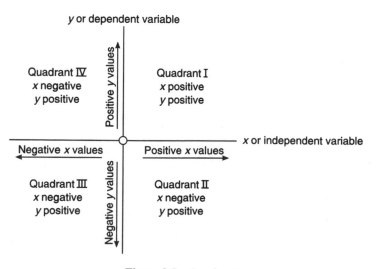

Figure 2.5   Quadrants

many of the graphs used will concentrate on quadrant I given that many economic variables can take only positive values. (It makes little sense, after all, to talk of negative Q_d and P values in the context of economics.) Occasionally we may use quadrant II and less frequently quadrants III and IV.

> ***Student activity 2.3***
> On a single graph plot the following points:
>
> A(6,10)
> B(6,−10)
> C(−6,−10)
> D(−6,10)

2.3 Functions

In the situation examined in Sec. 2.2 we can readily obtain a graph of the data that we have collected. Frequently, however, we may wish to examine some economic relationship without the hindrance of specific numbers. This may at first seem odd, but we may wish to consider the underlying relationship between two variables such as P and Q that will apply no matter what the actual price and quantity numerical values. In other words, we may wish to study the general rather than the specific case. In such an economic analysis we first need to specify which variables we are examining. Mathematically, the first step is to establish a suitable *function*. If, for example, we denote the price of a good as P and the quantity demanded as Q_d then we can write:

$$Q_d = f(P) \tag{2.1}$$

In such an expression we are indicating that Q_d is a function of P and would read this as 'Q_d is a function of P', or 'Q_d equals eff P'. The implications of this expression are important. The term shown in Eq. (2.1) does not imply that Q_d equals f multiplied by P. Rather the symbol $f(\ )$ is the standard notation for indicating that there is some (as yet undefined) relationship between the variables. The variable inside the brackets is referred to as the *argument* of the function. We are implying here that quantity demanded is in some way determined by price. Given a numerical value of P, therefore, we can somehow derive the value for Q_d (as we did in the Activity 2.2). A function provides us with a method, or rule, for deriving the value of one variable given a value for the other. Formally we say that the function f provides a *mapping* rule from P to Q_d. Naturally, until we provide specific numerical values we may not know precisely what this mapping rule is. Further than this, however, there is a hidden assumption behind a functional expression: that for any given value of P there is only *one* unique value for Q_d that can be determined. This is an important point and deserves clarification. Let us generalize a function such that:

$$Y = f(X) \tag{2.2}$$

that is, some variable Y is a function of some other variable X. Let us assume that we can express such a function diagrammatically as in Fig. 2.6.

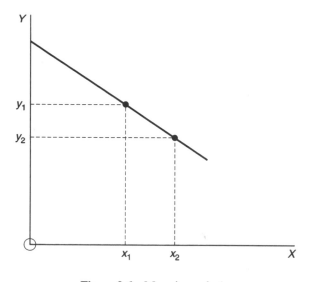

Figure 2.6   Mapping rule 1

We have a diagrammatic representation of the function and we can see that for any given value of X we can determine a single, unique value for Y. X_1, for example, gives rise to a value for Y of Y_1 and a value X_2 gives rise to a value of Y_2. Let us now examine Fig. 2.7. Here we have a different kind of relationship between X and Y, but we still have a functional relationship. We see that for any given value of X there is still only one unique value for Y. X_1, for example, still gives rise to only one Y value, Y_1. The fact that Y_1 can also result from a different X value, X_2, does not prevent the relationship being a functional one. Figure 2.8, however, shows a relationship where Y is *not* a function of X because for certain values of X more than one value of Y results. Two or more variables may be related, therefore, but not necessarily in a functional form. An example of this is given by the equation $y = \sqrt{x}$. If we set $x = 100$ then y will equal the square root. However, the square root of 100 could be either $+10$ or -10 (since both when squared will give 100). Thus we obtain two y values from the same x value.

The function expressed in Eq. (2.1) involves two types of variable: a *dependent* and an *independent* variable. The independent variable is enclosed in the function brackets—here P is

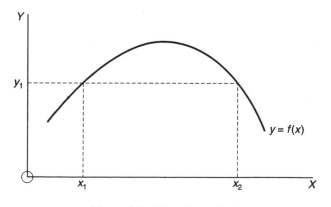

Figure 2.7   Mapping rule 2

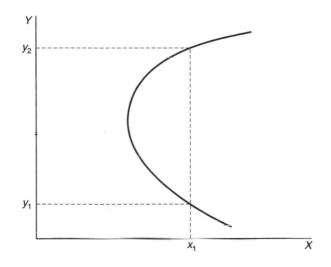

Figure 2.8   Non-functional relationship

independent—while the dependent variable appears on the left-hand side of the function equation. The distinction between the two types of variables is itself important. As the name suggests, an independent variable is one that does not depend on other variables (or, to be more specific, on other variables detailed in the function). A dependent variable, by definition, does. However, we must distinguish between the economic and mathematical implications of dependency. In mathematical terms a function simply establishes some rule or method for linking the two variables together; it does not examine why the variables move together in the stated way. In terms of economics, however, the choice of dependent/independent variable is usually of critical importance: it defines *causality*. We are implicitly assuming by our choice of variables that the value of the independent variable causes a change in the value of the dependent variable. (Naturally, in terms of economic analysis we will wish to progress further and establish exactly what this causal link is and why it occurs.) It will be worth ensuring that the distinction between mathematical and economic dependency is understood.

Consider the situation between two economic variables that we define as:

W = annual percentage increase in average wage rates
I = annual rate of inflation (i.e. the increase in the price of goods and services)

We could express the relationship in the form:

$$I = f(W)$$

that is, the rate of inflation is dependent on the rate of wage increases. This implies, in an economic context, that W 'causes' I. This may seem logically reasonable given that for most goods the labour input cost will be an important component of total costs. If these costs rise, businesses are likely to raise their prices to maintain profitability. However, we could equally denote:

$$W = f(I)$$

that is, inflation determines the rate of wage increases. Once again this seem intuitively logical since the workforce may ask for higher wages if they notice that the prices of goods they wish to buy as consumers are increasing. It is important to realize that mathematics *per se* has no role to play in helping us decide which of these two functions (or some other alternative) is most appropriate. We must use our knowledge of economics together with any empirical economic analysis that has been undertaken to determine the appropriate direction of such causality. This aspect of functions leads us to ascertain exactly why we bother with them in the first place. After all, you may think, a function in the form of Eq. (2.1) appears to do little to help our economic understanding of some relationship. We are not, after all, specifying the exact form of the functional relationship between P and Q_d. Such notation, however, does offer a convenient, shorthand way of expressing some economic relationship or, perhaps more importantly, what we *believe* to be some economic relationship. To illustrate this point let us return to the example we introduced in the last chapter. There we suggested that Q_d would be affected not only by the price charged but by a number of other factors also. In functional form we could write:

$$Q_d = f(P, P_c, P_s, Y) \tag{2.3}$$

that is, the quantity demanded is a function of several independent variables: the price of the product (P), the price of complementary goods (P_c), the price of substitute goods (P_s) and consumer income (Y). Such an expression makes explicit at the start of any economic analysis that we wish to undertake the key assumptions underpinning the analysis. We assume, given the functional specification, that these four variables are the only factors affecting the dependent variable—or at least the only factors that we are explicitly considering in our current economic model. Naturally, this is a convenient simplifying assumption that other economists may wish to challenge. However, by using the functional notation we are stating unequivocally what our initial assumptions are. We can then progress to deduce patterns of economic behaviour based on these assumptions. We may well be challenged on the validity of these assumptions—on the structure of the functional relationship specified—but we cannot be challenged on the deductive conclusions derived from these assumptions (providing, of course, that our logic and reasoning is correct).

2.4 Functional notation

Although the usual method of denoting a functional relationship is in the form $Y = f(X)$, there are a number of other notational forms that we need to be aware of since functions appear in a number of forms in the economics literature. Other common ways of representing functions are:

$$Y = f(X)$$
$$Y = g(X)$$
$$Y = y(X)$$

All state equally that Y is a function of X and it is frequently a matter of personal preference as to which method of notation is used. One important point at this stage that can cause initial confusion relates to the fact that even though the function has no numerical values we can still undertake arithmetic operations on it. Consider, for example, a function such that:

$$Y = f(X)$$

Recollect that we have said that such a function represents a (currently unspecified) mapping rule to obtain Y, given a value for X, even though we do not know the precise form of the function; that is:

$$2Y = 2f(X)$$

still represents the same function (i.e. the same mapping rule) since a given X value will provide the same Y value. All that we have done is to multiply both parts of the functional expression by the same number, leaving the underlying relationship unchanged. We could, of course, have divided rather than multiplied, or subtracted or added or indeed undertaken most forms of arithmetic on the function (even though it currently involves no numbers). We shall frequently be making use of this as we progress.

2.5 Linear functions

While the expression of an economic relationship in functional form may be a useful first step in economic analysis we will wish to go further in explicitly examining the form of the relationship. Typically, we will wish to examine the algebraic form of the function (the explicit equation) and we may also wish to represent this relationship diagrammatically in the form of a graph. We shall first examine those relationships that are *linear* in form. Let us examine a simple illustration.

Consider a firm manufacturing some product for sale. We wish to examine the costs incurred in producing quantities of this item. It is logical to begin with:

$$TC = f(Q) \tag{2.4}$$

where TC represent total costs incurred and Q represents units of output produced.

> ***Student activity 2.4***
> Why is Q set as the independent variable in this function? What other independent variables would you consider including to make the function more realistic? (Solution on p. 321.)

Note that we imply that total costs depend upon output. We can logically (albeit simplistically) assume that the firm will incur two separate types of costs. The first will be a set-up cost: a factory will have to be built, machinery acquired and resources obtained before production can begin. We refer to these costs as *fixed* costs since they will be unaffected by the precise quantity of the product we actually decide to produce—that is, they will be independent of Q. The second type of cost will be directly related to what we actually produce: the more we produce, the more costs we incur for labour, materials, energy and so on. These costs are referred to as *variable* costs. Denoting fixed costs as a and variable costs as b we therefore have an equation such that:

$$TC = a + bQ \tag{2.5}$$

where a and b are referred to as the parameters of the equation. The values that these take will give the equation its specific form and shape. While this equation does not (yet) involve specific numerical values, we can logically restrict the values that apply to a and b using not mathematics but our knowledge of economics. We can set:

$$a > 0$$
$$b > 0$$

that is, both costs can reasonably be assumed to be greater than zero. Naturally, we may wish to go one stage further and examine the precise effect of specific numerical values. Let us assume that, for the firm in question, fixed costs are £100 000 and variable costs are £5 per item produced. We then have an equation:

$$\text{TC} = 100 + 5Q \tag{2.6}$$

where both TC and Q are measured in thousands (£s and units respectively). As we shall soon discover, Eq. (2.6) is readily recognized as a linear equation and its graph can be obtained with a minimum of two pairs of coordinates. That is, if we derive two sets of coordinates for the equation and draw these on a graph we can join these two points together with a straight line which will then represent the linear equation (2.6). To obtain the two sets of coordinates we must define what is known as the *domain* of Q (the x, or independent, variable). The domain simply identifies the numerical limits for Q within which we wish to examine the economic relationship in Eq. (2.6). Assume that we limit Q to take a maximum value of 50 (measured in 000s units). A logical lower limit would be $Q = 0$. The domain of Q would then be $0 \leq Q \leq 50$. That is, Q varies between (and including) 0 and 50. To determine the two sets of coordinates required for the graph it would then be logical to find the coordinates when $Q = 0$ and again when $Q = 50$. By substituting each value of Q in turn into Eq. (2.6) we can obtain the corresponding values for TC (and hence the two sets of coordinates):

$$\text{TC} = 100 + 5Q$$
$$\text{TC} = 100 + 5(0) = 100$$

$$\text{TC} = 100 + 5Q$$
$$\text{TC} = 100 + 5(50) = 100 + 250 = 350$$

that is, when $Q = 0$, $\text{TC} = 100$ and then when $Q = 50$, TC takes the value 350. Therefore our two points have coordinates (0, 100) and (50, 350) and can be plotted onto the corresponding graph, shown in Fig. 2.9.

The two points plotted have been joined together by a straight line (hence the term 'linear' equation). You should be able to appreciate why we have done this. If we know that an equation results in a straight-line graph, then we can derive any two points on that line from the equation. Joining those two points together gives us the only straight line that can be drawn between those two points, hence giving the line of the equation. It is also important to realize that the graph and the original equation provide exactly the same information. Both allow us to quantify the value taken by the dependent variable (in this case total costs) for any given value for the independent variable (here quantity produced).

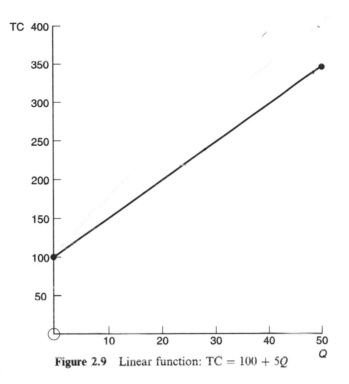

Figure 2.9   Linear function: TC $= 100 + 5Q$

Student activity 2.5
In the example we have just examined assume that:

(i) Fixed costs increase by £50 000. Draw the new TC function on a graph, together with the original function.
(ii) Variable costs now also increase by £2. Draw this third TC function on the same graph.

What observations can you make about the change on the graph as the a term and the b term change? (Solution on p. 321.)

2.6 Non-linear functions

It will be apparent, even from an elementary study of economics, that it is far too simplistic to assume that all economic relationships can be represented as linear functions. While this type of function has a number of useful properties as far as mathematical economic analysis is concerned, many such relationships can be realistically represented only through the use of *non-linear* functions. The exact form of non-linear functions can be extremely variable. We shall examine a number of common types and we shall be returning to some of these later in more detail.

Drawing a graph of a non-linear function follows the same principles as that of a linear function but with one major exception: whereas for a linear function we required only two sets of x, y coordinates for a non-linear function we require more. A rule of thumb that usually works is to determine about 10 sets of coordinates. This is usually sufficient to determine the shape of the non-linear function reasonably accurately. A second, minor, difference is that while we join the coordinates for a linear function together with a straight line for a non-linear function we join the coordinates as best as we can with a curve. Let us illustrate with a function:

$$y = 50 - x^3$$

with $-10 \leq x \leq 10$. By substituting a range of x values into the equation and solving for y we can obtain a series of coordinates. The calculations are:

x	y
-10	1050
-8	562
-6	266
-4	114
-2	58
0	50
2	42
4	-14
6	-166
8	-462
10	-950

Note that we have taken 11 x values and spaced them equally over the x domain. This provides a set of 11 x. y coordinates which can be used to obtain the graph shown in Fig. 2.10. Notice that we have drawn a smooth curve through the points rather than join them with a straight line.

2.7 Polynomial functions

We have already seen that the general form of a linear function can be represented as:

$$Y = a + bX \tag{2.7}$$

It will be useful to examine the structure of this equation in some detail in order to derive a general mathematical pattern. It is possible to represent each term in such an equation in terms of X. Equation (2.7) can be rewritten as:

$$Y = aX^0 + bX^1 \tag{2.8}$$

given that $X^0 = 1$ and $X^1 = X$. There may appear to be little point in rewriting Eq. (2.7) in this way but it does enable us to establish the pattern of polynomial equations (the term literally means 'many terms'). The pattern that becomes evident is:

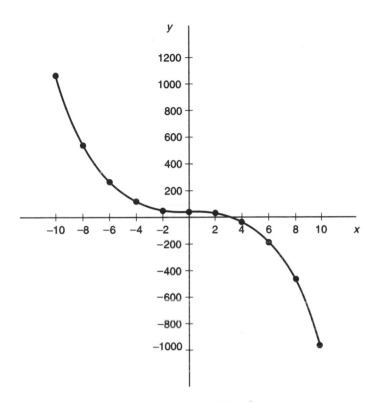

Figure 2.10 $y = 50 - x^3$

$$Y = a \quad (\text{since } Y = aX^0 = a \text{ given that } X^0 - 1) \tag{2.9}$$
$$Y = a + bX \tag{2.10}$$
$$Y = a + bX + cX^2 \tag{2.11}$$
$$Y = a + bX + cX^2 + dX^3 \tag{2.12}$$

and so on, adding a new and higher power X term each time. In general, a polynomial function can be written as:

$$Y = a + b_1X + b_2X^2 + b_3X^3 + \ldots + b_nX^n \tag{2.13}$$

We have already established that a polynomial of degree 1 [where the 1 refers to the highest power of X in the function, as in Eq. (2.10)] is a linear function. A polynomial of degree 2 (as in Eq. (2.11)) is referred to as a *quadratic* function while that of degree 3 (Eq. (2.12)) as a *cubic* function. We shall be examining the use of such polynomials in more detail as we progress.

For now it is sufficient to know that a quadratic function will typically follow a pattern shown in Figs 2.11(a) and (b). Which of the two patterns is followed will depend upon the exact parameters of the quadratic equation. A cubic function will typically follow the sort of pattern shown in Fig. 2.12.

One important point takes us back to the four quadrants that are technically available for any graph. We may decide, for example, that in our illustration of a total cost function it might be more realistic to use, say, a quadratic function rather than a linear one. Considering Figs 2.11(a) and 2.11(b) we appear to have difficulties, however, in using such a function to model the

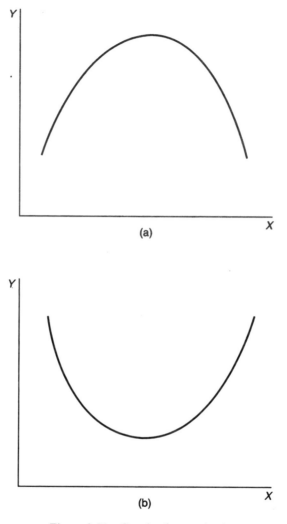

Figure 2.11   Graph of a quadratic

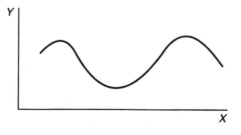

Figure 2.12   Cubic function

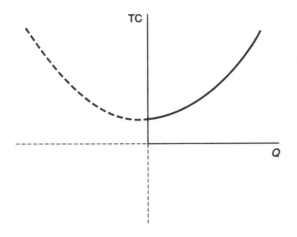

Figure 2.13   TC $= f(x)$ as a function

relationship between TC and Q. If we examine Fig. 2.11(a), the implications are that as output (on the X axis) increases, TC (on the Y axis) increases at first but then decreases. This does not seem a realistic pattern of behaviour for TC. Equally, with Fig. 2.11(b), TC at first decreases as output increases and then increases again. This does not seem unduly realistic either. However, through careful consideration of the existence of four quadrants and the economic implications of each we might use the relationship shown in Fig. 2.13.

We still have a quadratic function but, given the economic logic of the problem, our interest will be solely in quadrant I, which would effectively be the only part of the graph we would actually construct. We retain the important features of the quadratic function whilst retaining the economic logic of the problem under examination. Such manipulation is both common and useful in economics.

> **Student activity 2.6**
>
> Plot each of the functions shown below on one graph, with X from 0 to 50. What observations can you make about the three functions?
>
> (i) $Y = 100 + 12X - 0.3X^2$
> (ii) $Y = 500 + 12X - 0.3X^2$
> (iii) $Y = 100 + 12X + 0.3X^2$
>
> (Solution on p. 322.)

2.8 Other non-linear functions

The variety of other types of non-linear functions in addition to polynomials that we may encounter in economics is considerable. We shall focus attention here on two common groups: exponential and logarithmic functions (which we examine in the next section) and non-linear functions derived from linear functions. Let us return to Eq. (2.6)—the linear function showing the relationship between TC and Q:

$$TC = f(Q) = 100 + 5Q$$

It is frequently the case in economics that we may wish to derive a related function from an equation such as this and such derived functions may well be non-linear even though the original function is linear. For example, we may wish to derive a function showing average costs of production rather than the total. Given that the definition of an average cost (ATC) is the total cost divided by the quantity produced we have:

$$\text{ATC} = \frac{\text{TC}}{Q} = \frac{100 + 5Q}{Q} = \frac{100}{Q} + 5 \tag{2.14}$$

which is clearly non-linear even though the function from which it was derived is linear.

Student activity 2.7
Plot this function on a graph, with Q from 0 to 50. (Take care when Q approaches 0.) What happens to ATC as Q gets larger over the range shown? How do you explain this in terms of economics?
(Solution on p. 323.)

2.9   Exponential and logarithmic functions

One further group of non-linear functions of special interest in economic analysis involves the use of exponential and logarithmic relationships. Such functions are particularly useful in examining economic growth problems and problems involving economic dynamics. We shall be returning to these functions in more detail later. For the moment we shall simply examine their basic features. We have already seen that polynomial functions involve a variable raised to some power. Mathematically, the value of the power is referred to as the *exponent*. Thus X^2 is said to be of exponent 2 and it is also evident that in such a case the exponent is a constant: no matter what the value of X, we always raise this value to the power 2. There is no reason, however, why the exponent itself could not be variable. When this occurs we have an exponential function. The simplest form of this type of function can be expressed as:

$$T = f(X) = b^X \tag{2.15}$$

where the b parameter is denoted as the fixed base of the exponent. Typically in economics we might use X to denote a time variable and in such a case might replace the symbol X with t. The properties of such an exponential function are of considerable use in economic modelling. Let us consider the following:

$$Y = f(t) = 1.5^t \tag{2.16}$$

We wish to examine the relationship for $t = 0$ to 5. In order to do so we must ensure an adequate understanding of how we can mathematically manipulate exponents; a short digression will be profitable at this stage. When dealing with exponents a number of simple rules can be developed which simplifies the mathematics and helps our understanding of the resulting calculation. Consider the following two values:

$$X^3 \quad \text{and} \quad X^4$$

and assume we wish to undertake some basic arithmetic involving these.

Rule 1 $X^m \times X^n = X^{(m+n)}$ As an illustration assume we require $X^3 \times X^4$. This can be rewritten as:

$$(X \times X \times X) \times (X \times X \times X \times X) = X \times X \times X \times X \times X \times X \times X = X^7$$

Rule 2 $(X^m)^n = X^{mn}$ Assume we require $(X^3)^2$. This can be rewritten as $X^3 \times X^3$ which, using Rule 1, gives X^6 (that is, X^{3+3}).

Rule 3 $X^m/X^n = X^{(m-n)}$ Assume we require X^4/X^3. This is:

$$\frac{X^4}{X^3} = \frac{X \times X \times X \times X}{X \times X \times X} = X^1 = X$$

This leads logically on to Rule 4.

Rule 4 $X^{-n} = 1/X^n$ Suppose, for Rule 3, we require X^2/X^4. Applying Rule 3 we know this gives X^{-2} since:

$$\frac{X^2}{X^4} = \frac{X \times X}{X \times X \times X \times X} = \frac{1}{X \times X} = \frac{1}{X^2} = X^{-2}$$

It is worth noting that this type of notation is frequently used. For example, we will usually write X^{-1} rather than $1/X$, although both are the same.

Rule 5 $X^{1/n} = \sqrt[n]{X}$.   Assume we had an expression such as $X^{1/2}$. Using Rule 1 we know that:

$$X^{1/2} \times X^{1/2} = X^{(1/2+1/2)} = X^1$$

However, the interpretation of a square root of some number, X (denoted by $\sqrt{X}$) is that we have a second number, say Y, which when multiplied by itself gives the original number X. Thus we would say that 2 is $\sqrt{4}$ since $2^2 = 4$. We can, therefore, rewrite $X^{1/2}$ as $\sqrt{X}$ since this is also the definition of a square root. In fact, this rule can be generalized such that

$$X^{m/n} = \sqrt[n]{X^m}$$

Rule 6 $X^{-1/n} = 1/\sqrt[n]{X}$ Assume we had $X^{-1/4}$. Setting $n = 4$ and using Rule 4 we then have:

$$X^{-1/4} = \frac{1}{X^{1/4}}$$

but using Rule 5, $X^{1/4} = \sqrt[4]{X}$. Hence

$$X^{-1/4} = \frac{1}{\sqrt[4]{X}}$$

Again, this can be generalized to:

$$X^{-m/n} = \frac{1}{\sqrt[n]{X^m}}$$

Student activity 2.8
Using the rules we have just examined simplify the following expressions:

(i) $8^6 \times 8^3$
(ii) $(7^2)^3$
(iii) $8^6/8^3$
(iv) $8^3/8^6$
(v) $5^{-1/3}$
(vi) $8^6 + 8^3$
(vii) $(10^3 \times 10^5)^2/10^4$

(Solution on p. 323.)

We can now return to the exponential function we were examining earlier. We had $Y = 1.5^t$, where t took values between 0 and 5. To graph this function we can now tabulate appropriate sets of coordinates using the rules we have just introduced:

t	Y	
0	1.5^0	$= 1$
1	1.5^1	$= 1.5$
2	1.5^2	$= 2.25$
3	1.5^3	$= 3.375$
4	1.5^4	$= 5.0625$
5	1.5^5	$= 7.59375$

and these produce a graph as in Fig. 2.14.

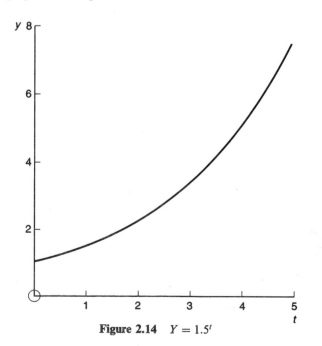

Figure 2.14 $Y = 1.5^t$

In fact, we can generalize such an exponential function into the form:

$$Y = f(t) = ab^{ct} \qquad (2.17)$$

where a, b and c are the parameters of the function, in this example taking the values $a = 1$, $b = 1.5$, $c = 1$. One specific example of this is frequently used in economics, where the b parameter is replaced by the mathematical constant e, which is known as an irrational number and always takes the same value: 2.718 28. We cannot, at the moment, justify why such a number should be used—we must wait until certain other topics have been discussed before explaining this. However, the use of functions such as:

$$Y = f(t) = e^{0.25t} \qquad (2.18)$$

are common in mathematical economic models and this type of equation is evaluated and graphed in exactly the same way as before.

2.10 Logarithms and logarithmic functions

We next turn to the use of logarithms and logarithmic functions. You may recollect (with some dismay) encountering logarithms in your earlier studies of mathematics. In fact, they are an invaluable aid to the economist both in terms of facilitating certain complex arithmetical calculations and in developing mathematical economic models. Again we shall review their basic principles here before proceeding. You will find it useful to have a pocket calculator with logarithmic facilities available for this section. A logarithm is the power to which a given base number must be raised in order to obtain a specified numerical value. Thus, we say that the logarithm of 100 is 2 when using base 10. This probably makes more sense if we show that:

$$100 = 10^2$$

since we see that, using the base number of 10, we must raise this to the power 2 in order to obtain the number in question of 100. Conventionally we would say that 2 is the log of 100. Similarly we would say that the log of 1000 was 3 ($1000 = 10^3$), the log of 10 000 was 4 ($10\,000 = 10^4$) and so on. Logs of other numbers have the same logic but may be less obvious. For example, we can determine that the log of 56 is 1.7482 (you could check this on your own calculator). Finally, we may know the log value and wish to determine the actual number of which this is the logarithm. For example, suppose we knew that the log of some number is 1.2095. What is the number for which this is the logarithm? Effectively we have:

$$X = 10^{1.2095}$$

so calculating the value of 10 to this power will provide the result. Such a process is known as finding the *antilog* of 1.2095 (and an appropriate key should be available on your pocket calculator to confirm the result of 16.199). So far, we have assumed that our logarithms have used a base of 10 (referred to as common logarithms). While computationally this is frequently very convenient we could actually use any number as the base for the logarithm calculations. For theoretical model building there is an alternative to base 10 that is useful. This is the constant e (with a value of 2.718 28). Using e as the base results in what is known as a natural logarithm, usually denoted either as ln or $\log_e$ to distinguish it from base 10 logarithms. (You will probably find both common and natural logarithm keys on your calculator.) As with exponents, there are a number of common and useful rules when dealing with logarithms (and the rules apply both to common and natural logarithms). We state these to be:

Rule 1 $\log(XY) = \log X + \log Y$

Rule 2 $\log(X/Y) = \log X - \log Y$

Rule 3 $\log X'' = n \log X$

Rule 4 $\log(\sqrt[n]{X}) = (\log X)/n$

> **Student activity 2.9**
> Evaluate the expressions shown below using the relevant logarithm rule(s). Confirm your solution by first using common logarithms and antilogs and then recalculating the solution using natural logarithms and antilogs.
>
>   (i) 173×56.2
> (ii) $173/56.2$
> (iii) 173^5
> (iv) $\sqrt[3]{173}$
>
> (Solution on p. 324.)

A simple illustration of the usefulness of logarithms in economic models may be of benefit at this stage. Consider the production function shown below:

$$Q = f(K, L) = AK^\alpha L^\beta \tag{2.19}$$

This function is known as the Cobb–Douglas production function and shows that production, Q, is a function of the input of capital, K, and labour, L. A, α and β are the parameters of the function (as we shall see later the sum of α and β indicates the returns to scale effect). However, the function in its current form is not particularly easy to manipulate or develop further. As we have already seen, linear functions have certain properties that make them attractive to use in models, not least because they are easier to use and understand. However, let us apply some of the logarithm rules we have just introduced to the production function (and we shall use logarithms to base e). Taking logarithms we have:

$$\ln Q = \ln A + \alpha \ln K + \beta \ln L \tag{2.20}$$

$$\text{or} \quad Q' = A' + \alpha K' + \beta L' \tag{2.21}$$

(using the prime symbol ($'$) to denote a logarithmic variable) which, on inspection, can be seen to have been transformed into a linear format. Not only is Eq. (2.21) easier to examine and understand but any numerical calculations required are more readily derived from the transformed function than the original. This use of logarithms to transform non-linear functions into a linear format is particularly common in economics.

Student activity 2.10
Assume that some variable Y changes over time. It has an initial value in period 1 of 100 and grows at 10 per cent each subsequent period.

(i) Calculate the Y value up to period 10 and plot Y against time.
(ii) Take the logarithm of Y and plot this against time.
(iii) What observations do you make about the logarithmic relationship and how do you explain this?

(Solution on p. 324.)

2.11 Functions involving more than one independent variable

The Cobb–Douglas production function leads to the next topic we examine in this chapter: functions involving more than one independent variable. It is entirely logical that we should wish to use such functions in economic models. After all, the purpose of modelling is to try to construct a theoretical model representing some real-world economic system. Given that such systems are typically complex the models we develop will need to be able to cope with multiple independent variables. Let us consider in detail the function:

$$Q_d = f(P_x, P_s) \tag{2.22}$$

which is a demand function indicating that the quantity demanded of good X, Q_d, is a function of the price of that good, P_x, and the price of a substitute good, P_s. It is clear from the function that in order to determine the value of the dependent variable we now require a value for both of the independent variables. Figure 2.15 illustrates the principles involved.

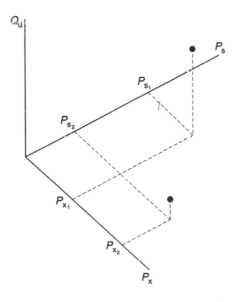

Figure 2.15 $Q_d = f(P_x, P_s)$

The diagram shows Q_d on the vertical axis and the two price variables on the *two* horizontal axes that we now require. A particular combination of values for the two price variables, say P_{x_1} and P_{s_1}, will give Q_d a unique value, say Q_{d_1}, and hence we can plot the corresponding point at the relevant three-dimensional coordinates $(P_{x_1}, P_{s_1}, Q_{d_1})$. We could equally plot a second point with different coordinates and so on. If we were to construct a sufficient number of such points then we could derive a graph of the function which would normally take the form of some three-dimensional *surface* rather than a two-dimensional *line* as it has been up to now. While we would not usually wish to do this for a specific numerical function, it will actually be informative to do so this once, in order to reinforce the principles involved in dealing with these multivariable functions. Figure 2.16 illustrates the kind of surface we might obtain for such a demand function.

The diagram may at first appear somewhat complex but will repay close attention. The three-dimensional surface that is shown represents the coordinates for the three variables in the function. As we progress through the text we shall be examining ways in which we can analyse a surface such as this. For the moment it is quite revealing to examine a simple approach that we might take. It is evidently not a straightforward task to examine the diagram and reach general conclusions about economic behaviour. Assume instead that we wish to examine the behaviour of Q_d with respect to P_x. Clearly we cannot just forget about P_s since it forms part of the demand function. What we can do, however, is to transform the three-dimensional diagram into a two-dimensional one. Assume that, as in Fig. 2.17, we take a series of 'slices' through the diagram and that these slices are parallel to the P_x axis. We could then 'transfer' these slices to a two-dimensional graph as in Fig. 2.18. In such a way we can then build up a series of two-dimensional pictures showing the relationship between Q_d and P_x for different values of P_s. You will be able to appreciate how we can do this from Fig. 2.17. Each slice corresponds to a constant value for P_s—in our example, at 2 and then at 4. Of course, what we are effectively doing is holding this variable constant in order to examine the economic relationship between the other two. In principle, of course, this extends readily beyond three variable functions to functions involving any number of variables. While we would not be able to produce a corresponding graph for more than a three-variable function, the principles of examining slices of the function's surface (the slices are more formally known as *planes*) remain the same. You will probably have already encountered such principles in your study of economics even if they have not been explained in mathematical terms.

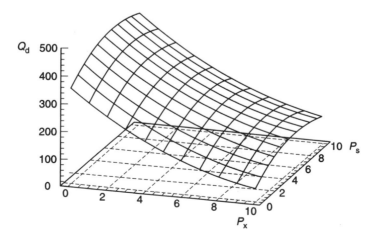

Figure 2.16 $Q_d = f(P_x, P_s)$

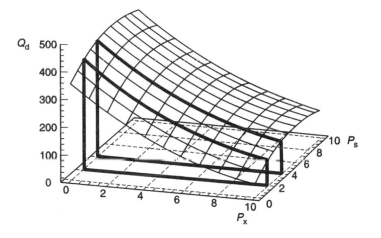

Figure 2.17 $Q_d = f(P_x, P_s)$

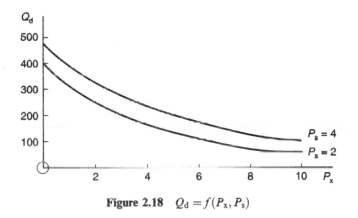

Figure 2.18 $Q_d = f(P_x, P_s)$

2.12 Inverse functions

Finally in this chapter we consider the inverse function. Let us return to the example with which we started this chapter—that relating price and quantity demanded. Assume a function such that:

$$Q_d = f(P) = 100 - 5P \tag{2.23}$$

Now consider a situation where the firm wishes to derive a related function from this. It requires a function for total revenue (TR). Clearly, total revenue will simply be the product of price per unit times quantity demanded:

$$TR = P \times Q_d$$

but since we already have an expression for Q_d in Eq. (2.23) this becomes:

$$TR = P(100 - 5P) = 100P - 5P^2 \tag{2.24}$$

where

$$TR = f(P)$$

and we have a mapping rule to determine TR given some value for P. However, assume that instead of determining TR from P we wished to determine TR from Q_d instead. From the perspective of a TR function this makes sense as revenue will depend on quantity demanded as well as price. To proceed, we can find the inverse of Eq. (2.23). Since:

$$Q_d = 100 - 5P$$

we can rearrange this to get:

$$5P = 100 - Q_d$$
$$P = 20 - 0.02Q_d \qquad (2.25)$$

where Eq. (2.25) is the inverse of Eq. (2.23). Note that we are not implying that $P = f(Q)$ but have rearranged the original function into an equivalent form. We now have again:

$$TR = P \times Q_d$$

but substituting Eq. (2.25) for P now gives:

$$TR = f(Q) = (20 - 0.02Q_d)Q_d = 20Q_d - 0.02Q_d^2 \qquad (2.26)$$

It is important to realize that both Eqs (2.24) and (2.26) will generate the same TR values for a specific P, Q_d combination.

2.13   Summary

In this chapter we have begun to examine how mathematics can be applied in economics. We have examined and developed the fundamental principles of terminology and concepts that we shall require from now on (and which we assume you have now acquired). In the next chapter we shall immediately begin to put some of these principles to work as we examine a number of common mathematical models. We shall be using the mathematics we have introduced so far to reveal aspects of these models—and the implicit economic behaviour patterns—that are not evident from any other perspective. As was said in the introductory chapter, a number of detailed exercises occur at the end of this (and subsequent) chapter. You should ensure that you attempt a number of these before proceeding. Not only do they reinforce what we have covered here but many of them introduce questions and aspects that we develop in the next chapter.

Worked example

Finally, to reinforce the concepts introduced in this chapter we look at a worked example using the principles introduced thus far. After we have introduced the problem (but before you examine the worked solution) you might wish to tackle the problem yourself and then compare your solution with that shown.

A firm has been analysing its revenue and cost situations. A demand function for its product has been derived as:

$$Q = f(P) = 125 - P$$

and its total costs, TC, as:

$$TC = f(Q) = 500 + 0.5Q^2$$

The firm wishes to use graphs to:

(i) Derive a profit function $PR = f(Q)$ where PR is profit defined as the difference between TR and TC
(ii) Use this profit function to determine the level of output which maximizes profit
(iii) Use this profit function to determine the breakeven level of output (where total costs are just equal to total revenue)
(iv) Determine the price to be set which will generate profit-maximizing output

Output is not expected to exceed 100 units.

Solution

Since we require a profit function where $PR = f(Q)$ we must have:

$$PR = TR - TC$$

and we require a function for TR and TC expressed in terms of Q. This implies that we require the inverse function of the demand function (since this is expressed in terms of P). The inverse function will be derived from:

$$Q = 125 - P$$

and this can be rearranged to give:

$$P = 125 - Q$$
$$TR = f(Q) = P \times Q = (125 - Q) \times Q = 125Q - Q^2$$

and since $TC = 500 + 0.5Q^2$ this gives:

$$PR = TR - TC$$
$$= (125Q - Q^2) - (500 + 0.5Q^2)$$
$$= -500 + 125Q - 1.5Q^2$$

The corresponding graph for the profit function for $0 \leq Q \leq 100$ is shown in Fig. 2.19.

We see from the graph that the profit function is quadratic and rises to reach a maximum value when $Q = 40$ (although our solution from the graph might not be exactly correct given the

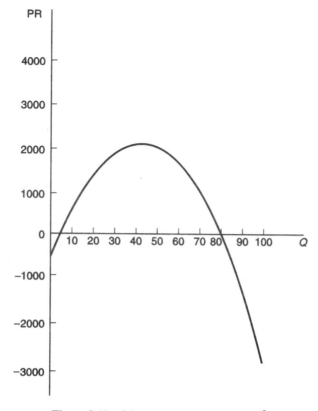

Figure 2.19 $PR = -500 + 125Q - 1.5Q^2$

limitations of the axis scales). We can also comment on the function. We note that the function takes a negative value when $Q = 0$ (implying the firm is making a financial loss). From our knowledge of economics this is logical since we know the firm faces fixed costs of 500 and, by definition, these costs are incurred even when $Q = 0$. Since, also by definition, TR must equal 0 when $Q = 0$ this implies that $PR = -500$ at zero output. We also see that the firm will continue to make a loss until the PR curve crosses the x axis (technically this is the breakeven position where $PR = 0$). This occurs when $Q = 5$ (again approximately given the graph). We also note, however, that a second breakeven level of output occurs when $Q = 79$. You may wish to consider the economic explanation for this situation (and indeed the shape of the PR function itself). It is also instructive to show the relationship between the three functions: PR, TR and TC. All three functions are shown in Fig. 2.20. All three are quadratic (although with TC taking the opposite shape to PR and TR). The TR function starts from 0 while the TC function starts at 500 (linked to PR starting at -500). Notice that where TR and TC intersect is also where PR crosses the x axis—the two breakeven points, in other words. Notice also that PR reaches its maximum at the point where the gap between TR and TC reaches its widest.

Finally, we require the price that will equate to the profit-maximizing level of output. Since $Q = 40$ at the point of profit maximization we can use:

$$P = 125 - Q \quad \text{and set} \quad Q = 40$$

to give $P = 85$ as the price which will equate to the profit-maximizing level of output.

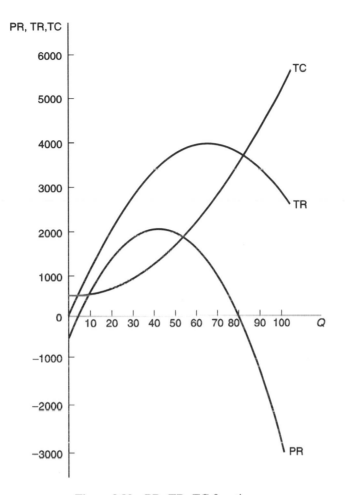

Figure 2.20 PR, TR, TC functions

Exercises

2.1 For each of the following relationships obtain a graph for the range of X values indicated. Determine which of these is a function and which is not:

(i) $Y = 8 + 2X$, $X = 0$ to 20
(ii) $Y = 8 + 4X$, $X = 0$ to 20
(iii) $Y = 8 + 0.5X$, $X = 0$ to 20
(iv) $Y = 20X - 0.02X^2$, $X = 0$ to 1000
(v) $Y = 10 + \sqrt{X}$, $X = 0$ to 100
(vi) For each of the above attempt to derive the inverse function.

2.2 Return to Eq. (2.6) where we had:

$$TC = f(Q) = 100 + 5Q$$

(i) If Q changes from 10 units to 11, what is the corresponding change in TC?
(ii) If Q changes from 40 to 41 units, what is the corresponding change in TC?
(iii) What is the economic interpretation of this change in TC?
(iv) How realistic is it that TC changes by the same amount regardless of the actual level of production?

2.3 Assume a function such that:

$$TC = f(Q) = 500 + 20Q - 6Q^2 + 0.6Q^3$$

where Q ranges from 0 to 15.

(i) Plot this function and comment upon its shape.
(ii) Derive functions for:

Average total costs (ATC)
Average variable costs (AVC)
Average fixed costs (AFC)

and plot these functions on one graph.
(iii) Comment on the economic explanation for the shape of the ATC function.

2.4 Assume that we have a function linking consumer's expenditure, C, to income, Y:

$$C = 2500 + 0.75Y$$

which is valid for income in the range 0 to £25 000.

(i) Plot this function.
(ii) Plot a second function on the graph such that:

$$C = Y$$

What does this function represent? What does the point where the two functions intersect represent?
(iii) Given that by definition any income not consumed is saved, that is $Y = C + S$, derive a savings function of the form:

$$S = f(Y)$$

and plot this on the graph with the consumption function.

2.5 The market for a particular product is characterized by the following demand and supply functions:

$$Q_d = f(P) = 25 - 4P + 0.2P^2$$
$$Q_s = f(P) = -5 + 2P - 0.01P^2$$

(i) Plot both functions on one graph for $P = 0$ to 50.
(ii) In economic terms, over what range for P do these functions represent logical patterns of behaviour?
(iii) Given that total revenue (TR) is defined as the quantity demanded multiplied by the price per unit, derive a function such that:

$$TR = f(P)$$

and plot this over the range for P that represents logical patterns of behaviour. Comment on the shape of this function.

2.6 A firm expects that over the next decade its annual output will increase by 3 per cent per year because of achievements in productivity. Its current annual output is 100 000 units.

(i) For each of the next 10 years calculate the annual output if this rate of growth is sustained.
(ii) Show that this rate of growth can be represented by:

$$\text{Output} = 100\,000(1.03)^t$$

where t is the number of years from the present.

2.7 A Cobb–Douglas production function is given as:

$$Y = 0.6L^{0.3}K^{0.7}$$

where Y represents production
L the input of labour
K the input of capital

(i) Assume that K is fixed at 5 units. Plot the function for $L = 0$ to 10.
(ii) On the same graph plot the function if K changes to 7.5 and then to 10 units.
(iii) Repeat (i) and (ii) but now with L fixed at 5, 7.5 and 10 and K variable from 0 to 10.
(iv) Comment on the shape of the functions you have produced.

2.8 Plot the functions shown in (i) and (ii) below on one graph and those in (iii) and (iv) on a second graph. Use t from 0 to 10. What effect does the negative exponent term have?

(i) $Y = e^{0.25t}$
(ii) $Y = e^{0.3t}$
(iii) $Y = e^{-0.25t}$
(iv) $Y = e^{-0.3t}$

2.9 For the two functions shown in Eqs (2.23) and (2.24), plot each over the range $P = 0$ to 15 and comment upon their relationship.

2.10 Return to the function shown in Eq. (2.23). Assume this now changes to:

$$Q_d = 150 - 5P$$

(i) Plot this on the same graph as Eq. (2.23) and comment on the change in economic behaviour that this represents. What factors might have caused such a change?
(ii) The function now changes to:

$$Q_d = 150 - 10P$$

Plot this on the same graph and comment upon the change in economic behaviour and the factors that might be behind this.

3 Linear models in economics

We have already seen that linear functions are particularly attractive because they are easy both to use and understand. Equally, there are a considerable number of areas of economic analysis where we can approximate some relationship using a linear function. It is not surprising, therefore, that a considerable number of economic models are built on linear functions and in this chapter we shall examine some of the more common of these, developing our mathematical skills as we do so. In particular we shall be examining the concept of *equilibrium* from both a mathematical and an economic viewpoint.

Learning objectives

By the time you have completed this chapter you should be able, for a linear function or a set of functions, to:

- Derive and explain the intercept/constant
- Derive and explain the slope/gradient
- Find the equilibrium solution using both algebra and graphs
- Sketch a simple model
- Determine the solution to a variety of common economic models

3.1 Linear functions

Let us return to the linear function we introduced in the previous chapter. This and its corresponding graph (Fig. 3.1) are shown below:

$$TC = f(Q) = a + bQ = 100 + 5Q \tag{3.1}$$

The function relates to a total cost equation where we determined that fixed costs were 100 and variable costs 5 per unit produced. It is clear that there are two parameters to this, and any other, linear equation: a and b. The numerical values taken by these parameters will vary, but in general each will fall into one of three categories:

(i) $a < 0$	(i) $b < 0$
(ii) $a = 0$	(ii) $b = 0$
(iii) $a > 0$	(iii) $b > 0$

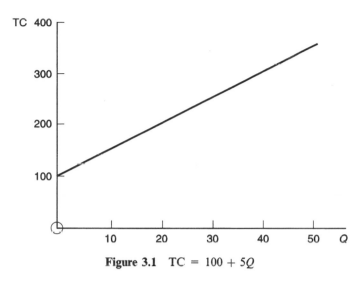

Figure 3.1 TC $= 100 + 5Q$

It is evident that, in our example, both parameters fall into category (iii). However, let us examine the general principles involved. The a parameter is generally referred to as the *intercept* (or constant) of the function. Referring to Fig. 3.1, it is clearly no coincidence that the line representing this function starts from a point on the vertical axis equal to 100, the value of a. Inspection of the linear function reveals that this will always be the case—that the line will intercept the y axis at a value equal to a. Generalizing to $Y = a + bX$, if we set X to zero then clearly $Y = a$. The line on the graph will always intercept the vertical axis at this value. Given that a could be negative, zero or positive, then we clearly have three possibilities, as shown in Fig. 3.2. The value taken by a will move the line up or down the vertical, Y, axis. The second parameter of the function, b, refers to the *slope* or gradient of the line. Literally, it indicates the steepness taken by the line. As we shall see, the gradient is particularly important in economic analysis and will repay further detailed attention here. Let us examine Fig. 3.3.

If we examine the linear function $Y = a + bX$ we see two points on the line with coordinates respectively of (x_1, y_1) and (x_2, y_2).

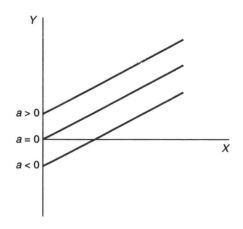

Figure 3.2 Change in a

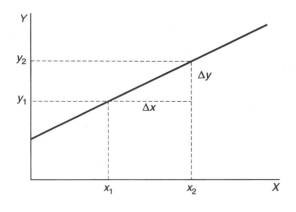

Figure 3.3 $Y = a + bX$

We have:

$$y_1 = f(x_1) = a + bx_1 \tag{3.2}$$
$$y_2 = f(x_2) = a + bx_2 \tag{3.3}$$

If we now wish to determine the change in Y that has occurred due to the change in X we have:

Change in X : $x_1 - x_2$

Change in Y : $y_1 - y_2 = (a + bx_1) - (a + bx_2)$

$$= a + bx_1 - a - bx_2$$
$$= bx_1 - bx_2$$
$$= b(x_1 - x_2)$$

This implies that the change in Y is equal to b times the change in X. We introduce a new symbol, Δ (pronounced 'delta'), which is used in economics to indicate a change in the variable we are examining. Here we have:

$$\Delta y = y_1 - y_2 \quad \text{and} \quad \Delta x = x_1 - x_2$$

so we now have:

$$\Delta y = b\Delta x$$

giving

$$b = \frac{\Delta y}{\Delta x} \tag{3.4}$$

that is the slope b is given by the ratio of the change in Y to the change in X, where the expression $\Delta y / \Delta x$ is often referred to as the difference quotient. We can also confirm from this that, for a linear function, the slope is constant—always equal to b. The implication is equally important for economics: the rate of change of Y to a change in X remains the same anywhere on the line representing the function. We shall see the implications of this shortly. As we have seen, the numerical value of b could be negative, zero or positive. The three alternatives are shown in Fig. 3.4.

A linear function with a positive slope moves upwards, as we view it, from left to right. A function with a negative slope moves down (the change in Y brought about by a change in X represents a decrease in the Y value). Finally, a zero value for b indicates a line parallel to the X axis. Here a change in X brings about no change in Y; Y is actually independent of X in such a case.

Student activity 3.1
Consider the following pairs of linear functions:

(i) $Y = -75 + 12X$
      $Y = -100 - 6X$
(ii) $Y = 75 - 15X$
      $Y = 75 + 10X$
(iii) $Y = 100 - 5X$
      $Y = 100 - 10X$
(iv) $Y = -100 + 12X$
      $Y = -100 + 6X$

Without drawing a detailed graph, sketch each pair of equations in terms of their relative intercepts and slopes.
(Solutions on p. 326.)

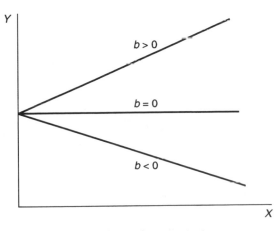

Figure 3.4 Change in b

3.2 A simple breakeven model

Let us now develop and examine the first of our linear models: that relating to breakeven analysis. We already have a linear function representing total costs. Equally we could introduce a linear function showing the revenue obtained from selling the goods produced. If we assume that the firm in question operates under conditions of perfect competition, then we know it has to sell at whatever price is fixed by the market, denoted by P. A little logic also reveals that at zero output the firm's revenue will also be zero: in other words, the a parameter equals zero. This gives rise to a function:

$$TR = f(Q) = PQ \qquad (3.5)$$

where TR refers to total revenue with parameters $a = 0$, $b = P$. If we now define the breakeven point as the level of output where total costs are equal to total revenue, then clearly we are seeking a point where:

$$TC = TR$$

and visually this would be illustrated in Fig. 3.5 where we are seeking to establish the value for q_1—the level of output at which the firm breaks even and where, by definition, TC = TR.

As a slight, but important, digression it is worth noting that the expression TC = TR does not represent a functional relationship in the way we have previously discussed, but is rather a requirement we are imposing on the model and is often referred to as a *conditional equality*. Clearly, we are not implying that $TC = f(TR)$ with this expression, but rather indicating that we seek a position where the two functions take identical values.

While we could examine this in numerical terms (as we shall shortly do to reinforce the key principles), we are more interested in establishing general conclusions from this simple model. After all, numerical values will vary from one firm to another or over time. We seek to establish the general principles that apply to a breakeven analysis model so that they can be applied to any such situation regardless of the precise numerical parameters used. Let us indulge in some simple algebra. We require:

$$TC = TR$$

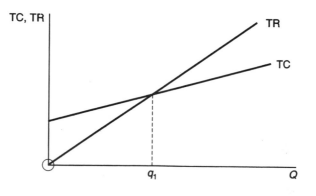

Figure 3.5 Breakeven point

However:

$$TC = f(Q) = a + bQ$$

and

$$TR = f(Q) = \quad pQ$$

so if we require TC = TR then:

$$TC = TR$$
$$a + bQ = pQ$$
$$a \quad = pQ - bQ$$
$$a \quad = Q(p - b)$$

and rearranging gives:

$$Q = \frac{a}{p - b} \tag{3.6}$$

where Q is the quantity such that total costs and total revenue will be equal.

This leads us to the conclusion that, in general, the breakeven level of output can be found by:

$$\frac{a}{p - b} = \frac{\text{fixed costs}}{\text{price} - \text{variable costs}}$$

since, in this model, a represents fixed costs and b represents variable costs, and we have an immediate illustration of the usefulness of mathematics in evaluating economic models. We have used some simple mathematics to reach a conclusion that would have been difficult to establish in any other way. We can readily confirm our conclusion using a simple numerical example. If the firm we have examined sells its product for a price of £10 per unit then we have:

$$\text{Breakeven point} = \frac{a}{p - b} = \frac{100}{10 - 5} = 20 \text{ units}$$

Equally, confirmation that this is, in fact, the correct solution can be obtained by substitution of $Q = 20$ into both the TC and TR equations. We have:

$$TC = 100 + 5(20) = 200$$
$$TR = 10(20) \quad = 200$$

confirming that our solution method is correct.

> **Student activity 3.2**
> Assume the firm now faces the following situation:
>
> $$TR = 12Q$$
>
> that is, the price charged per unit increases to £12. Plot this new function on the same graph as TR = $10Q$, and TC = $100 + 5Q$. Determine the new breakeven point using the general solution obtained in Eq. (3.6). Explain, in economic terms, why the breakeven level of output has fallen.
> (Solution on p. 326.)

3.3 Simultaneous equations

In fact, the method whereby we require a solution to two equations is a situation that occurs frequently. It will be worth while deriving a general solution method for the other models we shall be examining. If we have two linear equations such that:

$$Y_1 = a_1 + b_1 X \tag{3.7}$$
$$Y_2 = a_2 + b_2 X \tag{3.8}$$

and we require a solution such that $Y_1 = Y_2$, then we can derive the following:

$$
\begin{aligned}
Y_1 &= Y_2 \\
a_1 + b_1 X &= a_2 + b_2 X \\
a_1 - a_2 &= b_2 X - b_1 X \\
a_1 - a_2 &= X(b_2 - b_1) \\
\frac{a_1 - a_2}{b_2 - b_1} &= X
\end{aligned}
\tag{3.9}
$$

This expression (Eq. (3.9)) allows us to find the solution to X that satisfies both equations simultaneously. To find the corresponding Y value we have:

$$Y_1 = a_1 + b_1 X$$

and using Eq. (3.9) we then have:

$$
\begin{aligned}
Y_1 &= a_1 + b_1 \frac{a_1 - a_2}{b_2 - b_1} \\
&= a_1 \frac{b_2 - b_1}{b_2 - b_1} + \frac{b_1 a_1 - b_1 a_2}{b_2 - b_1} \\
&= \frac{a_1 b_2 - a_1 b_1 + a_1 b_1 - a_2 b_1}{b_2 - b_1} \\
&= \frac{a_1 b_2 - a_2 b_1}{b_2 - b_1}
\end{aligned}
\tag{3.10}
$$

which, by definition, must give the same value for Y_2. Summarizing this then gives:

$$X = \frac{a_1 - a_2}{b_2 - b_1}$$

and

$$Y_1 = Y_2 = \frac{a_1 b_2 - a_2 b_1}{b_2 - b_1}$$

Therefore we now have a general method for deriving the solution for the problem we have already examined. We had:

$$TC = 100 + 5Q$$
$$TR = 10Q$$

so here we have:

$$a_1 = 100 \qquad b_1 = 5$$
$$a_2 = 0 \qquad b_2 = 10$$

Using the two solution equations we have:

$$X = \frac{a_1 - a_2}{b_2 - b_1} = \frac{100 - 0}{10 - 5} = 20 \qquad (= Q \text{ in the context of our problem})$$

$$Y = \frac{a_1 b_2 - a_2 b_1}{b_2 - b_1} = \frac{100(10) - 0(5)}{10 - 5} = \frac{1000}{5} = 200 \qquad (= \text{TC} = \text{TR})$$

Student activity 3.3
For each set of functions derive the simultaneous equations' solution and sketch each pair of equations.

(i) $Y = 100 - 18X$
     $Y = -75 + 17X$
(ii) $Y = 100 - 10X$
     $Y = -50 + 5X$
(iii) $Y = -20 + 3X$
     $Y = 200 - 5X$
(iv) $Y = -60 + 3X$
     $Y = 50 - 2X$

(Solution on p. 327.)

Two points are worth noting at this stage. The first is that there is no guarantee that an equation system actually has a solution. Consider two equations such that:

$$Y = 100 + 5X$$
$$Y = 200 + 5X$$

Clearly, the two functions have the same slope and, in graphical terms, would be parallel to each other. Consider further that, since a simultaneous solution is effectively determining the point at which the two lines intersect, no such solution actually exists. The second point is that the equations in a model for which we require a simultaneous solution must be *functionally independent* of each other; that is, one equation must not be a function of another. Consider the two equations:

$$Y = 100 + 5X \tag{3.11}$$
$$-2.75Y = -275 - 13.75X \tag{3.12}$$

At first it may appear that we have two different equations and hence can find a unique solution. In fact, however, the second equation is a function of the first (it equals -2.75 times the first function). So we actually have only one functional equation. Given that we have two unknowns, X and Y, no unique solution is possible. Naturally, in more complex equation systems it will not always be readily apparent that we face such problems. Fortunately we shall be developing methods for determining whether a unique solution to a set of linear equations is possible in Chapter 4.

> *Student activity 3.4*
> Plot Eqs (3.11) and (3.12) on a graph for $X = 0$ to 100. Comment on the relationship between the two. Using the method of simultaneous equations attempt to find the values for X and Y for these two equations.

3.4 Deriving linear equations from graphs

We have seen how a linear equation and the corresponding graph are effectively identical: both provide the same information about the relationship between X and Y albeit in a different form. We have seen how to obtain the graph of a linear function. How do we reverse the process? Given a graph, how do we obtain the corresponding linear equation? Let us return to the example we introduced in Table 2.1 in Chapter 2 reproduced below.

TABLE 2.1 Prices and quantities over a 4-month period

	Month 1	*Month 2*	*Month 3*	*Month 4*
Price per unit (£)	5	7	9	10
Quantity demanded (daily average 000s)	75	65	55	50

It was from these coordinates that we obtained the graph shown in Chapter 2. We now know that the slope of such a function is constant. It does not matter where on the line we measure the slope, we arrive at the same value. We are seeking a function of the form:

$$Y = a + bX$$

where Y is Q_d and X is P. We can use the difference quotient to obtain the slope of the function between any two X, Y points. Let us choose the relevant two points as (7, 65) and (9, 55). We then have:

$$b = \frac{\Delta y}{\Delta x} = \frac{65 - 55}{7 - 9} = \frac{10}{-2} = -5$$

Given b we can now obtain a since:

$$Y = a + bX = a - 5X$$

and when $X = 7$, $Y = 65$, then:

$$65 = a - 5(7) = a - 35$$

which on rearranging gives $a = 100$ and an equation:

$$Y = 100 - 5X$$

It is, of course, worth checking against the other (X, Y) combinations to see that this equation is correct.

3.5 Market demand and supply

The next linear model we shall examine is the familiar one of market supply and demand. We have already discussed the type of demand function that is likely to exist for some good.

$$Q_d = f(P_x, P_c, P_s, Y, T) \tag{3.13}$$

The quantity demanded, Q_d, of some good, X, will be a function of the price charged, P_x, the price of complementary goods, P_c, the price of substitute goods, P_s, consumer income, Y, and consumer tastes, T. Note that our attention is focused upon market demand and supply and that, further, we assume that the market operates under competitive conditions. Naturally, the more complex we wished the model to be (and the more realistic), then the more independent variables we could introduce into the function. By doing this, however, we make the function more difficult to use in terms of deducing patterns of economic behaviour. At this stage we shall assume that our prime interest lies in examining the relationship between the quantity demanded of the good and its price. Effectively we are assuming that all other variables in the function remain constant (recollect the discussion on functions of more than one independent variable in the previous chapter). If we further assume that the demand function takes a linear form, then we have:

$$Q_d = f(P) = a + bP \tag{3.14}$$

For a normal good we would expect the parameters of the function to be $a > 0$ and $b < 0$. This will then give the familiar demand line shown in Fig. 3.6.

The line slopes downwards with the negative slope equal to b and intercepts the vertical axis at a. Equally we can develop a function for market supply. At its simplest the function will be:

$$Q_s = f(P) = c + dP \tag{3.15}$$

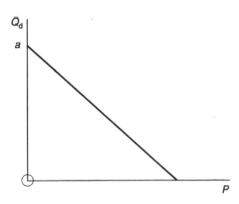

Figure 3.6   Demand function $Q_d = a + bP$

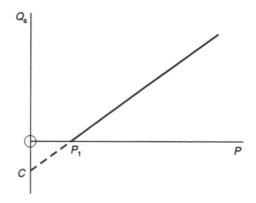

Figure 3.7   Supply function $Q_s = c + dP$

Here we can expect the slope to be positive (an increase in price leads to an increase in supply and hence $d > 0$) while the intercept will take a negative value ($c < 0$).

> *Student activity 3.5*
> Why, in economic terms, does the intercept of the supply function take a negative value?

The immediate logic of this may be less apparent until we examine Fig. 3.7. This shows a typical, linear supply function. We see that the function starts at a point on the horizontal axis below the origin. This implies, quite logically, that supply of the good will not commence until the price has reached some minimum level. Firms will simply be unwilling to supply this good at a price below P_1. Mathematically, this requires a negative constant in the supply function. It is evident that we shall wish to examine both functions together to build a simple economic model of supply and demand. To ensure that we recognize which parameters relate to which function we shall adopt the subscript notation:

$$Q_d = a_1 + b_1 P \qquad (3.16)$$
$$Q_s = a_2 + b_2 P \qquad (3.17)$$

with subscript 1 referring to the parameters of the first equation and so on.

3.6   A partial equilibrium model

We are now in a position to consider this model, to derive a number of principles of economic behaviour from it and to introduce the concept of equilibrium. You will already be aware that in such a market model equilibrium is defined as:

$$Q_d = Q_s \qquad (3.18)$$

that is, where the quantity of the good demanded by consumers is exactly matched by the quantity of the good supplied. In terms of our analysis such an equilibrium position is formally known as a *partial* equilibrium since we are examining only one good available in the market and not the totality of goods available (where we would be trying to establish a *general* equilibrium). Therefore we have a model comprising:

$$Q_d = Q_s$$
$$Q_d = a_1 + b_1 P$$
$$Q_s = a_2 + b_2 P$$

Mathematically, we require values for the three variables, Q_d, Q_s, P, that satisfy all three equations simultaneously. Effectively, however, since we insist by definition that the two quantity variables must be equal, we shall require the values for P and Q that satisfy the model. Such values, naturally, are known as the *equilibrium* values: the equilibrium price, P_e, and the equilibrium quantity, Q_e. An examination of the appropriate graph (Fig. 3.8) for such a system reveals that the solution we seek will occur at the intersection of the two functions and that only one such solution exists (there is, after all, only one point where two straight lines can cross). You should also ensure that you understand why such a position will be an equilibrium.

> *Student activity 3.6*
> Explain in detail why, under the conditions shown, the price can deviate only temporarily from the equilibrium level P_e.

At a price below P_e demand will exceed supply and there will be a shortage of the good in the market. Under shortage conditions the price will rise and as it does so the quantity demanded will decrease while that supplied will increase. Equally, if the price exceeds P_e there will be excess supply and pressure will arise for the price to fall, thereby stimulating quantity demanded but reducing quantity supplied. The only stable position, therefore, will be at the equilibrium point where both quantity supplied and demanded are equal. Algebraically, of course, we already have the ability to determine the general solution to such a model. We derived in Section 3.3 the general solution to two simultaneous equations as·

$$X = \frac{a_1 - a_2}{b_2 - b_1}$$
$$Y = \frac{a_1 b_2 - a_2 b_1}{b_2 - b_1}$$

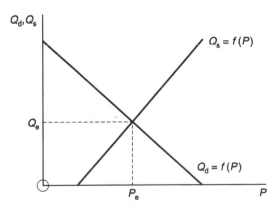

Figure 3.8 Market equilibrium

for two linear equations of the form $Y = f(X)$. In the context of our market model, Q is the dependent variable and P the independent. Hence the equilibrium can be found from:

$$P_e = \frac{a_1 - a_2}{b_2 - b_1} \tag{3.19}$$

$$Q_e = \frac{a_1 b_2 - a_2 b_1}{b_2 - b_1} \tag{3.20}$$

where P_e and Q_e denote the equilibrium values of the two variables. The equilibrium solution expression is worth further inspection. The parameters of the model have already been specified in terms of general value:

$$a_1 > 0 \qquad b_1 < 0$$
$$a_2 < 0 \qquad b_2 > 0$$

Looking at Eqs (3.19) and (3.20) we see that the denominator in the equations, $b_2 - b_1$, must be positive, given the restrictions on the values taken by b_1 and b_2. As b_2 is positive and b_1 negative, then subtracting a negative number from a positive must leave a positive result. Equally, in Eq. (3.19) the numerator must also be positive given the restrictions on a_1 and a_2. Hence P_e must also be positive. Examination of Eq. (3.20) also leads to the general conclusion that in order for Q_e to be positive (which makes sense economically) we must have the additional restriction:

$$a_1 b_2 - a_2 b_1 > 0$$
or
$$a_1 b_2 \qquad > a_2 b_1$$

With the restrictions on the parameters that we have specified we have derived a simple mathematical method for determining the solution for any linear partial equilibrium market model. The importance of this should not be underestimated. We have not found it necessary to use numerical examples to develop the general principles that we have obtained. Indeed the use of specific numerical examples would rarely allow us to make such generalized deductions about economic behaviour. We have been able to show, for the simple model considered, what general conditions are required in order to establish an economically meaningful equilibrium solution.

> **Student activity 3.7**
> Return to activity 3.3. Apply the principles we have just developed to determine which sets of equations will lead to an economically meaningful market equilibrium.
> (Solution on p. 329.)

3.7   An excise tax in a competitive market

We can develop our market model further in order to examine a particular aspect of economic behaviour. Consider the situation where a government decides to impose a sales tax on the good. Assume that such a tax is imposed as a constant amount (known as an excise tax) regardless of the price. Thus the government might impose a tax of £2 on each bottle of whisky, £1 on each pack of cigarettes or 10 pence on a litre of leaded petrol. We wish to determine the general effects of such a policy. This brings us to a form of analysis that is particularly important in economics: *comparative static analysis*. Effectively, we wish to determine two equilibrium positions: one in the market where no tax is imposed and one in the market after the imposition of the tax. We shall thus have two static positions and, literally, we shall be able to compare these to deduce the effect on the equilibrium brought about by the change that has been introduced into the model—in this case the tax imposed. Such comparative static analysis is frequently adopted in economic analysis to allow us to ascertain the effect that a specific change in a model will have on the solution to that model. Clearly, the demand equation will be unchanged. However, on the supply side we must now incorporate the effect of the tax imposed. The firm supplying the good will receive the market price, P, per item sold. However, from this it must pay the government the tax that has been imposed. Let us denote this by t. From the supply side, therefore, we have:

$$P_t = P - t \tag{3.21}$$

where P_t (the difference between the market price P and the excise tax t) is the price that is actually relevant to the firm's supply decisions. We now have a supply function such that:

$$Q_s = a_2 + b_2 P_t \tag{3.22}$$

which can be rewritten using Eq. (3.21) as:

$$Q_s = a_2 + b_2(P - t) \tag{3.23}$$

and the complete model becomes:

$$Q_d = Q_s$$
$$Q_d = a_1 + b_1 P$$
$$Q_s = a_2 + b_2(P - t)$$

with restrictions on the values of the parameters such that:

$$a_1 > 0 \qquad b_1 < 0$$
$$a_2 < 0 \qquad b_2 > 0$$

and

$$t \geq 0$$

Graphically, we might expect a situation as illustrated in Fig. 3.9. The imposition of the tax affects the price from the suppliers' perspective. Suppliers will now require a higher market price to supply the same quantity of the good given that part of this price will go to the government and not the firm. Effectively, therefore, the supply function will shift to the right. The effect on equilibrium will be an increase in the equilibrium price (from P_1 to P_2) and a decrease in the equilibrium quantity (Q_1 to Q_2). We can confirm this logic through some simple algebra.

We require:

$$Q_d = Q_s$$

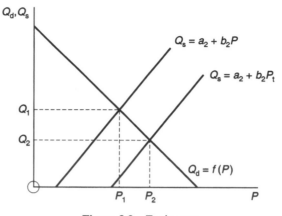

Figure 3.9 Excise tax

Hence:

$$a_1 + b_1 P = a_2 + b_2(P - t)$$
$$a_1 + b_1 P = a_2 + b_2 P - b_2 t$$
$$a_1 - a_2 = b_2 P - b_1 P - b_2 t$$
$$a_1 - a_2 + b_2 t = b_2 P - b_1 P$$
$$a_1 - a_2 + b_2 t = P(b_2 - b_1)$$

or

$$P = \frac{a_1 - a_2 + b_2 t}{b_2 - b_1}$$

giving

$$P_e = \frac{a_1 - a_2}{b_2 - b_1} + \frac{b_2 t}{b_2 - b_1} \tag{3.24}$$

and having found P we can determine the equilibrium quantity by substituting Eq. (3.24) into the demand (or supply) function:

$$Q_e = a_1 + b_1 P$$
$$= a_1 + b_1 \left(\frac{a_1 - a_2}{b_2 - b_1} + \frac{b_2 t}{b_2 - b_1} \right)$$
$$= \frac{a_1(b_2 - b_1) + b_1(a_1 - a_2 + b_2 t)}{b_2 - b_1}$$
$$= \frac{a_1 b_2 - a_1 b_1 + b_1 a_1 - b_1 a_2 + b_1 b_2 t}{b_2 - b_1}$$
$$= \frac{a_1 b_2 - b_1 a_2 + b_1 b_2 t}{b_2 - b_1}$$
$$Q_e = \frac{a_1 b_2 - b_1 a_2}{b_2 - b_1} + \frac{b_1 b_2 t}{b_2 - b_1} \tag{3.25}$$

Therefore Eqs (3.24) and (3.25) again provide us with a general solution for the market model involving an excise tax. This general solution may look complex but, again, careful examination proves particularly revealing. Let us compare these two equations with those derived earlier for the market model without the tax.

<table>
<tr><td>Market model without tax</td><td>Market model with tax</td></tr>
<tr><td>$$P_e = \frac{a_1 - a_2}{b_2 - b_1}$$</td><td>$$P_e = \frac{a_1 - a_2}{b_2 - b_1} + \frac{b_2 t}{b_2 - b_1}$$</td></tr>
<tr><td>$$Q_e = \frac{a_1 b_2 - a_2 b_1}{b_2 - b_1}$$</td><td>$$Q_e = \frac{a_1 b_2 - b_1 a_2}{b_2 - b_1} + \frac{b_1 b_2 t}{b_2 - b_1}$$</td></tr>
</table>

We see quite clearly that the two general solutions are similar. The difference is that for both P_e and Q_e we have an added element involving t, the tax levied. In fact if we set $t = 0$ we see that Eqs (3.24) and (3.25) become identical to Eqs (3.19) and (3.20). Let us examine these elements in more detail. With reference to the restrictions on the function parameters we see that the denominator, $b_2 - b_1$, must be positive and hence in Eq. (3.24) the expression:

$$\frac{b_2}{b_2 - b_1}$$

must be positive also.

Therefore we now know that for $t > 0$ the effect of the tax on the equilibrium price must be positive. The new equilibrium price must be higher than the non-tax P_e. Further inspection reveals that the expression must also be less than 1 since $b_2 - b_1$ will be larger than b_2. Hence the increase in P_e must be less than the tax imposed. Let us now examine the tax element in Eq. (3.25). We have:

$$\frac{b_1 b_2}{b_2 - b_1}$$

and since the denominator is positive and the numerator negative the whole expression must be negative. In other words, the effect on the equilibrium quantity will be negative. The equilibrium quantity after the imposition of a tax must be lower than it was. Hence we know that the imposition of such a tax will raise the equilibrium price but by less than the amount of tax imposed. Naturally, this higher price will lead to a fall in the equilibrium quantity. Once again, therefore, we have a clear demonstration of the usefulness of mathematics in evaluating a change in an economic model. We are able to deduce the effects of such a tax on any market model that fits the general structure identified (that is, has parameters that take numerical values consistent with the restrictions we introduced).

The models we have examined thus far are clearly restrictive in that they consider only a partial equilibrium situation involving one good. We could extend our analysis to examine markets relating to two, or more, goods using the approach developed thus far. We shall wait before doing this, however, in order to develop certain mathematical skills that will make the task much easier.

3.8 Elasticity

We have seen how the slope of a linear function measures the change in Y to a change in X. Frequently in economics we may wish to compare such slopes between two or more functions. Consider two demand functions, say for electricity and gas by domestic consumers. We may pose the question: by how much will demand change if the price increases by, say, £0.1 per energy unit? One problem with such an approach is that we immediately encounter difficulties in terms of units of measurement. Gas demand is likely to be measured in therms but electricity in kilowatt-hours. Equally the price per unit may differ, making the price change of £0.1 relatively larger for one product. Clearly, the slope again will be of little direct use.

The way around this in economics is to examine not the slope of such functions directly but rather their *elasticity*. We need to develop a method of facilitating such a comparison that is independent of units of measurement. This is what elasticity tries to provide. The simplest approach would be to express such changes in percentages rather than absolute terms, that is, comparing the percentage change in Q_d with the corresponding percentage change in P. Units of measurement then become irrelevant. In fact we can define elasticity in such a way:

$$E_d = \frac{\text{percentage change in } Q_d}{\text{percentage change in } P} \tag{3.26}$$

where E_d denotes the (price) elasticity of demand. To calculate a percentage change is straightforward. Given that we have $Q_d = f(P)$, then if we have two values for P (P_1 and P_2) we can derive two comparable values for Q_d (Q_1 and Q_2). The percentage change in, say, Q_d is then:

$$\frac{Q_2 - Q_1}{Q_1} \times 100$$

or to generalize:

$$\frac{\Delta Q}{Q} \times 100$$

and we therefore have:

$$E_d = \frac{\Delta Q / Q \times 100}{\Delta P / P \times 100}$$

which simplifies to:

$$E_d = \frac{\Delta Q / Q}{\Delta P / P}$$

$$= \frac{\Delta Q}{Q} \times \frac{P}{\Delta P}$$

$$= \frac{\Delta Q}{\Delta P} \times \frac{P}{Q} \tag{3.27}$$

Given that the demand function will be:

$$Q_d = a + bP$$

then $\Delta Q = b \Delta P$, giving $b = \Delta Q / \Delta P$. Hence:

$$E_d = \frac{bP}{Q} \qquad (3.28)$$

Consider a demand function: $Q_d = 100 - 10P$. We wish to determine the elasticity of demand when $P = 4$. Clearly, when $P = 4$ then $Q = 60$ and with $b = -10$ we have:

$$E_d = \frac{-10(4)}{60} = -0.67$$

What does this mean? It indicates that at this particular price some given percentage change in the price will bring about a percentage change in Q_d of -0.67 times the percentage change in price. To confirm this let us assume that P changed by 1 per cent, that is, from 4 to 4.04. The new Q_d will be:

$$Q_d = 100 - 10(4.04) = 59.6$$

and the percentage change in Q_d:

$$\frac{59.6 - 60}{60} \times 100 = \frac{-0.4}{60} \times 100 = -0.67$$

Consider further the effect on total revenue, which is given by:

$$TR = P \times Q = P(100 - 10P) = 100P - 10P^2$$

Using $P_1 = 4$ and $P_2 = 4.04$ we have:

$$TR_1 = 240 \qquad \text{and} \qquad TR_2 = 240.784$$

In other words, even though the price has risen and the quantity demanded has fallen, the total revenue from the reduced volume of sales has actually increased. We also note that elasticity can normally be expected to be negative and the sign is usually ignored. Thus, we would report an elasticity of 0.67 in this example and the negative sign would be taken for granted.

> *Student activity 3.8*
> Explain in terms of economics why TR has increased in the example above even though the price has risen.
> (Solution on p. 329.)

Clearly, such an outcome in terms of revenue will depend upon the exact-price elasticity figure that applies to a particular situation. In general, however, we can denote three general values for the price elasticity of demand (ignoring the negative sign):

$$E_d < 1$$
$$E_d = 1$$
$$E_d > 1$$

These three categories indicate the responsiveness of quantity demanded to a proportionate change in price. With elasticity less than 1 (referred to as an inelastic position), then, as we have seen, a proportionate change in P leads to a smaller proportionate change in Q_d. Equally, if the elasticity is greater than 1 (highly elastic), there will be a greater proportionate change in Q_d. When elasticity equals 1 (unitary elasticity), a proportionate change in price brings about the same proportionate change in Q_d. Although we have introduced elasticity here in terms of a demand function, the concept is equally useful to many other functions in economics; we shall be returning to this important topic later in the text. We should note that the evaluation of elasticity is strictly appropriate for considering infinitesimally small changes in the price.

> **Student activity 3.9**
> Calculate, and interpret, the elasticity of demand for $Q_d = 100 - 10P$ when:
>
> (i) $P = 8$
> (ii) $P = 2$
>
> Comment on the implications for the individual firm considering raising its price at each of these two levels.
> (Solution on p. 329.)

3.9 A simple national income model

Having seen how we can apply mathematical analysis to microeconomics we now turn to macroeconomic examples. We begin by assuming the simplest national income model but will gradually develop this model in the rest of this chapter. We start with a model that assumes a closed economy (no foreign trade), no government sector, no inflation and the availability of unused resources. We define national income as comprising two elements: consumption and investment:

$$Y = C + I \tag{3.29}$$

where Y denotes national income
  C consumption expenditure
  I investment expenditure

Let us make the further assumptions that:

$$C = f(Y) = a + bY$$
$$I = i \tag{3.30}$$

where i is some constant value. It will be worth discussing the implications of these in more detail. We have already distinguished between dependent and independent variables. We now distinguish between *endogenous* and *exogenous* variables. Simply, an exogenous variable takes its value from outside the model we are investigating. An endogenous variable, on the other hand, has its value determined from within the model. In this model I is exogenous—its value, i, is determined from outside the model—while Y and C are both endogenous. Let us now examine Eq. (3.30) in more detail. This function is an important one in macroeconomic theory and is known as the *consumption function*. It is evident that, as with other models we have examined thus far, Eq. (3.30) is a simplification of the real-world consumption function which we would expect to include many more independent variables: previous consumption expenditure, wealth, interest rates, levels of government activity and so on. However, it will suffice for the moment to allow us to examine some of the more important principles. It would appear sensible to restrict the two parameters of this function such that:

$$a > 0 \quad \text{and} \quad 0 < b < 1$$

First, we require the intercept of the function to be positive. Even if income is zero, some consumption still takes place—funded either from borrowing against future income or from savings derived from past income (a is often referred to as autonomous consumption). We also restrict the slope of the function to be positive and to lie between zero and 1. The positive restriction on b implies that as Y increases so does C (that is, $0 < b$). This appears logical, but equally we can restrict the maximum value for b to be less than 1. Consider the meaning of b in this context. It represents the change in C that occurs for a given change in Y. If Y increases by, say, £100, then we are restricting the increase in C to be a proportion less than this amount. In fact, the slope of the consumption function is more normally referred to as the *marginal propensity to consume* (mpc). Its value is an indication of the extra consumption arising from extra income. The mpc is given by:

$$\text{mpc} = \frac{\Delta C}{\Delta Y} = b \tag{3.31}$$

while the average propensity to consume (apc) is given by:

$$\text{apc} = \frac{C}{Y} = \frac{a + bY}{Y} = \frac{a}{Y} + b \tag{3.32}$$

which clearly is clearly larger than the mpc since both a and Y are positive. Let us now consider equilibrium in the model. We have, therefore:

$$Y = C + I$$
$$C = a + bY$$

and substituting we derive:

$$Y = a + bY + I$$
$$Y - bY = a + I$$
$$Y(1 - b) = a + I$$
$$Y_e = \frac{a + I}{1 - b} \tag{3.33}$$

Substituting Eq. (3.33) back into the consumption function (3.30) we have:

$$C = a + bY$$
$$= a + b\frac{a + I}{1 - b}$$

and multiplying a by $1 - b/1 - b$ we then have

$$\begin{aligned} C &= \frac{a(1-b)}{1-b} + \frac{ab+bI}{1-b} \\ &= \frac{a-ab+ab+bI}{1-b} \\ C_e &= \frac{a+bI}{1-b} \end{aligned}$$

(3.34)

Thus we have:

$$Y_e = \frac{a+I}{1-b} \qquad \text{and} \qquad C_e = \frac{a+bI}{1-b}$$

as the equilibrium levels of national income and consumers' expenditure.

> ### Student activity 3.10
> Given the restrictions on the equation parameters, what are the implications for the feasible values of Y_e and C_e?
> (Solution on p. 330.)

We note that both endogenous variables (Y and C) can now be determined from known values (given that a and b are parameters and I is exogenous). Note also that given the restrictions on the parameter values the resulting equilibrium values for Y and C must be positive and that C must be less than Y. One further interesting aspect is readily introduced. Let us undertake a comparative static analysis. Let us assume that in time period 1 investment takes some fixed value, I_1. Equilibrium national income will then be:

$$Y_1 = \frac{a+I_1}{1-b}$$

In period 2 investment changes to I_2. The new level of national income is given by:

$$Y_2 = \frac{a+I_2}{1-b}$$

Accordingly we have the change in income:

$$\begin{aligned} Y_1 - Y_2 &= \frac{a+I_1}{1-b} - \frac{a+I_2}{1-b} \\ &= \frac{a+I_1-a-I_2}{1-b} \\ &= \frac{I_1-I_2}{1-b} \\ \Delta Y &= \frac{1}{1-b}\Delta I \\ \frac{\Delta Y}{\Delta I} &= \frac{1}{1-b} = \frac{1}{1-\text{mpc}} \end{aligned}$$

(3.35)

which you may recognize as the familiar Keynesian investment multiplier (usually denoted by k). Moreover, consideration of the parameter restrictions on b indicates that k must be positive; hence an increase in exogenous investment will lead to an increase in income and vice versa. The multiplier k also lies in the range greater than 1 but less than ∞, implying that a given change in I will lead to a greater—but finite—change in Y.

> **Student activity 3.11**
> Assume the following national income model:
>
> $$Y = C + I$$
> $$C = 1000 + 0.8Y$$
> $$I = 250$$
>
> (i) Determine the equilibrium level of national income.
> (ii) Determine the value of k and interpret the result.
> (iii) Assume the mpc changes to 0.75. Calculate the new equilibrium income and explain the change that has occurred in the equilibrium income level.
> (Solution on p. 330.)

It is important to appreciate exactly how the multiplier effect works (we shall be returning to the multiplier concept a number of times through the text). It may at first appear odd that some change in investment can lead to a larger change in income. The key to the puzzle lies in the model formulation. A change in investment has, first, an immediate effect on Y, given Eq. (3.29), and then a subsequent effect on C through Eq. (3.30). However, the process does not stop there. Given that C has now changed, this again changes Y (via Eq. (3.29)), which again changes C, which changes Y, which ... Eventually, of course, the process stops, given that each successive change in Y and C becomes smaller and smaller.

> **Student activity 3.12**
> For the national income model in the last activity, assume that, from equilibrium, I now changes from 250 to 260. Calculate the round-by-round changes in Y and C that occur. What do you observe happening to the successive changes? (Use a spreadsheet.)
> (Solution on p. 331.)

We can also derive the savings function for this model. Given that income must either be spent or saved we have:

$$Y = C + S$$

where S is savings and it follows that $S = f(Y)$ giving:

$$Y = C + S$$
$$Y = (a + bY) + S$$
$$S = Y - (a + bY) = -a + (1 - b)Y$$

as the savings function. Note that the function has a negative intercept and that for low levels of Y S will be negative. Notice also that we have confirmation that at equilibrium income S must equal I. Since at equilibrium:

$$Y = C + I$$

and $Y = C + S$ it follows that $S = I$. That is, the injections into the model, I, must exactly equal the leakages out of the model, S.

3.10   The national income model in diagram form

It is now a simple task to represent the model in the form of a graph. If we examine Fig. 3.10 we can confirm the analysis we have just completed. We have a line representing $I = i$ (which is parallel to the Y axis to indicate a constant value). We have the consumption function $C = f(Y)$ and a line representing $C + I$ to show the actual total of consumption and investment expenditure. We also have a line starting from the origin which represents $Y = C + I$—the level of planned consumption and investment expenditure. Naturally, our equilibrium position must occur somewhere on this line and we see that when $C + I$ intersects with this line we have established Y_e and C_e. The graph also allows us to confirm the general impact on the equilibrium of a change in any of the parameters. We can readily see, for example, that an increase in I will increase the intercept of the $C + I$ line (that is, will push the line higher up the vertical axis). This will have the effect of increasing equilibrium income, Y_e. Similarly, if mpc falls the slope of the $C = f(Y)$ line falls and Y_e will fall also.

> ***Student activity 3.13***
> For the model used in the last activities ($C = 1000 + 0.8Y$ and $I = 250$) use a graph to confirm the equilibrium position.

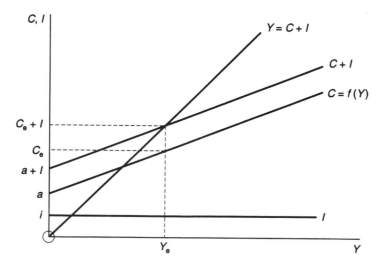

Figure 3.10   National income equilibrium

3.11 A national income model including a government sector

We are now in a position to make the national income model more realistic by including first a government sector and, later, a foreign trade sector. Introducing a government sector has a twofold effect. First, the government itself will act as a consumer, introducing spending into the economic system. Second, in order to spend the government will need to raise revenue through the tax system. We shall make two assumptions: the first that the level of government activity, G, is itself exogenous and the second that tax is raised through a fixed rate imposed on income. Thus our model now becomes:

$$Y = C + I + G \qquad (3.36)$$
$$Y_d = Y - T \qquad (3.37)$$
$$T = tY \qquad (3.38)$$
$$C = a + bY_d \qquad (3.39)$$

Equation (3.37) indicates that disposable income, Y_d, is income Y less taxes T. Equation (3.38) shows that tax is a proportion, t, of income and the new consumption function shows C as a function of disposable income. If we denote t in fractional terms then we would add as parameter restriction such that:

$$0 < t < 1$$

that is, the government must take less than 100 per cent of income in tax! If we substitute Eqs (3.37) and (3.38) into the consumption function (3.39) we have:

$$C = a + b(Y - tY)$$

which gives:

$$Y = C + I + G$$
$$Y = a + b(Y - tY) + I + G$$
$$Y - b(Y - tY) = a + I + G$$
$$Y - bY - btY = a + I + G$$
$$Y(1 - b - bt) - a + I + G$$
$$Y[1 - b(1 - t)] = a + I + G$$
$$Y_e = \frac{a + I + G}{1 - b(1 - t)} \qquad (3.40)$$

If we compare this with the equation for equilibrium income in our earlier model (Eq. (3.33)), we see that if $G = 0$ and $t = 0$ (i.e. there was no government sector) the two expressions for equilibrium income would be the same. We can continue in a similar vein and derive the equation for equilibrium consumption. Substituting Eq. (3.40) into Eq. (3.39) we have:

$$C = a + b(Y - tY)$$
$$C = a + b\left[\frac{a + I + G}{1 - b(1 - t)} - t\left(\frac{a + I + G}{1 - b(1 - t)} \right) \right]$$

Multiplying a by $1 - b(1 - t)/1 - b(1 - t)$ and multiplying the term in square brackets through by b we have:

$$C = \frac{a[1 - b(1 - t)]}{1 - b(1 - t)} + \frac{ba + bI + bG}{1 - b(1 - t)} - \frac{bta + btI + btG}{1 - b(1 - t)}.$$

$$C = \frac{a - ab + abt}{1 - b(1 - t)} + \frac{ba + bI + bG}{1 - b(1 - t)} - \frac{bta + btI + btG}{1 - b(1 - t)}$$

$$C = \frac{a + bI + bG - btI - btG}{1 - b(1 - t)}$$

$$C = \frac{a + b[I + G - t(I + G)]}{1 - b(1 - t)} \quad \text{or} \quad \frac{a + (I + G)(b - bt)}{1 - b(1 - t)} \tag{3.41}$$

Once again if we compare Eq. (3.41) with its earlier counterpart, Eq. (3.34), we see that without G and t the equations are again identical. Equally, we could derive the equation for the final endogenous variable T, although this is left as an activity for you to check your own ability to manipulate a model in this way.

> ### Student activity 3.14
> Derive a corresponding expression for T. Confirm that an increase in G will lead to an increase in T.
> (Solution on p. 331.)

Once again, if we wish to examine the parameter restrictions that we imposed on the model we see that Y, C and T must all be positive. Finally, in this model let us return to the multiplier. Following the same principles as before let us assume that G changes from G_1 to G_2, but with all other factors remaining constant. This gives:

$$Y_1 = \frac{a + I + G_1}{1 - b(1 - t)}$$

$$Y_2 = \frac{a + I + G_2}{1 - b(1 - t)}$$

$$Y_1 - Y_2 = \frac{a + I + G_1}{1 - b(1 - t)} - \frac{a + I + G_2}{1 - b(1 - t)}$$

$$\Delta Y = \frac{1}{1 - b(1 - t)} \Delta G \tag{3.42}$$

where we see the new multiplier. Again, a quick confirmation reveals that if $t = 0$ then the new multiplier is the same as in the first model. Given that both b and t are required to be positive in the model we can also see that the denominator in the new multiplier is larger than in the old; hence the value of the multiplier will be less in this model than in the model without a government sector. We can rationalize this quite easily. An increase in one of the exogenous variables will now lead to a smaller increase than before in Y since some of the increase will 'leak out' of the system in terms of taxation revenue. However, on inspection it is evident that k is still greater than 1.

> ### Student activity 3.15
> What effect will an increase in t have on k?
> (Solution on p. 331.)

3.12 A national income model with a government sector and foreign trade

In terms of economic policy governments are generally concerned about the effect of their own activities on the equilibrium level of national income. Equally, they have a keen interest in the balance of trade and its effect. Let us expand the government model by introducing foreign trade in the form of exports, X, and imports, M. We shall assume that exports are exogenous (not unduly unrealistic given that demand for goods that we produce will frequently be determined by factors outside our national economy). We also assume that imports are endogenous and take the form:

$$M = f(Y_d) = mY_d \tag{3.43}$$

where m represents the marginal propensity to import. The equilibrium condition is now met when:

$$Y = C + I + G + X - M \tag{3.44}$$

and we have:

$$Y_d = Y - t \tag{3.45}$$
$$T = tY \tag{3.46}$$
$$C = a + bY_d \tag{3.47}$$
$$M = mY_d \tag{3.48}$$

Substituting as appropriate we then derive:

$$Y = C + I + G + X - M$$
$$C = a + bY_d = a + b[Y(1-t)]$$
$$M = mY_d = mY(1-t)$$

giving at equilibrium:

$$Y = a + b[Y(1-t)] + (I + G + X) - mY(1-t)$$
$$Y = a + bY - btY - mY + mtY + (I + G + X)$$
$$Y(1 - b + bt + m - mt) = a + I + G + X$$
$$Y = \frac{a + I + G + X}{1 - b + bt + m - mt} \tag{3.49}$$

and we see the new multiplier is given by:

$$k = \frac{1}{1 - b + bt + m - mt} = \frac{1}{1 - (1-t)(b-m)} \tag{3.50}$$

Student activity 3.16
Confirm that the new multiplier would return to that shown in Eqs (3.41) and (3.35) if first
m and then t took a zero value.

Clearly, our model is now more complex and we could examine a variety of potential policy
issues. However, let us focus on the balance of trade. Let us define:

$$B = X - M$$

as the balance of trade being the difference between exports and imports. Let us assume that the
government is considering altering its own spending level, G, and wishes to evaluate the impact
on the balance of trade, that is, to assess ΔB. Given that exports are exogenous, clearly the
impact in the model will occur through a change in income, consumption and then imports. Let
us assume that $\Delta G > 0$, that is the government increases its own spending. We know that:

$$\begin{aligned}
\Delta M &= m\Delta Y_d \\
&= m\Delta Y(1 - t) \\
&= m(1 - t)k\Delta G \qquad \text{(since } \Delta Y = k\Delta G)
\end{aligned}$$

and therefore $\Delta M > 0$ since m, t, k are > 0 in the model, $\Delta G > 0$ by definition and $t < 1$. Hence
an increase in G must lead to an increase in M and, in this model, a worsening of the balance of
trade position. Exactly how much worse is, of course, a matter of the precise values taken by the
parameters. What is worth noting, however, is that we conclude that ΔM will be affected not
only by the marginal propensity to import, m, but also by the income tax rate, t, and the
marginal propensity to consume, b (which is hidden in the k term). In terms of policy instru-
ments, therefore, the government would be able to affect the change in M through alterations in
t as well as G. We must, however, wait before examining in detail how this can be done.

3.13 Summary

We have seen in this chapter a number of examples of the usefulness of mathematics in deriving
general conclusions about economic behaviour from an economic model. None of the examples
we have introduced has actually involved numerical values and yet we have been able to derive
important policy conclusions from our applications of a combination of mathematical and
economic logic. Naturally, there are severe limitations in the realism of the models we have
examined. This does not negate, however, the importance of mathematics. As we shall see as we
progress through the text, expansions to all these models are readily incorporated once we have
developed the necessary skills.

Worked example

The minister of finance in the government is keen to try to raise additional revenue through
taxation. She has identified one industrial sector in the economy and is considering introducing
an excise tax of £3 per unit sold. The relevant demand and supply functions are:

$$Q_d = 250 - 8P$$
$$Q_s = -50 + 4P$$

Someone has suggested that if the tax were doubled to £6 per unit then the government would raise twice as much tax revenue. Using the functions given can we assess the accuracy of this suggestion? Additionally, can we suggest an excise tax amount which would maximize the tax revenue obtained by the government?

We can denote the tax revenue raised as T so we have:

$$T = tQ_e$$

where t is the unit tax and Q_e the equilibrium quantity. From Eq. (3.25) we know the equilibrium solution will be:

$$Q_e = \frac{a_1 b_2 - b_1 a_2}{b_2 - b_1} + \frac{b_1 b_2 t}{b_2 - b_1}$$

Here we have, for a tax of £3:

$$Q_e = \frac{250(4) - (-8)(-50)}{4 - (-8)} + \frac{(-8)(4)(3)}{4 - (-8)}$$
$$= \frac{1000 - 400}{12} - \frac{96}{12} = 42$$

and we then have:

$$T = tQ_e = 3(42) = 126$$

as the tax revenue raised.

If $t = £6$ we then have:

$$Q_e = \frac{250(4) - (-8)(-50)}{4 - (-8)} + \frac{(-8)(4)(6)}{4 - (-8)}$$
$$= \frac{1000 - 400}{12} - \frac{192}{12} = 34$$

and we then have:

$$T = tQ_e = 6(34) = 204$$

as the tax revenue raised.

While the tax revenue has increased it clearly has not doubled as the tax imposed has. It is also clear that we have the same principles at work as with elasticity of demand.

With regard to the second part to the problem we are required to offer advice on a tax that will maximize the total tax revenue. We know that in general:

$$T = tQ_e$$

In this case Q_e simplifies to:

$$Q_e = 50 - 1.33t$$

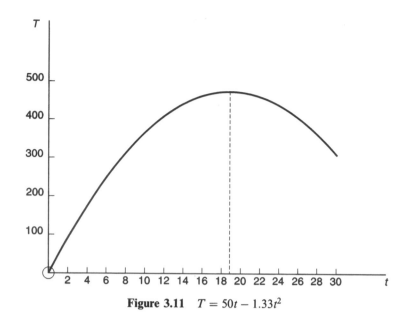

Figure 3.11 $T = 50t - 1.33t^2$

so we have:

$$T = 50t - 1.33t^2$$

which we recognize as a quadratic taking the inverted U shape from Chapter 2. If we now plot this function we can use the graph to identify the maximum T position. The corresponding graph in shown in Figure 3.11 where we see the maximum value of T occurs when t is approximately 19 (in fact, the t value is 18.75 using solution techniques we shall develop later in the text).

Exercises

3.1 On a weekly basis a small firm producing a certain product has overheads of £12 000. The product costs £15 per unit to produce and, because the firm is small, all output can be sold at a unit price of £22. Determine:

    (i) The breakeven level of output.
    (ii) The new breakeven level of output if the selling price falls to £20.
    (iii) The new breakeven level if fixed costs change to £20 000.
    (iv) The new breakeven level if variable costs change to £16.

3.2 Assume the following market model:

$$Q_d = 500 - 9P$$
$$Q_s = -100 + 6P$$

    (i) Sketch the model.
    (ii) Determine the equilibrium price and quantity.
    (iii) If a tax of £5 per unit sold is now imposed, calculate the new equilibrium price and quantity.

(iv) Sketch the new equilibrium.
(v) What proportion of the tax is paid by the consumer?
(vi) What revenue does the government raise through imposition of the tax?

3.3 Assume that the demand function changes to:

$$Q_d = 500 - 10P$$

(i) Sketch both demand functions and the supply function.
(ii) What would you expect to happen to the equilibrium price:
    (a) before tax?
    (b) after tax?
(iii) Calculate the new equilibrium price before and after tax.
(iv) What proportion of the tax is paid by the consumer?
(v) What has happened to the revenue raised from the tax?
(vi) How do you explain (iv) and (v)?

3.4 Assume a simple national income model with:

$$C = f(Y) = 750 + 0.75Y \qquad \text{and} \qquad I = 500$$

(i) Calculate the equilibrium levels of income, consumption and saving.
(ii) Calculate k and interpret the result.
(iii) If I changed to 510, what would be the effect on (i)?

3.5 In the model in Exercise 3.4 assume that the mpc changes to 0.8. Explain in detail the effect you would expect this to have on the equilibrium position. Calculate the new equilibrium to confirm your logic.

3.6 The simple national income model now includes a government sector with $G = 150$ and $t = 0.25$. Calculate the new equilibrium and the new value for k. Why has the value for k decreased? What are the implications of this?

3.7 In Exercise 3.6 we now add a foreign trade sector such that $X = 200$ and $M = 0.15Y_d$. Calculate the new equilibrium and explain the changes that have occurred from your answer to Exercise 3.6.

3.8 For the model in Exercise 3.6 find the level of G that will give a balanced budget (that is, $G = T$).

3.9 For the model in Exercise 3.7 find the level of G that will balance foreign trade (that is, $X = M$).

4 Matrix algebra

In the previous two chapters we have seen the need for, and usefulness of, economic models presented as sets of linear equations. Not only can we develop a suitable theoretical model using such equations but we can also find the unique solution to such a model and begin the process of deducing the implications and consequences of the model and its parameters. The problem with the approach we have taken thus far is that it is both tedious and restrictive. Frequently we wish to assess the impact of some change in the underlying conditions on the model we have developed. Typically one of the parameter values in the model will be changed and we wish to assess the effect this has on the solution. With simultaneous equations it is necessary to recalculate the entire set of equations to determine the new solution. This makes the task of comparative static analysis both tedious and time consuming. Additionally, it is apparent that the simple models we have developed so far in the text—involving only two or, at most, three equations—are far too restrictive in terms of economic theory and model building. It is clear that we shall require the facility to develop mathematical models involving considerably more variables or equations than this. Once we wish to extend our basic models, however, determining the solution using the simultaneous equations approach becomes impractical. Consider the calculations necessary for, say, a 10-equation system. For these reasons we require an alternative method of handling large systems of linear equations and of finding the unique solution to such sets of equations. Such a method is readily available through the use of *matrix algebra*. In this chapter we shall introduce and develop the appropriate tools for dealing with matrix algebra and in the next we shall use matrix algebra to develop a number of common economic models.

Learning objectives

By the time you have finished this chapter you should be:

- Familiar with matrix notation
- Able to manipulate matrices and vectors using matrix arithmetic
- Able to determine the inverse of a matrix
- Able to use the inverse matrix to find the solution to a set of linear equations
- Able to derive and use determinants

4.1 The terminology of matrix algebra

A matrix can be thought of simply as a rectangular array, or table, of numbers, numerical coefficients, parameters or variables. Assume that a firm operates on a regional basis and last year achieved the sales levels shown in Table 4.1. For example, in the North region sales of

TABLE 4.1   Number of units of each product sold by region

Region	Product		
	X	Y	Z
North	1000	500	750
South	750	400	600
Midlands	100	50	80

product X were 1000 units, of product Y 500 units and of product Z 750 units. The matrix representing these data would be:

$$\text{Sales matrix } \mathbf{A} = \begin{bmatrix} 1000 & 500 & 750 \\ 750 & 400 & 600 \\ 100 & 50 & 80 \end{bmatrix}$$

Conventionally, a matrix is denoted using a capital letter—$\mathbf{A}$ in this case—marked in bold type and the values comprising the matrix denoted using square brackets [ ]. A matrix is, therefore, simply a format for showing the data relating to the problem. Note that the matrix makes no reference to the variables we are using in the problem: regions and sales levels. It is our task to remember what the rows and columns of the matrix actually represent and also to remember, where appropriate, units of measurement being used. We could also use a matrix to denote a set of variables rather than numbers. We may have a matrix, $\mathbf{P}$, denoting the selling price for each product in each region:

$$\text{Price matrix } \mathbf{P} = \begin{bmatrix} p_{NX} & p_{NY} & p_{NZ} \\ p_{SX} & p_{SY} & p_{SZ} \\ p_{MX} & p_{MY} & p_{MZ} \end{bmatrix}$$

It is evident that matrix notation offers a convenient shorthand for describing large sets of data or variables. No matter how many regions or how many products, we could simply refer to matrix $\mathbf{A}$ and $\mathbf{P}$ rather than to a cumbersome multidimensional table of data. The potential usefulness of such notation in economic models is self-evident.

The dimensions of a matrix

The dimension, or size, of a matrix is defined in terms of the number of rows (denoted by m) and the number of columns (n) comprising the matrix. In this example, matrix $\mathbf{A}$ is referred to as a 3×3 matrix as it has three rows and three columns. Conventionally the first number in the dimension refers to the number of rows and the second to the number of columns. Note also that matrix $\mathbf{A}$ is symmetrical (that is, $m = n$). Such a matrix is known as a square matrix. The items making up the matrix—in this example set of numbers representing product sales in each region—are referred to as the elements of the matrix, or as the cells of the matrix. Each element can be uniquely identified by its row and column position using a suitable subscript notation:

$$\mathbf{A} = \begin{bmatrix} a_{11} & a_{12} & a_{13} \\ a_{21} & a_{22} & a_{23} \\ a_{31} & a_{32} & a_{33} \end{bmatrix}$$

Thus a_{23}, for example, refers to the matrix element in row 2, column 3 (here $a_{23} = 600$). It is also conventional to represent a matrix and its elements in a shorthand fashion:

$$\mathbf{A} = [a_{ij}] \qquad i = 1, 2, 3; \; j = 1, 2, 3$$

or in general as:

$$\mathbf{A} = [a_{ij}] \qquad i = 1, 2, \ldots, m; \; j = 1, 2, \ldots, n$$

Vectors

One special type of matrix is that consisting of a single row or a single column. Such a matrix is more generally referred to as a *vector*. A column vector would appear as:

$$\mathbf{c} = \begin{bmatrix} c_1 \\ c_2 \\ \vdots \\ c_m \end{bmatrix}$$

and a row vector as:

$$\mathbf{r}' = [r_1 r_2 \ldots r_n]$$

Note that we distinguish a vector by using a lower-case letter and that, conventionally, a row vector is distinguished from a column vector by using the prime ($'$) symbol. One point to remember is that effectively a matrix is made up of a set of vectors. The sales matrix $\mathbf{A}$, for example, could be broken into three column vectors (with each column representing sales of one product) or into three row vectors (with each vector representing sales in a particular region). This ability to manipulate a matrix as a series of vectors becomes useful at later stages of matrix algebra.

Scalars

One final term must be defined before we proceed to develop the use of matrices and matrix algebra. This is the term *scalar*, which represents not an array or matrix of numbers but only a single number, or a constant that we shall occasionally wish to use in conjunction with some matrix.

4.2 Special matrices

There are three special types of matrix that we introduce. The first of these is the identity matrix, denoted by $\mathbf{I}$ which is a square matrix that consists solely of the values 1 and 0. The values of 1 occur in what is known as the main diagonal of the matrix, that is, the diagonal running from the top-left corner to the bottom-right corner. All other elements of the identity matrix take the value zero. So, for example, an identity matrix of size three would be:

$$\mathbf{I} = \begin{bmatrix} 1 & 0 & 0 \\ 0 & 1 & 0 \\ 0 & 0 & 1 \end{bmatrix}$$

Second, a null matrix, **N**, is one where all the elements take a zero value. Note that, unlike the identity matrix, the null matrix is not required to be square. Finally, there is the transpose matrix. Such a matrix is created by interchanging the rows and columns of some matrix. For example, let us return to the sales matrix, **A**:

$$\mathbf{A} = \begin{bmatrix} 1000 & 500 & 750 \\ 750 & 400 & 600 \\ 100 & 50 & 80 \end{bmatrix}$$

If we let row 1 of **A** become column 1 of a new matrix, row 2 become column 2 and row 3 become column 3, we have:

$$\mathbf{A}' = \begin{bmatrix} 1000 & 750 & 100 \\ 500 & 400 & 50 \\ 750 & 600 & 80 \end{bmatrix}$$

where $\mathbf{A}'$ is the transpose of **A**. In this example, the columns would now represent the regions and the rows would represent the different products.

4.3 Matrix algebra

The importance of matrices in economics is not simply in terms of their usefulness in presenting data, variables or equations in a compact form but rather in their ability to allow us to perform complex manipulations and algebra relatively easily. Just as we can carry out arithmetic on ordinary numbers so we can undertake the equivalent arithmetic on matrices. In the rest of this chapter we shall focus upon a number of such types of matrix arithmetic:

- Matrix addition
- Matrix subtraction
- Multiplication by a scalar
- Matrix multiplication
- Matrix division (known as determining a matrix 'inverse')

We shall look at each in turn. While much of the arithmetic we perform on matrices is similar to that carried out on numbers, we should be cautious about inferring that exactly the same rules apply to matrix algebra as apply to ordinary algebra. As we shall see, there are important differences.

4.4 Matrix addition

We can add two matrices provided that they have the same dimensions—that they are compatible for addition. Assume that matrix **A** used earlier represents sales for last year and that we have a corresponding matrix, **B**, that represents sales achieved this month:

$$\mathbf{B} = \begin{bmatrix} 10 & 50 & 30 \\ 20 & 10 & 0 \\ 10 & 20 & 10 \end{bmatrix}$$

If we now require the total sales to date (that is, last year's sales plus this month's), we can add the two matrices simply by adding their corresponding elements. Thus:

$$C = A + B = \begin{bmatrix} 1000 & 500 & 750 \\ 750 & 400 & 600 \\ 100 & 50 & 80 \end{bmatrix} + \begin{bmatrix} 10 & 50 & 30 \\ 20 & 10 & 0 \\ 10 & 20 & 10 \end{bmatrix}$$

$$C = \begin{bmatrix} 1000+10 & 500+50 & 750+30 \\ 750+20 & 400+10 & 600+0 \\ 100+10 & 50+20 & 80+10 \end{bmatrix} = \begin{bmatrix} 1010 & 550 & 780 \\ 770 & 410 & 600 \\ 110 & 70 & 90 \end{bmatrix}$$

In general, therefore, we have:

$$C = [c_{ij}] = [a_{ij}] + [b_{ij}] \tag{4.1}$$

Given that a vector can be regarded as a particular type of matrix then this addition process can be applied equally to vectors, providing they are compatible. Note also that:

1 The **C** matrix resulting from the addition will be of the same size as the **A** and **B** matrices.

2 $A + B = B + A$ (4.2)

3 $(A + B) + C = A + (B + C)$, that is, that when adding matrices the order in which we add is irrelevant to the result.

> ### Student activity 4.1
> For the three matrices shown below determine which of the following can be undertaken and find the resulting matrix:
>
> $$D + E$$
> $$E + D$$
> $$D + F$$
> $$F + E$$
>
> where
>
> $$D = \begin{bmatrix} 15 & 7 & 11 \\ 6 & 4 & 7 \\ 4 & 3 & 2 \end{bmatrix}$$
>
> $$E = \begin{bmatrix} 10 & 5 & 4 \\ -3 & 6 & 1 \\ 11 & 9 & 2 \end{bmatrix}$$
>
> $$F = \begin{bmatrix} -2 & 3 & 6 \\ 4 & 7 & 4 \end{bmatrix}$$
>
> (Solution on p. 332.)

4.5 Matrix subtraction

Matrix subtraction is as straightforward as matrix addition. Again, as with addition, the two matrices to be subtracted must be compatible. In this case we have:

$$\mathbf{C} = [c_{ij}] = [a_{ij}] - [b_{ij}] \tag{4.3}$$

Student activity 4.2
Using **C** and **B** derive the original **A** matrix (the sales matrix) we have been using.

4.6 Multiplication by a scalar

As we have seen, a scalar is a single number or constant. When we multiply a matrix by a scalar the effect is to multiply each element in the matrix by that number. Assume that the firm has decided to establish regional sales targets for the future. Sales of each product in each region are to increase by 10 per cent over and above last year's levels (as shown in **A**). We require the new sales target matrix. Given that the new sales levels will be 110 per cent of the existing levels the scalar takes a value of 1.1. Each element in turn in the matrix is then multiplied by the scalar:

$$\mathbf{B} = 1.1 \times \mathbf{A} = 1.1 \begin{bmatrix} 1000 & 500 & 750 \\ 750 & 400 & 600 \\ 100 & 50 & 80 \end{bmatrix} = \begin{bmatrix} 1100 & 550 & 825 \\ 825 & 440 & 660 \\ 110 & 55 & 88 \end{bmatrix}$$

Note that in general if we denote the scalar as k then:

(a) $$k\mathbf{A} = \mathbf{A}k \tag{4.4}$$
(b) $$k[a_{ij}] = [ka_{ij}] = [a_{ij}]k \tag{4.5}$$

In the terminology of matrix algebra, this implies that it is immaterial whether we *pre*multiply the matrix with the scalar or whether we *post*multiply the matrix with the scalar.

Student activity 4.3
Using the appropriate scalar, transform **B** above back into the original **A** matrix first by premultiplying and then by postmultiplying.
   As an additional activity derive a matrix showing the extra sales to be achieved per product per region in order to meet the sales target set.

4.7 Matrix multiplication

The potential advantages of using matrix notation for large-scale economic models start to become apparent when we look at matrix multiplication. To illustrate the process, we shall first consider the multiplication of a matrix and a vector.

Multiplying a vector and a matrix

Let us return to the sales matrix we have been using:

$$A = \begin{bmatrix} 1000 & 500 & 750 \\ 750 & 400 & 600 \\ 100 & 50 & 80 \end{bmatrix}$$

Let us further assume the following column vector, **b**:

$$b = \begin{bmatrix} 10 \\ 12 \\ 18 \end{bmatrix}$$

which represents the current market price of each of the three products. Thus, product X sells for £10, product Y for £12 and product Z for £18. We wish to calculate the current total sales revenue in each region. In terms of ordinary arithmetic we would follow a simple process. For each region in turn we would calculate the sum of the number of units of each product sold multiplied by the market price. Thus, for North region we would have:

$$(1000 \times 10) + (500 \times 12) + (750 \times 18) = £29\,500$$

Let us denote the vector and matrix by their cell references:

$$A = \begin{bmatrix} a_{11} & a_{12} & a_{13} \\ a_{21} & a_{22} & a_{23} \\ a_{31} & a_{32} & a_{33} \end{bmatrix} \qquad b = \begin{bmatrix} b_1 \\ b_2 \\ b_3 \end{bmatrix}$$

We now multiply each row in the **A** matrix by the column vector **b** and total the result. The product of this multiplication will be given by:

$$[a_{11}b_1 + a_{12}b_2 + a_{13}b_3 \qquad a_{21}b_1 + a_{22}b_2 + a_{23}b_3 \qquad a_{31}b_1 + a_{32}b_2 + a_{33}b_3]$$

where

$$\begin{aligned} a_{11}b_1 + a_{12}b_2 + a_{13}b_3 &= 1000(10) + 500(12) + 750(18) = 29\,500 \\ a_{21}b_1 + a_{22}b_2 + a_{23}b_3 &= 750(10) + 400(12) + 600(18) = 23\,100 \\ a_{31}b_1 + a_{32}b_2 + a_{33}b_3 &= 100(10) + 50(12) + 80(18) = 3\,040 \end{aligned}$$

giving

$$Ab = r = \begin{bmatrix} 29\,500 \\ 23\,100 \\ 3\,040 \end{bmatrix}$$

where **r** represents a total revenue vector with the elements relating to sales revenue in a particular region.

Student activity 4.4

Assume that the organization has data on the per unit cost of each of the products sold:

Product X   £8

Product Y   £11

Product Z   £15

  (i) Show these data in vector form.

 (ii) Derive a vector showing the total product cost for the sales achieved in each region.

(iii) Derive a vector showing the total profit per region.

(iv) Construct a single matrix showing the price, cost and profit per product.

(Solution on p. 332.)

Multiplying two matrices

Multiplying two matrices is as straightforward as the example shown of multiplying a vector and a matrix. Assume we have two matrices:

$$A = \begin{bmatrix} a_{11} & a_{12} \\ a_{21} & a_{22} \end{bmatrix} \qquad B = \begin{bmatrix} b_{11} & b_{12} & b_{13} \\ b_{21} & b_{22} & b_{23} \end{bmatrix}$$

and we wish to determine the product of **AB**. If we regard matrix A as consisting of two row vectors, then we can perform exactly the same arithmetic as before. We take each row in turn in the **A** matrix and multiply by each column in turn in the **B** matrix, calculating the total of each row/column multiplication as we proceed. This results in matrix **C**:

$$C = AB = \begin{bmatrix} a_{11}b_{11} + a_{12}b_{21} & a_{11}b_{12} + a_{12}b_{22} & a_{11}b_{13} + a_{12}b_{23} \\ a_{21}b_{11} + a_{22}b_{21} & a_{21}b_{12} + a_{22}b_{22} & a_{21}b_{13} + a_{22}b_{23} \end{bmatrix} \qquad (4.6)$$

This process of multiplying rows and columns from the two matrices is readily applied to any two matrices of any size, although, naturally, the arithmetic for large matrices quickly becomes tedious.

Student activity 4.5

Returning to the matrices in activity 4.1, find the following:

 (i) **DE**

(ii) **ED**

(Solution on p. 332.)

There are a number of important points about matrix multiplication that we need to be aware of. First, the two matrices to be multiplied must be compatible. It is clear that—given the nature of the multiplication process—the number of columns in the first matrix must be the same as the number of rows in the second matrix. In all the examples thus far the two matrices have been compatible. Not all matrices will be, however. Second, the size of the matrix resulting from the multiplication will be determined by the sizes of the two matrices being multiplied. This matrix will have the same number of rows as the first matrix and the same number of columns as the second. If, for example, we multiply a 5×4 matrix by a 4×2 matrix the result will be a 5×2 matrix. Third, the process of multiplying larger matrices together follows the same structure as in the simple examples used earlier—summing the products of multiplying successive rows by successive columns. To determine the position of the resulting elements we use the row/column combinations that have been used in the calculation; that is, if we denote the product matrix as **C** we have:

$$C = \begin{bmatrix} c_{11} & c_{12} & \cdots & c_{1n} \\ c_{21} & c_{22} & \cdots & c_{2n} \\ \vdots & \vdots & & \vdots \\ c_{m1} & c_{m2} & \cdots & c_{mn} \end{bmatrix}$$

and the value of any cell, c_{ij}, will be the product of multiplying row i of the first matrix and column j of the second. Thus each value produced from the multiplication takes its place according to the **A** row and **B** column used to produce it. Fourth, it is important to note that, unlike ordinary algebra, the order of matrix multiplication is critical. In ordinary arithmetic the product of 2×5 is exactly the same as that of 5×2. In matrix algebra, however, this is generally not the case (as you will have realized in the Activity 4.5); that is:

$$AB \neq BA \tag{4.7}$$

However, the following property of multiplication does hold:

$$(AB)C = A(BC) \tag{4.8}$$

that is, the sequence of multiplication is immaterial.

4.8 Using matrix algebra to represent economic models

Collecting together the aspects of matrix algebra we have examined thus far, we are now in a position to show how we can represent the linear economic models we have previously developed in matrix form. (The next step will be to show how we can use matrix algebra to find the solution to such models.) Let us return to the example we used earlier involving a sales matrix and a price vector. We show the sales matrix in numerical terms but the price vector simply in terms of the three variables:

$$A = \begin{bmatrix} 1000 & 500 & 750 \\ 750 & 400 & 600 \\ 100 & 50 & 80 \end{bmatrix} \qquad p = \begin{bmatrix} p_1 \\ p_2 \\ p_3 \end{bmatrix}$$

Similarly, we can represent the total sales revenue vector that we derived in Sec. 4.7 as:

$$r = \begin{bmatrix} r_1 \\ r_2 \\ r_3 \end{bmatrix}$$

The relationship between sales, prices and revenue can then be conveniently represented as:

$$\mathbf{Ap} = \mathbf{r}$$

There are two aspects to the matrix representation of such an economic model to note. The first is that the matrix representation of the model remains the same no matter how large—in terms of equations or variables—the model becomes. We have a compact method of notation for the economic models we wish to examine. Second, the matrix notation actually represents a series of equations. In this example we would have:

$$\mathbf{Ap} = \mathbf{r}$$
$$a_{11}p_1 + a_{12}p_2 + a_{13}p_3 = r_1$$
$$a_{21}p_1 + a_{22}p_2 + a_{23}p_3 = r_2$$
$$a_{31}p_1 + a_{32}p_2 + a_{33}p_3 = r_3$$

It will be instructive to consider a second example of this as it is central to much of what we shall be doing in the next chapter. Consider the market equilibrium model:

$$Q_d = Q_s$$
$$Q_d = a_1 + b_1 P$$
$$Q_s = a_2 + b_2 P$$

Let us rearrange these equations so that the endogenous variables are collected together on the left-hand side while the exogenous values are on the right. We then have:

$$Q_d - Q_s = 0$$
$$Q_d - b_1 P = a_1$$
$$Q_s - b_2 P = a_2$$

and in matrix format this can be written as:

$$\mathbf{Ax} = \mathbf{b}$$

$$\begin{bmatrix} 1 & -1 & 0 \\ 1 & 0 & -b_1 \\ 0 & 1 & -b_2 \end{bmatrix} \begin{bmatrix} Q_d \\ Q_s \\ P \end{bmatrix} = \begin{bmatrix} 0 \\ a_1 \\ a_2 \end{bmatrix}$$

You should confirm for yourself that the matrix representation is identical to the equation system. The next stage is to determine the solution to such a model. In order to be able to do this we need to introduce the last aspect of matrix algebra—the matrix inverse.

Student activity 4.6
Represent the following two models in matrix format:

(i) $Y = C + I$
$\quad C = a + bY$

where I is exogenous;
(ii) $Y = C + I + G$
$C = a + bY_d$
$T = tY$
$Y_d = Y - T$
where I and G are exogenous.

(Solution on p. 333.)

4.9 Matrix inversion

The inverse matrix has much the same meaning as the inverse, or reciprocal, of a normal number. The inverse of the number 10, for example, is:

$$\frac{1}{10} \quad \text{or} \quad 10^{-1}$$

One property of such an inverse is that:

$$10 \times 10^{-1} = 1$$

that is, a number multiplied by its inverse equals 1. In matrix terms the inverse of matrix $\mathbf{A}$ is denoted as $\mathbf{A}^{-1}$ and has the equivalent property:

$$\mathbf{AA}^{-1} = \mathbf{I} \tag{4.9}$$

or alternatively:

$$\mathbf{A}^{-1}\mathbf{A} = \mathbf{I} \tag{4.10}$$

that is, a matrix pre- or postmultiplied by its inverse will result in an identity matrix. (Readers should not be tempted at this stage to assume, however, that the inverse of a matrix will simply be $1/\mathbf{A}$. The analogy with normal arithmetic is not appropriate, as we shall see). The following properties of inverse matrices must be noted:

- Only a square matrix can have an inverse.
- Not all square matrices will have an inverse. A matrix that has an inverse is said to be non-singular and a matrix that has no inverse is said to be singular.
- If an inverse exists it is unique.
- Inverses have the following properties:

$$(\mathbf{A}^{-1})^{-1} = \mathbf{A} \tag{4.11}$$

$$(\mathbf{AB})^{-1} = \mathbf{B}^{-1}\mathbf{A}^{-1} \tag{4.12}$$

$$(\mathbf{A}')^{-1} = (\mathbf{A}^{-1})' \tag{4.13}$$

Before we look at methods of determining the inverse of a matrix it is worth examining their use in order to be aware of their importance.

The use of a matrix inverse

Let us return to the sales matrix and price vector that we used earlier in the chapter. We had:

$$\mathbf{Ap} = \mathbf{r}$$

where:

$$\mathbf{A} = \begin{bmatrix} 1000 & 500 & 750 \\ 750 & 400 & 600 \\ 100 & 50 & 80 \end{bmatrix}$$

and represents sales in the three regions last year, $\mathbf{p}$ represents the price vector and $\mathbf{r}$ represents the sales revenue vector. Let us assume that the firm has set a sales revenue target for next year of:

Region 1   £35 500
Region 2   £26 250
Region 3   £3 450

and is investigating the implications of such a target for pricing policy. For simplicity, we shall assume that sales levels stay the same (that is, that the $\mathbf{A}$ matrix remains unchanged), although in practice we could readily simulate the effect of different growth rates in sales on the pricing policy. Management now wish to determine the market prices that must be charged for the three products, given the sales figures and the revenue targets. In matrix terms we require the appropriate values for the $\mathbf{p}$ vector given the values for $\mathbf{A}$ and $\mathbf{r}$. Using what we know about the matrix inverse we can rearrange the model:

$$\mathbf{Ap} = \mathbf{r}$$
$$\mathbf{A}^{-1}\mathbf{Ap} = \mathbf{A}^{-1}\mathbf{r}$$

but as $\mathbf{A}^{-1}\mathbf{A} = \mathbf{I}$, then:

$$\mathbf{Ip} = \mathbf{A}^{-1}\mathbf{r}$$

Let us examine the term $\mathbf{Ip}$ in more detail. Given that the $\mathbf{A}$ matrix is of size 3×3, the $\mathbf{A}$ inverse matrix and the $\mathbf{I}$ matrix must also be of the same size. If we multiply out $\mathbf{Ip}$ we have:

$$\mathbf{Ip} = \begin{bmatrix} 1 & 0 & 0 \\ 0 & 1 & 0 \\ 0 & 0 & 1 \end{bmatrix} \begin{bmatrix} p_1 \\ p_2 \\ p_3 \end{bmatrix} = \begin{bmatrix} p_1 \\ p_2 \\ p_3 \end{bmatrix}$$

that is, multiplication of a vector by an identity matrix leaves the vector unchanged. Our model, therefore, can be written as:

$$\mathbf{p} = \mathbf{A}^{-1}\mathbf{r} \tag{4.14}$$

that is, by multiplying the **A** inverse by the **r** vector we can obtain the numerical values for **p** that will satisfy the model. Given that such matrix notation is simply a shorthand way of representing a set of equations, what we have derived is a method of solving a simultaneous set of equations using matrix algebra and the matrix inverse. The potential of matrix algebra using the inverse in this way cannot be overemphasized as the solution method is applicable to any size matrix and the equation system it represents. To find the solution to the model we shall state (and later show the derivation) that the inverse of the **A** matrix is:

$$\mathbf{A}^{-1} = \begin{bmatrix} 0.016 & -0.02 & 0 \\ 0 & 0.04 & -0.3 \\ -0.02 & 0 & 0.2 \end{bmatrix}$$

Using this inverse we can now solve for the **p** vector values:

$$\mathbf{p} = \mathbf{A}^{-1}\mathbf{r} = \begin{bmatrix} 0.016 & -0.02 & 0 \\ 0 & 0.04 & -0.3 \\ -0.02 & 0 & 0.2 \end{bmatrix} \begin{bmatrix} 33\,500 \\ 26\,250 \\ 3\,450 \end{bmatrix}$$

giving

$$\mathbf{p} = \begin{bmatrix} 11 \\ 15 \\ 20 \end{bmatrix}$$

that is, the prices that must be charged to meet these sales targets are: £11 for product X, £15 for product Y and £20 for product Z. The matrix inverse, therefore, can be used to determine the solution to a set of simultaneous equations. The advantages of the inverse method in terms of both economic theory and analysis are evident. Having seen the usefulness of the matrix inverse we now turn our attention to the method of derivation.

Student activity 4.7

(i) Using the **p** vector just obtained confirm that **Ap** = **r**.
(ii) Assume that the firm has now set regional sales targets as:

Region 1 £35 000
Region 2 £27 400
Region 3   £3 595

Determine the new set of prices.
(Solution on p. 333.)

4.10 Calculating the matrix inverse

The matrix inverse is of particular importance in the development of theoretical economic models. In such models we are concerned not with the unique numerical solution to a specific application but rather in deriving the general conclusions relevant to such a model. Matrix algebra and the matrix inverse, as we shall see in detail in the next chapter, are ideally suited to such requirements. To find the inverse is a matter of alternative methods available. One method which—in numerical calculation terms—is reasonably efficient is the Gauss–Jordan elimination method and we shall examine this first. However, it is also necessary to be familiar with a second method which is technically less efficient. This is the method of determinants. Determinants are widely used in mathematical economics and have an important role in theoretical analysis as we shall shortly discover.

The Gauss–Jordan elimination method

This method (similar to the approach taken when we were solving a set of simultaneous equations in Chapter 3) operates through a sequence of simple stages. First, we create what is known as an augmented matrix. This consists of the matrix for which we wish to find an inverse—matrix A—and the equivalent identity matrix. In this example we have:

$$\begin{bmatrix} 1000 & 500 & 750 & 1 & 0 & 0 \\ 750 & 400 & 600 & 0 & 1 & 0 \\ 100 & 50 & 80 & 0 & 0 & 1 \end{bmatrix}$$

where the left-hand part of the augmented matrix is **A** and the right-hand part the corresponding **I** matrix. We now undertake a series of arithmetic operations on the rows of this augmented matrix. Upon completion the **A** part of this matrix will have been transformed into an identity matrix and what was the identity matrix will have been transformed into the inverse matrix. (You are advised to confirm the detailed arithmetic for yourself as we progress using a pocket calculator.) To begin the transformation of **A** into **I** we take the first row and require that $a_{11} = 1$ (which is the value of the first diagonal element of the **I** matrix that we wish to create). This is achieved by dividing the entire row by the current a_{11} coefficient. This gives:

$$\text{Row } 1 \div 1000 \quad 1 \quad 0.5 \quad 0.75 \quad 0.001 \quad 0 \quad 0$$

We now have to change the a_{21} coefficient into 0 (to correspond to the value required in the **I** matrix) and we use the new row 1 to achieve this. We take the new first row, multiply by -750 (the a_{21} coefficient with reversed sign) and add this to the current row 2:

$-750 \times$ row 1	-750	-375	-562.5	-0.75	0	0
$+$ Row 2	750	400	600	0	1	0
New row 2	0	25	37.5	-0.75	1	0

We perform the same process on row 3, multiplying the new row 1 by -100 (the a_{31} coefficient with reversed sign) and adding the result to the existing row 3. This gives:

$-100 \times$ row 1	-100	-50	-75	-0.1	0	0
$+$ Row 3	100	50	80	0	0	1
New row 3	0	0	5	-0.1	0	1

to give a result at this stage of:

Row 1	1	0.5	0.75	0.001	0	0
Row 2	0	25	37.5	-0.75	1	0
Row 3	0	0	5	-0.1	0	1

We see that the effect of this arithmetic has been to transform the first column of the augmented matrix into a column appropriate for an identity matrix. We now repeat this process by transforming column 2 into an identity matrix format. This is achieved by dividing row 2 by the a_{22} coefficient (changing it to the value 1) and using this new row 2 to alter row 1 and row 3 (to zero). Performing this arithmetic (and you are strongly urged to do this for yourself) produces the matrix:

Row 1	1	0	0	0.016	−0.02	0
Row 2	0	1	1.5	−0.03	0.04	0
Row 3	0	0	5	−0.1	0	1

We see that the first two columns are now in identity matrix format. Finally, we transform column 3 by using row 3. We divide row 3 by the a_{33} coefficient and using the new row 3 to alter row 1 and row 2 (changing the a_{i3} coefficients to zero). This gives a matrix:

Row 1	1	0	0	0.016	−0.02	0
Row 2	0	1	0	0	0.04	−0.3
Row 3	0	0	1	−0.02	0	0.2

giving:

$$\mathbf{A}^{-1} = \begin{bmatrix} 0.016 & -0.02 & 0 \\ 0 & 0.04 & -0.3 \\ -0.02 & 0 & 0.2 \end{bmatrix}$$

The original $\mathbf{A}$ matrix has now been transformed into an $\mathbf{I}$ matrix and the $\mathbf{I}$ matrix into the inverse of $\mathbf{A}$ that was given in Sec. 4.9. Because of its repetitive and sequential nature this process is readily extended to larger-sized matrices (and is also ideally suited to solution via computer spreadsheet; indeed a number of commercial spreadsheets have an inbuilt matrix inverse function which performs such arithmetic automatically). As we stated earlier in this section, however, while this method may be a more efficient way of arriving at a numerical result the alternative method of using determinants is necessary if we are to introduce certain key theoretical aspects.

To summarize the calculations:

1 Create an augmented matrix consisting of the $\mathbf{A}$ matrix (m by n, where $m = n$) and an identity matrix of the same size.
2 Divide the first row of the matrix through by the a_{11} coefficient.
3 Taking each subsequent row in turn multiply the new row 1 by the a_{i1} coefficient and subtract this from the existing ith row (to set the a_{i1} in the ith row to zero).
4 Repeat the calculation for each remaining row, 2 to m, in the $\mathbf{A}$ matrix:
   • Divide the row by its a_{ii} coefficient
   • Taking every other row in turn multiply the new row i by the relevant a_{ij} coefficient of the row being adjusted and subtract this from the existing ith row (to set the corresponding a in the row to zero)

Student activity 4.8
Confirm the following using the original **A** matrix and the inverse that we have found:

(i) $\mathbf{A}\mathbf{A}^{-1} = \mathbf{I}$
(ii) $\mathbf{A}^{-1}\mathbf{A} = \mathbf{I}$
(iii) $(\mathbf{A}^{-1})^{-1} = \mathbf{A}$

Return to the matrices **D** and **E** from the first activity in this chapter. Find the inverse of each and confirm your calculations through the use of (i) above.
(Solution on p. 334.)

4.11 Determinants

A determinant is a scalar associated with some square matrix. For a simple 2×2 matrix, **A**, the determinant would be defined as:

$$|\mathbf{A}| = \begin{vmatrix} a_{11} & a_{12} \\ a_{21} & a_{22} \end{vmatrix} = a_{11}a_{22} - a_{21}a_{12} \tag{4.15}$$

where $|\mathbf{A}|$ is the standard notation for denoting a determinant. For example, suppose we had matrix **A** as:

$$\mathbf{A} = \begin{bmatrix} 1 & 2 \\ 3 & 4 \end{bmatrix}$$

Then $|\mathbf{A}| = 1 \times 4 - 3 \times 2 = -2$, that is, the determinant of matrix A equals -2. Such a determinant is known as a second-order determinant, given that it is associated with a 2×2 matrix, **A**. Determinants of an order higher than 2 can be evaluated using the *Laplace expansion*. Assume a matrix such that:

$$\mathbf{A} = \begin{bmatrix} a_{11} & a_{12} & a_{13} \\ a_{21} & a_{22} & a_{23} \\ a_{31} & a_{32} & a_{33} \end{bmatrix}$$

Then its determinant, $|\mathbf{A}|$, is found by expanding the first row in the manner:

$$|\mathbf{A}| = a_{11}\begin{vmatrix} a_{22} & a_{23} \\ a_{32} & a_{33} \end{vmatrix} - a_{12}\begin{vmatrix} a_{21} & a_{23} \\ a_{31} & a_{33} \end{vmatrix} + a_{13}\begin{vmatrix} a_{21} & a_{22} \\ a_{31} & a_{32} \end{vmatrix} \tag{4.16}$$

At first sight this may look somewhat daunting but such an expansion follows a simple set of rules. This third-order determinant comprises three parts, each of which consists of an element from the first row of the matrix (given that we are expanding the first row to obtain the determinant) and a 2×2 determinant. If we examine the first of these subdeterminants, we can see that it consists of the remaining cells of the A matrix after row 1 and column 1 have been deleted. Similarly, the second subdeterminant consists of those cells remaining after row 1 and column 2 have been deleted. Finally, the third subdeterminant is obtained from cells after row 1 and column 3 have been deleted. Such subdeterminants are more generally referred to as the *minors* of the elements of **A**. The calculation of a determinant using this approach is now a matter of simple arithmetic. Let us return to the sales matrix, **A**, that we were using in the previous section:

$$\mathbf{A} = \begin{bmatrix} 1000 & 500 & 750 \\ 750 & 400 & 600 \\ 100 & 50 & 80 \end{bmatrix}$$

The determinant of **A** can now be calculated as:

$$|\mathbf{A}| = a_{11} \begin{vmatrix} a_{22} & a_{23} \\ a_{32} & a_{33} \end{vmatrix} - a_{12} \begin{vmatrix} a_{21} & a_{23} \\ a_{31} & a_{33} \end{vmatrix} + a_{13} \begin{vmatrix} a_{21} & a_{22} \\ a_{31} & a_{32} \end{vmatrix}$$

giving:

$$|\mathbf{A}| = 1000 \begin{vmatrix} 400 & 600 \\ 50 & 80 \end{vmatrix} - 500 \begin{vmatrix} 750 & 600 \\ 100 & 80 \end{vmatrix} + 750 \begin{vmatrix} 750 & 400 \\ 100 & 50 \end{vmatrix}$$

and calculating the values of the resulting 2×2 determinants we have:

$$|\mathbf{A}| = 1000(2000) - 500(0) + 750(-2500) = 125\,000$$

> *Student activity 4.9*
> Find the determinants of matrices **D** and **E** used in the previous activity.
> (Solution on p. 335.)

This process of calculating the value of the determinant can be extended to even higher-order determinants. To do so, however, it is worth introducing a new concept—that of a cofactor. Let us denote the minor of a particular element of the determinant, a_{ij}, as M_{ij}. The expansion expression that we had earlier can be written as:

$$|\mathbf{A}| = a_{11}M_{11} - a_{12}M_{12} + a_{13}M_{13} \tag{4.17}$$

The cofactor, C_{ij}, of a_{ij} is defined as:

$$C_{ij} = (-1)^{i+j}M_{ij} \tag{4.18}$$

and the determinant can be rewritten as:

$$|\mathbf{A}| = a_{11}C_{11} + a_{12}C_{12} + a_{13}C_{13} \tag{4.19}$$

It can be seen that:

$$C_{11} = (-1)^{1+1}M_{11} = (-1)^2 M_{11} = +M_{11}$$
$$C_{12} = (-1)^{1+2}M_{12} = (-1)^3 M_{12} = -M_{12}$$
$$C_{13} = (-1)^{1+3}M_{13} = (-1)^4 M_{13} = +M_{13}$$

In other words, a cofactor is simply the corresponding minor with either a plus sign (if $i + j$ is even) or a minus sign (if $i + j$ is odd) attached. For higher-order determinants we can now provide a general expression for the expansion. If we had a matrix **A** which was of size 4×4:

$$\mathbf{A} = \begin{bmatrix} a_{11} & a_{12} & a_{13} & a_{14} \\ a_{21} & a_{22} & a_{23} & a_{24} \\ a_{31} & a_{32} & a_{33} & a_{34} \\ a_{41} & a_{42} & a_{43} & a_{44} \end{bmatrix}$$

then its determinants would be given by:

or

$$|\mathbf{A}| = a_{11}C_{11} + a_{12}C_{12} + a_{13}C_{13} + a_{14}C_{14}$$
$$= a_{11}M_{11} - a_{12}M_{12} + a_{13}M_{13} - a_{14}M_{14}$$

In general, therefore, we can define the determinant as:

$$|\mathbf{A}| = \Sigma a_{1j}C_{1j}, \qquad j = 1, 2, \ldots, n \tag{4.20}$$

A slight digression may be necessary for those of you who have not encountered the symbol Σ. This is known as a summation operator (and called 'sigma') and indicates that we are to add together whatever appears immediately after the symbol. Thus, in the example above we are to add together the $a_1 C_1$ terms for all the columns in the matrix. In fact, the Laplace expansion has one particularly useful property. This is that the determinant can be found by expanding *any* row or *any* column. No matter which row or column we use for the expansion we will arrive at the same determinant value. The expansion can, therefore, be undertaken across any row or down any column of the matrix. Expanding by a chosen row, i for example, would give:

$$|\mathbf{A}| = \Sigma a_{ij}C_{ij}, \qquad j = 1, 2, \ldots, n$$

and by a chosen row, j, would give:

$$|\mathbf{A}| = \Sigma a_{ij}C_{ij}, \qquad i = 1, 2, \ldots, m$$

> ***Student activity 4.10***
> Referring back to the sales matrix, **A**, calculate the value of the determinant using:
>
> (i) row 3,
> (ii) column 2.

Properties of a determinant

Determinants have a number of properties which prove useful in mathematical economics. Among these are:

1 The determinant of a matrix **A** has the same value as that of its transpose, $\mathbf{A}'$:

$$|\mathbf{A}| = |\mathbf{A}'| \tag{4.21}$$

2 Multiplying a single row or column of a matrix by a scalar will cause the value of the determinant to be multiplied by the scalar:

$$k\mathbf{A} = k|\mathbf{A}| \tag{4.22}$$

3 If one row (or one column) is a multiple of another row (or column) the value of the determinant is zero; that is, if two rows or columns are linearly dependent the value of the determinant is zero.

4 The expansion of a determinant by what are known as its *alien cofactors* will result in a value of zero for the determinant; that is, if we expand a determinant along a specific row (or column) but use the cofactors of a different row (or column) the value of the determinants will be zero. This may seem an illogical process to want to undertake but we shall see its relevance shortly when we examine the calculation of the matrix inverse using determinants.

To illustrate, assume a 3×3 matrix:

$$\mathbf{A} = \begin{bmatrix} a_{11} & a_{12} & a_{13} \\ a_{21} & a_{22} & a_{23} \\ a_{31} & a_{32} & a_{33} \end{bmatrix}$$

If we now decide to find the determinant by expanding with the second row elements but using the cofactors of the first row elements we have:

$$a_{21}C_{11} + a_{22}C_{12} + a_{23}C_{13} = 0$$

Alternatively:

$$\Sigma a_{2j}C_{1j} = 0. \qquad j = 1, 2, 3$$

> **Student activity 4.11**
> Confirm from your own calculation for the sales matrix **A** that expanding by these alien cofactors results in a value of zero.

4.12 Calculating the matrix inverse using determinants

We are now in a position to use the determinant to calculate the matrix inverse. Let us return to the **A** matrix:

$$\mathbf{A} = \begin{bmatrix} a_{11} & a_{12} & a_{13} \\ a_{21} & a_{22} & a_{23} \\ a_{31} & a_{32} & a_{33} \end{bmatrix}$$

We can also define a matrix of the associated cofactors:

$$\mathbf{C} = \begin{bmatrix} C_{11} & C_{12} & C_{13} \\ C_{21} & C_{22} & C_{23} \\ C_{31} & C_{32} & C_{33} \end{bmatrix}$$

which, of course, would be determined from the relevant minors:

$$\mathbf{M} = \begin{bmatrix} M_{11} & -M_{12} & M_{13} \\ -M_{21} & M_{22} & -M_{23} \\ M_{31} & -M_{32} & M_{33} \end{bmatrix}$$

Transposing the $\mathbf{C}$ matrix we obtain:

$$\mathbf{C}' = \begin{bmatrix} C_{11} & C_{21} & C_{31} \\ C_{12} & C_{22} & C_{32} \\ C_{13} & C_{23} & C_{33} \end{bmatrix}$$

where $\mathbf{C}'$ is known as the adjoint of $\mathbf{A}$ and is denoted as adj $\mathbf{A}$. We state that the inverse of $\mathbf{A}$ is given by:

$$\mathbf{A}^{-1} = \frac{1}{|\mathbf{A}|} \text{adj } \mathbf{A} \tag{4.23}$$

Because of the importance of the determinant method of calculating the inverse in theoretical analysis it is worth showing the derivation of this expression. Let us first examine a 2×2 matrix. Assume an $\mathbf{A}$ matrix such that:

$$\mathbf{A} = \begin{bmatrix} a_{11} & a_{12} \\ a_{21} & a_{22} \end{bmatrix}$$

Then:

$$\mathbf{C} = \begin{bmatrix} a_{22} & -a_{21} \\ -a_{12} & a_{11} \end{bmatrix}$$

and

$$\text{adj } \mathbf{A} = \begin{bmatrix} a_{22} & -a_{12} \\ -a_{21} & a_{11} \end{bmatrix}$$

We have seen that:

$$|A| = \begin{vmatrix} a_{11} & a_{12} \\ a_{21} & a_{22} \end{vmatrix} = a_{11}a_{22} - a_{21}a_{12}$$

and that $\mathbf{A}\mathbf{A}^{-1} = \mathbf{I}$. If:

$$\mathbf{A}^{-1} = \frac{1}{|\mathbf{A}|} \text{adj } \mathbf{A}$$

then:

$$\mathbf{A}\mathbf{A}^{-1} = \frac{\mathbf{A} \text{ adj } \mathbf{A}}{|\mathbf{A}|}$$

$$= \frac{1}{|\mathbf{A}|} \begin{bmatrix} a_{11} & a_{12} \\ a_{21} & a_{22} \end{bmatrix} \begin{bmatrix} a_{22} & -a_{12} \\ -a_{21} & a_{11} \end{bmatrix}$$

which by matrix multiplication gives:

$$\mathbf{A}\mathbf{A}^{-1} = \frac{1}{|\mathbf{A}|} \begin{bmatrix} a_{11}a_{22} - a_{12}a_{21} & -a_{12}a_{11} + a_{12}a_{11} \\ a_{22}a_{21} - a_{22}a_{21} & -a_{21}a_{12} + a_{22}a_{11} \end{bmatrix}$$

$$= \frac{1}{|\mathbf{A}|} \begin{bmatrix} a_{11}a_{22} - a_{12}a_{21} & 0 \\ 0 & a_{11}a_{22} - a_{12}a_{21} \end{bmatrix}$$

and since $|\mathbf{A}| = a_{11}a_{22} - a_{12}a_{21}$ this gives:

$$\mathbf{A}\mathbf{A}^{-1} = \frac{1}{a_{11}a_{22} - a_{12}a_{21}} \begin{bmatrix} a_{11}a_{22} - a_{12}a_{21} & 0 \\ 0 & a_{11}a_{22} - a_{12}a_{21} \end{bmatrix}$$

Remembering that the determinant of $\mathbf{A}$ is a scalar ($= a_{11}a_{22} - a_{12}a_{21}$) this gives:

$$\mathbf{A}\mathbf{A}^{-1} = \begin{bmatrix} 1 & 0 \\ 0 & 1 \end{bmatrix} = \mathbf{I}$$

which is the definition of an inverse matrix. We can expand this to look at a 3×3 matrix. We have:

$$\mathbf{A} = \begin{bmatrix} a_{11} & a_{12} & a_{13} \\ a_{21} & a_{22} & a_{23} \\ a_{31} & a_{32} & a_{33} \end{bmatrix}$$

and

$$\mathbf{C}' = \begin{bmatrix} C_{11} & C_{21} & C_{31} \\ C_{12} & C_{22} & C_{32} \\ C_{13} & C_{23} & C_{33} \end{bmatrix}$$

Let us determine the product of $\mathbf{A}\mathbf{C}'$:

$$\mathbf{X} = \mathbf{A}\mathbf{C}' = \begin{bmatrix} a_{11} & a_{12} & a_{13} \\ a_{21} & a_{22} & a_{23} \\ a_{31} & a_{32} & a_{33} \end{bmatrix} \begin{bmatrix} C_{11} & C_{21} & C_{31} \\ C_{12} & C_{22} & C_{32} \\ C_{13} & C_{23} & C_{33} \end{bmatrix}$$

Therefore x_{11}, for example, will be:

$$x_{11} = a_{11}C_{11} + a_{12}C_{12} + a_{13}C_{13}$$

or alternatively this can be written as:

$$x_{11} = \Sigma a_{1j}C_{1j}, \qquad j = 1, 2, 3$$

Similarly, x_{21} will be:

$$x_{21} = a_{21}C_{11} + a_{22}C_{12} + a_{23}C_{13}$$
$$= \Sigma a_{2j}C_{1j}, \qquad j = 1, 2, 3$$

and the remaining elements of the resulting **X** matrix can also be expressed using summation notation as:

$$\mathbf{X} = \mathbf{A}\mathbf{C}' = \begin{bmatrix} \Sigma a_{1j}C_{1j} & \Sigma a_{1j}C_{2j} & \Sigma a_{1j}C_{3j} \\ \Sigma a_{2j}C_{1j} & \Sigma a_{2j}C_{2j} & \Sigma a_{2j}C_{3j} \\ \Sigma a_{3j}C_{1j} & \Sigma a_{3j}C_{2j} & \Sigma a_{3j}C_{3j} \end{bmatrix}$$

There are two aspects to note. First, the main diagonal elements represent the expansion of $|\mathbf{A}|$ that we have already used. Second, the remaining off-diagonal elements represent the expansion by alien cofactors. You will remember that one of the properties of determinants stated earlier was that such an expansion will result in a value of zero. We can therefore rewrite this product matrix as:

$$\mathbf{A}\mathbf{C}' = \begin{bmatrix} |\mathbf{A}| & 0 & 0 \\ 0 & |\mathbf{A}| & 0 \\ 0 & 0 & |\mathbf{A}| \end{bmatrix}$$

In turn, remembering that $|\mathbf{A}|$ is a scalar, this gives:

$$\mathbf{A}\mathbf{C}' = |\mathbf{A}| \begin{bmatrix} 1 & 0 & 0 \\ 0 & 1 & 0 \\ 0 & 0 & 1 \end{bmatrix} = |\mathbf{A}|\,\mathbf{I}$$

Rearranging gives:

$$\mathbf{A}\mathbf{C}' = |\mathbf{A}|\,\mathbf{I}$$

$$\frac{1}{|\mathbf{A}|}\mathbf{A}\mathbf{C}' = \mathbf{I}$$

Next, we premultiply both sides by $\mathbf{A}^{-1}$:

$$\frac{\mathbf{A}^{-1}\mathbf{A}\mathbf{C}'}{|\mathbf{A}|} = \mathbf{A}^{-1}\mathbf{I}$$

but since $\mathbf{A}^{-1}\mathbf{A} = \mathbf{I}$ and $\mathbf{A}^{-1}\mathbf{I} = \mathbf{A}^{-1}$ we have:

$$\frac{\mathbf{I}\mathbf{C}'}{|\mathbf{A}|} = \mathbf{A}^{-1}$$

or

$$\mathbf{A}^{-1} = \frac{1}{|\mathbf{A}|}\mathbf{C}' = \frac{1}{|\mathbf{A}|}\,\text{adj } \mathbf{A}$$

since $\mathbf{C}'$ is the adjoint of $\mathbf{A}$. To illustrate the use of the inverse expression let us return to our original example where:

$$\mathbf{A} = \begin{bmatrix} 1000 & 500 & 750 \\ 750 & 400 & 600 \\ 100 & 50 & 80 \end{bmatrix}$$

The determinant of **A** was calculated earlier as 125 000. The **C** matrix for this **A** matrix will be:

$$\mathbf{C} = \begin{bmatrix} 2000 & 0 & -2\,500 \\ -2500 & 5\,000 & 0 \\ 0 & -37\,500 & 25\,000 \end{bmatrix}$$

$$\text{adj } \mathbf{A} = \begin{bmatrix} 2000 & -2500 & 0 \\ 0 & 5000 & -37\,500 \\ -2500 & 0 & 25\,000 \end{bmatrix}$$

Therefore:

$$\mathbf{A}^{-1} = \frac{1}{|\mathbf{A}|} \text{adj } \mathbf{A}$$

$$= \frac{1}{125\,000} \begin{bmatrix} 2000 & -2500 & 0 \\ 0 & 5000 & -37\,500 \\ -2500 & 0 & 25\,000 \end{bmatrix}$$

giving:

$$\mathbf{A}^{-1} = \begin{bmatrix} 0.016 & -0.02 & 0 \\ 0 & 0.04 & -0.3 \\ -0.02 & 0 & 0.2 \end{bmatrix}$$

again confirming that this is the inverse to the **A** matrix.

Thus, the use of determinants allows us to calculate the inverse of a matrix and thereby determine the solution to a set of linear equations. It is apparent, however, that the use of determinants is somewhat more cumbersome than the Gauss–Jordan method and the question arises: why bother with determinants when we have a computationally more efficient method of finding the inverse? The answer to this takes us back to one of the main elements of this text and of mathematical economics in general. As we shall see in the next chapter, the use of determinants is essential if we are to fully evaluate a theoretical—as opposed to a numerical—economic model. When we attempt to assess the implications and predictions of such a theoretical model we shall find that the determinant method is indispensable.

There is also an additional reason why the determinant method may be useful. In some cases it may be easier to determine the numerical inverse using determinants. You will remember from the Laplace transformation that, to calculate the determinant of some matrix, we can expand along any row or any column. Consider the equation system detailed below:

$$\mathbf{Ax} = \mathbf{b}$$

where

$$\mathbf{A} = \begin{bmatrix} 2 & 3 & -1 \\ 5 & -4 & 2 \\ 0 & 0 & 2 \end{bmatrix} \qquad \mathbf{x} = \begin{bmatrix} x_1 \\ x_2 \\ x_3 \end{bmatrix} \qquad \mathbf{b} = \begin{bmatrix} 15 \\ 70 \\ 40 \end{bmatrix}$$

and we wish to solve for **x**. On inspection of the **A** matrix it is apparent that the calculation of the determinant using row 3 will involve very little arithmetic, given the two zero coefficients, whereas the Gauss–Jordan method requires arithmetic manipulation of the entire matrix.

4.13 The determinant and non-singularity

When the concept of an inverse was first introduced we stated that inverses exist only for square matrices but that not every square matrix will have an inverse. A matrix without an inverse is said to be singular and the determinant of such a matrix will clearly have a zero value. We also stated, when summarizing the properties of determinants, that if a row (column) is a multiple of another row (column) in the matrix its determinant will take a zero value. Given our use of matrix algebra to represent, and solve, economic models, this feature of determinants is of particular importance. We have focused upon the use of the inverse matrix in finding the solution to a set of linear equations. It is clear that, if a matrix is singular—that is, if one row/equation is dependent upon another—then there can be no unique solution to the equation system represented by that matrix, and we can readily see this from the value of the determinant.

Consider the following equation system:

$$X_1 + X_2 = 6$$
$$2X_1 + 2X_2 = 12$$

It is clear that the two equations are not independent, the second being a multiple of the first, and that we cannot find a unique solution. In matrix form we would have:

$$\begin{bmatrix} 1 & 1 \\ 2 & 2 \end{bmatrix} \begin{bmatrix} x_1 \\ x_2 \end{bmatrix} = \begin{bmatrix} 6 \\ 12 \end{bmatrix}$$

and the determinant of the **A** matrix is:

$$(1 \times 2) - (2 \times 1) = 0$$

that is, the matrix is singular and hence has no inverse and the equation system has no unique solution.

Consider now the following equation system:

$$X_1 + X_2 = 6$$
$$2X_1 + 2X_2 = 10$$

It is clear that these two equations are inconsistent in that there are no values for X_1 and X_2 that satisfy both equations simultaneously. Graphically, the two equations would appear as parallel lines and given that a simultaneous solution occurs where two such lines cross it is clear there can be no solution. Again, given that we have the same **A** matrix, this matrix is singular and again we know from the value of the determinant that no unique solution exists. In general, therefore, with a set of simultaneous equations, when the number of equations equals the number of unknowns a unique solution can be obtained only where no equation is either inconsistent or dependent on one of the others. This would be readily recognized from the value of the corresponding determinant being equal to 0. It is tempting to underestimate the usefulness of determinants in this context. In the illustrative examples used it is clear, without calculating a determinant value, that no solution exists. However, for larger-scale problems and in particular for economic models, which consist of theoretical parameters rather than numerical values, such a situation will be far less obvious and the use of the determinant in this way proves invaluable.

> **Student activity 4.12**
> Consider the equation system:
>
> $$4X_1 + 3X_2 + 5X_3 = 74$$
> $$3X_1 + X_2 + 3X_3 = 42$$
> $$-X_1 + 3X_2 + X_3 = 22$$
>
> Show through the use of determinants that this system has no unique solution. (Solution on p. 335.)

4.14 Cramer's rule

Matrix inversion provides, as we have seen over the last few sections, a general method of finding the solution to a set of linear equations expressed in the form:

$$\mathbf{Ax} = \mathbf{b}$$

For certain applications there is a simpler method available—known as Cramer's rule—based on the determinant approach, which we shall develop in this section. The general solution to the **x** vector in the equation system is given as:

$$\mathbf{x} = \mathbf{A}^{-1}\mathbf{b} = \frac{1}{|\mathbf{A}|}\text{adj }\mathbf{Ab} \tag{4.24}$$

For the 3×3 matrix problem we have been examining this can be rewritten as:

$$\begin{bmatrix} x_1 \\ x_2 \\ x_3 \end{bmatrix} = \frac{1}{|\mathbf{A}|} \begin{bmatrix} C_{11} & C_{12} & C_{13} \\ C_{21} & C_{22} & C_{23} \\ C_{31} & C_{32} & C_{33} \end{bmatrix} \begin{bmatrix} b_1 \\ b_2 \\ b_3 \end{bmatrix}$$

$$= \frac{1}{|\mathbf{A}|} \begin{bmatrix} C_{11}b_1 + C_{12}b_2 + C_{13}b_3 \\ C_{21}b_1 + C_{22}b_2 + C_{23}b_3 \\ C_{31}b_1 + C_{32}b_2 + C_{33}b_3 \end{bmatrix}$$

$$= \frac{1}{|\mathbf{A}|} \begin{bmatrix} \Sigma C_{i1}b_i \\ \Sigma C_{i2}b_i \\ \Sigma C_{i3}b_i \end{bmatrix} \quad \text{for} \quad i = 1, 2, 3$$

which gives:

$$\begin{bmatrix} x_1 \\ x_2 \\ x_3 \end{bmatrix} = \begin{bmatrix} \Sigma C_{i1}b_i \\ \Sigma C_{i2}b_i \\ \Sigma C_{i3}b_i \end{bmatrix}$$

that is, any of the (unknown) x values can be determined by evaluating the appropriate cofactor expression. Cramer's rule takes us one stage further than this, however. Let us define a new determinant $|\mathbf{A}_1|$ such that:

$$|\mathbf{A}_1| = \begin{bmatrix} b_1 & a_{12} & a_{13} \\ b_2 & a_{22} & a_{23} \\ b_3 & a_{32} & a_{33} \end{bmatrix}$$

that is, $|\mathbf{A}_1|$ is simply the $|\mathbf{A}|$ determinant where the first column has been replaced by the **b** vector. Using the Laplace expansion on the b column we have:

$$\begin{aligned} |\mathbf{A}_1| &= b_1C_{11} + b_2C_{21} + b_3C_{31} \\ &= \Sigma b_iC_{i1}, \qquad i = 1,2,3 \\ &= \Sigma C_{i1}b_i, \qquad i = 1,2,3 \end{aligned}$$

So we now have:

$$x_1 = \Sigma C_{i1}b_i = \frac{1}{|\mathbf{A}|}|\mathbf{A}_1|$$

In the same way we could define $|\mathbf{A}_2|$ with the **b** vector replacing column 2 of $|\mathbf{A}|$, and $|\mathbf{A}_3|$ where the **b** vector replaces the third column of the **A** determinant. This would give:

$$x_2 = \frac{1}{|\mathbf{A}|}|\mathbf{A}_2|$$

$$x_3 = \frac{1}{|\mathbf{A}|}|\mathbf{A}_3|$$

Generalizing this we can state Cramer's rule as:

$$x_i = \frac{|\mathbf{A}_i|}{|\mathbf{A}|} \tag{4.25}$$

that is, the value of the ith x value is given by the ratio of the two determinants. Let us illustrate by returning to the sales matrix:

$$\mathbf{A} = \begin{bmatrix} 1000 & 500 & 750 \\ 750 & 400 & 600 \\ 100 & 50 & 80 \end{bmatrix}$$

and
$$\mathbf{b} = \begin{bmatrix} 33\,500 \\ 26\,250 \\ 3\,450 \end{bmatrix}$$

which represents the sales revenue targets for each region. The determinant of $\mathbf{A}$ was calculated earlier as $125\,000$. The following further determinants are required:

$$|\mathbf{A}_1| = \begin{bmatrix} 33\,500 & 500 & 750 \\ 26\,250 & 400 & 600 \\ 3\,450 & 50 & 80 \end{bmatrix} = 1\,375\,000$$

$$|\mathbf{A}_2| = \begin{bmatrix} 1000 & 33\,500 & 750 \\ 750 & 26\,250 & 600 \\ 100 & 3\,450 & 80 \end{bmatrix} = 1\,875\,000$$

$$|\mathbf{A}_3| = \begin{bmatrix} 1000 & 500 & 33\,500 \\ 750 & 400 & 26\,250 \\ 100 & 50 & 3\,450 \end{bmatrix} = 2\,500\,000$$

Solving for x we therefore have:

$$x_1 = \frac{1}{|\mathbf{A}|}|\mathbf{A}_1| = \frac{1\,375\,000}{125\,000} = 11$$

$$x_2 = \frac{1}{|\mathbf{A}|}|\mathbf{A}_2| = \frac{1\,875\,000}{125\,000} = 15$$

$$x_3 = \frac{1}{|\mathbf{A}|}|\mathbf{A}_3| = \frac{2\,500\,000}{125\,000} = 20$$

confirming the solution to this equation system. The advantages of Cramer's rule are that it removes the need for the matrix inverse calculations and it allows us to solve for an individual x value if we do not require all the x solutions.

4.15   Summary

In this chapter we have introduced the basic concepts and techniques associated with matrix algebra. We have seen that matrix algebra can be used to represent linear economic models in a convenient and compact way. We have also seen that, through the use of the matrix inverse, we can readily determine the solution (if it exists) to a set of linear equations. In the next chapter we shall be considering the use of matrix algebra in developing a number of theoretical economic models and examining the deductions that can be derived from such matrix representation. It is imperative that you have an adequate grasp of the key principles of matrix algebra introduced in this chapter before proceeding. To this end, you should ensure that you can complete the exercises at the end of this chapter.

Worked example

A firm produces three products—A, B, C—for sale both in the domestic market and in the export market and for sale to other firms to use in their own production process. Last year domestic sales were, respectively, 50, 60, 80. Export sales were 25, 40, 20. Sales to other firms were 10, 20, 30. This year domestic sales are expected to increase by 5 per cent and export sales by 10 per cent. Sales to other firms are expected to remain the same. The firm offer the products at the same price in all three markets. Prices are currently £3, £4, £5. Production costs for the three products are £2, £3, £4.

Using matrix algebra we require the following:

(a) A profit vector for last year.
(b) A projected profit vector for this year.
(c) Costs are expected to rise this year by 10%. If profit levels are to be maintained what prices must the firm charge?

Solution

First we must derive the relevant matrices and vectors for the data given. We have:

$$S = \begin{bmatrix} 50 & 60 & 80 \\ 25 & 40 & 20 \\ 10 & 20 & 30 \end{bmatrix}$$

as the last year's sales vector where the columns represent the three products and the rows the domestic market, the export market, and sales to other firms respectively. With a price vector, p, of:

$$p = \begin{bmatrix} 3 \\ 4 \\ 5 \end{bmatrix}$$

we have a revenue vector, r, of:

$$r = Sp = \begin{bmatrix} 790 \\ 335 \\ 260 \end{bmatrix}$$

Given a unit cost vector, u, of:

$$u = \begin{bmatrix} 2 \\ 3 \\ 4 \end{bmatrix}$$

we then have a cost vector, c, of:

$$c = Su = \begin{bmatrix} 600 \\ 250 \\ 200 \end{bmatrix}$$

and a profit vector, **v**, of:

$$\mathbf{v} = \mathbf{r} - \mathbf{c} = \begin{bmatrix} 190 \\ 85 \\ 60 \end{bmatrix}$$

(b) The projected profit matrix for this year can be derived in the same way but now using an **S** matrix of:

$$\mathbf{S} = \begin{bmatrix} 52.5 & 63 & 84 \\ 27.5 & 44 & 22 \\ 10 & 20 & 30 \end{bmatrix}$$

$$\text{and } \mathbf{v} = \begin{bmatrix} 199.5 \\ 93.5 \\ 60 \end{bmatrix}$$

(c) We have:

$$\mathbf{v} = \mathbf{Sp} - \mathbf{Su}$$

or

$$\mathbf{Sp} = \mathbf{v} + \mathbf{Su}$$

giving

$$\mathbf{p} = \mathbf{S}^{-1}(\mathbf{v} + \mathbf{Su})$$

as the **p** vector required in order to keep profit levels at the projected values. However, we have a new **u** vector of:

$$\mathbf{u} = k\mathbf{u} = 1.1 \begin{bmatrix} 2 \\ 3 \\ 4 \end{bmatrix} = \begin{bmatrix} 2.2 \\ 3.3 \\ 4.4 \end{bmatrix}$$

and hence **Su** as:

$$\mathbf{c} = \mathbf{Su} = \begin{bmatrix} 693 \\ 302.5 \\ 220 \end{bmatrix}$$

giving

$$\mathbf{v} + \mathbf{Su} = \begin{bmatrix} 892.5 \\ 396.0 \\ 280.0 \end{bmatrix}$$

$\mathbf{S}^{-1}$ is derived as:

$$\begin{bmatrix} 0.050794 & -0.012120 & -0.133330 \\ -0.034920 & 0.042424 & 0.066667 \\ 0.006349 & -0.024240 & 0.033333 \end{bmatrix}$$

and then:

$$\mathbf{p} = \mathbf{S}^{-1}(\mathbf{v} + \mathbf{Su}) = \begin{bmatrix} 3.20 \\ 4.30 \\ 5.93 \end{bmatrix}$$

as the new price levels required to maintain profit levels given the cost increases and the sales increases.

Exercises

4.1 Using the sales matrix A, confirm that:

$$|\mathbf{A}| = |\mathbf{A}'|$$

4.2 Confirm that:

$$k\mathbf{A} = \mathbf{A}k$$

using some numerical value for the scalar.

4.3 In the chapter the cofactor matrix C for the sales matrix A was given as:

$$\mathbf{C} = \begin{bmatrix} 2000 & 0 & -2\,500 \\ -2500 & 5\,000 & 0 \\ 0 & -37\,500 & 25\,000 \end{bmatrix}$$

Confirm that it is correct.

4.4 At the end of Sec. 4.12 an equation system is given. Find the solution by expanding row 3 of the A matrix.

4.5 Return to the sets of equations that were given in Student activity 3.1. Reformulate these into a matrix format and find the numerical solution using the Gauss–Jordan method. Compare these solutions with those obtained using the determinant approach.

4.6 Return to the numerical exercises given at the end of Chapter 3. Formulate each of them into a matrix format and solve using one of the methods shown in this chapter.

4.7 Find the inverse of the following matrix:

$$\begin{bmatrix} 0.7 & -0.1 & 0 \\ -0.1 & 0.6 & -0.05 \\ -0.25 & -0.25 & 0.8 \end{bmatrix}$$

This solution will be required in the next chapter.

4.8 For the following matrices complete the matrix arithmetic indicated (where possible):

$$A = \begin{bmatrix} 3 & 1 & 4 \\ 5 & -1 & 6 \\ 0 & 2 & 3 \end{bmatrix} \qquad B = \begin{bmatrix} 7 & 2 & 3 \\ -1 & 2 & 2 \\ 5 & 9 & 1 \end{bmatrix} \qquad C = \begin{bmatrix} 2 & 3 & 1 \\ 0 & 4 & 2 \\ 0 & 0 & 1 \end{bmatrix}$$

(i) AB

(ii) BA

(iii) ABC

(iv) BAC

(v) $(AB)^{-1}$

(vi) $|AC|$

(vii) $|CA|$

(viii) $(CBA)^{-1}$

5 Economic applications of matrix algebra

In the previous chapter we examined the techniques of matrix algebra and saw that these allow the ready formulation of linear economic models and, through the matrix inverse, the solution of such economic models. In this chapter we shall examine a number of economic models and show how through the use of matrix methods we can deduce a number of important conclusions from the inherent relationships. We shall then examine the area of input–output analysis which relies extensively on the use of matrix algebra for the numerical solution of input–output models. Input–output models are, in fact, an ideal illustration of how matrix algebra can be used both to develop a theoretical model and then to put that model to practical use by finding its numerical solution and examining the economic policy implications of the solution. The application of matrix algebra to theoretical economic models is a particularly important area in mathematical economics. While we frequently wish to determine the solution to some numerical problem we are often more interested in the underlying principles behind such a solution: what conditions must exist for a solution to be economically valid and what the implications of the solution are. We begin by returning to two simple microeconomic models that we introduced in Chapter 3.

Learning objectives

By the end of this chapter you should be able to:

- Use matrix algebra to represent and solve market models
- Use matrix algebra to represent and solve national income models
- Understand an input–output table
- Use matrix algebra to analyse input–output models

5.1 A partial equilibrium market model

Earlier, in Chapter 3, we developed a simple partial equilibrium market model which we present as:

$$Q_d = Q_s \tag{5.1}$$
$$Q_d = a_1 + b_1 P \tag{5.2}$$
$$Q_s = a_2 + b_2 P \tag{5.3}$$

where a_1, a_2, b_1 and b_2 are appropriate parameters for the linear demand and supply equations and we restrict their values to those that are sensible in an economic context. As we have seen, it is useful to be able to derive the general implications from such a model and we shall use the appropriate matrix algebra techniques to determine the appropriate equilibrium and examine its inherent implications. We can rearrange the model into a form more convenient for matrix representation. Collecting variables onto the left-hand side and single parameters (the exogenous elements of the model) onto the right, we can rewrite the model as:

$$1Q_d - 1Q_s + 0P = 0 \tag{5.4}$$
$$1Q_d + 0Q_s - b_1P = a_1 \tag{5.5}$$
$$0Q_d + 1Q_s - b_2P = a_2 \tag{5.6}$$

This can be expressed in the matrix format of $\mathbf{Ax} = \mathbf{b}$ as:

$$\begin{bmatrix} 1 & -1 & 0 \\ 1 & 0 & -b_1 \\ 0 & 1 & -b_2 \end{bmatrix} \begin{bmatrix} Q_d \\ Q_s \\ P \end{bmatrix} = \begin{bmatrix} 0 \\ a_1 \\ a_2 \end{bmatrix} \tag{5.7}$$

and we require a solution to the $\mathbf{x}$ vector (that is, we require the equilibrium values for Q_d, Q_s and P). The solution for the $\mathbf{x}$ vector is then:

$$\mathbf{x} = \mathbf{A}^{-1}\mathbf{b}$$

and since $\mathbf{A}^{-1} = (1/|\mathbf{A}|)\text{adj }\mathbf{A}$:

$$\mathbf{x} = \frac{1}{|\mathbf{A}|}\text{adj }\mathbf{A}\,\mathbf{b} \tag{5.8}$$

Therefore the solution to the parameter model can be determined using the inverse to the $\mathbf{A}$ matrix (derived using the determinant approach). Before we find such an inverse, we must first test that a unique solution exists for this equation system. You will remember from the previous chapter that we stated that such a system will have a unique solution where $|\mathbf{A}| \neq 0$. The determinant of the $\mathbf{A}$ matrix in our system is readily found.

> *Student activity 5.1*
> Find the determinant of $\mathbf{A}$ by expanding the third row.

We have a 3×3 matrix so we can expand, say, the first column:

$$|\mathbf{A}| = 1\begin{vmatrix} 0 & -b_1 \\ 1 & -b_2 \end{vmatrix} - 1\begin{vmatrix} -1 & 0 \\ 1 & -b_2 \end{vmatrix} + 0\begin{vmatrix} -1 & 0 \\ 1 & -b_2 \end{vmatrix}$$
$$= 1[0 - (-b_1)] - 1(b_2 - 0) + 0$$
$$= b_1 - b_2$$

If the equation system has a unique solution then:

$$|\mathbf{A}| = b_1 - b_2 \neq 0$$

Given that b_1 and b_2 are the slopes of the demand and supply equations respectively, this implies that $b_1 \neq b_2$ and thus the two equations cannot have the same slope if there is to be a unique solution. To find $\mathbf{A}^{-1}$ we now require adj $\mathbf{A}$. This can be derived by using the cofactor matrix:

$$\mathbf{C} = \begin{bmatrix} \begin{vmatrix} 0 & -b_1 \\ 1 & -b_2 \end{vmatrix} & -\begin{vmatrix} 1 & -b_1 \\ 0 & -b_2 \end{vmatrix} & \begin{vmatrix} 1 & 0 \\ 0 & 1 \end{vmatrix} \\ -\begin{vmatrix} -1 & 0 \\ 1 & -b_2 \end{vmatrix} & \begin{vmatrix} 1 & 0 \\ 0 & -b_2 \end{vmatrix} & -\begin{vmatrix} 1 & -1 \\ 0 & 1 \end{vmatrix} \\ \begin{vmatrix} -1 & 0 \\ 0 & -b_1 \end{vmatrix} & -\begin{vmatrix} 1 & 0 \\ 1 & -b_1 \end{vmatrix} & \begin{vmatrix} 1 & -1 \\ 1 & 0 \end{vmatrix} \end{bmatrix}$$

$$= \begin{bmatrix} b_1 & b_2 & 1 \\ -b_2 & -b_2 & -1 \\ b_1 & b_1 & 1 \end{bmatrix}$$

giving adj $\mathbf{A} = \mathbf{C}'$ as:

$$\mathbf{C}' = \begin{bmatrix} b_1 & -b_2 & b_1 \\ b_2 & -b_2 & b_1 \\ 1 & -1 & 1 \end{bmatrix}$$

The general equilibrium solution, therefore, is given by:

$$\mathbf{x} = \frac{1}{|\mathbf{A}|} \text{adj } \mathbf{A} \ \mathbf{b}$$

$$\begin{bmatrix} Q_d \\ Q_s \\ P \end{bmatrix} = \frac{1}{b_1 - b_2} \begin{bmatrix} b_1 & -b_2 & b_1 \\ b_2 & -b_2 & b_1 \\ 1 & -1 & 1 \end{bmatrix} \begin{bmatrix} 0 \\ a_1 \\ a_2 \end{bmatrix}$$

Simplifying the expression we have:

$$\begin{bmatrix} Q_d \\ Q_s \\ P \end{bmatrix} = \begin{bmatrix} \dfrac{b_1}{b_1 - b_2} & \dfrac{-b_2}{b_1 - b_2} & \dfrac{b_1}{b_1 - b_2} \\ \dfrac{b_2}{b_1 - b_2} & \dfrac{-b_2}{b_1 - b_2} & \dfrac{b_1}{b_1 - b_2} \\ \dfrac{1}{b_1 - b_2} & \dfrac{-1}{b_1 - b_2} & \dfrac{1}{b_1 - b_2} \end{bmatrix} \begin{bmatrix} 0 \\ a_1 \\ a_2 \end{bmatrix}$$

giving:

$$Q_d = \frac{-a_1 b_2}{b_1 - b_2} + \frac{a_2 b_1}{b_1 - b_2} \tag{5.9}$$

$$Q_s = \frac{-a_1 b_2}{b_1 - b_2} - \frac{a_2 b_1}{b_1 - b_2} \tag{5.10}$$

$$P = \frac{-a_1}{b_1 - b_2} + \frac{a_2}{b_1 - b_2} \tag{5.11}$$

While these solutions are perfectly adequate it will be instructive to take them one stage further. Let us multiply each expression through by -1 and rearrange slightly (and you are strongly encouraged to do this yourself to confirm the results). We then have:

$$Q_d = \frac{a_1 b_2 - a_2 b_1}{b_2 - b_1} \tag{5.12}$$

$$Q_s = \frac{a_1 b_2 - a_2 b_1}{b_2 - b_1} \tag{5.13}$$

$$P = \frac{a_1 - a_2}{b_2 - b_1} \tag{5.14}$$

It can be seen that at the equilibrium solution Q_d and Q_s take the same value. Using the determinant we saw earlier that there will be a unique solution to this system, providing the two slopes are not the same. This does not guarantee, however, that the solution we obtain will be a meaningful one in an economic context. There is nothing in the model, for example, to prevent negative or zero values for P and Q. To make sense in an economic context both P and Q_d/Q_s must be greater than zero. Let us consider the values for the four parameters in the equations. For P this implies that both the numerator $(a_1 - a_2)$ and the denominator $(b_2 - b_1)$ take positive values and hence the ratio of these two must also result in a positive number, that is, at equilibrium $P > 0$. For Q a similar logic applies. The denominator is positive so in order for $Q > 0$ the numerator must be positive also; that is, $a_1 b_2 - a_2 b_1 > 0$ and therefore $a_1 b_2 > a_2 b_1$ in order for Q to take an economically meaningful value. You may also wish to compare the results we have obtained through the application of matrix algebra with those we obtained in Chapter 3 through the use of normal algebra. You will see that they are identical.

> **Student activity 5.2**
> Return to the equation systems shown in Student activity 3.3. Assuming that each system represents a market model confirm the solutions using matrix algebra.

5.2 The effect of an excise tax on market equilibrium

Earlier, in Chapter 3, we saw the effect that the imposition of an excise tax would have on the market equilibrium under competitive market conditions and we compared that equilibrium with the one without the imposition of the tax. We saw that such a tax—where a fixed tax is imposed per unit of the product sold—would raise the equilibrium price and reduce the equilibrium quantity. Let us examine this model via the use of matrix algebra. Assume that the tax levied per unit sold is denoted as t and is exogenous to the model. Then we have:

$$Q_d = Q_s$$
$$Q_d = a_1 + b_1 P$$
$$Q_s = a_2 + b_2 (P - t) \tag{5.15}$$

again with all the parameters restricted to taking the usual values. The supply equation can be rewritten into a more convenient form as:

$$Q_s = a_2 + b_2(P - t)$$
$$= a_2 + b_2 P - b_2 t$$
$$= (a_2 - b_2 t) + b_2 P \qquad (5.16)$$

Comparison with the market model developed in the previous section reveals that the new supply equation has the same slope as before (b_2) but with a different intercept ($a_2 - b_2 t$). Given that $b_2 t > 0$ in terms of our initial model specification, then the second supply function will have a larger negative intercept than the first and will lie parallel and below the original on a graph. (Of course, this already allows us to predict that with a given and fixed demand equation the imposition of such an excise tax will change the equilibrium position to one where Q is lower and P higher than before.) What, however, are the general implications for equilibrium? Again, developing the methods of the previous section the answer to such a question is straightforward. We can rewrite the tax model as:

$$Q_d - Q_s = 0$$
$$Q_d - b_1 P = a_1$$
$$Q_s - b_2 P = a_2 - b_2 t \qquad (5.17)$$

and in matrix form:

$$\mathbf{Ax = b}$$

where

$$\begin{bmatrix} 1 & -1 & 0 \\ 1 & 0 & -b_1 \\ 0 & 1 & -b_2 \end{bmatrix} \begin{bmatrix} Q_d \\ Q_s \\ P \end{bmatrix} = \begin{bmatrix} 0 \\ a_1 \\ a_2 - b_2 t \end{bmatrix} \qquad (5.18)$$

Inspection of this matrix formulation with that of the previous section reveals that the only difference lies in the one cell of the **b** vector, reflecting the tax element, and this immediately illustrates one of the benefits of using matrix algebra. We do not have to rework the new model to determine the relevant basic principles and equilibrium conditions. We simply have to follow through the (relatively minor) changes in the matrix structure. The general solution to the model, therefore, will be:

$$\mathbf{x = A^{-1} b}$$

where $\mathbf{A}^{-1}$ is exactly as before. To find the solution, therefore, we have:

$$\begin{bmatrix} Q_d \\ Q_s \\ P \end{bmatrix} = \begin{bmatrix} \dfrac{b_1}{b_1 - b_2} & \dfrac{-b_2}{b_1 - b_2} & \dfrac{b_1}{b_1 - b_2} \\ \dfrac{b_2}{b_1 - b_2} & \dfrac{-b_2}{b_1 - b_2} & \dfrac{b_1}{b_1 - b_2} \\ \dfrac{1}{b_1 - b_2} & \dfrac{-1}{b_1 - b_2} & \dfrac{1}{b_1 - b_2} \end{bmatrix} \begin{bmatrix} 0 \\ a_1 \\ a_2 - b_2 t \end{bmatrix}$$

giving:

$$Q_d = Q_s = \frac{-a_1 b_2 + b_1 a_2 - b_1 b_2 t}{b_1 - b_2} \tag{5.19}$$

$$P = \frac{-a_1 + a_2 - b_2 t}{b_1 - b_2} \tag{5.20}$$

Once again it will be instructive to multiply through by -1 to get:

$$Q_d = Q_s = \frac{a_1 b_2 - b_1 a_2 + b_1 b_2 t}{b_2 - b_1} = \frac{a_1 b_2 - b_1 a_2}{b_2 - b_1} + \frac{b_1 b_2 t}{b_2 - b_1} \tag{5.21}$$

$$P = \frac{a_1 - a_2 + b_2 t}{b_2 - b_1} = \frac{a_1 - a_2}{b_2 - b_1} + \frac{b_2 t}{b_2 - b_1} \tag{5.22}$$

Let us examine the equilibrium position, and its implications *vis-à-vis* the earlier market model. It is apparent, examining P first, that the equilibrium price is as before but with an extra element involved:

$$\frac{b_2 t}{b_2 - b_1}$$

thanks to the imposition of the excise tax. Since all the elements of this expression are greater than zero then the value of this expression will be positive also. This implies that the equilibrium price after the imposition of an excise tax will always be higher than the equilibrium price without the tax. It is also apparent from this expression that since $t < 1$ then:

$$\frac{b_2 t}{b_2 - b_1} < t$$

so that the increase in the equilibrium price brought about by the excise tax will always be less than the full amount of the tax. In other words, part of the tax will be incurred by the consumer of the product and part by the supplier, the exact proportions depending on the b_1 and b_2 parameter values. Let us now turn to the equilibrium quantity. Again it is evident that the difference between the new equilibrium and that prevailing before the imposition of the tax is given by:

$$\frac{b_1 b_2 t}{b_2 - b_1}$$

It is apparent that the denominator will be positive (thanks to the usual restrictions on the model parameters) while the numerator will be negative. This implies that the new equilibrium quantity must always be less than that prevailing before the excise tax. You may also realize that the results we have just obtained are the same as those from Chapter 3 for this model.

> *Student activity 5.3*
> Return to Exercise 3.2 in Chapter 3. Work through the model we have developed in this section by substituting the appropriate numerical parameters, and thereby find the solution.

5.3   A simple national income model

Let us return to the simplest national income model that we examined in Chapter 3. We had a two-equation system such that:

$$Y = C + I \tag{5.23}$$
$$C = a + bY \tag{5.24}$$

where Y = income
C = consumption
I = investment

The second equation represents a linear consumption function and we would additionally specify that $0 < b < 1$ and $a > 0$. The Y and C variables are endogenous—that is, they are determined from within the model—while I is exogenous—it is determined independently of this model. If we rewrite the model into a form suitable for matrix representation we have:

$$Y - C = I$$
$$-bY + C = a$$

which can be written as:

$$Ax = b$$

where

$$\begin{bmatrix} 1 & -1 \\ -b & 1 \end{bmatrix} \begin{bmatrix} Y \\ C \end{bmatrix} = \begin{bmatrix} I \\ a \end{bmatrix} \tag{5.25}$$

and the solution to the model—the equilibrium values for Y and C—will be given by:

$$x = A^{-1} b$$

We first require $|A|$ to establish the conditions necessary for a unique solution. We have:

$$|A| = 1 - b \neq 0$$

which confirms that b (the marginal propensity to consume) cannot equal 1 if there is to be a solution to the model. To determine A^{-1} we now require adj A:

$$C = \begin{bmatrix} 1 & b \\ 1 & 1 \end{bmatrix} \quad \text{and} \quad C' = \begin{bmatrix} 1 & 1 \\ b & 1 \end{bmatrix}$$

giving:

$$A^{-1} = \frac{1}{1-b} \begin{bmatrix} 1 & 1 \\ b & 1 \end{bmatrix} = \begin{bmatrix} \dfrac{1}{1-b} & \dfrac{1}{1-b} \\ \dfrac{b}{1-b} & \dfrac{1}{1-b} \end{bmatrix}$$

and thereby giving a solution of:

$$\mathbf{x} = \mathbf{A}^{-1}\mathbf{b} = \begin{bmatrix} \dfrac{1}{1-b} & \dfrac{1}{1-b} \\[2mm] \dfrac{b}{1-b} & \dfrac{1}{1-b} \end{bmatrix} \begin{bmatrix} I \\ a \end{bmatrix}$$

$$= \begin{bmatrix} \dfrac{I}{1-b} + \dfrac{a}{1-b} \\[3mm] \dfrac{Ib}{1-b} + \dfrac{a}{1-b} \end{bmatrix} = \begin{bmatrix} \dfrac{I+a}{1-b} \\[3mm] \dfrac{a+bI}{1-b} \end{bmatrix} = \begin{bmatrix} Y \\ C \end{bmatrix} \qquad (5.26)$$

The solution to the simple model, therefore, is readily determined from the matrix expression above. What is more revealing, however, are the contents of $\mathbf{A}^{-1}$. If we examine these in detail it is readily apparent that we have the respective multipliers for the model that we originally derived using ordinary algebra in Chapter 3. The inverse neatly summarizes these impact multipliers in an obvious way. We have:

$$\begin{bmatrix} Y \\ C \end{bmatrix} = \begin{bmatrix} \dfrac{1}{1-b} & \dfrac{1}{1-b} \\[2mm] \dfrac{b}{1-b} & \dfrac{1}{1-b} \end{bmatrix} \begin{bmatrix} I \\ a \end{bmatrix} \qquad (5.27)$$

This can be shown as:

	I	a
Y	Multiplier for Y given I	Multiplier for Y given a
C	Multiplier for C given I	Multiplier for C given a

(5.28)

Thus, the multiplier impact of a change in I on the equilibrium level of income, Y, will be given by the corresponding cell of the $\mathbf{A}^{-1}$ matrix—here $1/(1-b)$—and similarly for any other impact we wish to assess. The potential usefulness of this approach is further evidenced if we consider a slightly more developed national income model.

5.4 A national income model with government activity

Let us consider the model:

$$Y = C + I + G \tag{5.29}$$
$$C = a + bY_d \tag{5.30}$$
$$T = tY \tag{5.31}$$
$$Y_d = Y - T \tag{5.32}$$

with:

$$a > 0$$
$$0 < b < 1$$
$$0 < t < 1$$

and I and G exogenously determined. Rewriting this we have:

$$Y = C + I + G$$
$$C = a + b(Y - T) \tag{5.33}$$
$$T = tY$$

and in matrix form as:

$$\mathbf{Ax = b}$$

$$\begin{bmatrix} 1 & -1 & 0 \\ -b & 1 & b \\ -t & 0 & 1 \end{bmatrix} \begin{bmatrix} Y \\ C \\ T \end{bmatrix} - \begin{bmatrix} I + G \\ a \\ 0 \end{bmatrix} \tag{5.34}$$

Before finding the solution to the model using the $\mathbf{A}$ inverse we need to test for the conditions necessary for a unique solution. Finding $|\mathbf{A}|$ by expanding the first row we have:

$$|\mathbf{A}| = 1 \begin{vmatrix} 1 & b \\ 0 & 1 \end{vmatrix} + 1 \begin{vmatrix} -b & b \\ -t & 1 \end{vmatrix}$$
$$= 1 + (-b) + bt = 1 - b + bt$$

Therefore, for a unique solution to exist $1 - b + bt \neq 0$. This is the same as:

$$1 \neq b - bt$$
$$1 \neq b(1 - t)$$

and, by definition of the model parameters, $b(1 - t)$ cannot equal 1. We now proceed to find the inverse of the $\mathbf{A}$ matrix. We have:

$$\mathbf{C} = \begin{bmatrix} \begin{vmatrix} 1 & b \\ 0 & 1 \end{vmatrix} & -\begin{vmatrix} -b & b \\ -t & 1 \end{vmatrix} & \begin{vmatrix} -b & 1 \\ -t & 0 \end{vmatrix} \\ -\begin{vmatrix} -1 & 0 \\ 0 & 1 \end{vmatrix} & \begin{vmatrix} 1 & 0 \\ -t & 0 \end{vmatrix} & -\begin{vmatrix} 1 & -1 \\ -t & 0 \end{vmatrix} \\ \begin{vmatrix} -1 & 0 \\ 1 & b \end{vmatrix} & -\begin{vmatrix} 1 & 0 \\ -b & b \end{vmatrix} & \begin{vmatrix} 1 & -1 \\ -b & 1 \end{vmatrix} \end{bmatrix}$$

giving:

$$\mathbf{C} = \begin{bmatrix} 1 & b - bt & t \\ 1 & 1 & t \\ -b & -b & 1-b \end{bmatrix} \quad \text{and} \quad \mathbf{C}' = \begin{bmatrix} 1 & 1 & -b \\ b - bt & 1 & -b \\ t & t & 1-b \end{bmatrix}$$

which in turn gives:

$$\mathbf{A}^{-1} = \frac{1}{1 - b(1-t)} \begin{bmatrix} 1 & 1 & -b \\ b - bt & 1 & -b \\ t & t & 1-b \end{bmatrix}$$

$$= \begin{bmatrix} \dfrac{1}{1 - b(1-t)} & \dfrac{1}{1 - b(1-t)} & \dfrac{-b}{1 - b(1-t)} \\[2ex] \dfrac{b - bt}{1 - b(1-t)} & \dfrac{1}{1 - b(1-t)} & \dfrac{-b}{1 - b(1-t)} \\[2ex] \dfrac{t}{1 - b(1-t)} & \dfrac{t}{1 - b(1-t)} & \dfrac{1-b}{1 - b(1-t)} \end{bmatrix} \qquad (5.35)$$

At this stage, of course, we could derive the expressions for the equilibrium values for Y, C and T. Our interest, however, is rather in the inverse matrix and the multiplier expressions it contains. As a general statement it becomes clear, considering both this model and the previous national income model, that the inverse matrix coefficients are the multiplier coefficients linking the endogenous to the exogenous variables. If we denote the inverse coefficients as α, then a particular coefficient, α_{ij}, links the ith endogenous variable with the jth exogenous variable in the model. Thus $(b - bt)/[1 - b(1 - t)]$, for example, links Y with $(I + G)$. In general we would have for a three-equation model:

$$\begin{bmatrix} y_1 \\ y_2 \\ y_3 \end{bmatrix} = \begin{bmatrix} \alpha_{11} & \alpha_{12} & \alpha_{13} \\ \alpha_{21} & \alpha_{22} & \alpha_{23} \\ \alpha_{31} & \alpha_{32} & \alpha_{33} \end{bmatrix} \begin{bmatrix} x_1 \\ x_2 \\ x_3 \end{bmatrix} \qquad (5.36)$$

where x represents the exogenous variables in the model, y the endogenous and the α matrix shows the multiplier coefficients linking each x to each y. It should be apparent that such an approach to multiplier analysis is readily extended to any sized model, given the two-dimensional nature of the inverse $\mathbf{A}$ matrix (which represents the multiplier coefficients).

> *Student activity 5.4*
> Determine the appropriate expressions for the equilibrium values for Y, C and T. Compare these with those we derived in Chapter 3.

5.5 Input–output analysis

Finally in this chapter we turn to, what is for us, a new area of economic analysis—that relating to input–output economics. This is an area of economic study that provides an ideal illustration of the uses of matrix algebra both from the viewpoint of developing a theoretical model and then applying that model to numerical problems to ascertain the policy implications of the model solution. The principles of input–output economics are straightforward. Let us assume a simplified economy consisting of three broad 'industry' groups: agriculture (A), production (P) and services (S). We shall focus initially on the production sector. Over a given time period, say a year, this sector will produce a given output of goods and these goods will be used in a variety of ways—in terms of input–output economics we say that this output has a number of destinations. The destination of this output can be grouped into two broad categories:

1 Output going to other industries
2 Output going to final consumers

It is evident that some of the output from production will be used by other industries in their own productive activities. For example, this sector may produce tractors which are used by the agriculture sector to enable that sector to produce its own output, food. It may equally produce, say, microcomputers which are used in the service sector. In short, some of this industry's output is used as an input into another industry. On the other hand, some of the output of the production sector will be used directly by the final consumer. Motor vehicles, for example, will be used by the individual consumer. If we now turn to consider the other side of the production process—inputs as opposed to outputs—it is clear that production will require two broad categories of inputs. These will comprise:

1 Inputs from other industries
2 Inputs of primary factors of production

As we have seen, a particular industry will use as inputs into its own production process the output of other sectors of the economy. Similarly, there will be certain primary factors of production that will be required: land, labour, capital, for example. Therefore, the various sectors of an economy can be linked together in terms of their inputs and outputs. Let us now consider the numerical example shown in Table 5.1.

We must ensure that the structure and information content of the table is clearly understood before proceeding. Across the top of the table we show the output destinations. Taking agriculture as an example the total output of this sector (£100 billion) is used in the following way:

1 £30 billion by the sector itself (e.g. farmers growing barley to feed to cattle)
2 £30 billion by the production sector (e.g. meat sold to food companies to turn into burgers)
3 £30 billion for private consumption (people buying food)
4 £10 billion for export.

In terms of national income accounting this output of £100 billion must be matched exactly by inputs of £100 billion. These are shown down the columns of the table. Using agriculture as our example again this sector uses £100 billion of outputs in the following way:

1 £30 billion from agriculture itself (as we have already seen)
2 £10 billion from production
3 £25 billion from services
4 £10 billion of imports
5 £10 billion of labour
6 £15 billion of capital.

TABLE 5.1   Input–output table (in £ billions)

Inputs	Outputs A	P	S	C	I	G	X	Total
A	30	30	0	30	0	0	10	100
P	10	120	25	70	30	25	20	300
S	25	75	100	100	70	60	70	500
M	10	15	50	50	25	0	0	150
L	10	30	175	0	0	15	0	230
K	15	30	150	0	0	0	0	195
Total	100	300	500	250	125	100	100	1475

A = agriculture

P = production

S = services

C = private consumption

I = investment

G = consumption by government

X = exports of goods and services

M = imports of goods and services

L = labour (measured in terms of wages and salaries)

K = capital (measured in terms of profit)

We could examine the input–output pattern of the other sectors in exactly the same way. There are a number of important points to note about such an input–output table at this stage:

1 It is evident that, although our example is an oversimplified representation, the input–output structure can easily be expanded into a more realistic model. We could introduce additional industry sectors, we could subdivide the final demand categories, we could subdivide the primary factors of production. The basic structure of our simple model, however, will remain the same no matter how large the table becomes and is, therefore, eminently suitable for manipulation through matrix algebra.

2 There are obvious difficulties of categorization and definition in such an approach. Although these are not our prime concern in this text it is worth noting that such measurement difficulties do exist and in practice pose a severe problem for input–output analysis.

3 It is clear from the table that there is also a linkage between the primary factors of production and final demand. In our example, final demand consumers require imports and labour.

The next stage in the development of a suitable model is to transform the data in Table 5.1 into a set of input–output coefficients. Our interest lies primarily in the links between the various sectors of the economy, and these can best be expressed in proportionate terms rather than in absolute terms as currently shown in Table 5.1. This can be achieved by showing, for a particular sector, the proportion of total inputs that came from each sector of economic activity. In the case of agriculture, for example, we can calculate the proportion of the total required from agriculture, production, services, imports, labour and capital. These proportions—referred to as the input–output coefficients—are shown in Table 5.2.

TABLE 5.2 Input–output table: input–output coefficients

Inputs	Outputs						
	A	P	S	C	I	G	X
A	0.30	0.10	0.00	0.12	0	0	0.10
P	0.10	0.40	0.05	0.28	0.24	0.25	0.20
S	0.25	0.25	0.20	0.40	0.56	0.60	0.70
M	0.10	0.05	0.10	0.20	0.20	0	0
L	0.10	0.10	0.35	0	0	0.15	0
K	0.15	0.10	0.30	0	0	0	0
Total	1.00	1.00	1.00	1.00	1.00	1.00	1.00

For our three industry sectors (A, P, S) Table 5.2 effectively shows the input requirements for one unit of output of a particular sector. Thus, for example, for each unit of output from production a number of different inputs are required: 0.1 units of agriculture, 0.4 units of production, 0.25 units of services, 0.05 units of imports, 0.1 units of labour and 0.1 units of capital. We are now in a position to develop a matrix representation of the basic input–output model. First let us define vector $\mathbf{t}$ as the total outputs of the industry sectors. From Table 5.1 we have:

$$\mathbf{t} = \begin{bmatrix} t_1 \\ t_2 \\ t_3 \end{bmatrix} = \begin{bmatrix} 100 \\ 300 \\ 500 \end{bmatrix}$$

Let us denote $\mathbf{f}$ as a vector of final demand for the outputs of the industry sectors. In our model this would comprise the total of $C + I + G + X$ to give:

$$\mathbf{f} = \begin{bmatrix} f_1 \\ f_2 \\ f_3 \end{bmatrix} = \begin{bmatrix} 40 \\ 145 \\ 300 \end{bmatrix}$$

Similarly we define $\mathbf{y}$ as the total demand for primary factors of production, $\mathbf{h}$ as the vector of primary factors of production required by final users and $\mathbf{g}$ as the vector of final demand totals:

$$\mathbf{y} = \begin{bmatrix} y_1 \\ y_2 \\ y_3 \end{bmatrix} = \begin{bmatrix} 150 \\ 230 \\ 195 \end{bmatrix} \qquad \mathbf{h} = \begin{bmatrix} h_1 \\ h_2 \\ h_3 \end{bmatrix} = \begin{bmatrix} 75 \\ 15 \\ 0 \end{bmatrix}$$

and

$$\mathbf{g} = \begin{bmatrix} 250 & 125 & 100 & 100 \end{bmatrix}$$

Turning now to Table 5.2 which shows the input–output coefficients we define four matrices. $\mathbf{A}$ is a matrix of the interindustry coefficients, $\mathbf{B}$ a matrix of the industry/final demand

TABLE 5.3   Input–output block structure

Inputs	Outputs								Total
	A	P	S	C	I	G	X		
A P S	A			B				f	t
M L K	C			D				h	y
Total	t			g					

coefficients, **C** a matrix of the industry/factors of production coefficients and **D** a matrix of the factors of production/final demand coefficients. This gives:

$$\mathbf{A} = \begin{bmatrix} 0.30 & 0.10 & 0.00 \\ 0.10 & 0.40 & 0.05 \\ 0.25 & 0.25 & 0.10 \end{bmatrix} \quad \mathbf{B} = \begin{bmatrix} 0.12 & 0.00 & 0.00 & 0.10 \\ 0.28 & 0.24 & 0.25 & 0.20 \\ 0.40 & 0.56 & 0.60 & 0.70 \end{bmatrix}$$

$$\mathbf{C} = \begin{bmatrix} 0.10 & 0.05 & 0.10 \\ 0.10 & 0.10 & 0.35 \\ 0.15 & 0.10 & 0.30 \end{bmatrix} \quad \mathbf{D} = \begin{bmatrix} 0.20 & 0.20 & 0.00 & 0.00 \\ 0.00 & 0.00 & 0.15 & 0.00 \\ 0.00 & 0.00 & 0.00 & 0.00 \end{bmatrix}$$

Combining these coefficient matrices and the total vectors together would give the block structure shown in Table 5.3.

To see how we can proceed from this stage we shall represent the relationships inherent in the input–output structure as simple linear equations. Let us examine the outputs of the agriculture sector (which we denote as sector 1). From Table 5.2 we have:

$$t_1 = 0.30t_1 + 0.10t_2 + 0t_3 + f_1$$

This is readily confirmed from the vector definition:

$t_1 = 100, t_2 = 300, t_3 = 500$ and $f_1 = 40$. This gives:
$$t_1 = 0.30(100) + 0.10(300) + 0(500) + 40 = 30 + 30 + 0 + 40 = 100$$

Similarly, for the other two industry sectors we have:

$$t_1 = 0.30t_1 + 0.10t_2 + 0t_3 + f_1$$
$$t_2 = 0.10t_1 + 0.40t_2 + 0.05t_3 + f_2$$
$$t_3 = 0.25t_1 + 0.25t_2 + 0.10t_3 + f_3$$

In matrix format this can be written as:

$$\mathbf{t} = \mathbf{At} + \mathbf{f}$$

which in turn can be written as:

$$t - At = f$$
$$t(I - A) = f$$
$$t(I - A)(I - A)^{-1} = (I - A)^{-1}f$$
$$t = (I - A)^{-1}f \qquad (5.37)$$

where $(I - A)^{-1}$ is known as the input–output inverse. Providing the $I - A$ matrix is non-singular this implies that for a given f vector we can readily determine the corresponding t vector.

Before applying this to our problem it is worth reviewing the implications of this model so far. What we have derived is a matrix expression that allows us to determine—for a given level of final demand—what the corresponding total outputs of the various industry sectors must be. Further than this we can readily calculate the effect on total output for a given change in the f vector. For example (and as we shall demonstrate later), assume the government intends reducing the level of its own demand in the economy from £100 billion to, say, £90 billion. All other components of final demand are assumed to remain constant. The matrix expressions we have derived will allow us to determine the exact effect this will have on the various industry sectors. Similarly, if exports are anticipated to increase by 10 per cent, the impact on the three industry sectors can be calculated. Potentially, therefore, the model provides an extremely powerful economic planning and analysis tool. Let us return to our numerical example to illustrate this. $I - A$ will be given as:

$$I - A = \begin{bmatrix} 1 & 0 & 0 \\ 0 & 1 & 0 \\ 0 & 0 & 1 \end{bmatrix} - \begin{bmatrix} 0.30 & 0.10 & 0.00 \\ 0.10 & 0.40 & 0.05 \\ 0.25 & 0.25 & 0.20 \end{bmatrix} = \begin{bmatrix} 0.70 & -0.10 & 0.00 \\ -0.10 & 0.60 & -0.05 \\ -0.25 & -0.25 & 0.80 \end{bmatrix}$$

The inverse to this matrix can then be derived as:

$$(I - A)^{-1} = \begin{bmatrix} 1.470\,126\,0 & 0.251\,572\,3 & 0.015\,723\,3 \\ 0.290\,880\,5 & 1.761\,006\,0 & 0.110\,062\,9 \\ 0.550\,314\,5 & 0.628\,930\,8 & 1.289\,308\,0 \end{bmatrix}$$

and we can confirm the logic of the model from the original input–output table:

$$t = (I - A)^{-1}f = \begin{bmatrix} 1.470\,126\,0 & 0.251\,572\,3 & 0.015\,723\,3 \\ 0.290\,880\,5 & 1.761\,006\,0 & 0.110\,062\,9 \\ 0.550\,314\,5 & 0.628\,930\,8 & 1.289\,308\,0 \end{bmatrix} \begin{bmatrix} 40 \\ 145 \\ 300 \end{bmatrix} = \begin{bmatrix} 100 \\ 300 \\ 500 \end{bmatrix}$$

This, however, is not unduly useful given that we already have the original input–output table. However, let us return to one of the earlier illustrative examples. Assume that the government intends reducing its expenditure in terms of final demand. The government final demand for production output is expected to fall from its current level of £25 billion to £20 billion and for services output is expected to fall from £60 billion to £55 billion. The new final demand vector (f_2) therefore, *ceteris paribus*, will be:

$$f_2 = \begin{bmatrix} 40 \\ 140 \\ 295 \end{bmatrix}$$

and using the input–output inverse we can readily determine the new **t** vector, t_2, which will be given by:

$$\begin{bmatrix} 1.470\,126\,0 & 0.251\,572\,3 & 0.015\,723\,3 \\ 0.290\,880\,5 & 1.761\,006\,0 & 0.110\,062\,9 \\ 0.550\,314\,5 & 0.628\,930\,8 & 1.289\,308\,0 \end{bmatrix} \begin{bmatrix} 40 \\ 140 \\ 295 \end{bmatrix} = \begin{bmatrix} 98.7 \\ 290.6 \\ 490.4 \end{bmatrix}$$

Therefore, the precise changes such a decrease in government final demand would have on the three industry sectors can be quantified readily. We see that total output of agriculture will fall to £98.7 billion, production to £290.6 billion and services to £490.4 billion as a result of a £5 billion reduction in government purchases of both production and services output.

> *Student activity 5.5*
> Explain why the reduction in the total output in each sector is larger than the initial reduction in *G*. Why has output of agriculture fallen even though the government purchases no output from this sector?

As we might expect from our understanding of macroeconomic multipliers, the largest impact of such a change in final demand is on the two sectors directly affected. Notice also that, because of the interrelationships between the various sectors, total output of the agriculture sector also decreases, even though it is not directly affected by government changes. Having found the new **t** vector we could determine the impact these changes in total outputs have on the rest of the input–output table. We know, for example, that agriculture's output requires a 10 per cent input from labour (*L*). This is currently £10 billion. However, since the new agriculture output has fallen to £98.7 billion this implies the new labour input will fall to £9.87 billion. Similar calculations are readily undertaken on the rest of the inputs for all three sectors. Should we require further detail of the precise impact of such a policy then we could use the new **t** vector with the original input–output coefficients to construct the full, new, input–output table. It should be apparent that the use of the input–output inverse in this way provides an especially powerful tool of economic analysis and economic policy. The economic policy maker is able to assess in considerable detail alternative macroeconomic strategies and their impact on specific sectors of the economy. We could now, for example, compare the effects of this change in *G* with—what may be an alternative policy—some change in *C*. (This may be brought about, for example, by a change in government tax policy.) One further point to note at this stage is that we could have carried out the analysis not on the various totals but rather on the various changes in the totals—undertaking marginal analysis in other words. Here, for example, we could have used an **f** vector such that:

$$\Delta\mathbf{f} = \begin{bmatrix} 0 \\ -5 \\ -5 \end{bmatrix}$$

and the **t** vector would now show changes in total outputs rather than the totals themselves. For comparative static analysis this may be more convenient than examining the totals as we did previously.

> *Student activity 5.6*
> Confirm that such an **f** vector will produce the same results in the **t** vector as before.

We can readily expand the application of this analysis. So far, we have determined the change in total outputs that will be required as the result of some change in the final demand vector. From an economic planning viewpoint what may be equally important is an assessment of the effect such a change in **f** will have on the demand for primary factors of production. The economic policy maker may, for example, be interested in the change in demand for labour (i.e. in employment levels) that such a change in final demand will bring about. Earlier we derived a matrix expression for the **t** vector:

$$\mathbf{t} = (\mathbf{I} - \mathbf{A})^{-1}\mathbf{f}$$

and in a similar way we can derive an equivalent expression for **y**, the vector of demand for primary factors of production. In terms of a linear equation system we have for the imports, labour and capital sectors respectively:

$$y_1 = 0.10t_1 + 0.05t_2 + 0.10t_3 + h_1$$
$$y_2 = 0.10t_1 + 0.10t_2 + 0.35t_3 + h_2$$
$$y_3 = 0.15t_1 + 0.10t_2 + 0.30t_3 + h_3$$

which in matrix form gives:

$$\mathbf{y} = \mathbf{Ct} + \mathbf{h}$$

However, as we also have:

$$\mathbf{t} = (\mathbf{I} - \mathbf{A})^{-1}\mathbf{f}$$

this gives:

$$\mathbf{y} = \mathbf{C}(\mathbf{I} - \mathbf{A})^{-1}\mathbf{f} + \mathbf{h} \tag{5.38}$$

In other words, we can again use the input–output inverse to quantify the effects on the **y** vector of a given change in the **f** vector. To illustrate the calculations let us return to the earlier example where the *G* element in the final demand vector was reduced. If we express the new **f** vector in terms of marginal changes we have:

$$\Delta\mathbf{f} = \begin{bmatrix} 0 \\ -5 \\ -5 \end{bmatrix} \quad \text{and} \quad \Delta\mathbf{h} = \begin{bmatrix} 0 \\ 0 \\ 0 \end{bmatrix}$$

since no change has occurred in terms of final demand for primary inputs. We now require the product of the **C** matrix multiplied by the input–output inverse. The product of this is:

$$\mathbf{C}(\mathbf{I} - \mathbf{A})^{-1} = \begin{bmatrix} 0.10 & 0.05 & 0.10 \\ 0.10 & 0.10 & 0.35 \\ 0.15 & 0.10 & 0.30 \end{bmatrix} \begin{bmatrix} 1.470\,126\,0 & 0.251\,572\,3 & 0.015\,723\,3 \\ 0.290\,880\,5 & 1.761\,006\,0 & 0.110\,062\,9 \\ 0.550\,314\,5 & 0.628\,930\,8 & 1.289\,308\,0 \end{bmatrix}$$

$$= \begin{bmatrix} 0.216\,588\,1 & 0.176\,100\,6 & 0.136\,006\,3 \\ 0.368\,710\,7 & 0.421\,383\,6 & 0.463\,836\,5 \\ 0.414\,701\,3 & 0.402\,515\,7 & 0.400\,157\,2 \end{bmatrix}$$

and multiplying by the $\Delta \mathbf{f}$ vector gives:

$$\Delta \mathbf{y} = \begin{bmatrix} -1.56 \\ -4.43 \\ -4.01 \end{bmatrix}$$

Interpretation of the $\Delta \mathbf{y}$ vector is straightforward. The demand for imports will fall by £1.56 billion, for labour by £4.43 billion and for capital by £4.01 billion. In the context of the original problem, we could also determine the precise effect on each industry's labour requirements by returning to the original input–output coefficients. Finally, to complete the model we can develop the final matrix forms relating to the input–output table. We already have:

$$\mathbf{t} = (\mathbf{I} - \mathbf{A})^{-1} \mathbf{f}$$

and
$$\mathbf{y} = \mathbf{C}(\mathbf{I} - \mathbf{A})^{-1} \mathbf{f} + \mathbf{h}$$

These can be written in an equivalent form as:

$$\mathbf{t} = (\mathbf{I} - \mathbf{A})^{-1} \mathbf{B}\mathbf{g}$$

since $\mathbf{f} = \mathbf{B}\mathbf{g}$, and as:

$$\mathbf{y} = [\mathbf{C}(\mathbf{I} - \mathbf{A})^{-1}\mathbf{B} + \mathbf{D}]\mathbf{g} \tag{5.39}$$

since $\mathbf{h} = \mathbf{D}\mathbf{g}$. Effectively this means that we can determine the new $\mathbf{t}$ and $\mathbf{y}$ vectors not only from introducing a change in the $\mathbf{f}$ vector but also a change in the $\mathbf{g}$ vector (which relates to the final demand for primary factors). This would allow us to develop the following structure of coefficients:

$$\begin{array}{c|c} (\mathbf{I} - \mathbf{A})^{-1} & (\mathbf{I} - \mathbf{A})^{-1}\mathbf{b} \\ \hline \mathbf{C}(\mathbf{I} - \mathbf{A})^{-1} & \mathbf{C}(\mathbf{I} - \mathbf{A})^{-1}\mathbf{B} + \mathbf{D} \end{array} \tag{5.40}$$

where the coefficients can be interpreted in the same general way as the multipliers that were discussed in Sec. 5.5. The two matrix expressions on the left will show the multiplier (or cumulative) impact of a change in the $\mathbf{f}$ vector (or any element of the $\mathbf{f}$ vector) on $\mathbf{t}$ and $\mathbf{y}$ respectively. The two matrix expressions on the right will show the multiplier impact of a change in the $\mathbf{g}$ vector on $\mathbf{t}$ and $\mathbf{y}$ respectively. Thus, these coefficients can be readily used to pinpoint a single multiplier impact on any of the elements in the $\mathbf{t}$ and $\mathbf{y}$ vectors arising from any element in the $\mathbf{f}$ and $\mathbf{g}$ vectors. For example, if we wished to determine the multiplier effect of a change in consumption, C, on total demand for imports, M, this is readily achieved through the appropriate multiplier coefficient. It can be seen, therefore, that input–output analysis provides the economic policy maker with a potentially extremely powerful comparative analysis tool. Through the use of matrix algebra, the input–output model can readily be constructed and, through the use of the input–output inverse, the solution to a numerical model can readily be found.

5.6 Summary

In this chapter and in Chapter 4 we have examined the area of matrix algebra and its potential application in the study of mathematical economics. In particular in this chapter we have seen how matrix algebra can be used to examine the fundamental relationships inherent in a theoretical economic model and deduce the important implications of the model. We also saw that, in the area of input–output analysis and the development of macroeconomic models in general, the use of matrix algebra readily allows comparative static analysis to be undertaken into an economic structure. The use of matrix methods allows the ready identification of economic multipliers and thereby the policy implications arising from the solution of a numerical model can be determined.

Worked example

We have a simple national income model where:

$$Y = C + I$$
$$C = a + bY$$

but where:

$$I = c + dr$$

where r is the rate of interest. We place restrictions on the parameters such that:

$$a > 0$$
$$0 < b < 1$$
$$c > 0$$
$$d < 0$$

For the investment function, this comprises a fixed level of investment, c, and a variable investment which is inversely linked to the rate of interest. We also add a monetary sector to the model.

$$M_s = m$$
$$M_d = m_1 + m_2 r + m_3 Y$$

M_s is the money supply which is assumed to be exogenous to the model. M_d is the demand for money in the economy linked to both the rate of interest and the level of income. We place restrictions on the parameters such that:

$$m_1 > 0$$
$$m_2 < 0$$
$$m_3 > 0$$
$$m > m_1$$

Demand for money is inversely linked to the rate of interest, positively linked to the level of income and the autonomous demand for money, m_1, is less than the fixed supply.

We wish to derive the equilibrium expressions for Y and r using matrix algebra. We also wish to assess the effect of an increase in M_s on the equilibrium values of Y and r.

Solution

We have:

$$Y = C + I$$
$$C = a + bY$$
$$I = c + dr$$
$$M_s = m$$
$$M_d = m_1 + m_2 r + m_3 Y$$

Since we require $Y = C + I$ we then have:

$$Y = a + bY + c + dr$$
$$(Y - bY) - dr = a + c$$
$$(1 - b)Y - dr = a + c$$

or in matrix form:

$$\begin{bmatrix} 1 - b & -d \end{bmatrix} \begin{bmatrix} Y \\ r \end{bmatrix} = \begin{bmatrix} a + c \end{bmatrix}$$

We also require at equilibrium:

$$M_s = M_d$$
$$m = m_1 + m_2 r + m_3 Y$$
$$m_3 Y + m_2 r = m - m_1$$

which again in matrix form gives:

$$\begin{bmatrix} m_3 & m_2 \end{bmatrix} \begin{bmatrix} Y \\ r \end{bmatrix} = \begin{bmatrix} m - m_1 \end{bmatrix}$$

Collecting both matrix expressions together we then have:

$$\begin{bmatrix} 1 - b & -d \\ m_3 & m_2 \end{bmatrix} \begin{bmatrix} Y \\ r \end{bmatrix} = \begin{bmatrix} a + c \\ m - m_1 \end{bmatrix}$$

or $\mathbf{Ax} = \mathbf{b}$.

The equilibrium values for $\mathbf{x}$ (Y and r) will be given by:

$$\mathbf{x} = \mathbf{A}^{-1} \mathbf{b}$$

We now require the inverse to the **A** matrix:

$$\mathbf{A}^{-1} = \frac{1}{|\mathbf{A}|}\text{adj }\mathbf{A}$$

$$|\mathbf{A}| = m_2(1-b) + dm_3$$

$$\text{adj }\mathbf{A} = \begin{bmatrix} m_2 & d \\ -m_2 & 1-b \end{bmatrix} \qquad \text{(from the transposed cofactor matrix)}$$

This then gives

$$\begin{bmatrix} Y \\ r \end{bmatrix} = \frac{1}{m_2(1-b)+dm_3} \begin{bmatrix} m_2 & d \\ -m_2 & 1-b \end{bmatrix} \begin{bmatrix} a+c \\ m-m_1 \end{bmatrix}$$

which gives:

$$Y = \frac{(a+c)m_2 + d(m-m_1)}{m_2(1-b)+dm_3}$$

and

$$r = \frac{(a+c)(-m_2) + (m-m_1)(1-b)}{m_2(1-b)+dm_3}$$

as the equilibrium values for Y and r.

To assess the impact of an increase in the money supply, $M_s = m$, we can use the equilibrium expressions just derived. For Y, given the parameter restrictions that we imposed, an increase in m will change the numerator through the term $d(m-m_1)$. d is required to be negative and $(m-m_1)$ is required to be positive so there will be a negative effect on the numerator as M_s increases. The denominator, however, will also be negative since $m_2(1-b)$ will be negative and dm_3 will be negative also. With both the numerator and denominator effect negative the overall effect on Y must be positive. Hence an increase in M_s will lead to an increase in Y. But what of the effect on r? Using similar logic, the denominator will again be negative. The numerator will be affected through the expression $(m-m_1)(1-b)$ which, because of the original parameter restrictions, will be positive. Hence the overall effect on r will be negative. An increase in M_s will lead to a fall in r.

You may also wish to explore the impact of other changes on Y and r.

Exercises

5.1 Return to the national income model that we developed in Sec. 5.4. Assume that we now add a foreign trade sector to the model such that X represents exports and is exogenous while M represents imports and takes the functional form:

$$M = k + mY_d$$

Find the equilibrium expressions for Y, C, T and M.

5.2 Assume a simplified foreign trade model where two countries trade with each other but with no other country. It follows that exports from country 1 must be the imports for country 2 and vice versa. Assume the following model:

For country 1:

$$Y_1 = C_1 + I_1 + X_1 - M_1$$
$$C_1 = bY_1$$
$$M_1 = mY_1$$

For country 2:

$$Y_2 = C_2 + I_2 + X_2 - M_2$$
$$C_2 = bY_2$$
$$M_2 = mY_2$$
$$X_1 = M_2$$
$$X_2 = M_1$$

with I exogenous. Represent this model in a suitable matrix form. Find the equilibrium expressions for Y in each country.

5.3 Return to the input–output table shown in Table 5.1. The government is concerned about the level of economic growth in the economy and is trying to evaluate two alternate policies that could be adopted to stimulate a higher growth rate.

Policy 1 would lead to an increase in exports of the three sectors. Agricultural exports will rise by £2 billion, production exports by £3 billion and services exports by £5 billion.

Policy 2 would lead to a 5 per cent increase in private consumption, C, in each of the three sectors.
For each policy assess the effect on:

(i) Total output of each sector.
(ii) The demand for M, L, K.
(iii) The balance of trade $(X - M)$.
(iv) Obtain a complete new table, corresponding to that shown in Table 5.1.

5.4 Return to the exercises at the end of Chapter 3. Formulate each in matrix form and solve.

6 Non-linear models and differential calculus

Up to now our attention has been focused almost exclusively on the use of linear models in economic analysis. As you will appreciate from your study of economics, such models are frequently useful because of their simple mathematical structure; however, they are also quite limiting in the way they can be used to model economic behaviour. We clearly need to be able to develop *non-linear* models for use in economic analysis and it is to these that we now turn. In this chapter we shall illustrate how non-linear models can be developed and analysed. We shall focus our attention initially on one particular type of non-linear function—the quadratic—as this has a number of useful properties allowing us to illustrate many of the key features of non-linear models in general. We shall then turn to the important topic of *differential calculus* which provides us with the analytical skills we shall require to be able to cope with non-linear models in economic analysis.

Learning objectives

By the time you have completed this chapter you should be able to:

- Determine the roots and turning point of a quadratic function
- Understand what is meant by the derivative
- Be able to calculate the derivative for a range of common non-linear functions
- Understand what is meant by a non-differentiable function

6.1 Quadratic functions

Quadratic functions were introduced briefly in Chapter 2 as a type of polynomial function. You will remember that such a function takes the general form:

$$Y = f(X) = a + bX + cX^2 \tag{6.1}$$

where a, b and c are the numerical parameters of the function. We shall illustrate the key features of such functions with a simple economic model. Assume a firm faces a situation such that:

$$\text{TR} = f(Q) = 260Q \tag{6.2}$$

$$\text{TC} = g(Q) = 1125 + 10Q + 5Q^2 \tag{6.3}$$

where TR and TC represent total revenue and total costs respectively (both measured in £000s) and Q represents the units of output produced (measured in 000s). Figure 6.1 shows both these functions for $Q = 0$ to 50.

> **Student activity 6.1**
> Consider the form of the TR function shown in Eq. (6.2). What does this imply about the demand function faced by this firm and the market conditions under which the firm operates?
> (Solution on p. 335.)

A number of points become evident. The TR function, as we know, is linear while the TC function is quadratic. We have already seen how to interpret the parameters (a and b) of a linear function. Can we interpret the quadratic parameters in a similar way? On inspection we see that the quadratic function intercepts the vertical axis at 1125, the value for a in the quadratic equation. Clearly, as in a linear function, the a term indicates the intercept—where the quadratic function will cross the vertical axis. The other visual feature of a quadratic that we can identify is its general shape. Quadratic functions will take either a U shape or an inverted U shape (∩) and we can determine which of these shapes it will take by inspection of the c term in the equation. If the c term is positive (as in Eq. (6.3)), then the graph of the function will follow the U shape (although the U shape may not be immediately obvious from the graph since we use only quadrant I). If the c term is negative the shape will be that of ∩. Clearly this is useful when we wish to have a visual picture of the form of the quadratic we are dealing with but do not wish to bother drawing a detailed graph of the function. You will remember, however, that the other critical feature of a linear function was its slope or gradient—denoted for a linear function by the b term. For a quadratic function, however, and indeed for non-linear functions in general,

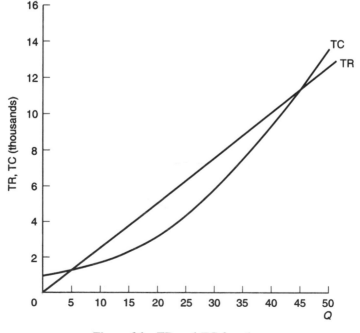

Figure 6.1   TR and TC functions

the slope is not as easily obtained. On inspection it is clear that the slope of the quadratic (and of any non-linear function) does not remain constant but changes depending whereabouts on the function we are—that is, it will vary depending on the value taken by X. For now, however, we have the problem of not being able to quantify the slope of a non-linear function directly by observation as we could for a linear function. We shall be returning to this shortly. Indeed it is this feature of a variable slope that makes non-linear functions so attractive and useful in economic analysis. Equally important is an appreciation of the implications of the economic relationship shown in Fig. 6.1 by the total cost function. The slope of the function must clearly measure the change in costs that occurs as we change output. It is also evident that this change in cost will vary depending on the level of output actually produced. When Q is low the slope is positive but as Q increases the slope becomes steeper, and hence more positive. In other words, the slope is gradually increasing as we increase output. It is worth stressing the importance of viewing such a function not simply in numerical terms but in terms of its economic implications also. We must constantly remind ourselves that all such functions represent some facet of economic behaviour and we should adopt the habit of automatically interpreting the mathematics in this context.

Clearly, not only will we wish to examine the slope but we will frequently wish to find a solution to such an economic model (as we did with earlier, linear, versions). In this example we require the breakeven level of output, defined as the level of output where TR = TC. It is evident from Fig. 6.1 that in this model there will be two such points and from the graph we see that these correspond to $Q = 5$ and $Q = 45$. However, such a graphical solution is not always possible or, indeed, desirable. We must turn to algebra as a general solution method. We have:

$$TR = TC \tag{6.4}$$

Hence:

$$TR - TC = 0$$
$$260Q - (1125 + 10Q + 5Q^2) = 0$$
$$260Q - 1125 - 10Q - 5Q^2 = 0$$
$$-1125 + 250Q - 5Q^2 = 0 \tag{6.5}$$

and we clearly require the values for Q that will cause the left-hand side of this equation to equal zero.

> **Student activity 6.2**
> Plot the equation we have just derived (Eq. 6.5) for $X = 0$ to 50. What economic interpretation would you give this function? What interpretation would you give the two points where the function crosses the X axis? What interpretation would you give to the point where $X = 25$?
> (Solution on p. 336.)

It may appear that finding such values algebraically (as opposed to graphically) will be no easy task. However, we can readily derive a suitable formula for finding such values for (almost) any quadratic function taking this general form. Let us denote the general form of a quadratic as:

$$a + bX + cX^2 = 0 \tag{6.6}$$

If we divide through by c (given that it cannot equal zero by definition of a quadratic), we have:

$$\frac{a}{c} + \frac{bX}{c} + X^2 = 0$$

and

$$\frac{bX}{c} + X^2 = -\frac{a}{c}$$

If we now add $b_2/4c^2$ to both sides and rearrange the expression to get:

$$X^2 + \frac{bX}{c} + \frac{b^2}{4c^2} = -\frac{a}{c} + \frac{b^2}{4c^2}$$

then the left-hand side can be simplified to:

$$\left(X + \frac{b}{2c}\right)^2 = -\frac{a}{c} + \frac{b^2}{4c^2}$$

and the right-hand side to:

$$\left(X + \frac{b}{2c}\right)^2 = -\frac{4ca}{4c^2} + \frac{b^2}{4c^2} = \frac{-4ac + b^2}{4c^2}$$

Taking the square root of both sides we then have:

$$X + \frac{b}{2c} = \pm\sqrt{\frac{-4ac + b^2}{4c^2}}$$

Note that the $\pm$ term is necessary because the square of both a positive and negative number will produce the same result. However, the square root of $4c^2 = 2c$ so:

$$X + \frac{b}{2c} = \pm\frac{\sqrt{-4ac + b^2}}{2c}$$

$$X = -\frac{b}{2c} \pm \frac{\sqrt{-4ac + b^2}}{2c}$$

$$= \frac{-b \pm \sqrt{b^2 - 4ac}}{2c} \tag{6.7}$$

which provides us with a general formula for providing the solution to a quadratic expression taking the form of Eq. (6.6). Note that in general the formula will provide two solution values for X: one when we evaluate the expression using the $+$ sign from the $\pm$ symbol and one when we use the $-$ sign. Effectively what Eq. (6.7) provides is a ready method of finding the X value for some quadratic function that will give $Y = 0$.

Student activity 6.3
Using this formula solve for the two X values for Eq. (6.5) and interpret the result.

Returning to our problem we have:

$$a = -1125$$
$$b = 250$$
$$c = -5$$

and substituting into Eq. (6.7) (taking care with negative values) we have:

$$
\begin{aligned}
Q &= \frac{-b \pm \sqrt{b^2 - 4ac}}{2c} \\
&= \frac{-250 \pm \sqrt{250^2 - 4(-1125)(-5)}}{2(-5)} \\
&= \frac{-250 \pm \sqrt{62\,500 - 22\,500}}{-10} = \frac{-250 \pm \sqrt{40\,000}}{-10}
\end{aligned}
$$

and evaluating first for $+$ and then for $-$ we have:

$$Q_1 = \frac{-250 + 200}{-10} = \frac{-50}{-10} = 5$$

$$Q_2 = \frac{-250 - 200}{-10} = \frac{-450}{-10} = 45$$

confirming that the two breakeven levels of output occur when $Q = 5$ and $Q = 45$.

> ### Student activity 6.4
> Assume a simple market model where:
>
> $$Q_d = 100 - 2P$$
> $$Q_s = -100 + 10P + 10P^2$$
>
> Sketch both functions together. Determine the (economically sensible) equilibrium price and quantity. Plot both functions on a graph to confirm your algebraic solution.
> (Solution on p. 336.)

In fact, the two values for Q that we have derived are more generally known as the *roots* of the quadratic expression from which they were derived. In general such values represent the value for X that generate a value of zero for the quadratic function. There is another way to view the two roots, however. Assume that we were to graph the quadratic function for which we have just found the roots. The roots (the values for X that cause the function to take a zero value) will correspond to the two points on the X axis where the function crosses. The roots, in other words, indicate where such a function crosses the X axis (much as the a term in a quadratic indicates where the function crosses the Y axis). Such an interpretation is not always useful in terms of the economic model we are examining although in this illustration, however, it clearly will be. Consider the economic meaning of the quadratic function in Eq. (6.5). On reflection it can be seen that this will represent a profit function for this firm given the definition of profit as the difference between total revenue and total costs. Let us now show this profit function on the same graph (Fig. 6.2) as the TR and TC functions.

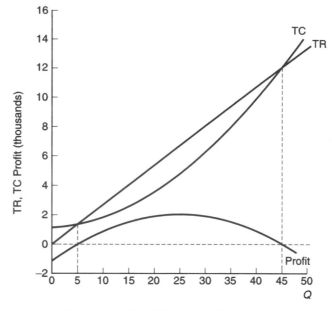

Figure 6.2   TR, TC and profit functions

The diagram will repay close inspection as it has a number of features that we shall develop over this and subsequent chapters of the text. The economic model we are now examining involves three functional relationships with one of these, for profit, derived from the other two. We see that the two roots of the profit function—at 5 and 45—are the points where the profit function crosses the horizontal axis. Clearly, in this model the breakeven points are where profit equals zero. (Note that, as must be the case, TR = TC at these two output levels.) The profit function also intercepts the vertical axis at −1125. It is evident that this represents the fixed cost the firm incurs even when it has a zero output. At such a point profit will be −1125 (i.e. the firm makes an operational loss). This loss-making situation continues up to an output level of 5, with the profit line below the horizontal axis (representing negative profit levels). This is confirmed on examination of the TC and TR lines with TC > TR for output up to 5. After this point profit becomes positive (TC < TR) and it is also evident that profit continues to increase with extra output up to 25. At this level of output the situation reverses and while profits are still being made with increased output the total profit is gradually declining. At $Q = 45$ we again encounter breakeven and after this level of output the firm is again in a loss-making situation. One point on the profit function will clearly be of considerable importance in economic analysis: the point where profit reaches its maximum (here at $Q = 25$).

The concept of profit maximization in particular and optimization in general are of critical importance in economic analysis. The topic is of such importance that we shall be spending much of the rest of this text examining optimization in a number of different ways. For the moment it is evident that in our model the optimum level of profit occurs at the top of the quadratic curve. It is also evident on reflection that such a point occurs when the slope of the profit function is zero. Consider that for $Q < 25$ the slope of the profit function is positive while for $Q > 25$ the slope is negative. At $Q = 25$ we encounter what we can refer to as a *turning point*: where the slope is about to change from positive to negative (or vice versa depending on the exact nature of the function). For a quadratic function such a turning point is readily obtained: it occurs midway between the two roots. Here we see that 25 is equidistant from 5 and 45. For other types of non-linear functions, however, we need a more general approach. While the analysis of the slope of such a non-linear function therefore appears to offer a method for determining such an optimum point, we clearly require a general-purpose method for evaluating the slope of any function. Before examining this, however, we need to consider one further aspect of quadratic functions.

Quadratic functions with no real roots

We should note that the algebraic method we have, through Eq. (6.7), of finding the roots of a quadratic equation will not necessarily find a solution. Recollect that one way of interpreting the roots is that they represent where the function crosses the X axis. Not all quadratic functions, however, will necessarily do this. Some may always lie above or below the X axis and if a function does not cross it cannot have roots. We would normally recognize that this had occurred on inspection of part of Eq. (6.7):

$$\frac{-b \pm \sqrt{b^2 - 4ac}}{2c}$$

Let us examine the term involving the square root. It is possible that the term $4ac$ could take a larger value than b^2. If this were to happen the result would be a negative number. As far as we are concerned the square root of a negative number cannot be found; hence we cannot find the roots of such a function. This would indicate that the function did not intercept the X axis.

> *Student activity 6.5*
> Return to the profit function we have been examining. Assume the firm's fixed costs increase to £4000. Reformulate the equation and attempt to find the roots. Graph this function to confirm that it always lies below the X axis.

6.2 The slope of linear and non-linear functions

As we have seen, the slope is an important concept in economic analysis. Let us return to the slope of a linear function. Figure 6.3 illustrates the principles involved.

We have some linear function and its slope can be determined graphically by locating two points, A and B, finding the corresponding X and Y values and expressing the change in Y as a ratio to the change in X:

$$\frac{\Delta y}{\Delta x} = \frac{y_2 - y_1}{x_2 - x_1} = \frac{BC}{CA} \tag{6.8}$$

and where we know that $\Delta y / \Delta x$ (the *difference quotient*) is equal to the b parameter in the linear function. We also know that the slope of a linear function is constant. In other words, point B in Fig. 6.3 could have been closer to, or further away from, point A and we would obtain the same value for the slope of the function. Let us now consider Fig. 6.4 which shows part of some non-linear function. Assume that for such a function we examine the slope between points A and B. Using the same principles we have the difference quotient as:

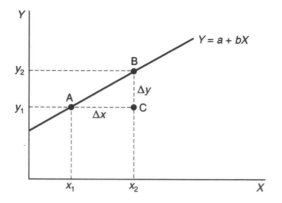

Figure 6.3 Slope of a linear function

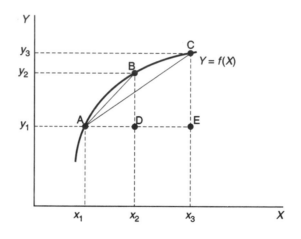

Figure 6.4 Slope of a non-linear function

$$\frac{\Delta y}{\Delta x} = \frac{y_2 - y_1}{x_2 - x_1} = \frac{BD}{DA} \tag{6.9}$$

On reflection, however, it is evident that this expression actually measures the slope of the (straight) line between points A and B and not the slope of the non-linear function between these two points. We see that there is actually a difference between the line AB and that of the non-linear curve between these two points. Therefore, while the difference quotient allows us to derive the slope of a linear function it will not suffice for a non-linear function. There is also another important point revealed. It is clear that if we were now to measure the slope of this function between points A and C the difference quotient would now change (to CE/EA) and it is evident that this slope is different from that given by BD/DA. In other words, as we have already indicated, the slope of a non-linear function is not constant but will change depending whereabouts on the curve we are: it will vary depending on the value of X. To see how we can proceed let us examine Fig. 6.5.

Assume that we wish to determine the slope of the non-linear function shown at a specific point on the curve, say point A. Assume further that we can draw a straight line so that the line

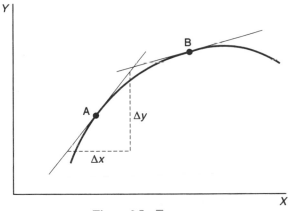

Figure 6.5 Tangents

literally just touched the curve at this one point and nowhere else. Such a line is known as *tangent*, and it is important to realize that a tangent line touches but does not cross the curve. Equally, there is only one possible tangent line for any single point on the curve. To determine the slope of the curve at point A we could now use the difference quotient to find the slope of the tangent line. Clearly, the slope of the tangent line and that of the curve at point A will be the same. In a similar way, if we required the slope of the curve at point B, we could determine its tangent line and then measure the slope of that line which would be the same as that of the curve at point B. How does this help? Clearly, we do not wish to have to resort to a clumsy graphical method every time we wish to determine the slope at some point on a non-linear function. Let us introduce a further concept.

In Fig. 6.6 we are still trying to determine the slope at point A through the use of the tangent line. However, let us return to the difference quotient. From point B_3 the slope of the line joining A to B_3 would be given by:

$$\frac{\Delta y}{\Delta x} \qquad \text{where } \Delta x = x_3 - x_0$$

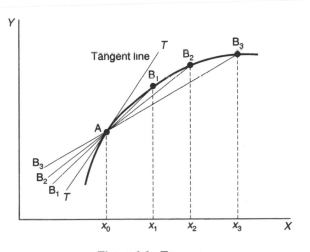

Figure 6.6 Tangents

Similarly the slope of the line B_2 would be given by:

$$\frac{\Delta y}{\Delta x} \qquad \text{where } \Delta x = x_2 - x_0$$

and that of the line B_1 as:

$$\frac{\Delta y}{\Delta x} \qquad \text{where } \Delta x = x_1 - x_0$$

You may be forgiven for wondering at this stage what on earth we are doing. However, consider what is happening as we move along our curve from point B_3 to B_2 to B_1. On inspection it is evident that the slope of each corresponding line is getting closer and closer to the slope of the tangent line that we actually require. In other words, as Δx gets smaller and smaller (the difference between the appropriate x value and x_0) we get closer and closer to the slope of the tangent line at point A. Clearly, we could get to a position where the value for Δx was so infinitesimally small that the slope of the line from A to the corresponding B point would be the same as the slope of the tangent line. Therefore, if we were to calculate the value of the difference quotient:

$$\frac{\Delta y}{\Delta x} \qquad \text{as } \Delta x \text{ approaches zero}$$

we derive the slope of the tangent line that we actually require. Formally we denote this as:

$$\lim_{\Delta x \to 0} \frac{\Delta y}{\Delta x} \tag{6.10}$$

which means the limit of $\Delta y / \Delta x$ as Δx approaches zero. The concept of a limit simply indicates the value that $\Delta y / \Delta x$ approaches as Δx itself approaches zero. This expression relates to the slope of the function at any point along its length and is formally referred to as the *derivative* of the function with respect to x. The notation appropriate for a derivative is:

$$\frac{dy}{dx} = \lim_{\Delta x \to 0} \frac{\Delta y}{\Delta x} \tag{6.11}$$

where dy/dx (pronounced dee-y by dee-x) is the symbolic expression of the derivative. It is important to note that the derivative symbol does not represent d times y divided by d times x but is simply the standard notation used to denote a derivative. The process of obtaining the derivative of a function is known as *differentiation* and the formal study of derivatives is a branch of mathematics referred to as *differential calculus*.

> *Student activity 6.6*
> Return to the profit function shown in Eq. (6.5). Assume that we require the slope of the function when $Q = 10$. Calculate the profit for this level of output and also for the following levels:
>
> $$Q = 11, 10.9, 10.75, 10.5, 10.1, 10.05, 10.01, 10.001$$

Taking Δy as the change in profit between $Q = 10$ and each other value of Q in turn and Δx as the change in output from $Q = 10$, calculate the difference quotient for each value of Q shown.

What comment can you make about the value of the difference quotient as Q approaches 10? What would you infer the slope of the function to be when $Q = 10$? (Solution on p. 337.)

6.3 The derivative

We may not appear to be much further forward in terms of actually finding a value for the slope of some function. In fact, we now have all the concepts we need to put the finishing touches to our discussion. Let us return to the profit function we had earlier:

$$\text{Profit} = -1125 + 250Q - 5Q^2$$

which we recollect is a quadratic following the inverted U shape. Clearly, in terms of our general discussion Q represents the X variable and profit the Y variable. Returning to Fig. 6.6, we can assume this to represent some part of the profit function and that we wish to determine the slope of the profit function at point A. How can we proceed? First, let us rewrite the function in terms of X and Y to avoid confusion:

$$Y = -1125 + 250X - 5X^2 \tag{6.12}$$

At point A, $X = x_0$ and Y will be given by:

$$y_0 = -1125 + 250x_0 - 5x_0^2 \tag{6.13}$$

If we now examine point B_3, we see that $X = x_3$. Let us denote x_3 as $x_0 + k$, that is, as the original X value plus some change, denoted by k. Y will be given as:

$$y_3 = -1125 + 250(x_0 + k) - 5(x_0 + k)^2 \tag{6.14}$$

To determine the slope of the line AB_3 we require:

$$
\begin{aligned}
\frac{\Delta y}{\Delta x} &= \frac{y_3 - y_0}{x_3 - x_0} = \frac{y_3 - y_0}{(x_0 + k) - x_0} = \frac{y_3 - y_0}{k} \\
&= \frac{[-1125 + 250(x_0 + k) - 5(x_0 + k)^2] - [-1125 + 250x_0 - 5x_0^2]}{k} \\
&= \frac{-1125 + 250x_0 + 250k - 5x_0^2 - 5k^2 - 10x_0 k + 1125 - 250x_0 + 5x_0^2}{k} \\
&= \frac{250k - 5k^2 - 10x_0 k}{k} = 250 - 5k - 10x_0 \tag{6.15}
\end{aligned}
$$

However, using the logic we introduced to derive the concept of a limit, as k gets smaller (i.e. as $\Delta x \to 0$) then Eq. (6.11) will become:

$$\lim_{\Delta x \to 0} \frac{\Delta y}{\Delta x} = 250 - 10x_0 \tag{6.16}$$

which, if we now generalize for any value of X and not simply for x_0, gives:

$$\frac{dy}{dx} = \lim_{\Delta x \to 0} \frac{\Delta y}{\Delta x} = 250 - 10X \qquad (6.17)$$

that is, the derivative of the profit function is given by the expression $250 - 10X$. It will be worth reviewing what we have accomplished. We started out by seeking some general method of determining the slope of a non-linear function. We saw that difficulties arise as the slope of such a function will differ depending where on the appropriate curve we are (i.e. depending on which value for X we are considering). Through the use of some logic and some simple mathematical manipulations we have shown that the slope at a point on some non-linear function will be the same as that of the (unique) tangent line to that point. Similarly, as we take successively smaller changes in X we can approximate to this tangent line and hence to the slope of the point on the curve. This principle of a limit leads directly to the definition of a derivative of the original function.

> *Student activity 6.7*
> Using Eq. (6.17) calculate the slope of the profit function when $X = 10$. Compare this with your result from the previous activity.
>   What is the economic interpretation of the derivative value you have obtained?

Let us return to our example and examine in detail what we have achieved. We had the original function:

$$Y = -1125 + 250X - 5X^2$$

and obtained:

$$\frac{dY}{dX} = 250 - 10X$$

where Y represents profit and X output. One important point to note at this stage is that the derivative of a function of X is itself a function of X, that is:

$$Y = f(X) = -1125 + 250X - 5X^2$$

and
$$\frac{dY}{dX} = g(X) = 250 - 10X$$

However, to denote that the derivative is actually derived from Eq. (6.5) the standard notation used is:

$$\frac{dY}{dX} = f'(X) \qquad (6.18)$$

where f' (f prime) denotes the derivative of a function of X. This point also helps explain what the derivative represents and how it can be used. For Eq. (6.5) we know, from our earlier discussion on functions in Chapter 2, that we can obtain a value for the function given some value for X. For example, if $X = 10$ we have:

$$Y = f(X) = -1125 + 250X - 5X^2$$
$$= f(X = 10) = -1125 + 250(10) - 5(10)^2 = 875$$

Similarly, for the derivative when $X = 10$ we have:

$$\frac{dY}{dX} = f'(10) = 250 - 10(10) = 150$$

What does this value of 150 represent? Recollect how we obtained the derivative expression. It measures the slope of the original function at a given point. Here the given point is $X = 10$ so dY/dX measures the slope of the original function at this point. When $X = 10$ the profit function has a slope of 150. Consider further the meaning of the slope in the context of the profit function. At a level of output of 10 then a change in output will bring about a change in profit of 150 times the change in output. The derivative therefore allows us to determine the slope of the original function anywhere along its length (i.e. for any given value of X).

> **Student activity 6.8**
> Using the difference quotient calculate the slope for the profit function between $Q = 9.99$ and $Q = 10$. Calculate the slope using the derivative for $Q = 9.99$. Why is there a difference between the two?
>   Calculate the slope when $Q = 15$, $Q = 25$, $Q = 35$.
> (Solution on p. 337.)

There is one important point to note, however. The interpretation of the slope value is strictly correct only for *infinitesimally* small changes in X (recollect the limit concept). Technically the slope of 150 is strictly applicable only when $X = 10$. If X were 11 or 9 then the slope of the profit function would not be 150 (although, of course, we could find its precise value from the derivative function as before). It will be instructive to show both the original function and its derivative on the same graph. We do this in Fig. 6.7. A number of points are worth noting. First, we remember that the original function has a positive slope where $X < 25$ and a negative slope for $X > 25$. It can be seen from the line representing dY/dX that this is confirmed. The derivative (measuring the slope of the original function) takes positive values up to $X = 25$ and negative values thereafter. Remember also that we started our discussion searching for a method of finding the point where the slope of the profit function was zero. This, in our example, represented the level of output at which the firm will maximize profit. We have already seen that such a point occurs when $X = 25$. This can now be confirmed using the derivative. We see from Fig. 6.7 that the slope of the profit function (as shown by the derivative) takes a zero value when $X = 25$. At this level of output the derivative line crosses the X axis and must, therefore, take a zero value. This point on the profit function where the slope is zero is frequently referred to as a *stationary* point (since the slope is neither positive nor negative). Note also that the slope of the derivative (which is itself a linear function) is negative. We see this also from Eq. (6.17) since the derivative, which is a linear function, has a slope of -10. How can this be interpreted? It is an indication of the rate of change of the slope of the original (profit) function. Given that, as we know, the original function is changing from a positive to a negative slope, it is clear that the direction of change of the slope is negative. This is confirmed by the slope of the derivative. This brings us to a further development. We have stated that the derivative is itself a function of X. As such we could find the derivative of this function—i.e. an expression showing the slope of this function at any point. In other words we have:

$$Y = f(X)$$
$$\frac{dY}{dX} = f'(X)$$

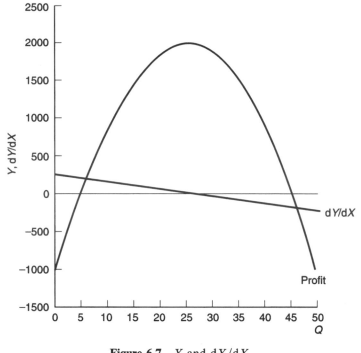

Figure 6.7 Y and dY/dX

and we could determine the derivative of dY/dX. In this case algebra is not actually required. We know that dY/dX is itself a linear function and therefore has a constant slope represented by the b parameter (at -10). The derivative of dY/dX is known as the *second* derivative and is denoted by:

$$\frac{d^2 Y}{dX^2} = f''(X) \tag{6.19}$$

(pronounced as dee two Y by dee X squared and as f double prime). Note that, as before, the second derivative notation is not an indication of division or of squaring but simply the standard form of notation. Collecting these together we have:

$$Y = f(X) = -1125 + 250X - 5X^2$$
$$\frac{dY}{dX} = f'(X) = 250 - 10X$$
$$\frac{d^2 Y}{dX^2} = f''(X) = -10$$

We shall shortly examine the use of the second derivative.

Student activity 6.9
Assume that a firm faces a marginal cost (MC) function:

$$MC = 50 - 10Q + Q^2$$

where Q represents units of output.

(i) Using the methods developed find the derivative of this function.

(ii) Using the derivative calculate the point where the MC function takes a minimum value (where the slope is zero).

(iii) Attempt to find the roots of the MC function

(iv) Graph this function and comment on the suitability of the equation for representing typical economic behaviour in the context of marginal costs.

(Solution on p. 338.)

6.4 Rules of differentiation

Although we have developed a method for finding the derivative of a function it is clear that the approach thus far—in terms of finding a numerical value—is both clumsy and time consuming. Clearly, we do not wish to have to go through the mathematical contortions of the previous section every time we wish to find the derivative of some function. Fortunately, we can develop some simple rules for differentiating the kind of functions that we encounter in economic analysis. We shall not show the derivation of these rules but simply illustrate their use. Readers who might be interested in such derivations are referred to one of the standard calculus texts available. For the illustrative function we shall be using we shall assume that all functions are of the form $Y = f(X)$ and that we require $f'(X)$.

Derivative of a power

Assume a function of the form:

$$f(X) = -5X^2$$

This can be generalized to:

$$f(X) = kX^n \tag{6.20}$$

where k and n are any real numbers. Then $f'(X)$ is determined by:

$$f'(X) = nkX^{n-1} \tag{6.21}$$

For example:

$$f'(-5X^2) = (2) - 5X^{2-1} = -10X^1 = -10X$$

since $k = 5$ and $n = 2$. This rule can be applied to any function that can be expressed in the form of Eq. (6.20). For example:

$$
\begin{aligned}
f(X) &= 15X^6 & f'(X) &= 90X^5 \\
f(X) &= 0.3X^{1/2} & f'(X) &= 0.15X^{-1/2} \\
f(X) &= 250X & f'(X) &= 250 \\
f(X) &= -1125 & f'(X) &= 0
\end{aligned}
$$

The last two examples require comment. $f(X) = 250X$ is clearly linear with a slope of 250. The derivative confirms this by producing a derivative function that takes a constant value equal to 250. Similarly, $f(X) = -1125$ is not actually a function of X at all (and would be represented by a line parallel to the X axis—i.e. a zero slope). The derivative confirms the slope of such an expression to be zero: Y will not change as X changes. This will apply to any constant.

Student activity 6.10
For the functions shown below obtain the first and second derivatives. Plot the original function and the first derivative together for $X = 0$ to 10.

  (i) $Y = 0.6X^3$
  (ii) $Y = 12X^6$
  (iii) $Y = 7X^{1/3}$
  (iv) $Y = \frac{1}{3}X^{-1/3}$

(Solution on p. 339.)

Derivative of sums and differences of power functions

If we have some function that comprises the sums and/or differences of other functions then the derivative is simply the sum of the individual derivatives. In fact we have already used this rule. Let:

$$f(X) = -1125 + 250X - 5X^2$$

Then:

$$f'(X) = \frac{d}{dX}(-1125) + \frac{d}{dX}(250X) + \frac{d}{dX}(-5X^2)$$

$$= 0 + 250 - 10X = 250 - 10X$$

Student activity 6.11
Assume a total cost function such that:

$$TC = 500 + 50Q - 5Q^2 + \frac{1}{3}Q^3$$

  (i) Obtain the derivative of this function.
  (ii) Interpret the derivative function in the context of economics.
  (iii) Find the value for Q that gives the minimum for the derivative function.
  (iv) Obtain a function for average cost.
  (v) Plot all three functions on one graph.

(Solution on p. 340.)

Derivative of a product of functions

If Y is the product of two functions such that:

$$Y = f(X) = g(X)h(X)$$

then the derivative is given as:

$$f'(X) = g(X)h'(X) + h(X)g'(X) \qquad (6.22)$$

For example, let $g(X) = 6X^2 + 5X$ and let $h(X) = 2X^4 - 10$. We then have:

$$Y = f(X) = (6X^2 + 5X)(2X^4 - 10)$$

Then:

$$g(X) = 6X^2 + 5X \qquad \text{and} \qquad g'(X) = 12X + 5$$
$$h(X) = 2X^4 - 10 \qquad \text{and} \qquad h'(X) = 8X^3$$

and

$$
\begin{aligned}
f'(X) &= (6X^2 + 5X)(8X^3) + (2X^4 - 10)(12X + 5) \\
&= 48X^5 + 40X^4 + 24X^5 - 120X + 10X^4 - 50 \\
&= 72X^5 + 50X^4 - 120X - 50
\end{aligned}
$$

Student activity 6.12
Confirm the derivative obtained by first expanding in full the original function $(6X^2 + 5X)(2X^4 - 10)$ and then using the first rule of differentiation.

Derivative of a quotient of functions

If Y is a function given by:

$$Y = f(X) = \frac{g(X)}{h(X)} \qquad (6.23)$$

then:

$$f'(X) = \frac{g'(X)h(X) - h'(X)g(X)}{h(X)^2} \qquad (6.24)$$

For example, let $g(X)$ and $h(X)$ take the values as in the last rule. We then have:

$$Y = f(X) = \frac{6X^2 + 5X}{2X^4 - 10}$$

and

$$f'(X) = \frac{(12X+5)(2X^4 - 10) - 8X^3(6X^2 + 5X)}{(2X^4 - 10)^2}$$
$$= \frac{(24X^5 + 10X^4 - 120X - 50) - (48X^5 + 40X^4)}{(2X^4 - 10)^2}$$
$$= \frac{-24X^5 - 30X^4 - 120X - 50}{(2X^4 - 10)^2}$$

> **Student activity 6.13**
> Assume a function such that
>
> $$Y = \frac{2X^4 - 10}{6X^2 + 5X}$$
>
> Obtain the first derivative.
> (Solution on p. 341.)

Derivative of a function of a function (the chain rule)

If we have a function that is itself a function of X such that:

$$Y = f(g(x))$$

then the derivative is given by:

$$\frac{dY}{dX} = \frac{dY}{dg} \frac{dg}{dX} \tag{6.25}$$

Assume we have a function such that:

$$Y = (10X^2 - 3X + 25)^2$$

and we denote:

$$g(X) = 10X^2 - 3X + 25$$

Then we can write:

$$Y = g^2$$

Now:

$$\frac{dg}{dX} = g'(X) = 20X - 3$$

and

$$\frac{dY}{dg} = f'(g^2) = 2g$$

We then have:

$$\frac{dY}{dX} = 2g(20X - 3) = 2(10X^2 - 3X + 25)(20X - 3)$$
$$= (20X^2 - 6X + 50)(20X - 3)$$
$$= 400X^3 - 120X^2 + 1000X - 60X^2 + 18X - 150$$
$$= 400X^3 - 180X^2 + 1018X - 150$$

> *Student activity 6.14*
> Confirm this last derivative by first expanding the original function $Y = (10X^2 - 3X + 25)^2$
> and then differentiating using the first rule of differentiation.

Derivative of a logarithmic function

The derivative of a natural (base e) log function:

$$Y = f(X) = \ln X \tag{6.26}$$

is given by:

$$f'(X) = \frac{1}{X} \tag{6.27}$$

Functions involving logarithms in economic analysis (usually to the base e because of their more useful theoretical properties) typically involve more complex functions than those shown. In such cases we can combine this rule with previous rules where appropriate. Consider the function:

$$Y = f(X) = \ln(3X^2 - 5X + 10)$$

Let:

$$g(X) = 3X^2 - 5X + 10$$
$$f(X) = \ln[g(X)]$$

Using the log rule and the product rule we have:

$$f'(X) = \frac{1}{g(X)}g'(X) = \frac{1}{3X^2 - 5X + 10}(6X - 5)$$
$$= \frac{6X - 5}{3X^2 - 5X + 10}$$

Inverse function rule

Assume we have a function such that:

$$Y = f(X) = X^2$$

Then we have:

$$\frac{dY}{dX} = f'(X) = 2X$$

However, if we find the inverse of the original function we then have:

$$X = g(Y) = \sqrt{Y} = Y^{1/2}$$

and we have

$$\frac{dX}{dY} = g'(Y) = \frac{1}{2} Y^{-1/2} = \frac{1}{2\sqrt{Y}}$$

However:

$$2X = 2Y^{1/2}$$

Hence:

$$\frac{dY}{dX} = 2X = 2Y^{1/2} = 2\sqrt{Y}$$

and hence:

$$\frac{dX}{dY} = \frac{1}{dY/dX} \tag{6.28}$$

This result is known as the inverse function rule. Not all functions, however, will have an inverse that can be differentiated. In general, for a function to possess an inverse it must be *monotonic*. This simply means that if we have $Y = f(X)$ then if X increases then Y must increase/decrease successively. In other words, an increase in X will always lead to an increase/decrease in Y. A linear function, for example, is monotonic but a quadratic is not (Y will change in one direction with respect to X and then in the opposite direction). Effectively in the context of differential calculus a monotonic function will always have the same type of slope—either always negative or always positive. These rules can be neatly summarized in tabular form (Table 6.1).

6.5 Non-differentiable functions

We must recognize, however, that not all functions can be differentiated. Recollect that by differentiating we are finding an expression that allows us to quantify the slope of the original function for any value of X (and recollect this is the equivalent of finding the slope of the tangent line at that point). Consider the situations illustrated in Figs 6.8 and 6.9.

Figure 6.8 shows a discontinuous function where the function takes a 'jump' at X_0, and clearly there will be no unique tangent at this point. Similarly in Fig. 6.9 while the function is continuous there is a definite 'kink' at point X_0 where, again, there would be no unique tangent.

TABLE 6.1 Derivative rules

Expression	Function $y = f(x)$	Derivative $f'(x)$
Constant	$y - a$	0
Power term	$y = x^n$	$nx^{(n-1)}$
Constant times power term	$y = kx^n$	$knx^{(n-1)}$
Sum or difference	$y = g(x) \perp h(x)$	$g'(x) \pm h'(x)$
Product	$y = g(x)h(x)$	$g(x)h'(x) + h(x)g'(x)$
Quotient	$y = g(x)/h(x)$	$\dfrac{g'(x)h(x) - h'(x)g(x)}{h(x^2)}$
Chain rule	$y = f(g(x))$	$\dfrac{\mathrm{d}Y}{\mathrm{d}g}\dfrac{\mathrm{d}g}{\mathrm{d}X}$
Natural logarithm	$y = \ln X$	$\dfrac{1}{X}$

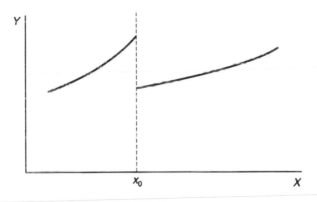

Figure 6.8 Discontinuity

Fortunately we are usually able to develop suitable economic models with functions that are differentiable using the rules we have developed.

> **Student activity 6.15**
> Plot the following function for $X = 0$ to 2 in steps of 0.2. Comment on whether you think it can be differentiated.
>
> $$Y = 2 + \sqrt[3]{(x - 1)^2}$$
>
> (Solution on p. 341.)

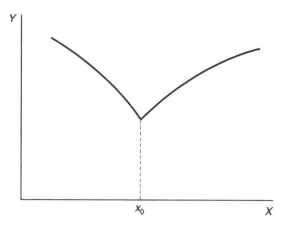

Figure 6.9 Non-differentiable function

6.6 Summary

In this chapter we have begun to examine the principles involved in using non-linear functions in economic analysis. We have seen that such functions involve two key principles: that of slope and that of optimization. Both these principles are of critical importance in economic theory, as we shall demonstrate in the next chapter. In order to be able to deal with these we introduced the basic of differential calculus and saw that for any function we can obtain the derivative: a function showing the slope of the original relationship under examination. In the next chapter we shall examine the opportunities differential calculus offers economic analysis. You should ensure, however, before proceeding that you have an adequate technical grasp of the topic.

Worked example

A firm has noted that its short-run production function linking production and number of workers employed is given by:

$$Q = -0.05L^3 + 3L^2$$

with $0 \leq L \leq 50$ where Q is production and L is the number of workers employed. Capital is assumed fixed in the short run. The firm is interested in assessing the impact on production of variations in the number of workers employed and in trying to determine the number of workers to employ which will lead to maximum production. The firm is also interested in an explanation of its situation in this context.

Solution

The firm's interest is in assessing how production, Q, varies the number of workers employed, L, varies. Effectively, this implies the firm is interested in assessing changes in Q brought about by changes in L and it is clear that the derivative will be appropriate since dQ/dL will provide a function showing the relationship between the changes in the two variables. We have:

$$\frac{dQ}{dL} = -0.15L^2 + 6L$$

We observe that the derivative is a quadratic with a zero intercept and will follow the inverted U shape giving a situation as in Fig. 6.10. Initially, as L increases so does dQ/dL: as the firm increases labour then total production increases (since dQ/dL represents additional production from additional labour). After some point, L_0, however, the derivative decreases in value: additional labour actually leads to a reduction in total production. This is predictable from economic theory. The law of diminishing returns (or diminishing marginal product) indicates that once the size of the labour input reaches a certain critical level (in part dependent on the available capital stock which is fixed in the short run) then the additional output from additional labour will gradually decrease until the increase in labour actually has a negative impact on total production.

We can confirm this through a graph of the original production function as in Fig. 6.11 which also shows the derivative. In fact it becomes more appropriate to refer to the derivative of the production function as the marginal product of labour (MP_L). We see that MP_L reaches its maximum at point L_m which coincides with a point on the production function where diminishing returns begin to set in. We also see that at the point where Q reaches its maximum MP_L is zero and after this level of L MP_L is negative and hence Q will actually decline after this point. We have, as yet, no tools other than the graph for obtaining a maximum value mathematically for the production function. However, we now know that $MP_L = 0$ at the maximum production point. We can then use the derivative:

$$MP_L = -0.15L^2 + 6L = 0$$

Using the roots approach we find:

$$L_1 = 0$$
$$L_2 = 40$$

and both from Fig. 6.11 and by substituting back into the production function we confirm that maximum production will occur when $L = 40$.

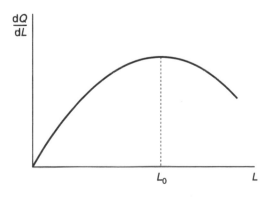

Figure 6.10 $dQ/dL = -0.15L^2 + 6L$

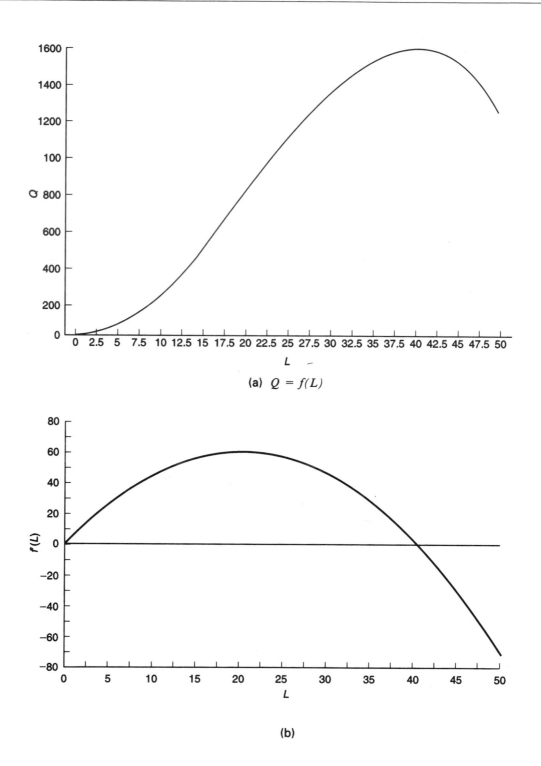

(a) $Q = f(L)$

(b)

Figure 6.11a and b

Exercises

6.1 Find the roots of the following functions using the quadratic formula and the turning points using the derivatives:

(i) $Y = -100 - 10X + 2.5X^2$
(ii) $Y = -100 + 50X - 5X^2$
(iii) $Y = -250 + 50X - 5X^2$
(iv) $Y = 250 + 50X - X^2$

6.2 A firm has analysed demand for its product and obtained a demand function of the form:

$$Q_d = 100 + \frac{5}{P}$$

(i) Find the derivative of this function.
(ii) Calculate the slope when $P = 2$ and when $P = 5$. What observations can you make about the behaviour of the slope with respect to price?
(iii) What use do you think could be made of the derivative in this context?

6.3 Return to the TC and TR functions we were examining in the chapter:

$$TR = 260Q$$
$$TC = 1125 + 10Q + 5Q^2$$

(i) Find a derivative of the TR and TC functions.
(ii) What economic interpretation would you give to each of these?
(iii) Calculate the slope of the TR and TC functions at the profit-maximizing level of output $(Q = 25)$.
(iv) How do you explain your result in (iii)?
(v) The selling price of the firm's product now increases to 300. What would you expect to happen to the profit-maximizing level of output?
(vi) Calculate the new profit-maximizing level of output.
(vii) The firm's fixed costs now increase to 1500. Calculate the new profit-maximizing level of output. How do you explain your result?

6.4 For each of the following functions find the first and second derivatives:

(i) $Y = X^3 + 4X^2 - 9X + 10$
(ii) $Y = (5X - 10)(2X - 3)$
(iii) $Y = \dfrac{5X - 10}{2X - 3}$
(iv) $Y = (5X - 10)^4$
(v) $Y = (10X^3 - 12)(2X + 5)$
(vi) $Y = \dfrac{10X^3 - 12}{2X + 5}$
(vii) $Y = \dfrac{(10X^3 - 12)^2}{2X + 5}$
(viii) $Y = \sqrt{X - 1}$
(ix) $Y = 10\sqrt{X - 1}$

6.5 A firm's cost function is given by:

$$TC = 500 + 20Q - 6Q^2 + 0.6Q^3$$

(i) Find an expression for marginal costs.
(ii) Find an expression for average costs.
(iii) Draw a graph of these two functions.
(iv) What do you notice about their intersection?
(v) Find this intersection algebraically.

6.6 The market for a particular product is characterized by the following demand and supply functions:

$$Q_d = 25 - 3P + 0.2P^2$$
$$Q_s = -5 + 3P - 0.01P^2$$

(i) Sketch both these functions.
(ii) Find the equilibrium position algebraically.
(iii) Calculate total revenue at this point.

6.7 A Cobb–Douglas production function is given as:

$$Y = 0.6L^{0.3}K^{0.7}$$

(i) If K is fixed at 10 units, derive a production function for labour.
(ii) Find the derivative of this function.
(iii) What is the economic meaning of this derivative?
(iv) Plot this derivative together with the labour production function for $L = 1$ to 10. Comment on the behaviour of the two functions.
(v) Repeat the analysis but now with labour fixed at 10.

7 Derivatives and economics

In the previous chapter we introduced the important concept of the derivative. In this chapter we continue to explore how derivatives can be used in economic models and this task will occupy us for much of the rest of the text. Economic analysis is frequently concerned with relationships between variables and in particular the changes that occur in one variable when another—related—variable changes. The derivative, as we have seen, is mathematically concerned with the same and it is evident that we can use the derivative to examine such economic relationships. In this chapter we illustrate a number of common areas of economic application and see how the ability to use the derivative frequently allows us to develop more complex—and realistic—economic models as well as reaching important conclusions about those models.

Learning objectives

By the end of this chapter you should be able to:

- Use the principles of calculus to help sketch typical functions
- Calculate elasticity using the derivative
- Explain the use of the derivative in the context of economic marginality
- Derive marginal expressions from a number of common economic models

7.1 Curve sketching

We can immediately begin to use the principles inherent in the first and second derivatives as an aid in curve sketching. As we have seen, it is frequently useful to sketch (as opposed to drawing a detailed graph) some economic function so that we have a picture of the corresponding relationship. Consider the function:

$$Q_d = \frac{100}{P} \tag{7.1}$$

where P = price per unit
 Q_d = quantity demanded

Clearly, this is a demand function, but what form will it take? Let us begin to put various pieces of information together. First it is sensible in an economic context to restrict the values of P to be non-negative ($P \geq 0$). If this is the case then it is clear by inspection that Q_d will take larger values as P decreases and that Q_d will tend to infinity as P approaches zero. Equally, as P

increases Q_d will approach, but never reach, zero. Similarly, the first derivative of the function is:

$$f'(P) = \frac{-100}{P^2} \tag{7.2}$$

and we see that with $P \geq 0$ then the first derivative must always take a negative value. Recollecting that the first derivative relates to the slope of the function, this indicates that the slope of Eq. (7.1) is always negative (hardly surprising for a demand function, but useful confirmation nevertheless). Moreover, we see from inspection of the derivative that the slope will take larger (negative) values when P decreases and smaller (negative) values as P increases. In other words, the function has a larger negative slope for lower prices than for higher. The second derivative confirms this. We have:

$$f''(P) = \frac{200}{P^3} \tag{7.3}$$

which, again for $P \geq 0$, can only give positive values. Since the second derivative represents the rate of change in the first derivative (which in turn represents the gradient of the original function) we see that the function's slope is decreasing as P increases. Putting all these deductions together we can produce a sketch (Fig. 7.1) of Eq. (7.1).

Student activity 7.1
(i) Plot both the demand function and its derivative for $P = 1.00$ to 2.00 in units of 0.1.
(ii) The function:

$$D = 400/W^2$$

shows the demand for labour, D, as a function of the wage rate, W. Obtain a sketch of this function. Confirm your sketch by drawing a detailed graph for $W = 5$ to 10 for both the function and its derivative.
(Solution on p. 342.)

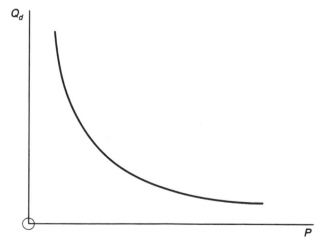

Figure 7.1   Sketch of $Q_d = 100/P$

7.2   Elasticity

However, although using the derivative to sketch some economic function is quite useful it can hardly justify the use of differential calculus in economics by itself. We can begin to appreciate its usefulness when we turn to the concept of elasticity, or, more formally, price elasticity of demand. We examined elasticity earlier in Chapter 3 but only in the context of linear functions. We are now in a position to investigate the concept for any type of demand function. Let us examine the following demand function:

$$Q_d = f(P) = 250 - 10P \tag{7.4}$$

We recognize this as a linear demand function and that its slope will be:

$$\frac{dQ_d}{dP} = -10 \tag{7.5}$$

We also have the general elasticity expressions:

$$E_d = \frac{\Delta Q}{\Delta P} \frac{P}{Q} \tag{7.6}$$

However, we saw in the previous chapter that for a function such as $Q_d = f(P)$ the limit of $\Delta Q / \Delta P$ as $\Delta P \to 0$ is actually the derivative of that function. In other words, when ΔP is infinitesimal we have:

$$E_d = \frac{dQ_d}{dP} \frac{P}{Q} \tag{7.7}$$

where dQ_d/dP is the derivative of the demand function with respect to P. Since the change in P that we are evaluating is infinitesimally small, E_d is technically known as *point* elasticity. It is important to realize that such an elasticity is independent of any units of measurement and facilitates a comparison of the responsiveness of quantity demanded to a change in price for any demand function. Let us return to Eq. (7.4) and use the elasticity formula to examine demand responsiveness. Assume that $P = 5$. We see from Eq. (7.4) that the corresponding Q_d will be 200. Elasticity will then be calculated as:

$$E_d = \frac{dQ_d}{dP} \frac{P}{Q} = -10 \times \frac{5}{200} = -0.25$$

We would conclude that the price elasticity of demand at this particular price level is 0.25, but what does this imply? It indicates that at the current price level a change in price (where the change is technically infinitesimally small) will bring about a corresponding proportionate change in Q_d of 0.25 of the change in price. Let us examine a simple illustration. Assume that the price changes from 5 to 5.1. We note that the percentage change in P, therefore, is 2 per cent and the corresponding percentage change in Q_d is:

$$P = 5 \qquad Q_d = 200$$
$$P = 5.1 \qquad Q_d = 199$$

$$\text{Percentage change in } Q_d = \frac{200 - 199}{200} \times 100 = 0.5\%$$

which we can confirm is 0.25 of the change in the price. It is important to realize that we are now using elasticity to examine proportionate changes, not absolute changes. In terms of economics we would denote the demand for this product at this price as inelastic: quantity demanded is relatively unresponsive to a change in price—a proportionate change in price has brought about a smaller proportionate change in Q_d. However, let us now consider elasticity at a different point on the same demand curve.

> **Student activity 7.2**
> Calculate elasticity when $P = 15$. How do you interpret this? Calculate the proportionate changes in P and Q_d as P changes from 15 to 15.1. Calculate the change in total revenue that has occurred at each of the price levels ($P = 5$ and $P = 15$).

Adopting a similar approach we have:

$$P = 15 \qquad Q_d = 100$$

and

$$E_d = -10 \times \frac{15}{100} = -1.5$$

which indicates that a change in price at this point on the curve will bring about a proportionate change in Q_d of 1.5 times the price change. In such a case we would denote that demand at this point was relatively elastic—responsive to a price change. To briefly summarize the possibilities we have:

$\|E_d\| < 1$	Inelastic	Demand is relatively unresponsive to a change in price
$\|E_d\| > 1$	Elastic	Demand is relatively responsive to a change in price
$\|E_d\| = 1$	Unitary	Demand responds proportionately to a change in price

The symbol around the E_d term— | | —is known as a *modulus* and indicates that we are interested only in the absolute value of E_d not in whether it is positive or negative.

> **Student activity 7.3**
> For the demand function we are examining Eq. (7.4) determine what price must be charged for the elasticity to equal −1.
> (Solution on p. 342.)

It is important to note that the elasticity value changes even though the slope of the linear function is constant. This occurs because elasticity is concerned with relative rather than absolute changes. Naturally, the same principles of price elasticity of demand can be applied to any type of demand function—linear or otherwise. One demand function worth noting at this stage returns us to Eq. (7.1) where we had:

$$Q_d = \frac{100}{P}$$

Here we have:

$$E_d = \frac{dQ_d}{dP} \frac{P}{Q} = \frac{-100}{P^2} \frac{P}{Q}$$

$$= \frac{-100}{PQ}$$

which if we substitute Eq. (7.1) for Q gives:

$$E_d = \frac{-100}{P(100/P)} = \frac{-100}{100} = -1$$

that is, for this demand function point elasticity of demand is -1 at any price. The demand function has unitary elasticity anywhere along its length. As a further example consider the function:

$$Q_d = f(P) = \frac{a}{P^b} \tag{7.8}$$

If a and b are > 0, then the demand function will have a constant elasticity of $-b$.

> *Student activity 7.4*
> Show that the elasticity of this type of demand function will be $-b$. Sketch the demand function.
> (Solution on p. 343.)

7.3   Other types of elasticity

Although we have focused simply upon price elasticity of demand in the previous section, the principles of elasticity are applicable to a number of different situations. For example, we have the following types.

Elasticity of supply

$$E_s = \frac{dQ_s}{dP} \frac{P}{Q_s} \tag{7.9}$$

which would denote the relative responsiveness of quantity supplied to a change in price.

Cross-elasticity of demand

Assume we had a demand function such that:

$$Q_{dx} = f(P_y) \tag{7.10}$$

that is, where the quantity demanded of good X was a function of the price of good Y. Such a situation could arise, for example, if the two products were close substitutes or where X was regarded as a complementary good to Y. We can then define the cross-elasticity of demand for X as:

$$E_z = \frac{dQ_{dx}}{dP_y} \frac{P_y}{Q_{dx}}$$
(7.11)

and E_z would indicate the relative responsiveness of demand for good X in relation to a change in the price of good Y.

Income elasticity of demand

In a similar way we may have a demand function such that:

$$Q_d = f(Y)$$
(7.12)

where Y represents consumer income. Income elasticity of demand would then be given by:

$$E_y = \frac{dQ_d}{dY} \frac{Y}{Q_d}$$
(7.13)

and would indicate the relative responsiveness of quantity demanded to a change in consumer income.

> **Student activity 7.5**
> For the functions shown below obtain an expression for the appropriate elasticity and calculate the elasticity at the point required. Interpret your result.
>
> (i) $Q_s = -10 + 5P$
> $P = 5$
> (ii) $Q_{dx} = 200 - 3P_y$
> $P_y = 10$
> (iii) $Q_{dx} = 200 + 3P_y$
> $P_y = 10$
>
> What type of good is Y in (ii) and (iii)?
> (Solution on p. 343.)

7.4   The derivative and the concept of marginality

We have seen that the derivative allows us to determine the rate of change in some Y variable as the X variable changes for virtually any type of functional relationship. We have also seen that in this context the derivative is readily interpreted as the slope of the function. It will by now be apparent that there is a direct connection between the derivative and the economic concept of marginality. In economics, analysis is frequently concerned with decisions taken at the margin. In one sense, this can be viewed as assessing the change that occurs in one economic variable as the result of some (marginal) change in another economic variable. Thus, we interpret marginal cost as the extra cost incurred by a firm as an extra unit of output is produced. Marginal revenue is the extra revenue earned by the firm from producing and selling an extra unit of output. Economic analysis is literally littered with such marginal changes: marginal propensity to consume, marginal cost, marginal propensity to import, marginal rate of substitution, marginal product, marginal utility and so on. In terms of differential calculus, the derivative can be interpreted as a marginal change in the Y variable given some (infinitesimally small) change in X, and hence is directly related to the marginal concepts so useful in economics. Throughout the rest of this chapter we shall be examining a number of such marginal relationships and using calculus to investigate them.

7.5 Total and marginal revenue

To illustrate marginal revenue let us assume a demand function such that:

$$Q_d = 625 - 25P$$

While such a functional form is typical of consumer theory where consumer behaviour responds to price, when we wish to examine the theory of the firm it is generally more appropriate to rewrite the demand function in the form:

$$P = f(Q_d) \quad \text{which here gives } P = 25 - 0.04Q_d \tag{7.14}$$

(We shall from now on simply denote Q_d as Q to help keep the notation simpler.) Given that a firm's total revenue (TR) will be determined by the quantity (Q) times the price per unit (P), we then have:

$$\begin{aligned} TR = f(Q) = PQ &= (25 - 0.04Q)Q \\ &= 25Q - 0.04Q^2 \end{aligned} \tag{7.15}$$

From the TR function we can readily obtain two related functions: average revenue (AR) and marginal revenue (MR). Average revenue is given as:

$$AR = \frac{TR}{Q} = \frac{25Q - 0.04Q^2}{Q} = 25 - 0.04Q = P \tag{7.16}$$

that is, average revenue is simply price per unit. Marginal revenue, on the other hand, is given by:

$$MR = \frac{d(TR)}{dQ} = 25 - 0.08Q \tag{7.17}$$

that is, marginal revenue is the derivative of the TR function—the slope of the TR function. Note that the AR and MR functions are both linear, with the MR function having the steeper (negative) slope. This implies that MR will always lie below the AR function on a graph. We are also able to re-examine the price elasticity of demand that we introduced in Sec. 7.1. We can re-express the relationships as:

$$\text{TR} = PQ = f(Q)Q \tag{7.18}$$

$$\text{MR} = \frac{d(\text{TR})}{dQ}$$

and using the differentiation product rule from the previous chapter we then have:

$$\text{MR} = \frac{d[f(Q)Q]}{dQ} = f(Q)(1) + Qf'(Q)$$

$$= f(Q) + Qf'(Q)$$

but since $P = f(Q)$ this gives:

$$\text{MR} = P + Q\frac{dP}{dQ} \tag{7.19}$$

From the earlier definition of elasticity, however, we had:

$$E_d = \frac{dQ}{dP}\frac{P}{Q}$$

which on rearranging gives:

$$Q\frac{dP}{dQ} = \frac{P}{E_d} \tag{7.20}$$

Therefore, using Eq. (7.9) we now have:

$$\text{MR} = P + \frac{P}{E_d} = P\left(1 + \frac{1}{E_d}\right) \tag{7.21}$$

Let us examine the implied relationship between MR and E_d. It is evident from Eq. (7.20) that since E_d is always negative then we reach the following conclusions (considering only the absolute value of E_d, $|E_d|$):

If $|E_d| > 1$ (elastic), then MR > 0 (since $1/|E_d| < 1$).
If $|E_d| < 1$ (inelastic), then MR < 0.
If $|E_d| = 1$ (unitary elastic), then MR $= 0$.

The implications of this are clear. If, at a particular price level, demand is elastic, then a change in price will lead to a proportionately greater change in quantity demanded and hence MR must be greater than zero. For example, a marginal decrease in P will lead to a proportionately larger increase in Q_d. TR will increase since, although the unit price is lower, extra sales more than compensate for this. Similar logic can be applied to inelastic and unitary elastic positions.

Student activity 7.6
Assume a current price of 5. Calculate E_d and MR. Now assume an initial price of 15. Repeat the calculations.
(Solution on p. 344.)

It is evident that the individual firm is able to use this type of information to assess the impact of a change in price on its revenue levels both total and marginal.

7.6 Marginal product and marginal revenue product

While we would normally regard a production function as involving two main variable inputs—labour and capital—at least in the short term we can regard some of the inputs as fixed and examine the implications of allowing the others to vary. Assume we have such a function where we have:

$$Q = g(L) \tag{7.22}$$

where Q represents output/production and L represents inputs of labour—i.e. we are assuming that the supply of capital is fixed. Naturally we can view the derivative of such a production function:

$$\frac{dQ}{dL} = g'(L) \tag{7.23}$$

as the marginal product of labour—the marginal product of the variable input. The marginal product simply indicates the marginal change in production arising from a marginal change in the labour input. We would normally expect a positive marginal product—that is, $g'(L) > 0$. However, the law of diminishing returns (or diminishing marginal product) implies that while the marginal product may be positive it will decrease as a function of labour input. In other words, the slope of the MP function will be negative. However, the slope of the MP function will also be the second derivative of the production function so that the assumption of diminishing marginal product implies that $g''(L) < 0$. We are also in a position to link marginal product to marginal revenue. Referring back to the previous section we had a total revenue function such that:

$$TR = f(Q)$$

and we now have a production function such that:

$$Q = g(L)$$

Clearly it should be possible to determine the change in TR that will occur as we change L—that is, the change in total revenue brought about by a change in the variable input, labour, via a change in output Q. Such a change will represent the marginal revenue product (MRP) of that input and would be denoted as:

$$MRP = \frac{d(TR)}{dL} \tag{7.24}$$

We have:

$$P = f(Q) = f(g(L)) \tag{7.25}$$

However, TR $= PQ$ and $Q = g(L)$; hence

$$\text{TR} = f(Q)g(L) = f(g(L))g(L)$$

Using the chain rule for differentiation on $f(g(L))$ we then have:

$$\frac{df(g(L))}{dL} = \frac{dP}{dL} = \frac{dP}{dQ}\frac{dQ}{dL} = f'(Q)g'(L)$$

so using the product rule:

$$\frac{d(\text{TR})}{dL} = g(L)\frac{d[f(g(L))]}{dL} + g'(L)f(g(L))$$
$$= g(L)f'(Q)g'(L) + g'(L)f(g(L))$$

However, from Eq. (7.22) MP $= g'(L)$ so that:

$$\frac{d(\text{TR})}{dL} = g(L)f'(Q)\text{MP} + \text{MP}f(g(L))$$
$$= \text{MP}[g(L)f'(Q) + f(g(L))]$$

which since:

$$P = f(g(L)) \qquad \text{and } Q = g(L)$$

gives

$$\frac{d(\text{TR})}{dL} = \text{MP}[Qf'(Q) + P]$$

but from Eq. (7.19) we have:

$$\text{MR} = Qf'(Q) + P$$

which gives:

$$\frac{d(\text{TR})}{dL} = \text{MP} \times \text{MR} = \text{MRP} \tag{7.26}$$

that is, the marginal revenue product is given by the marginal physical product multiplied by marginal revenue. Note that, importantly, we have derived such a relationship without any reference to numerical examples. The definition derived in Eq. (7.26), in other words, applies as a general result.

Student activity 7.7

Assume that we now have a production function where labour is fixed and:

$$Q = h(K)$$

where K is capital input. Derive a comparable equation to Eq. (7.26) for capital.

7.7 Total cost and marginal cost

Having seen how the derivative can be applied to revenue relationships let us now examine the cost side of the theory of the firm. It is evident that exactly the same principles can be applied. If we have a total cost function such that:

$$TC = f(Q) \tag{7.27}$$

it is evident that marginal cost (MC) will be given by:

$$MC = \frac{d(TC)}{dQ} = f'(Q) \tag{7.28}$$

It may also be apparent that if we break TC into fixed cost and variable cost elements then MC will be the same as marginal variable cost since fixed costs are independent of output, Q. We can also link marginal cost to marginal product. Assume as we did earlier that we have a production function:

$$Q = g(L)$$

If we define the cost per unit of labour as w, then variable cost (VC) will be:

$$VC = wL \tag{7.29}$$

that is, the cost per unit of labour multiplied by the number of units of labour employed. The marginal cost of another unit of labour is also w since:

$$\frac{d(VC)}{dL} = w \tag{7.30}$$

However, let us investigate instead the marginal cost with respect to output, Q; that is, we require:

$$\frac{d(VC)}{dQ}$$

Through the use of the chain rule this gives:

$$\frac{d(VC)}{dQ} = \frac{d(VC)}{dL} \frac{dL}{dQ}$$

However, $Q = g(L)$ and, therefore,

$$\frac{\mathrm{d}Q}{\mathrm{d}L} = g'(L)$$

If we note that, using the inverse function rule:

$$\frac{\mathrm{d}L}{\mathrm{d}Q} = \frac{1}{\mathrm{d}Q/\mathrm{d}L} = \frac{1}{g'(L)}$$

then we have:

$$\frac{\mathrm{d}(\mathrm{VC})}{\mathrm{d}Q} = \frac{\mathrm{d}(\mathrm{VC})}{\mathrm{d}L} \frac{1}{g'(L)} = \frac{w}{g'(L)}$$

which, since $g'(L)$ is the marginal product, gives:

$$\mathrm{MC} = \frac{\mathrm{d}(\mathrm{VC})}{\mathrm{d}Q} = \frac{w}{\mathrm{MP}} \qquad (7.31)$$

that is, marginal cost (MC) is equal to the marginal cost (w) of the variable input L divided by its marginal product. MC is simply the ratio of extra labour cost to extra output produced by that extra labour.

> **Student activity 7.8**
> Return to the production function for capital when labour is fixed. Derive a comparable expression to Eq. (7.31).

7.8 The consumption function

So far, all the applications of the derivative have been on the microeconomic side. The derivative is equally applicable to macroeconomic relationships. Consider the consumption function:

$$C = f(Y) \qquad (7.32)$$

where C is consumption and Y income. We can readily define:

$$\frac{\mathrm{d}C}{\mathrm{d}Y} = f'(Y) \qquad (7.33)$$

as the marginal propensity to consume—the change in consumption that occurs with a change in income. If we also note that by definition income that is not consumed is deemed to have been saved, we have an associated savings function:

$$S = g(Y) \qquad (7.34)$$

since $Y = C + S$ and that:

$$\frac{dS}{dY} = g'(Y) \tag{7.35}$$

is the marginal propensity to save. Furthermore, it is logical to state that:

$$\frac{dC}{dY} + \frac{dS}{dY} = 1 \tag{7.36}$$

that is, the change in consumption plus the change in savings must equal the change in income.

7.9   The national income multiplier

Finally in this chapter, let us consider how the derivative can help us assess one of the models we examined earlier in Chapter 3. We examine a macroeconomic national income model that involved a government sector but no foreign trade. We derived the value of the multiplier (Eq. (3.42)) in this model as:

$$\Delta Y = \frac{1}{1 - b(1 - t)} \Delta G$$

where b represented the marginal propensity to consume and t the tax rate levied on income, Y. Clearly the equation allows us to determine the effect of a change in government expenditure on the equilibrium level of national income. However, let us examine the multiplier in a slightly different context. How will a change in the tax rate, t, affect the multiplier (and hence the impact effect of G)? Clearly we could simply examine the multiplier expression and try to deduce what would happen if t increased or decreased. However, let us apply the principles we have been developing. If we denote the multiplier as k, then we have:

$$k = \frac{1}{1 - b(1 - t)} = \frac{1}{1 - b + bt} \tag{7.37}$$

We require the effect on k of a change in t, that is:

$$\frac{dk}{dt}$$

If we denote $x = 1 - b + bt$, then we have:

$$\frac{dx}{dt} = b$$

$$k = \frac{1}{x} = x^{-1}$$

$$\frac{dk}{dx} = -1x^{-2} = \frac{-1}{x^2} = \frac{-1}{(1 - b + bt)^2}$$

and through the chain rule: $\dfrac{dk}{dt} = \dfrac{dk}{dx}\dfrac{dx}{dt} = \dfrac{-1}{(1 - b + bt)^2} b = \dfrac{-b}{(1 - b + bt)^2}$ $\tag{7.38}$

which can be rewritten as:

$$\frac{\mathrm{d}k}{\mathrm{d}t} = -bk^2 \tag{7.39}$$

From this, given that b, the marginal propensity to consume, and k, the multiplier, will be positive in the model, we see that the rate of change in the multiplier as the tax rate changes will always be negative. In other words, a change in the tax rate will have an inverse effect on the multiplier. Increasing the tax rate will decrease the multiplier and vice versa.

Worked example

We shall return to the worked example we had in the previous chapter. There we had a firm facing a production function:

$$Q = -0.05L^3 + 3L^2$$

with $0 \leq L \leq 50$, where Q is production and L is the number of workers employed. We derived a $\mathrm{MP_L}$ function:

$$\mathrm{MP_L} = f'(Q) = -0.15L^2 + 6L$$

and derived that when $L = 40$ total production is maximized. Let us investigate a different aspect of the problem. The firm has now expressed interest not in marginal product of labour but in average product ($\mathrm{AP_L}$) and is interested in determining the level of output where $\mathrm{AP_L}$ is maximized.

Solution

$$\mathrm{AP_L} = Q/L$$

that is, production divided by the number of workers required to produce that output. Hence:

$$\mathrm{AP_L} = \frac{-0.05L^3 + 3L^3}{L} = -0.05L^2 + 3L$$

Again by inspection we see that $\mathrm{AP_L}$ is quadratic and will reach a maximum point. This point will have a slope equal to zero so we require:

$$\frac{\mathrm{dAP_L}}{\mathrm{d}L} = -0.1L + 3 = 0$$

giving $L = 30$ as the number of workers where average product will be greatest. The second derivative helps us to confirm this:

$$\frac{\mathrm{d^2AP_L}}{\mathrm{d}L^2} = -0.1$$

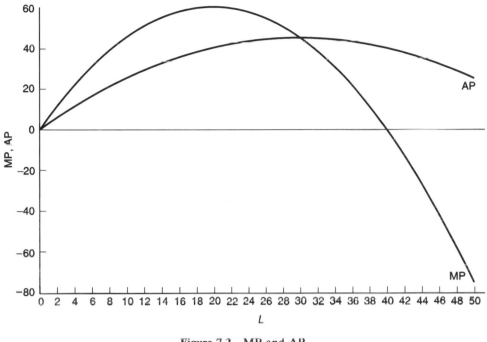

Figure 7.2 MP and AP

The second derivative is a negative constant implying the slope of AP_L (the first derivative) is decreasing with L. Hence $L = 30$ must equate to a maximum. AP_L will take its maximum value of 45 (units of production per worker) when we employ 30 workers. It will also be instructive to consider MP_L at this point:

$$MP_L = f'(Q) = -0.15L^2 + 6L$$

and when $L = 30$ $MP_L = 45$, that is, when average product is maximized, $MP = AP$. We shall see later in the text that this applies to production functions in general and not just to this specific numerical example. Figure 7.2 shows the two functions.

Exercises

7.1 Return to the national income model in Chapter 3 which involved both a government sector and foreign trade. From Eq. (3.50) which showed the multiplier for this model, determine the effect on the multiplier if the marginal propensity to import, m, changes.

7.2 We have the following market model:

$$Q_d = f(P) = 25 - 3P + 0.2P^2$$
$$Q_s = f(P) = -5 + 3P - 0.01P^2$$

(i) Derive an expression for elasticity of demand and of supply.

(ii) Calculate these two elasticities at the equilibrium price.

(iii) Derive an expression for marginal revenue.
(iv) Calculate marginal revenue at the equilibrium price.

7.3 A firm's demand function is given by:

$$P = f(Q) = aQ^b$$

(i) Derive an expression for elasticity.
(ii) Derive an expression for marginal revenue.

7.4 Assume a consumption function:

$$C = f(Y) = 100 + 2Y^{0.5}$$

(i) Sketch the shape of this function.
(ii) Comment on its general shape in the context of economic behaviour.
(iii) Derive an expression for marginal propensity to consume.
(iv) Comment on the behaviour of the mpc as Y increases. How do you explain this?
(v) Derive an expression for the marginal propensity to save.
(vi) Draw a graph for both the mpc and mps for Y up to 100. Comment on the relationship.

7.5 A firm's production function is given as:

$$Q = 6L^{0.3}$$

and a demand function:

$$P = 100 - 2Q$$

(i) Derive an equation for the marginal revenue product of labour.
(ii) Calculate the elasticity of demand when the marginal revenue is zero.

7.6 A firm's supply function is given as:

$$Q = -10 + 5P + 25\sqrt{P}$$

Calculate the elasticity of supply when $P = 20$, 60, 100.

7.7 A consumer derives utility from consumption of some good in the form:

$$U = 10X^{0.8}$$

where X denotes the quantity of the good consumed. Find an expression for marginal utility and interpret the result. Plot both the original function and the marginal function on a graph for X up to 10. Comment on the relationship.

7.8 Assume a production function:

$$Q = 100 + 0.1L^2 - 0.001L^3$$

with the wage rate set at 10. Find an expression for MC. Examine and comment upon its behaviour in relation to the production function. Plot both functions for L up to 65.

8 Optimization

In the previous two chapters we have examined the concept of the derivative and its general applicability in economics. One of the prime uses of differential calculus in economic analysis relates to the investigation of *optimization*. This concept is of particular importance and interest in economics at the macro and micro level. In the theory of the firm a business organization is assumed to desire to maximize profit. In cost theory the firm wishes to minimize costs. In consumer utility theory the individual consumer is assumed to want to maximize his or her utility derived from consumption. On the macro side, a government may wish to maximize the level of national income, to minimize the balance of trade deficit, to minimize inflation and/or unemployment, to maximize revenue from taxation. In this chapter we examine how we can determine such an optimum position. Fortunately, we already have all the tools we require to do this (courtesy of the principles of differential calculus that we have recently established). All that we require is to put these together.

Learning objectives

By the end of this chapter you should be able to:

- Find the stationary points of a function using the derivative
- Determine whether a stationary point represents a maximum or minimum using the second derivative
- Distinguish between local and global maxima and minima
- Locate points of inflection

8.1 An example of optimization

Let us return to a profit function that we were examining in Chapter 6. The function is shown below, together with the first and second derivatives and the corresponding diagram is shown in Fig. 8.1.

$$\text{Profit} = f(X) = -1125 + 250X - 5X^2 \tag{8.1}$$

$$f'(X) = 250 - 10X \tag{8.2}$$

$$f''(X) = -10 \tag{8.3}$$

where X represents the level of production.

163

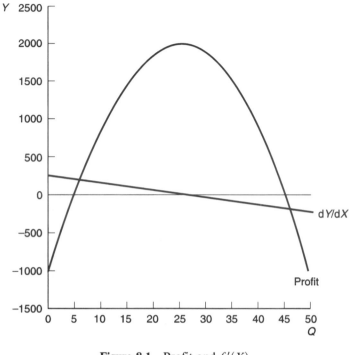

Figure 8.1   Profit and $f'(X)$

In an economic context we would wish to determine the level of output (X) where the firm maximizes profit. It can be seen from Fig. 8.1 that the point we require is the turning point of the profit function and that at this point the slope of the function will be zero. Given that the slope of the function is given by the first derivative we then require:

$$f'(X) = 250 - 10X = 0$$

which, on solving, gives $X = 25$ as the profit-maximizing level of output. Clearly, to find such an optimum point we simply set the first derivative to zero and solve. However, let us consider a further aspect to the problem. The point we have found $(X = 25)$ is technically a point where the slope of the original function is zero (often referred to as a *stationary* point). We were able to establish that this stationary point represented a *maximum* only because of our knowledge of economics (given that we seek a maximum point on the profit function) and by visual inspection of the relevant graph. In general, however, we might not be able to confirm that the stationary point is a maximum through simple inspection of the problem as it is evident that some functions could equally have a turning point that represented some minimum position. Clearly we require a general method for determining which type of optimum point the stationary position represents. This is readily achieved by examining the behaviour of the derivative itself. Returning to Fig. 8.1 we see that the first derivative (measuring the slope of the original function) behaves in a very specific way as X changes. The derivative gradually changes from positive values to negative values as X increases (obviously taking a zero value at some point as it does so). If we consider a function that had some minimum turning point (as illustrated in Fig. 8.2), we can see that the derivative will behave in exactly the opposite way: first taking negative values and then positive as X increases. Therefore, we can establish whether the stationary point

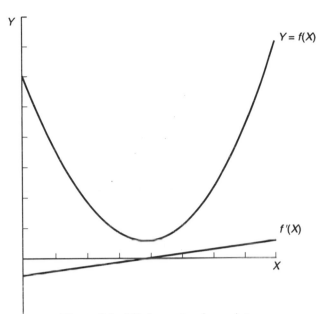

Figure 8.2   Minimum turning point

represents a maximum or minimum by inspecting the behaviour of the derivative. How do we do this without resorting either to a graph or to a series of arithmetic calculations to test the derivative values? The answer lies with the second derivative. Consider that any derivative shows the slope of a function. The second derivative, therefore, must show the slope of the function represented by the first derivative. Effectively, therefore, the second derivative can be interpreted as showing the rate of change of the first derivative and the direction of the change of the first derivative can be obtained by inspection of the sign of the second derivative. In our example, the second derivative has a negative sign, indicating that the slope of the first derivative is negative (sloping downwards from left to right). Such a first-derivative type can only occur if we have a stationary point representing a maximum since it indicates a change from a large positive slope to a small positive or negative slope. Conversely, if the second derivative had been positive then the stationary point would represent a minimum. We can summarize what we have found so far:

1 A stationary point occurs at the value(s) for X that gives a zero value for the first derivative, $f'(X)$.
2 This stationary point represents:

$$\text{a maximum if } f''(X) < 0$$
$$\text{a minimum if } f''(X) > 0$$

As we shall shortly see, these rules will need a slight modification to make them generally applicable to any function, but they will suffice for the moment. Point 1 is frequently referred to as the *first-order condition* to determine an optimum point while point 2 is referred to as the *second-order condition*. Use of these principles readily allows us to find a turning point for some function and to determine whether this point represents a maximum or minimum position.

Student activity 8.1
For the function:

$$Y = X^3 - 20X^2 + 13X - 50$$

find the turning points of the function and determine whether they represent a maximum or minimum.
(Solution on p. 345.)

8.2 Local and global maxima and minima

Let us progress by examining a slightly more complex function than those considered so far. Consider the function:

$$Y = 200 - 30X + 8X^2 - 0.5X^3 \tag{8.4}$$

For $X = 0$ to 12 the function and its first and second derivatives are shown in Figs 8.3 to 8.5. We have:

$$f'(X) = -30 + 16X - 1.5X^2 \tag{8.5}$$
$$f''(X) = 16 - 3X \tag{8.6}$$

Clearly in this example we have a function that has both a minimum and a maximum point. Using the first- and second-order conditions we first require:

$$f'(X) = -30 + 16X - 1.5X^2 = 0$$

to determine the stationary point(s). In this case the first derivative is itself a quadratic so to find the values for X that give $f'(X) = 0$ we clearly require the two roots of the quadratic function. Applying the relevant solution formula that we derived in Chapter 6 we obtain:

$$X_1 = 2.43 \quad \text{and} \quad X_2 = 8.24$$

These are the two X values where the original function takes a stationary value. It is important to note that we *cannot* now assume that $X_1 = 2.43$ is the minimum point simply because it takes a smaller value than X_2. We must examine the second-order conditions to determine whether the two stationary points represent a maximum or a minimum. We know that the stationary point represents:

a maximum if $f''(X) < 0$
a minimum if $f''(X) > 0$

With $X_1 = 2.43$ we then have:

$$f''(X_1) = 16 - 3(X_1) = 16 - 3(2.43) = 8.71$$

which, since the second derivative is positive, indicates that when $X = 2.43$, Y reaches a minimum position. Similarly, when $X_2 = 8.24$ we have:

$$f''(X_2) = 16 - 3(X_2) = 16 - 3(8.24) = -8.72$$

and, using the same logic, this value for X must indicate where Y takes a maximum value. The relationships between the original function, the two derivatives and the relevant X values are evident from Figs 8.3 to 8.5. Clearly the principles of the first- and second-order conditions can be applied to virtually any type of function to establish maximum and/or minimum points. In fact, this example establishes an important principle in terms of optimization. In terms of Eq.

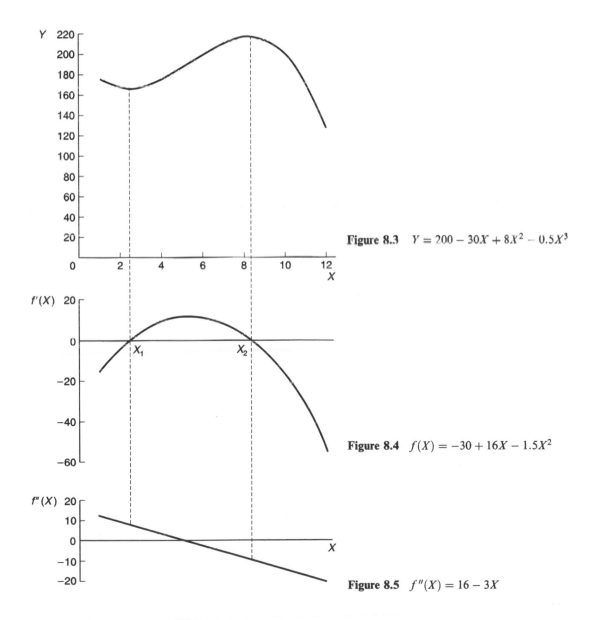

Figure 8.3 $Y = 200 - 30X + 8X^2 - 0.5X^3$

Figure 8.4 $f(X) = -30 + 16X - 1.5X^2$

Figure 8.5 $f''(X) = 16 - 3X$

(8.4) we have two stationary points, one representing a maximum and the other a minimum. In general, however, we may well face functions that give several such stationary points. Consider the function illustrated in Fig. 8.6.

It is evident that this function, in addition to having both maximum and minimum points, also has multiple maxima (and minima). Point A clearly represents a maximum position within that region of X values but a second, and higher, maximum also occurs at point C—similarly with points B and D in terms of minimum positions. Point A (and point D) is referred to as a *local*, or relative, optimum while point C (and B) is referred to as a *global* or absolute optimum. If we examine the first and second derivatives in Fig. 8.6, we see that the first- and second-order conditions are clearly being met for all such optimum points regardless of whether they are local or global. On reflection it is evident that these conditions are unable to distinguish between global optima and strictly must be viewed as the condition for finding a local optimum (or a series of local optima if there is more than one). At present we have no ready method of determining whether an optimum point represents a local or a global position. For the present the only method available is to compare all the local optima we may have found for some function and determine which of these generates the highest (or lowest) value for the Y variable. This optimum point would then represent the global.

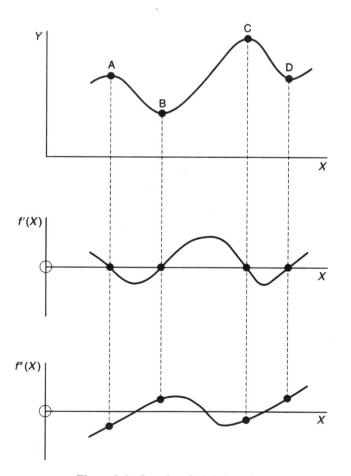

Figure 8.6 Local and global optima

8.3 Points of inflection

One further aspect of optimization must be considered before we progress to applying these principles to economic analysis. We have seen that when we have located a stationary point (where $f'(X) = 0$) then we can use the second derivative rule to determine whether this point represents a local maximum or minimum. As we have seen, if the second derivative is positive, the stationary point represents a local minimum while if it takes a positive value, the point represents a local maximum. Let us pose the question: what if the second derivative is neither positive nor negative but zero? In such a situation we face a position where the stationary point may represent not a maximum or minimum but what is referred to as a *point of inflection*.

Consider the function shown in Fig. 8.7. A point of inflection is shown at point A (shown with the corresponding tangent line superimposed). This is clearly a stationary point as the first derivative, $f'(X)$, takes a zero value; that is, the slope of the original function at this point is zero. The first derivative, however, is always non-negative so does not change its sign as we would normally

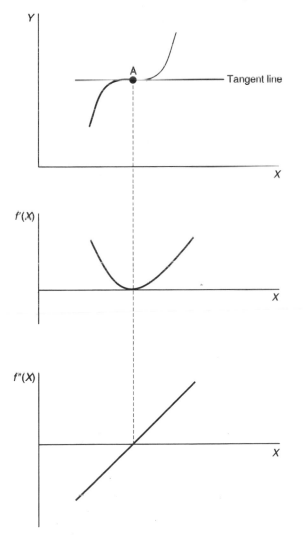

Figure 8.7 $Y = f(X)$: inflection point

expect (that is, the first derivative does not change from positive to negative values or from negative to positive values). Clearly at point A the second derivative will take neither a positive nor a negative value but will be zero. To illustrate the arithmetic involved let us consider the function:

$$Y = f(X) = 10 + (X - 4)^3 \tag{8.7}$$

where:

$$f'(X) = 3(X - 4)^2 \tag{8.8}$$
$$f''(X) = 6(X - 4) \tag{8.9}$$

The three functions are plotted in Fig. 8.8 over the range $X = 1$ to 7. To locate the point of inflection let us examine the second derivative (Eq. (8.8)). At such a point $f''(X) = 0$. Setting

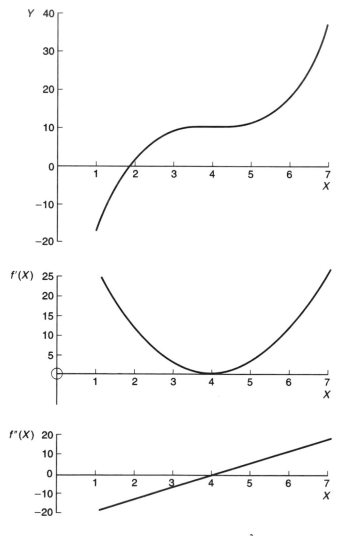

Figure 8.8 $Y = 10 + (X - 4)^3$

Eq. (8.9) to zero and solving gives $X = 4$. When $X = 4$ we see that the first derivative takes a value of zero, indicating that we have a stationary point on the original function. However, there exists another type of inflection point that we need to consider. This can arise at a *non-stationary* point on the original function. Consider Fig. 8.9. At point A we again have a point of inflection, where $f''(X) = 0$. However, at this value of X the slope of the original function is not zero (as indicated by the first derivative) and hence cannot be a stationary point. To summarize our discussion to date, therefore, we can say that a local optimum point must also be a stationary point but that a stationary point could be either a local optimum or a point of inflection. If the stationary point is a local optimum then we can use the first- and

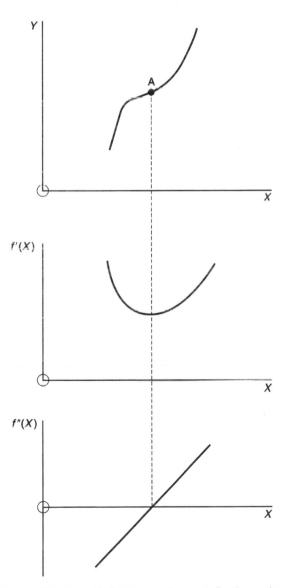

Figure 8.9 $Y = f(X)$: Non-stationary inflection point

second-order rules to determine both the X value at this point and whether we face a maximum or minimum local optimum.

8.4 Summary

This has been a relatively short chapter but the concepts relating to optimization are critical for the rest of what we cover in the text (and patently important for considerable areas of economic analysis). You should ensure that the concepts we have introduced are thoroughly understood before proceeding.

Worked example

A firm faces a total revenue function:

$$TR = 50Q - 2Q^2$$

and a total cost function:

$$TC = 20 + 0.25Q^3 - 10Q^2 + 100Q$$

For each of the following determine whether there the function has a maximum or minimum and if so of what type:

(a) Marginal cost
(b) Average fixed cost
(c) Average variable cost
(d) Marginal revenue
(e) Total revenue
(f) Profit

Solution

Taking each in turn:

(a) $MC = f'(TC) = 0.75Q^2 - 20Q + 100$
Setting $f'(MC)$ to zero and solving gives:

$$f'(MC) = 1.5Q - 20 \qquad \text{so } Q = 13.3$$

$f''(MC) = 1.5$ so when $Q = 13.3$ MC is at a minimum point.

(b) $AFC = FC/Q = 20/Q$
$f'(AFC) = -20/Q^2$

On inspection we see that as Q increases the term $-20/Q^2$ approaches zero but will in fact technically never reach zero. $f'(AFC)$ cannot then be solved for $f'(AFC) = 0$ and no maximum or minimum exists.

(c) $AVC = VC/Q = 0.25Q^2 - 10Q + 100$
This has a stationary point where $f'(AVC) = 0$:

$$f'(AVC) = 0.5Q - 10 = 0$$

so $Q = 20$ at this point. To check whether this represents a maximum or minimum we require the second derivative:

$$f''(AVC) = 0.5$$

so we confirm that when $Q = 20$ AVC reaches its minimum value.

(d) $MR = f'(TR)$ so we have:

$$MR = 50 - 4Q$$

This function reaches a stationary value when $f'(MR) = 0$:

$$f'(MR) = -4$$

which clearly cannot take a zero value. The MR function has no maximum or minimum value (a conclusion we can confirm on inspection of MR since this is a linear function).

(e) For total revenue we require:

$$f'(TR) = 0 = 50 - 4Q$$

giving $Q = 12.5$ (the optimum value for TR is found where $MR = 0$). Using the second derivative $f''(TR) = -4$ confirms that when $Q = 12.5$ TR will take a maximum value.

(f) Profit $= TR - TC$
Profit $= -0.25Q^3 + 8Q^2 - 50Q - 20$
We require $f'(Profit) = 0$:

$$f'(Profit) = -0.75Q^2 + 16Q - 50 = 0$$

and solving gives $Q_1 = 3.8$ and $Q_2 = 17.53$ as the two turning points. Using the second derivative:

$$f''(Profit) = -1.5Q + 16$$

substituting Q_1 gives $f''(Profit) = 10.3$, indicating that this value of Q gives a minimum profit. When Q_2 is substituted we derive $f''(Profit) = -10.3$, implying that this is a maximum.

Exercises

8.1 For the following functions determine the stationary point(s) and determine whether they represent a minimum or maximum and whether these are local or global extrema. You will also find it useful to graph most of these functions and their derivatives.

   (i) $Y = 10 - X^3$

  (ii) $Y = 100 + 5X + 0.05X^2$

 (iii) $Y = 50 - 30X + 10X^2 - 0.5X^3$

 (iv) $Y = X + 20/X$

  (v) $Y = (3X - 6)^3$

 (vi) $Y = 3X/(X + 2)^2$

(vii) $Y = X + 10X^{-1}$

(viii) $Y = 40X - 8X^2 + X^3$

 (ix) $Y = 20X^2 - \frac{1}{3}X^3$

  (x) $Y = 10 + 0.1(X - 5)^2$

 (xi) $Y = \sqrt{X} - 5X$

9 Optimization in economic analysis

Armed with the various principles and techniques introduced over the previous three chapters we are now in a position to examine some of the key models used in economic analysis which depend upon the concept of optimization. Some of these are likely to be familiar to you already—at least in terms of their general principles and verbal description. What we shall proceed to do is to establish key conclusions using differential calculus. We shall also be introducing certain models that can only be readily analysed through such mathematics.

Learning objectives

By the end of this chapter you should be able to:

- Confirm that MR = MC at profit maximization
- Use differential calculus to determine the profit-maximizing position for a firm in perfect competition and one in a monopoly
- Assess the effect of different taxes on profit maximization
- Determine the level of tax which will maximize tax revenue
- Apply differential calculus to production theory

9.1 Profit maximization

We begin with the most well-known model: that involving profit maximization for an individual firm. Profit is readily defined as the difference between total revenue (TR) and total costs (TC). If, as is usually assumed, revenue and costs can be expressed as functions of Q (output) then we have:

$$\text{Profit} = \text{TR} - \text{TC} \tag{9.1}$$
$$\text{TR} = r(Q) \tag{9.2}$$
$$\text{TC} = c(Q) \tag{9.3}$$

Hence:

$$\text{Profit} = r(Q) - c(Q) \tag{9.4}$$

From now on we shall use the symbol, π (pi), to represent Profit.

Note that Eq. (9.2) for total revenue is not dependent on the market conditions we may be examining. In other words, Eq. (9.2) is equally applicable to a firm in conditions of perfect competition or of monopoly since we do not specify the precise form of the function. Equally the precise form of the TC function is not specified either. To find the level of output that maximizes profit we require the first derivative:

$$\frac{d\pi}{dQ} = r'(Q) - c'(Q) = 0 \tag{9.5}$$

which is the same as:

$$r'(Q) = c'(Q) \tag{9.6}$$

which, given the economic meaning of the first derivative of the TR and TC functions, equates to:

$$MR = MC \tag{9.7}$$

that is, marginal revenue must equal marginal cost at the optimum point regardless of the market conditions under which the firm operates. For this level of output to be a (local) maximum, however, we also require:

$$\frac{d^2\pi}{dQ^2} = r''(Q) - c''(Q) < 0 \tag{9.8}$$

or

$$r''(Q) < c''(Q) \tag{9.9}$$

This indicates that the rate of change in MR must be less than the rate of change in MC. Graphically this implies that, for levels of output below the optimum, MC is less than MR while the reverse is true for levels of output that are greater than optimum. Clearly the exact optimum position depends upon the equation parameters. We now turn to examine these under two different sets of market conditions.

9.2 Profit maximization: perfect competition

Let us first examine a firm operating under conditions of perfect competition. One of the key assumptions about this model is that the individual firm is a price taker; that is, the price per unit is determined by the market and no individual firm—because of its small size *vis-à-vis* the total market—can directly influence this. In the context of mathematics this implies that the TR function is given as:

$$TR = PQ \tag{9.10}$$

that is, the quantity the individual firm is able to sell (Q) at the ruling price (P). Clearly, since P is a constant, Eq. (9.10) is linear. Equally, of course, the derivative of Eq. (9.10) is:

$$\frac{d(TR)}{dQ} = P = MR \tag{9.11}$$

which, since the derivative of TR is MR, indicates that $P = MR$. Given the basic principles established in Sec. 9.1, this indicates that for a firm in perfect competition to maximize profit the level of output must be set where $P = MC$. Figure 9.1 illustrates graphically the general relationships involved.

In Fig. 9.1(a) we see both the TR and TC functions. As we have just revealed, the TR function for this type of firm will be linear. The TC function follows the usual assumptions relating to returns to scale effects at different levels of output (you may recognize this type of function as a cubic). Figure 9.1(b) shows the corresponding profit function (graphically the difference between TR and TC at different levels of output). At points Q_2 and Q_4 we see that we have the breakeven level of output where profit $= 0$ (TR $=$ TC). For levels of output less than Q_2 or greater than Q_4 we see that profit is negative (TR $<$ TC) while between the two levels of output

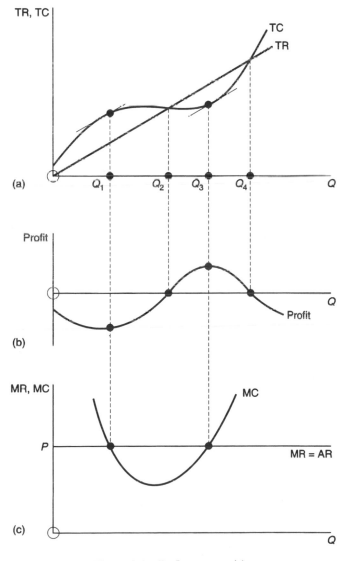

Figure 9.1   Perfect competition

profit is positive (TR > TC). The relevant first-order conditions require the derivative of profit to be zero. We see from Fig. 9.1(b) that this occurs at two points—Q_1 and Q_3. From Fig. 9.1(a) we see that the slopes of TR and TC are identical at these two output levels (as is confirmed from Fig. 9.1(c) which shows MR and MC—the relevant two first derivatives). However, we clearly need to distinguish between these two stationary points given that, as we see from Fig. 9.1(a), one level of output represents the minimum profit position while the other represents the maximum. The second-order condition (Eq. (9.9)) requires the revenue second derivative to be less than the cost second derivative. This implies that the slope of MR musts be less than the slope of MC at the profit-maximizing point. The slope of MR is zero no matter the level of output (MR is, after all, equal to P and parallel to the Q axis). We see that at output level Q_1 the MC curve—the rate of change in TC—has a negative slope and hence the slope of MC < the slope of MR. Conversely, at Q_3, MC has a positive slope and hence the slope of MC > the slope of MR; this satisfies the second-order condition for a maximum turning point.

Let us illustrate the general principles involved with a set of appropriate functions. First, let us assume that the prevailing market price for the product is 30. This gives a TR function such that:

$$\text{TR} = 30Q \tag{9.12}$$

Assume further that the TC function is given by:

$$\text{TC} = 100 + 20Q - 5Q^2 + 0.5Q^3 \tag{9.13}$$

The profit function is then:

$$\pi = -100 + 10Q + 5Q^2 - 0.5Q^3 \tag{9.14}$$

while we have:

$$\text{MR} = \frac{d(\text{TR})}{dQ} = 30 \tag{9.15}$$

$$\text{MC} = \frac{d(\text{TC})}{dQ} = 20 - 10Q + 1.5Q^2 \tag{9.16}$$

> ### *Student activity 9.1*
> Plot all these functions on an appropriate graph (as Fig. 9.1). Determine the profit-maximizing level of output. Calculate MC and MR when $Q = 7.5$ and again when $Q = 7.6$. Comment on the results. Confirm that the second-order conditions ((Eq. (9.9)) are satisfied. (Solution on p. 345.)

Note that the MC function gives a typical U-shaped curve, given that it is a quadratic function. We require the profit-maximizing level(s) of output. This requires the first derivative of the profit function (Eq. 9.14) to be set to zero and solved to give the stationary points of the function, giving $Q = -0.88$ and $Q = 7.55$. However, it is evident that one level of output represents a situation of minimum profit while the other of maximum profit. To determine which is which mathematically we require the second derivative:

$$\frac{d^2\pi}{dQ^2} = 10 - 3Q \tag{9.17}$$

With $Q = -0.88$ the second derivative is clearly positive (hence this represents the minimum point) while with $Q = 7.55$ the second derivative is negative, indicating a maximum stationary point.

9.3 Profit maximization: monopoly

Let us now consider the opposite market condition of monopoly. Clearly much of the structure of the problem will be similar. The cost functions facing the monopolist will be effectively the same as those facing the perfectly competitive firm. However, the TR function will differ since the monopolist (and indeed any firm facing a less than perfect competition situation) will be presented with a downward-sloping demand function; that is, in order to sell more of the product the monopolist will be required, *ceteris paribus*, to lower the price per unit. (This is in sharp contrast, of course, to the perfect competitive firm which can sell all it wishes at the prevailing price.) If we denote such a function in the form:

$$P = d(Q) = a - bQ \tag{9.18}$$

then we also have:

$$\text{TR} = r(Q) = PQ = (a - bQ)Q = aQ - bQ^2 \tag{9.19}$$

which now gives a quadratic TR function. This function can be seen to have a zero intercept and will take the standard inverted U shape since the parameter associated with the Q^2 term is negative. The appropriate relationships are shown in Fig. 9.2. Clearly the same logic applies as in the case of perfect competition. Figure 9.2(a) shows the TR and TC functions, with TR < TC for levels of output below Q_2 and above Q_4. The relevant profit function (together with break-even points) is shown in Fig. 9.2(b). The first-order condition requires the derivative of profit to be zero and clearly this will occur at Q_1 and Q_3 (where again from Fig. 9.2(a) we see that the slopes of TR and TC are equal at these points). These points are also confirmed from Fig. 9.2(c), which shows MC, MR and AR. Note that both AR and MR must be downward-sloping, linear functions given by Eq. (9.19). At points Q_1 and Q_3, MC = MR. To determine which level of output represents the maximum profit position we apply the second-order condition requiring the slope of MR to be less than the slope of MC. Clearly the slope of MR is negative for all Q. At point Q_1 the slope of MC is also negative but more so than MR. Conversely, at point Q_3 the slope of MC is positive while that of MR is still negative; hence this point must represent the profit-maximizing level of output. Note also from Fig. 9.2(c) that at this level of output the relevant price will be P_3 (since $P = \text{AR}$) and it can be seen that under such monopoly conditions $P > \text{MR}$ at the profit-maximizing level of output.

Again, to reinforce these principles, let us examine a numerical example. Assume that the monopoly firm faces a demand function such that:

$$P = d(Q) = 50 - 0.5Q \tag{9.20}$$

and

$$\text{TC} = 2 + 60Q - 8Q^2 + Q^3 \tag{9.21}$$

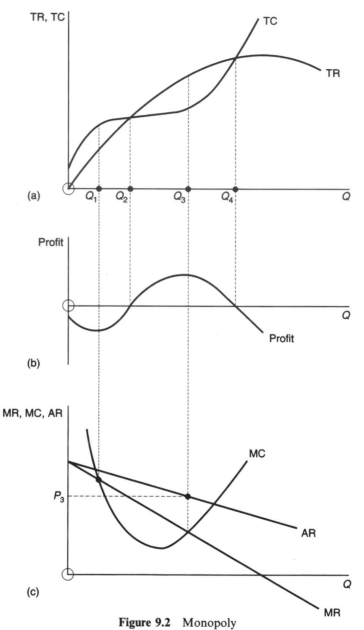

Figure 9.2 Monopoly

Student activity 9.2
Derive the relevant equations for profit, TR, MR and MC. Plot these on an appropriate graph (as in Fig. 9.1). Derive the profit-maximizing level of output. Derive the price and marginal revenue at this level of output. Explain why $P > MR$ at the profit-maximizing point for a monopolist.

Given Eq. (9.20) we have:

$$TR = PQ = 50Q - 0.5Q^2 \qquad (9.22)$$

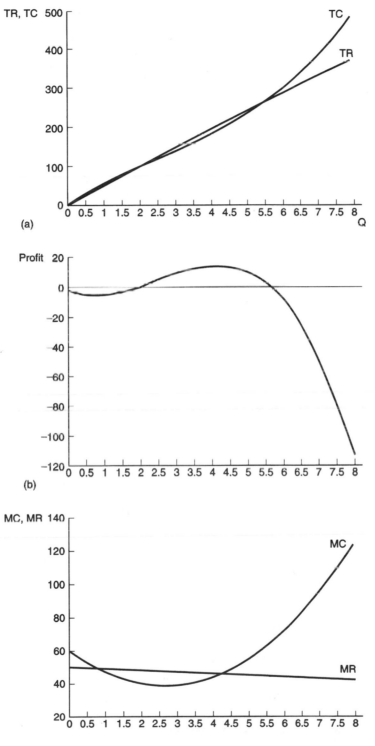

(a)

(b)

(c)

Figure 9.3

giving:

$$\text{Profit} = -2 - 10Q + 7.5Q^2 - Q^3 \qquad (9.23)$$

and

$$\frac{d(\text{TR})}{dQ} = 50 - Q \qquad (9.24)$$

$$\frac{d(\text{TC})}{dQ} = 60 - 16Q + 3Q^2 \qquad (9.25)$$

$$\frac{d\pi}{dQ} = -10 + 15Q - 3Q^2 \qquad (9.26)$$

Setting Eq. (9.26) to zero and solving gives $Q = 0.792$ and $Q = 4.208$. Taking the second derivative of Eq. (9.23) gives:

$$\frac{d^2\pi}{dQ^2} = 15 - 6Q \qquad (9.27)$$

and substituting the two Q values we see that $Q = 0.792$ represents minimum profit and $Q = 4.208$ maximum profit. Similarly from Eqs (9.20) and (9.24) we derive the price and marginal revenue as:

$$P = 50 - 0.5(4.208) = 47.896$$

and

$$\text{MR} = 50 - 4.208 = 45.792$$

confirming that $P > \text{MR}$. Figure 9.3 shows the relevant graphs.

9.4   The effect of tax on profit maximization

In earlier chapters we used comparative static analysis to examine the effect of the imposition of an excise tax on the market equilibrium. You may remember that in Chapter 3, Sec. 3.7, for example, we saw the effect such a tax would have in general on the market equilibrium under competitive conditions. Another aspect of this examination relates to the reasons why a government might impose such a tax on a product. Typically, the government will do so in order to raise revenue from the imposition of tax. Clearly, the logical question to be answered is: what effect will such a tax have on the profit-maximizing level of price and output? Let us begin by examining the effect of a lump-sum tax.

9.5   The imposition of a lump-sum tax

Such a tax is simply a fixed amount levied regardless of the quantity sold. Under monopoly conditions, for example, a government might view such a tax as an attractive method of penalizing supernormal profits arising from the existence of the monopoly. What effect will such a tax have? Clearly, we now have:

$$TR = r(Q) \tag{9.28}$$
$$TC = c(Q) \tag{9.29}$$
$$T = t \tag{9.30}$$

where T (and t) is the lump-sum imposed. We now need to distinguish between the profit earned by the firm and the profit retained after the tax has been paid. Retained profit will now be:

$$Profit = TR - TC - T$$
$$\pi = r(Q) - c(Q) - T \tag{9.31}$$

and, as usual, profit will be maximized where $d\pi/dQ = 0$ and $d^2\pi/dQ^2 < 0$. The first derivative will be:

$$\frac{d\pi}{dQ} = r'(Q) - c'(Q) = 0 \tag{9.32}$$

We see straightaway that this is effectively MR = MC and is identical to Eq. (9.5) (which related to market conditions prior to the imposition of the tax). Clearly, such a lump-sum tax will not affect the profit-maximizing level of output (and hence price), although it will affect the profit retained at this level of output. Logically, we can view such a lump-sum tax as an addition to the firm's fixed costs. For this reason it is easy to see why some governments favour this type of tax for a monopoly firm since they can argue that they are not interfering in the market equilibrium process. Given that Eq. (9.5) involves *marginal* costs then the optimum point will remain unaffected.

> **Student activity 9.3**
> Return to the activity 9.2. Confirm that a lump-sum tax of 2.5 will not affect the profit-maximizing level of output or the price for the monopolist. Calculate the retained level of profit and compare this with that earned before the tax.
> (Solution on p. 346.)

9.6 The imposition of a profit tax

Let us now examine the effect of a profit tax imposed on the firm. Such a tax typically takes some fixed percentage of the firm's profit. Again such a tax system is frequently attractive to governments since they can be seen to be actively taxing monopoly profits achieved. Clearly, we now need to distinguish between pre-tax and post-tax profit for the firm. Our model is then:

$$TR = r(Q)$$
$$TC = c(Q) \text{ as before}$$
and
$$T = t\pi \tag{9.33}$$

where π now represents the pre-tax profits earned at the profit-maximizing level of output and t the proportion of tax levied on these profits (with $0 < t < 1$). We now have:

$$\pi = r(Q) - c(Q) \tag{9.34}$$

and hence post-tax profit is given by:

$$\pi_t = r(Q) - c(Q) - t[r(Q) - c(Q)] \tag{9.35}$$

Clearly, from the firm's point of view it will seek to maximize post-tax profits. Rearranging Eq. (9.35) gives:

$$\pi_t = (1 - t)[r(Q) - c(Q)] \tag{9.36}$$

and hence we require:

$$\frac{d\pi_t}{dQ} = (1 - t)[r'(Q) - c'(Q)] = 0 \tag{9.37}$$

Since, by definition, $0 < t < 1$ then $(1 - t) > 0$ and hence we seek a value for Q such that:

$$r'(Q) - c'(Q) = 0 \tag{9.38}$$

Again, we recognize that the imposition of a profit tax will leave the profit-maximizing level of output unchanged since Eq. (9.38) is simply MR = MC yet again.

> *Student activity 9.4*
> Return to the activity 9.2. If the government imposes a profit tax of 60 per cent on the monopolist, confirm that the profit-maximizing level of output is unchanged. Compare the profit earned by the monopolist before the imposition of the tax with the post-tax profit.
> (Solution on p. 346.)

9.7 The imposition of an excise tax

Let us now consider the imposition of an excise, or sales, tax which typically takes the form of some fixed amount (£) per unit sold. Once again we have:

$$TR = r(Q)$$
$$TC = c(Q)$$

but now:

$$T = tQ \tag{9.39}$$

where T represents the total tax collected and t the per unit sales tax imposed. Retained profit π_t will now be:

$$\begin{aligned} \pi_t &= \text{TR} - \text{TC} - tQ \\ &= r(Q) - c(Q) - tQ \end{aligned} \tag{9.40}$$

Setting the first derivative to zero gives:

$$\frac{\mathrm{d}\pi_t}{\mathrm{d}Q} = r'(Q) - c'(Q) - t = 0 \tag{9.41}$$

which, on rearranging, gives:

$$\begin{aligned} r'(Q) &= c'(Q) + t \\ \text{MR} &= \text{MC} + t \end{aligned} \tag{9.43}$$

It can be seen that this type of tax, unlike the previous two types, will alter the profit-maximizing level of output. The tax imposed has the effect of shifting the MC function upwards by the amount of the per unit tax, t, imposed. Given the usual conditions associated with MR and MC, this must result in a profit-maximizing level of output which is lower than the non-tax model, and a price which is higher.

9.8 Maximizing taxation revenue

Following on from this investigation we can clearly raise an associated question. We know that an excise tax will affect the profit-maximizing level of output. From the government's viewpoint (since it is the government that imposes the tax) can we determine the optimum value for t, that is, the per unit tax to be imposed that will maximize tax revenue? We shall illustrate with reference to a simple market structure. Assume a monopoly firm facing the following TR and TC functions:

$$\text{TR} = b_1 Q + c_1 Q^2 \tag{9.44}$$
$$\text{TC} = a_2 + b_2 Q + c_2 Q^2 \tag{9.45}$$

with appropriate numerical restrictions on the parameters. The relevant TC function after the imposition of a tax will then be:

$$\begin{aligned} \text{TC}_t &= \text{TC} + tQ \\ &= (a_2 + b_2 Q + c_2 Q^2) + tQ \\ &= a_2 + (b_2 + t)Q + c_2 Q^2 \end{aligned} \tag{9.46}$$

and retained profit will be given by:

$$\pi_t = (b_1 Q + c_1 Q^2) - [a_2 + (b_2 + t)Q + c_2 Q^2] \tag{9.47}$$

To find the profit-maximizing level of output we require the first derivative of the profit function:

$$\frac{d\pi_t}{dQ} = b_1 + 2c_1 Q - [(b_2 + t) + 2c_2 Q]$$
$$= b_1 - (b_2 + t) + 2(c_1 - c_2)Q \qquad (9.48)$$

and rearranging gives:

$$Q = \frac{-b_1 + (b_2 + t)}{2(c_1 - c_2)} \qquad (9.49)$$

as the profit-maximizing level of output. Using this we then have:

$$T = tQ = t\left[\frac{-b_1 + (b_2 + t)}{2(c_1 - c_2)}\right]$$
$$T = \frac{-t(b_1 - b_2) + t^2}{2(c_1 - c_2)} \qquad (9.50)$$

To find the turning point of this function we require:

$$\frac{dT}{dt} = 0$$

and differentiating gives:

$$\frac{dT}{dt} = \frac{-(b_1 - b_2) + 2t}{2(c_1 - c_2)}$$

multiplying through by $2(c_1 - c_2)$ gives

$$\frac{dT}{dt} = -(b_1 - b_2) + 2t = 0 \qquad (9.51)$$

giving:

$$2t = b_1 - b_2$$
$$t = \frac{b_1 - b_2}{2} \qquad (9.52)$$

where Eq. (9.52) indicates the optimal rate of tax if the government wishes to optimize total taxation revenue. To determine whether this value of t gives a maximum or minimum turning point we require:

$$\frac{d^2 T}{dt^2} < 0$$

and from Eq. (9.51) this gives:

$$\frac{d^2 T}{dt^2} = \frac{2}{2(c_1 - c_2)} = \frac{1}{c_1 - c_2} < 0 \qquad (9.53)$$

which, given the usual restrictions on the numerical values for the parameters of this model ($c_1 < 0$, $c_2 > 0$) confirms that we have a maximum stationary point.

> **Student activity 9.5**
> Assume a market model where:
>
> $$TR = 125Q - Q^2$$
> $$TC = 500 + 5Q + 0.5Q^2$$
>
> Find the profit-maximizing level of output. Assume the government wishes to impose an excise tax. Find the optimal rate of tax. Calculate the new profit-maximizing level of output and price.
> (Solution on p. 347.)

Maximizing tax revenue in a competitive market

Finally, in the context of our examination of taxes, let us return to the model we derived in Sec. 3.7. There we had:

$$Q_d = Q_s \tag{9.54}$$
$$Q_d = a_1 + b_1 P \tag{9.55}$$
$$Q_s = a_2 + b_2(P - t) \tag{9.56}$$

with restrictions on the values of the parameters such that:

$$a_1 > 0 \qquad b_1 < 0$$
$$a_2 < 0 \qquad b_2 > 0$$

and

$$t > 0$$

where t represented the excise tax levied per unit of the product sold. We derived the general equilibrium to be:

$$P_e = \frac{a_1 - a_2}{b_2 - b_1} + \frac{b_2 t}{b_2 - b_1} \tag{9.57}$$

and

$$Q_e = \frac{a_1 b_2 - b_1 a_2}{b_2 - b_1} + \frac{b_1 b_2 t}{b_2 - b_1} \tag{9.58}$$

From the government's perspective we can also introduce a new function:

$$T = t Q_e \tag{9.59}$$

which represents a tax revenue function with T being the total tax revenue (at £t per unit sold for each Q_e unit). However, substituting Eq. (9.58) this becomes:

$$T = t\left(\frac{a_1b_2 - b_1a_2}{b_2 - b_1} + \frac{b_1b_2t}{b_2 - b_1}\right)$$

$$= \frac{(a_1b_2 - b_1a_2)t + b_1b_2t^2}{b_2 - b_1} \tag{9.60}$$

We then require the value for t that will generate the maximum value for T (total tax revenue). Clearly, in terms of the methodology we have developed, this requires:

$$\frac{dT}{dt} = 0 \quad \text{when} \quad \frac{d^2T}{dt^2} < 0$$

Taking the first derivative of Eq. (9.60) with respect to t we have:

$$\frac{dT}{dt} = \frac{a_1b_2 - b_1a_2 + 2b_1b_2t}{b_2 - b_1} = 0 \tag{9.61}$$

which gives:

$$a_1b_2 - b_1a_2 + 2b_1b_2t = 0$$
$$a_1b_2 - b_1a_2 = 2b_1b_2t$$

and therefore:

$$t = \frac{a_1b_2 - b_1a_2}{-2b_1b_2} \tag{9.62}$$

as the per unit excise tax to be levied to maximize total tax revenue. For this to be a maximum we require $d^2T/dt^2 < 0$ and from Eq. (9.61) we obtain:

$$\frac{d^2T}{dt^2} = \frac{2b_1b_2}{b_2 - b_1} < 0 \tag{9.63}$$

To illustrate, let us return to one of the examples we used in Chapter 3 (Exercise 3.2). We had:

$$Q_d = 500 - 9P \tag{9.64}$$
$$Q_s = -100 + 6P \tag{9.65}$$

Here we have the following values for the parameters:

$$a_1 = 500 \qquad b_1 = -9$$
$$a_2 = -100 \qquad b_2 = 6$$

and substituting into Eq. (9.62) gives:

$$t = \frac{a_1 b_2 - b_1 a_2}{-2 b_1 b_2}$$

$$= \frac{500(6) - (-9)(-100)}{-2(-9)(6)} = \frac{2100}{108} = £19.44$$

as the per unit tax required. To confirm this gives a maximum tax revenue we also require:

$$\frac{d^2 T}{dt^2} = \frac{2 b_1 b_2}{b_2 - b_1} < 0$$

$$= \frac{2(-9)(6)}{6 - (-9)} < 0$$

$$= \frac{-108}{15} < 0$$

confirming we have a maximum point on the tax revenue function.

> ***Student activity 9.6***
> Assuming this level of excise tax is imposed find:
>
> (i) The equilibrium price
> (ii) The equilibrium quantity
> (iii) The total tax revenue raised
>
> From Eq. (9.60) and using the numerical parameters for Eqs (9.64) and (9.65) derive a quadratic function for $T = f(t)$. Find the maximizing rate of excise tax directly from this function.
> (Solution on p. 347.)

9.9 The theory of production

Let us now apply the calculus principles that we have developed to the theory of production. Assume that, in the short run at least, we can regard a firm's production function as being of the form:

$$Q = g(L) \tag{9.66}$$

where Q refers to output and L to the labour input (other possible inputs being regarded as fixed in the short term). It is evident that the average product (AP) function will be given by:

$$AP = \frac{Q}{L} = \frac{g(L)}{L} \tag{9.67}$$

and that the marginal product (MP) function will be:

$$MP = \frac{dQ}{dL} = g'(L) \tag{9.68}$$

Let us investigate the maximum point on the AP function. To find such a point we require:

$$\frac{d(AP)}{dL} = 0$$

$$= \frac{d(Q/L)}{dL} = 0 \tag{9.69}$$

However, applying the quotient rule we then have:

$$\frac{Lg'(L) - g(L)}{L^2} = 0$$

which simplifies to:

$$Lg'(L) - g(L) = 0$$
$$Lg'(L) = g(L)$$
$$g'(L) = \frac{g(L)}{L}$$

but from Eqs (9.67) and (9.68) this can be rewritten as:

$$MP = g'(L) = \frac{g(L)}{L} = AP \tag{9.70}$$

In other words, the marginal product function passes through the point that is the maximum of the average product function. However, it may have occurred to you that we have strictly only found the turning point for AP given that we have not yet examined the second derivative to confirm that we have actually found the maximum. From Eq. (9.69) and applying both the quotient and product rules we obtain:

$$\frac{d^2(AP)}{dL^2} = \frac{L^2[Lg''(L) + g'(L) - g'(L)] - (2L)[Lg'(L) - g(L)]}{L^4}$$

$$= \frac{L^3 g''(L) - 2L^2 g'(L) + 2Lg(L)}{L^4}$$

$$= \frac{g''(L)}{L} - \frac{2g'(L)}{L^2} + \frac{2g(L)}{L^3} \tag{9.71}$$

However, we know that $Lg'(L) = g(L)$, so substituting gives:

$$\frac{d^2(AP)}{dL^2} = \frac{g''(L)}{L} - \frac{2g'(L)}{L^2} + \frac{2Lg'(L)}{L^3}$$

$$= \frac{g''(L)}{L} - \frac{2g'(L)}{L^2} + \frac{2g'(L)}{L^2} \tag{9.72}$$

Hence we require:

$$\frac{d^2(AP)}{dL^2} = \frac{g''(L)}{L} < 0 \tag{9.73}$$

However, it is sensible to consider only the range of values for which $L > 0$; hence we require $g''(L) < 0$. We know that:

$$g''(L) = \frac{d(MP)}{dL} \tag{9.74}$$

Hence for the MP function to cross the AP function at the latter's maximum point we simply require the slope of the MP function to be negative at this point. It is also instructive at this stage to consider the relationship between a mathematical exposition of these aspects of production with the graphical approach. Consider Figs 9.4 and 9.5 which show graphically a typical set of functions: a production function and the related MP and AP functions. Naturally, the shape of these functions is determined by the appropriate economic principles that we wish them to convey—the concept of diminishing marginal physical product, for example. It will be instructive, at this stage, to consider in detail how we can ensure that an appropriate mathematical representation of such a model can be obtained.

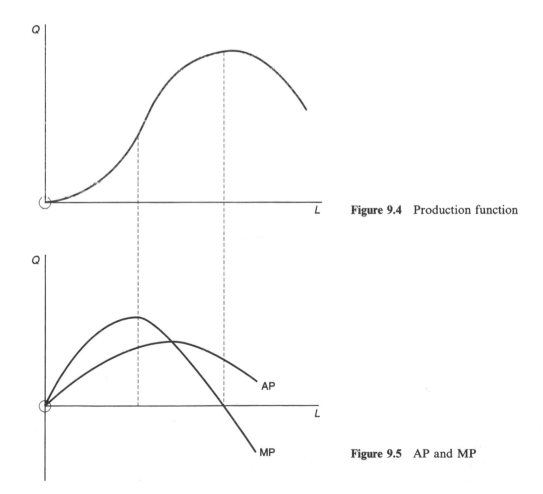

Figure 9.4 Production function

Figure 9.5 AP and MP

Let us assume for the purpose of illustration that we wish to represent the production function as a cubic function mathematically. We then have:

$$Q = g(L) = a + bL + cL^2 + dL^3 \tag{9.75}$$

$$MP = g'(L) = b + 2cL + 3dL^2 \tag{9.76}$$

$$AP = \frac{g(L)}{L} = \frac{a + bL + cL^2 + dL^3}{L} = \frac{a}{L} + b + cL + dL^2 \tag{9.77}$$

Let us examine the relevant parameters in terms of any restrictions we would require to place on these equations. First, it is evident that the production function itself should start from the origin (zero input = zero output). This requires $a = 0$. We also see that we require the MP function to start from the origin. From Eq. (9.76) this clearly requires $b = 0$ also. (Clearly, we could now simplify Eqs (9.75) to (9.77) if we wished by omitting all terms involving a or b.) It is also evident that MP takes a quadratic form (the inverse U), giving a maximum for MP that is positive when $L > 0$. We know that such a maximum point will occur when:

$$\frac{d(MP)}{dL} = \frac{d[g'(L)]}{dL} = g''(L) = 2c + 6dL = 0 \tag{9.78}$$

$$\frac{d^2(MP)}{dL^2} = g'''(L) = 6d < 0 \tag{9.79}$$

The first-order conditions will be satisfied when $L = -c/3d$. In order to meet the second-order conditions we clearly require $d < 0$, and since we would expect L to be non-negative this implies that $c > 0$. Summarizing, we have:

$$a = 0$$
$$b = 0$$
$$c > 0$$
$$d < 0$$

which reduces the three equations to the form:

$$Q = g(L) = cL^2 + dL^3 \tag{9.80}$$

$$MP = g'(L) = 2cL + 3dL^2 \tag{9.81}$$

$$AP = \frac{g(L)}{L} = cL + dL^2 \tag{9.82}$$

9.10   The theory of costs

In the context of our examination of production it will now be instructive to examine costs and, again, to apply the mathematical principles we have developed thus far. Consider the total costs function (TC) related to output (Q):

$$\text{TC} = c(Q) \tag{9.83}$$

$$\text{MC} = c'(Q) \tag{9.84}$$

$$\text{ATC} = \frac{c(Q)}{Q} \tag{9.85}$$

and, again, diagrammatically we would often expect to see the relationships as they are shown in Figs 9.6 and 9.7. We see that the TC function is one that is monotonically increasing—cost always increases with output (although naturally at different rates). This further implies that MC must always be positive and, as we see, MC takes the typical U shape. Let us consider the logic behind this. Clearly, as we have seen previously, there are direct links between costs and production. If we assume a simplified short-run function of the form:

$$\text{TC} = F + wL \tag{9.86}$$

where F represents fixed costs, L the labour input into the production process and w the wage rate per unit of labour, then we can in turn express MC as:

$$\text{MC} = c'(Q) = \frac{d(\text{TC})}{dQ} = \frac{d(\text{TC})}{dL}\frac{dL}{dQ}$$

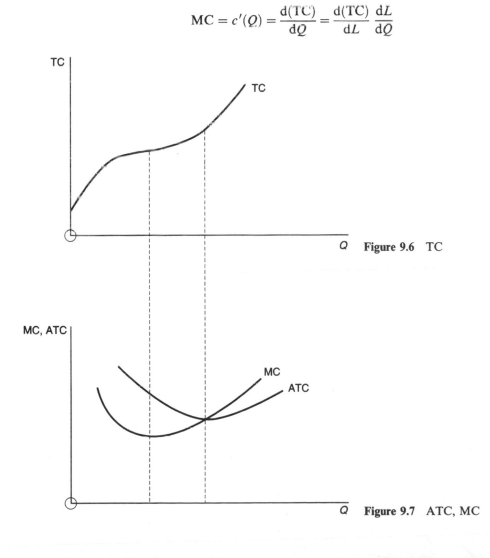

Figure 9.6   TC

Figure 9.7   ATC, MC

However, from Eq. (9.86), $d(TC)/dL = w$ and $dL/dQ = 1/MP$. Hence:

$$MC = \frac{w}{MP} \qquad (9.87)$$

that is, marginal cost is the wage rate divided by the marginal product of labour. Since, in the short term, w can be regarded as fixed, then MC will vary inversely with MP. In terms of the typical U shape for the MC function we can now see that as MP increases MC decreases and vice versa. Further, as MP approaches its maximum point MC will approach its minimum and logically when MP is at its maximum MC is at its minimum. It is evident that there is a direct relationship between the theory of production and the theory of cost. As with the production function, it will be instructive to consider numerical restrictions that we might wish to apply to a TC function. Consider the cubic function:

$$TC = a + bQ + cQ^2 + dQ^3 \qquad (9.88)$$

which gives:

$$MC = b + 2cQ + 3dQ^2 \qquad (9.89)$$

(which we recognize as a quadratic taking either the U or inverted U shape). Clearly the a term in Eq. (9.88) represents fixed costs and we would require $a > 0$. Since the TC function is monotonically increasing MC must take positive values for non-negative values for Q. This implies that the required minimum value for MC must be positive. The minimum is given when:

$$\frac{d(MC)}{dQ} = 2c + 6dQ = 0 \qquad (9.90)$$

and

$$\frac{d^2(MC)}{dQ^2} = 6d > 0 \qquad (9.91)$$

Therefore MC will have a minimum when $Q = -c/3d$ and when $d > 0$. Additionally, since we require $Q > 0$, then from Eq. (9.90) we also require $c < 0$. Taking $Q = -c/3d$ and substituting into Eq. (9.89) we then have:

$$MC = b + 2c\left(-\frac{c}{3d}\right) + 3d\left(-\frac{c}{3d}\right)^2$$

which we require to be positive. Simplifying this gives:

$$MC = b - \frac{2c^2}{3d} + \frac{3d(c^2)}{3d^2} = b - \frac{2c^2}{3d} + \frac{c^2}{3d} = b - \frac{c^2}{3d} = \frac{3db - c^2}{3d}$$

From this it is clear that the restrictions we have so far ($c < 0$ and $d > 0$) are insufficient to ensure a positive minimum value for MC. Additionally we require:

$$3db - c^2 > 0$$

which further implies that $b > 0$ and $3db > c^2$. Thus we require:

$$a > 0$$
$$b > 0$$
$$c < 0$$
$$d > 0$$
$$3db > c^2$$

to ensure the form of TC that we require to suit the economic model.

9.11 Relationship between the cost functions

Finally let us examine the relationship between the ATC and MC functions. If we have:

$$TC = c(Q) \quad \text{then ATC} = \frac{TC}{Q} = \frac{c(Q)}{Q} \tag{9.92}$$

Assume we wish to find the point where ATC is minimized. Following our usual approach we require the first derivative of ATC to be zero (and we can then solve for Q) and we require the second derivative to be positive to confirm that the turning point is a minimum. We then have, using the quotient rule:

$$\frac{d(ATC)}{dQ} = \frac{Qc'(Q) - c(Q)}{Q^2} = 0$$
$$Qc'(Q) - c(Q) = 0$$
$$Qc'(Q) = c(Q)$$
$$c'(Q) = \frac{c(Q)}{Q} \tag{9.93}$$

However, $MC = c'(Q)$ and $c(Q)/Q = ATC$ so we have:

$$MC = ATC \tag{9.94}$$

at the turning point of the ATC function; that is, the MC function intersects the ATC function at the latter's turning point. To confirm that this turning point represents a minimum we examine the second derivative:

$$\frac{d^2(ATC)}{dQ^2} = \frac{Q^2[Qc''(Q) + c'(Q) - c'(Q)] - [Qc'(Q) - c(Q)]2Q}{Q^4}$$
$$= \frac{Q^3 c''(Q) - 2Q^2 c'(Q) + 2Qc(Q)}{Q^4}$$
$$= \frac{c''(Q)}{Q} - \frac{2c'(Q)}{Q^2} + \frac{2c(Q)}{Q^3}$$

Given that MC = ATC, we have $c'(Q) = c(Q)/Q$ which can be written as $c(Q) = Qc'(Q)$. Substituting this gives:

$$
\begin{aligned}
\frac{d^2(\text{ATC})}{dQ^2} &= \frac{c''(Q)}{Q} - \frac{2c'(Q)}{Q^2} + \frac{2Qc'(Q)}{Q^3} \\
&= \frac{c''(Q)}{Q} - \frac{2c'(Q)}{Q^2} + \frac{2c'(Q)}{Q^2} \\
&= \frac{c''(Q)}{Q}
\end{aligned}
\tag{9.95}
$$

which we require to be positive for a minimum. Logically $Q > 0$ and hence we require $c''(Q) > 0$. However, $c''(Q)$ is simply the second derivative of TC or the derivative of MC. Therefore, for this point on the ATC function to represent a minimum we require MC to have a positive slope at this point. This confirms that MC will intersect ATC at the latter's minimum point.

9.12 Summary

In this chapter we have examined a number of areas of application of the principles of optimization to economics and derived a number of well-known principles as well as investigating a number of areas where we can only reach definitive conclusions through the use of calculus principles that we have developed. The topics we have examined are only a cross-section of those to which calculus could be applied.

Worked example

A firm produces a product at a single factory which it sells both in the domestic market and in the export market. Its cost function is given by:

$$TC = 10000 + 5Q$$

In the domestic market (d) it faces a demand function:

$$P_d = 250 - Q_d$$

and in the export market (x):

$$P_x = 200 - 2Q_x$$

(a) Determine the prices in the two markets that will maximize the firm's profit.
(b) The firm's export markets are in fact to other countries forming part of a customs union, or common market, and the firm has been told that it cannot price discriminate: that is, it must charge the same price in both its domestic market and its export market. Assess the new profit-maximizing level of output. Comment on the effect of the policy of non-price discrimination in this case.

Solution

(a) It is evident the firm faces two demand functions in its two markets and that we seek a profit-maximizing level of output in each. It appears logical to seek a solution where:

$$MC_d = MR_d$$

and
$$MC_x = MR_x$$

In fact, with only one production source (the one factory) $MC_d = MC_x$.

For the domestic market we then have:

$$TR_d = 250Q_d - Q_d^2$$
$$MR_d = f'(TR_d) = 250 - 2Q_d$$
$$MC = 5$$

and solving for Q_d when $MC = MR_d$ gives $Q_d = 122.5$ as the profit-maximizing level of output for the domestic market. For the export market we have:

$$TR_x = 200Q_x - 2Q_x^2$$

and

$$MR_x = f'(TR_x) = 200 - 4Q_x$$

Solving for $MC = MR_x$ gives $Q_x = 48.75$ as the profit-maximizing output for the export market. Total production for the firm will then be:

$$122.5 + 48.75 = 171.25$$

Note that the firm will actually discriminate in price terms between the two markets. For the domestic market we have:

$$P_d = 250 - Q_d$$

which for $Q_d = 122.5$ gives $P_d = 127.5$ as the domestic market price. For the export market we have:

$$P_x = 200 - 2Q_x$$

which gives $P_x = 102.5$ when $Q_x = 48.75$.

(b) If the firm is now told that it must charge the same price in both markets it will need to reassess its profit-maximizing position (particularly since in the domestic market it is able to earn considerably higher prices). From the two original demand functions we can rearrange these to give:

$$P_d = 250 - Q_d$$

becomes

$$Q_d = 250 - P_d$$

and

$$P_x = 200 - 2Q_x$$

becomes:

$$Q_x = 100 - 0.5P_x$$

Since $P_d = P_x$ because of the policy decision then we have:

$$Q_d = 250 - P$$

and

$$Q_x = 100 - 0.5P$$

Total quantity will now be $Q_d + Q_x$ to give:

$$Q = Q_d + Q_x = 250 - P + (100 - 0.5P) = 350 - 1.5P$$

or

$$P = 233.33 - \frac{2Q}{3}$$

The new TR function will then be:

$$TR = 233.33Q - \frac{2Q^2}{3}$$

and

$$f'(TR) = 233.33 - \frac{4Q}{3}$$

We still require $MC = MR$ and as $MC = 5$ we derive $Q = 171.225$ and with $f''(Q) = -4/3$ this is the new profit-maximizing level of output. What has also changed is the destination of the total output. For this level of output the price required will be $P = 119.18$ as the price charged in both markets.

From the two market demand functions we can determine that $Q_d = 130.82$ and $Q_x = 40.41$. Note that the new price is in between the two original (and different market prices) and the overall effect has been to decrease export sales and increase domestic sales.

You may also find it instructive to calculate the firm's profit in parts (a) and (b) and to consider through the use of the MR functions why the firm increases domestic sales at the expense of export.

Exercises

9.1 Assume a function of the form:

$$TC = 2000 + 10Q - 3Q^2 + 0.5Q^3$$

relating total costs to output.

    (i) Confirm that the function has 'sensible' numerical values for the parameters.
    (ii) Derive a function for marginal cost.
    (iii) Derive a function for average total cost.
    (iv) Derive a function for average fixed costs.
    (v) Find the level of output that minimizes MC.
    (vi) Find the level of output that minimizes ATC. Calculate ATC and MC at this level of output.
    (vii) Find the level of output that minimizes AFC. Comment.
    (viii) Plot MC, ATC, AFC on a single graph and comment upon their relationship.

9.2 Assume the firm in Exercise 9.1 above can sell all its output at a price of 200. Find the profit-maximizing level of output. Calculate profit for this level of output.

9.3 The government now imposes an excise tax, t, on sales of this product. Determine the value of t that will maximize total tax revenue. Calculate the new profit-maximizing level of output and the new profit level.

9.4 Assume a monopolist has the same TC function as in Exercise 9.1 above but faces a demand function:

$$P = 500 - 2.5Q$$

Find the profit-maximizing level of output.

9.5 For the monopolist find the revenue-maximizing level of output. Calculate the profit earned at this output level. Comment on why your solution to Exercise 9.4 is different.

9.6 The government imposes a lump-sum tax of 1000 on the monopolist. Confirm that this will not affect the optimum level of output. How would this affect the monopolist if he or she decided to maximize revenue instead?

9.7 The government now imposes a 20 per cent profit tax on the monopolist. Repeat the analysis in Exercise 9.6.

9.8 The government now imposes an excise tax. Determine the value of t that will maximize total tax revenue. Calculate the new profit-maximizing level of output and the new profit level.

9.9 Assume a production function:

$$Q = g(L) = 12L^2 - 0.75L^3$$

    (i) Confirm that the numerical values for the parameters take 'sensible' values.
    (ii) Derive an expression for AP.
    (iii) Derive an expression for MP.
    (iv) Find the optimum values for AP and MP.
    (v) Plot all three functions on a single graph.

9.10 Assume a production function of the form:

$$Q = h(K)$$

where K was capital input and L was fixed. Confirm that AP = MP when AP is at a maximum.

9.11 Assume a production function of the form:

$$Q = f(L) = 100 + 0.1L^2 - 0.001L^3$$

with a wage rate of £10 per unit of labour.

    (i) Derive the MP function.
   (ii) Derive the MC function.
  (iii) Plot both on a graph for L up to 75. Comment on the relationship between the two.

10 Functions of more than two variables

Over the past few chapters we have seen the importance and usefulness of differential calculus in economic analysis. The opportunities that such mathematical techniques offer the economist are extensive. However, the calculus methods introduced have focused only upon the simplest of functions: those taking the form $Y = f(X)$. Clearly, economics is frequently concerned with functions involving more than two variables and we need to be able to apply the useful principles we have developed to such functions. We begin by examining the principle of a *partial* derivative and then the concept of a total derivative.

Learning objectives

By the end of this chapter you should be able to:

- Calculate first- and second-order partial derivatives
- Calculate the total differential
- Calculate the total derivative
- Apply partial derivatives to a number of common economic models

10.1 Partial differentiation

Consider the function:

$$Y = f(X_1, X_2) \tag{10.1}$$
$$Y = -5 + 30X_1 - 3X_1^2 + 25X_2 - 5X_2^2 + X_1X_2 \tag{10.2}$$

This may represent, for example, the profit function of a firm producing two products—X_1 and X_2. As we have seen previously, it is possible to plot such a function as a three-dimensional graph. Equally, one approach frequently adopted in economics is to choose a fixed value for one of the X variables—say, X_2—and then to examine the relationship between Y and X_1. Figure 10.1 shows the three-dimensional picture we would obtain for this function while Fig. 10.2 shows the plot of Y and X_2 for certain fixed values of X_1. Clearly, our techniques of simple differentiation that we have developed will not suffice here since we have two X variables and the derivative applies only to one. However, the principles are readily extended to cover such multivariable functions.

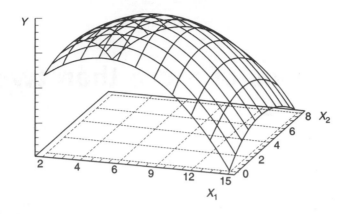

Figure 10.1 $Y = f(X_1, X_2)$

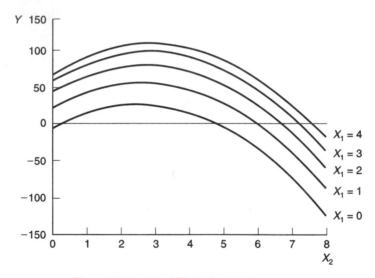

Figure 10.2 $Y = f(X_1, X_2)$ with X_1 constant

Recollect how we began the investigation of a simple derivative. We saw that the derivative indicated the change in Y given a change in X: in other words, the slope of the function at a specific X point. Consider the family of curves plotted in Fig. 10.2 for Y and X_2. Assume that we similarly wished to find the slope of each of these functions when, for example, $X_2 = 6$. Clearly, we would not wish to have to resort to the tedious approach of identifying the exact form of each associated function for each curve and then differentiating. It is apparent, however, that all these curves are related and that there should be some easier method of identifying the slopes. In fact, the approach we take is to obtain the *partial* derivative of the original multivariable function (Eq. (10.2)). Consider how we obtained Fig. 10.2. We assumed that the other X variable, X_1, could be treated not as a variable but as a constant, and we assigned it a series of fixed values (0, 1, 2, 3, 4). Remember, however, in our examination of calculus how we treated any constant in an expression that we wished to differentiate. It is clear, therefore, that we can obtain a derivative of Eq. (10.2) with respect to X_2, treating the other independent variable as a constant. Applying the basic rules that we have developed for differentiating we then get:

$$Y = -5 + 30X_1 - 3X_1^2 + 25X_2 - 5X_2^2 + X_1X_2$$

$$\frac{\partial Y}{\partial X_2} = 25 - 10X_2 + X_1 \tag{10.3}$$

It will be worth examining what we have just done. Differentiating the Y function in parts we see that we have:

Part	Derivative
-5	0
$30X_1$	0 (since X_1 is assumed constant)
$-3X_1^2$	0 (since X_1 is assumed constant)
$25X_2$	25
$-5X_2^2$	$-10X_2$
X_1X_2	X_1 (since X_1 is assumed constant)

Such an expression is referred to as a partial derivative of the original function and is denoted with the symbol $\partial Y/\partial X_2$ rather than the symbol dY/dX (this symbol is often referred to as 'the curly d'!). Such a partial derivative indicates the change in Y as the X_2 variable changes (and with the critical assumption that the other independent variable, X_1, remains unchanged).

> ***Student activity 10.1***
> Take $X_1 = 0, 1, 2, 3, 4$. Substitute each value in turn into the original function (Eq. (10.2)) to find $Y = f(X_2)$ for each X_1. Find the derivative of each of this series of functions and compare it with that for the partial derivative. Find the partial derivative $\partial Y/\partial X_1$. (Solution on p. 347.)

Therefore, we can find the partial derivative of Y with respect to each X variable in the function. Just as we denoted the ordinary derivative of:

$$Y = f(X)$$

as either dY/dX or $f'(X)$, so we have alternative notations for the partial derivatives. We have already seen that we can use the curly d. The alternative (and frequently preferred) notation is:

f_{X_1} to denote the partial derivative with respect to X_1.
f_{X_2} to denote the partial derivative with respect to X_2.

10.2 Second-order partial derivatives

It will probably come as no surprise to realize that, as with our earlier functions, we can readily obtain the second derivative of a multivariable function such as that in Eq. (10.2) and that such second-order partial derivatives have much the same interpretation as before. Consider the partial derivative:

$$\frac{\partial Y}{\partial X_2} = 25 - 10X_2 + X_1$$

which indicates the change in Y from some change in X_2, assuming X_1 fixed. Applying the same basic rules we can obtain the second-order partial derivatives with respect to X_2:

$$\frac{\partial^2 Y}{\partial X_2^2} = f_{X_2 X_2} = -10 \tag{10.4}$$

This second-order derivative tells us the rate at which the slopes of the family of curves in Fig. 10.2 change as X_2 changes. In this example we would note that the slope of Eq. (10.2) with respect to X_2 decreases as X_2 increases. Similarly, we can obtain the first- and second-order partial derivative with respect to X_1:

$$f_{X_1} = 30 - 6X_1 + X_2 \tag{10.5}$$
$$f_{X_1 X_1} = -6 \tag{10.6}$$

and this takes a similar interpretation. However, the matter of second-order derivatives for a multivariable function does not end there. Consider the first-order partial derivatives shown in Eqs (10.3) and (10.5). These in their own right are multivariable functions and it is clear that we could differentiate either with respect either to X_1 or X_2 in both cases. In the case of Eq. (10.3) we then have:

$$f_{X_2} = 25 - 10X_2 + X_1$$

and
$$f_{X_2 X_1} = 1 \tag{10.7}$$

while for Eq. (10.5) we have:

$$f_{X_1 X_2} = 1 \tag{10.8}$$

It is particularly important to be aware of what we have done. Taking Eq. (10.2)—the original multivariable function—we differentiated first with respect to X_2 (to get Eq. (10.3)). We then differentiated this function with respect to X_1 (to get Eq. (10.7)). Such a derivative is known as a *cross-partial* derivative. Similarly, the other cross-partial derivative is obtained by differentiating first with respect to X_1 and then with respect to X_2. You may have noticed that both cross-partial derivatives produce the same result (Eqs (10.7) and (10.8). In fact for any continuous function this will be the case, so the order of cross-differentiation is immaterial to the result produced (and can be a useful method for more complex functions of checking that your cross-partial derivative is actually correct). We shall be examining shortly the use of such cross-partial derivatives.

10.3 Differentials

In our examination of differential calculus we have treated the expression dY/dX as the symbol for a single item. We shall now explore the term as a ratio of the two terms dY and dX, where these individual terms are referred to as *differentials*. Consider the function:

$$Y = f(X)$$

Then, as we have seen on a number of occasions, we can investigate the effect of some small change in X, ΔX, on the Y value, ΔY. The ratio of the two changes we have referred to as the difference quotient is: $\Delta Y/\Delta X$. Using this we then have:

$$\Delta Y = \frac{\Delta Y}{\Delta X} \Delta X \qquad (10.9)$$

In our examination of calculus we then assumed that ΔX became infinitesimally small and we saw that the difference quotient, $\Delta Y/\Delta X$, will then become the derivative dY/dX as ΔX approached zero, giving:

$$\Delta Y = \frac{dY}{dX} \Delta X \qquad (10.10)$$

If we then denote the (infinitesimally) small changes in X and Y as dX and dY respectively, we then have:

$$dY = \frac{dY}{dX} dX = f'(X)dX \qquad (10.11)$$

where dX and dY are known as the differentials of X and Y. Note that we can find the differential of Y simply by multiplying the derivative of the function by the differential of X. Equally, dividing the differential of Y by the differential of X will equal the derivative of the function. For example, assume a function:

$$Y = 4X^2$$

Then:

$$\frac{dY}{dX} = 8X$$

and

$$dY = (8X)dX$$

which we could use to determine dY if we were given a specific value for X and a value for dX (which would be measured from the given X value).

10.4 The total differential

Clearly, we need to be able to apply the differential concept to partial derivatives also. Assume a function such that:

$$Y = f(A, B) \qquad (10.12)$$

where Y, A and B are variables. If we keep B constant then, following the previous procedure, we have:

$$\Delta Y = \frac{\partial Y}{\partial A} \Delta A \qquad (10.13)$$

which for infinitesimally small changes becomes:

$$dY = \frac{\partial Y}{\partial A} \, dA = f_A dA \tag{10.14}$$

and through the same logic if we keep A constant we have:

$$dY = \frac{\partial Y}{\partial B} \, dB = f_B dB \tag{10.15}$$

However, as we have seen, partial derivatives (and differentials) require one independent variable to be kept constant. Assume that we allowed both independent variables to change simultaneously. We could then have:

$$\Delta Y = \frac{\partial Y}{\partial A} \Delta A + \frac{\partial Y}{\partial B} \Delta B \tag{10.16}$$

$$dY = \frac{\partial Y}{\partial A} dA + \frac{\partial Y}{\partial B} dB \tag{10.17}$$

$$dY = f_A dA + f_B dB \tag{10.18}$$

Such an expression is referred to as the total differential. Let us illustrate with reference to the function we have been using:

$$Y = -5 + 30X_1 - 3X_1^2 + 25X_2 - 5X_2^2 + X_1 X_2$$

We have:

$$f_{X_1} = 30 - 6X_1 + X_2$$
$$f_{X_2} = 25 - 10X_2 + X_1$$

giving:

$$dY = (30 - 6X_1 + X_2)dX_1 + (25 - 10X_2 + X_1)dX_2 \tag{10.19}$$

Consider when $X_1 = 5$ and $X_2 = 2$. We wish to determine the effect on Y of:

- A change in X_1
- A change in X_2
- A change in *both* X_1 and X_2.

Let us examine each in turn.
Assume X_1 changes from 5 to 5.02. We then have:

$$dY = \frac{\partial Y}{\partial X_1} dX_1 = f_{X_1} dX_1 = (30 - 6X_1 + X_2)dX_1$$

where $X_1 = 5$, $X_2 = 2$ and $dX_1 = 0.02$. We then have:

$$dY = [30 - 6(5) + 2](0.02) = 0.04$$

which would be the (approximate) change in Y as X_1 changes between the two stated values. Similarly, assume X_2 changes from 2 to 2.02. We then have:

$$dY = \frac{\partial Y}{\partial X_2}dX_2 = f_{X_2}dX_2 = (25 - 10X_2 + X_1)dX_2$$

where $X_1 = 5$, $X_2 = 2$ and $dX_2 = 0.02$. We then have:

$$dY = [25 - 10(2) + 5]0.02 = 0.2$$

as the (approximate) change in Y as X_2 changes. Finally, if we wish to assess the effect of both changes in X simultaneously we have:

$$dY = (30 - 6X_1 + X_2)dX_1 + (25 - 10X_2 + X_1)dX_2$$

where

$$X_1 = 5$$
$$X_2 = 2$$
$$dX_1 = 0.02$$
$$dX_2 = 0.02$$

to give:

$$dY = [30 - 6(5) + 2](0.02) + [25 - 10(2) + 5](0.02) = 0.24$$

Partial derivatives and differentials then allow us to assess the impact on Y of changes in either of the X variables whether individually or together.

> **Student activity 10.2**
> From the original function calculate Y when $X_1 = 5$, $X_2 = 2$. Recalculate the solution when $X_1 = 5.02$, $X_2 = 2.02$. Comment on the change in Y.
>
> Obtain the total differential for the function:
>
> $$Y = 50 - 3X_1 + 6X_1^2 - 5X_2 - 10X_2^2 - 3X_1X_2$$
>
> (Solution on p. 348.)

10.5 The total derivative

So far we have considered a multivariable function where the X variables are independent of each other. In some economic models this may not be appropriate. We may have a situation, for example, where:

$$Z = f(X, Y) \tag{10.20}$$
$$Y = g(X) \tag{10.21}$$

where the X and Y variables are not independent but functionally related. In such a situation, a change in X will affect Z in two ways. It will affect Z directly (via function f) but also indirectly via function g. The total differential of such a function will be as before:

$$dZ = \frac{\partial Z}{\partial X} \, dX + \frac{\partial Z}{\partial Y} \, dY \qquad (10.22)$$

Dividing through by dX, the differential of X, we have:

$$\frac{dZ}{dX} = \frac{\partial Z}{\partial X} + \frac{\partial Z}{\partial Y} \frac{dY}{dX} = f_X + f_Y \frac{dY}{dX} \qquad (10.23)$$

where dZ/dX is known as the *total derivative* of Z with respect to X (where X is the independent variable in the function). Naturally we now need to be careful of distinguishing between the partial derivative with respect to X and the total derivative. The partial derivative indicates the direct effect of a change in X on Z while the total derivative measures both the direct and indirect (via $Y = g(X)$) effects on Z of a change in X. Consider the example:

$$Z = f(X, Y) = 4X^3 - Y^2 \qquad (10.24)$$

$$Y = g(X) = X^2 - 5 \qquad (10.25)$$

$$\frac{dZ}{dX} = f_X + f_Y \frac{dY}{dX} \qquad (10.26)$$

where

$$f_X = 12X^2$$

$$f_Y = -2Y$$

$$\frac{dY}{dX} = 2X \qquad \text{[the derivative of } (X^2 - 5)]$$

giving

$$\frac{dZ}{dX} = 12X^2 - 2Y(2X) = 12X^2 - 2(X^2 - 5)(2X)$$

$$= 12X^2 - (4X^3 - 20X)$$

where the first term, $12X^2$, represents the direct effect of a change in X on Z and the second term $(4X^3 - 20X)$ represents the indirect effects via $Y = g(X)$. The principle can be readily extended to more complex situations. Consider the function:

$$Z = f(X, Y) \qquad (10.27)$$

where

$$X = g(W) \qquad (10.28)$$

$$Y = h(W) \qquad (10.29)$$

The total derivative is then denoted as dZ/dW (since W is the independent variable in the set) giving:

$$\frac{dZ}{dW} = f_X \frac{dX}{dW} + f_Y \frac{dY}{dW} \qquad (10.30)$$

For example, consider:

$$Z = 10X^4 - 3Y^2 \tag{10.31}$$

$$X = g(W) = 12W - 10 \tag{10.32}$$

$$Y = h(W) = 2W^3 \tag{10.33}$$

Then:

$$f_X = 40X^3$$

$$f_Y = -6Y$$

$$\frac{dX}{dW} = 12$$

$$\frac{dY}{dW} = 6W^2$$

giving

$$\frac{dZ}{dW} = 40X^3(12) - 6Y(6W^2) = 480(12W - 10)^3 - 6(2W^3)(6W^2)$$

as the total derivative, showing how Z will change with respect to W.

Student activity 10.3
Find the total derivative for the function:

$$Z = 10X^{0.4}Y^{0.5}$$

where $Y = 0.8X^2$.
(Solution on p. 348.)

10.6 Implicit functions

Finally, before we turn to examine the use of all these principles in economic analysis, let us consider an implicit function. Consider a function such that:

$$Z = f(X, Y) \tag{10.34}$$

where we arbitrarily set the value of the function to some constant value, k. We then have:

$$Z = f(X, Y) = k$$

which, although not immediately obvious, implicitly defines Y as a function of X. Consider, for example, the function:

$$Z = X^2Y - 5Y \tag{10.35}$$

where we set $Z = 100$; then:

$$X^2 Y - 5Y = 100$$
$$Y(X^2 - 5) = 100$$
$$Y = g(X) = \frac{100}{X^2 - 5}$$

Using the principles of total differentiation we can obtain dY/dX for such an implicit function. Given that $Z = k$ (a constant), then dZ (the change in Z) must be zero by definition. So we have:

$$dZ = f_X dX + f_Y dY = 0 \qquad (10.36)$$

Dividing through by dX gives:

$$f_X + f_Y \frac{dY}{dX} = 0$$

and rearranging gives:

$$\frac{dY}{dX} = -\frac{f_X}{f_Y} \qquad (10.37)$$

Returning to the numerical example we have:

$$Z = X^2 Y - 5Y$$

with

$$f_X = 2XY$$
$$f_Y = X^2 - 5$$

and hence :

$$\frac{dY}{dX} = -\frac{2XY}{X^2 - 5}$$

10.7   Partial market equilibrium

To begin our examination as to how partial derivatives can be used in economic analysis we return to one of the earliest of our models—that relating to partial market equilibrium. The model is given as:

$$Q_d = Q_s \qquad (10.38)$$
$$Q_d = f(P) = a_1 + b_1 P \qquad (10.39)$$
$$Q_s = g(P) = a_2 + b_2 P \qquad (10.40)$$

with the restrictions that:

$$a_1, b_2 > 0$$
$$a_2, b_1 < 0$$

and we derived solutions for P_e and Q_e such that:

$$P_e = \frac{a_1 - a_2}{b_2 - b_1} \qquad (10.41)$$

$$Q_e = \frac{a_1 b_2 - a_2 b_1}{b_2 - b_1} \qquad (10.42)$$

We spent some time examining the effect on the solution of a change in one of the equation parameters (a_1, a_2, b_1, b_2). Let us now examine how this could be (much more easily) achieved through the application of the principles we have introduced in this chapter. Assume we wish to assess the effect of a change in a_1. Clearly this parameter is the intercept of the demand function and a change will shift the whole function upwards or downwards. Such a change would be brought about by some structural change in the *ceteris paribus* conditions surrounding the model — that is, a change in one of the factors other than price affecting the demand function (but which we have conveniently omitted from the function). If, for example, consumer income changed, then this would impact on the a_1 term. We wish to determine the effect of a change in a_1 on P_e; then we require:

$$\frac{\partial P_e}{\partial a_1} \qquad (10.43)$$

Since we can rewrite Eq. (10.41) as:

$$P_e = \frac{a_1 - a_2}{b_2 - b_1}$$
$$= a_1 \left(\frac{1}{b_2 - b_1} \right) - \frac{a_2}{b_2 - b_1} \qquad (10.44)$$

we then have:

$$\frac{\partial P_e}{\partial a_1} = \frac{1}{b_2 - b_1} \qquad (10.45)$$

If we examine this partial derivative we see that $(b_2 - b_1) > 0$, given the parameter restrictions, and hence the partial derivative itself must be positive. We conclude, therefore, that a change in the a_1 parameter will bring about a change in the same direction in P_e; that is, for example, an increase in a_1 will lead to an increase in P_e. Similarly if we examine the effect on Q_e we require $\partial Q_e / \partial a_1$. We have:

$$Q_e = \frac{a_1 b_2 - a_2 b_1}{b_2 - b_1}$$
$$= \frac{a_1 b_2}{b_2 - b_1} - \frac{a_2 b_1}{b_2 - b_1}$$

giving

$$\frac{dQ_e}{\partial a_1} = \frac{b_2}{b_2 - b_1} \qquad (10.46)$$

Again, given the parameter restrictions, this implies that a change in the a_1 parameter will bring about a change in Q_e in the same direction (i.e. an increase in a_1 will lead to an increase in Q_e). In the same way we can examine the impact of a change in the slope parameters. Consider, for example, that we wish to evaluate the effect of a change in the slope of the supply function. We now require:

$$\frac{\partial P_e}{\partial b_2} \quad \text{and} \quad \frac{\partial Q_e}{\partial b_2}$$

Using the quotient rule we have:

$$\frac{\partial P_e}{\partial b_2} = \frac{(b_2 - b_1)0 - (a_1 - a_2)1}{(b_2 - b_1)^2} = -\frac{a_1 - a_2}{(b_2 - b_1)^2} \tag{10.47}$$

which implies, given the parameter restrictions, that the partial derivative is less than zero. In other words, a change in b_2 will bring about a change in P_e of the opposite direction; an increase in the slope, for example, will lead to a decrease in P_e. Similarly for Q_e we have:

$$\frac{\partial Q_e}{\partial b_2} = \frac{(b_2 - b_1)a_1 - (a_1 b_2 - a_2 b_1)}{(b_2 - b_1)^2}$$

$$= -\frac{a_1 b_1 + a_2 b_1}{(b_2 - b_1)^2} = \frac{b_1(a_2 - a_1)}{(b_2 - b_1)^2} \tag{10.48}$$

and, once again given the parameter restrictions, we see that the partial derivative is negative, indicating an inverse relationship between a change in b_2 and Q_e.

> **Student activity 10.4**
> Repeat this analysis for the parameter a_2.
> (Solution on p. 348.)

We can readily extend these principles to a more general model. Consider the model:

$$Q_d = f(a_1, P) \tag{10.49}$$
$$Q_s = g(a_2, P) \tag{10.50}$$

where we do not specify the exact form of either of the two functions (i.e. whether they are linear, quadratic, cubic etc.). We simply indicate that both Q_d and Q_s are functions of price and a shift factor (a_1 and a_2 respectively). The only requirements that we impose are that we face the usual downward-sloping demand function and upward-sloping supply function. Clearly, for equilibrium we require:

$$f(a_1, P) = g(a_2, P) \tag{10.51}$$

Assume that we wish to determine the effect of a change in either a_1 or a_2 on equilibrium. Clearly a change in Q_d must be matched by an identical change in Q_s. Expressing this in terms of differentials, therefore, we have:

$$dQ_d = dQ_s \tag{10.52}$$

where

$$dQ_d = \frac{\partial Q_d}{\partial a_1}da_1 + \frac{\partial Q_d}{\partial P}dP = f_{a_1}da_1 + f_P dP \tag{10.53}$$

and

$$dQ_s = \frac{\partial Q_s}{\partial a_2}da_2 + \frac{\partial Q_s}{\partial P}dP = g_{a_2}da_2 + g_P dP \tag{10.54}$$

Substituting Eqs (10.53) and (10.54) into Eq. (10.52) gives:

$$f_{a_1}da_1 + f_P dP = g_{a_2}da_2 + g_P dP \tag{10.55}$$

Since we are interested in the effect of a change in one of the shift parameters on equilibrium price we can rewrite this as:

$$dP(f_P - g_P) = g_{a_2}da_2 - f_{a_1}da_1 \tag{10.56}$$

Hence:

$$dP = \frac{g_{a_2}da_2 - f_{a_1}da_1}{f_P - g_P} \tag{10.57}$$

Let us examine this in the context of some specific change. Assume, for example, that $da_1 > 0$ (that is, the demand function shifts upwards). Since we are introducing no change in the supply function we then have:

$$dP = -\frac{f_{a_1}da_1}{f_P - g_P}$$

Since $da_1 > 0$ this implies that $f_{a_1} > 0$ also (i.e. an increase in a_1 leads to an increase in Q_d, *ceteris paribus*). Further, given a downward-sloping demand function we must have $f_P < 0$ (an increase in price, *ceteris paribus*, means a lower quantity is demanded). Equally, $g_P > 0$ since we assume an upward-sloping supply function. Examining the dP expression we then see that the denominator must take a negative value while the numerator is positive. The whole expression is preceded by a negative sign implying that $dP > 0$. Therefore, we conclude that, for any downward-sloping demand curve no matter what its precise numerical form, a shift upwards in the function must lead to an increase in equilibrium price.

Student activity 10.5
Repeat this analysis for a_2.

10.8   A national income model

Let us return to the national income model we developed in Chapter 3. We had a model involving a government sector:

$$Y = C + I + G \tag{10.58}$$
$$Y_d = Y - T \tag{10.59}$$
$$T = tY \tag{10.60}$$
$$C = a + bY_d \tag{10.61}$$

and I and G are exogenous. We further restrict:

$$0 < t < 1$$
$$a > 0$$
$$0 < b < 1$$

We derived an expression for equilibrium income such that:

$$Y_e = \frac{a + I + G}{1 - b(1 - t)} \tag{10.62}$$

We may well wish to consider the impact on Y_e (and thereby on C_e and T_e) of a change in any of the parameters in the model or in the exogenous variables. Assume, for example, that we wish to assess the impact of a change in G. Taking the relevant partial derivative we have:

$$\frac{\partial Y_e}{\partial G} = \frac{1}{1 - b(1 - t)} \tag{10.63}$$

which, given the parameter restrictions, must be positive; that is, a change in G brings about a change in Y_e in the same direction. An increase in G leads to an increase in Y_e.

> ***Student activity 10.6***
> Investigate the impact of a change in I and a change in a.
> (Solution on p. 349.)

Clearly, the expression derived in Eq. (10.63) is a *multiplier*—the government expenditure multiplier in this case, showing the effect on equilibrium income of a change in G. It is evident that partial derivatives could be used to derive a whole series of such multipliers—showing the effect on Y_e of a change in any of the variables or coefficients. For example, the tax rate multiplier would be found from $\partial Y / \partial t$. From Eq. (10.62) we would have (using the quotient rule):

$$\frac{\partial Y}{\partial t} = \frac{-b(a + I + G)}{(1 - b(1 - t))^2} = \frac{-bY_e}{1 - b(1 - t)}$$

which from the model parameters must be less than zero. We can then readily assess the impact of a change in any of the model parameters in this way not just on equilibrium income but also on C and on T—for example, assessing the change in T that would occur through a change in G. You may wish to do this for the C_e and T_e expressions that we derived in Chapter 3 to gain further practice in the use of partial derivatives.

10.9   Elasticity of demand

When we first introduced calculus we saw that we could examine elasticity of demand for a simple demand function of the form $Q = f(P)$ through the expression:

$$E_d = \frac{dQ}{dP} \frac{P}{Q} \tag{10.64}$$

where dQ/dP was the derivative of the demand function. In the more general case, however, we might wish to examine a more complex demand function:

$$Q_a = f(P_a, P_b, Y) \qquad (10.65)$$

where Q_a = quantity demanded of good A
         P_a = price of good A
         P_b = price of some other good B
         Y = consumer income

It is clear that we would now wish to examine the effect of each variable on Q_d and that we will be able to derive three elasticity expressions. Assume, for example, that we had a function such that:

$$Q_d = 100 - 10P_a + 15P_b + 0.3Y \qquad (10.66)$$

and where $P_a = 5$, $P_b = 3$ and $Y = 200$.

Direct price elasticity

This will show the (proportionate) effect of a change in the price of the good itself:

$$E_{P_a} = \frac{\partial Q_d}{\partial P_a} \frac{P_a}{Q_d} \qquad (10.67)$$

This assumes that both P_b and Y are constant. If we wish to find the direct price elasticity for this numerical example we then have:

$$\frac{\partial Q_d}{\partial P_a} = -10 \qquad (10.68)$$

$$E_{P_a} = -10\frac{5}{155} = -0.32$$

At this particular price we have an inelastic demand.

Cross-price elasticity

Similarly, if we wish to find the elasticity with respect to a proportionate change in P_b we have:

$$E_{P_b} = \frac{\partial Q_d}{\partial P_b} \frac{P_b}{Q_d} \qquad (10.69)$$

assuming that now both P_a and Y are held constant. Here we can see that we are assessing the responsiveness of the demand for good A in the context of a change in the price of good B. With our numerical example we have:

$$E_{P_b} = 15\frac{3}{155} = +0.29$$

Note that since this cross-price elasticity is positive it implies that goods A and B are substitutes (at least at this level of prices). An increase in the price of good B will lead to an increase in the quantity demanded of good A, *ceteris paribus*. If this cross-price elasticity had been negative it would have indicated that the two goods were complementary. The size of the calculation again indicates a relatively inelastic situation.

Income elasticity

Finally, we can examine the income elasticity of demand—the responsiveness of demand to a change in consumer income, *ceteris paribus*. Following the same principles we have:

$$E_Y = \frac{\partial Q_d}{\partial Y} \frac{Y}{Q_d} \tag{10.70}$$

which for our example gives:

$$E_Y = 0.3 \frac{200}{155} = 0.39$$

Since the income elasticity is positive we would class good A as a normal good (demand increases with income). Had this elasticity been negative the good would be seen as inferior (an increase in income leads to a (proportionate) decrease in quantity demanded). Note also that, in all three cases, the absolute size of the elasticity can be assessed in the usual way (inelastic, perfectly elastic, highly elastic).

> **Student activity 10.7**
> Calculate and evaluate the elasticities for:
>
> $$P_a = 10, \qquad P_b = 2, \qquad Y = 100$$
>
> (Solution on p. 349.)

10.10 Production functions

We have previously examined production functions but have had to restrict our analysis to the short term so that we can assume that the supply of one of the two inputs is fixed. This was necessary to allow us to examine how output varied with the other input. Clearly, given the facility of partial derivatives this restrictive assumption is no longer necessary. Assume that we have a function:

$$Q = f(L, K)$$

where Q = production
  L = labour input
  K = capital input

Assume further that we generalize to examine a particular type of production function widely used in economic analysis, the Cobb–Douglas function. This takes the form:

$$Q = AL^\alpha K^\beta \tag{10.71}$$

where A is some positive constant and α and β are positive but less than 1. Let us first examine the two relevant marginal products: that of labour (MP_L) and of capital (MP_K). Clearly MP_L will relate to the extra production that can be obtained from an extra input of labour, but assuming the supply of capital is fixed. Similarly, MP_K will show how production changes with respect to a change in capital, assuming the labour input is fixed. We have, therefore:

$$MP_L = \frac{\partial Q}{\partial L} = \alpha A L^{\alpha-1} K^{\beta} \tag{10.72}$$

and

$$MP_K = \frac{\partial Q}{\partial K} = \beta A L^{\alpha} K^{\beta-1} \tag{10.73}$$

However, we also have from Eq. (10.72)

$$AL^{\alpha-1}K^{\beta} = (AL^{\alpha}K^{\beta})L^{-1} = \frac{Q}{L}$$

giving:

$$MP_L = \alpha \frac{Q}{L} \tag{10.74}$$

Since we can logically restrict our attention to values of Q and L which are positive and since, by assumption, $\alpha > 0$, then this implies that $MP_L > 0$. In other words, for the Cobb–Douglas production function an increase (decrease) in labour input will always lead to an increase (decrease) in production, *ceteris paribus*. We can similarly derive:

$$MP_K = \beta \frac{Q}{K} \tag{10.75}$$

and we reach the same conclusion regarding extra production arising from extra inputs of capital. However, it will be evident on reflection that we wish to examine these effects in more detail. Given that $MP_L > 0$ can we derive any conclusions about how MP_L changes as we change L (and obviously we wish to derive similar conclusions for MP_K)? Equally, however, we will wish to examine how the MP_L changes as we now allow K to change. All of this is readily achieved through our partial derivatives. Let us examine MP_L :

$$MP_L = \frac{\partial Q}{\partial L} = f_L = \alpha A L^{\alpha-1} K^{\beta} \tag{10.76}$$

We wish to examine the rate of change of this function first with respect to L and then again with respect to K. In the symbolism we have developed we require f_{LL} and f_{LK}. We then have:

$$f_{LL} = (\alpha - 1)\alpha A L^{\alpha-2} K^{\beta}$$

which from Eq. (10.74) gives

$$f_{LL} = (\alpha - 1)\alpha \frac{Q}{L^2} \tag{10.77}$$

which, since Q and $L > 0$ and since $0 < \alpha < 1$ by definition, must give $f_{LL} < 0$. In other words, while the MP_L is always positive it is also declining with increased labour input. Similarly we examine the change in MP_L as we now allow the capital input to change. We require f_{LK}. Since $f_L = \alpha A L^{\alpha-1} K^{\beta}$ then

$$f_{LK} = \alpha\beta A L^{\alpha-1} K^{\beta-1}$$
$$= \alpha\beta \frac{Q}{LK} \qquad (10.78)$$

which again, given our assumptions, must be positive; that is, MP_L will increase if we increase the input of capital. Naturally we could readily derive similar conclusions for MP_K.

> **Student activity 10.8**
> Obtain equivalent expressions for capital. Comment on f_{LK} and f_{KL}.
> (Solution on p. 349.)

Clearly, we may also wish to examine such changes not in absolute but in proportionate terms (this is analogous to elasticity of demand). In fact, this can be referred to as the elasticity of production. To determine this elasticity with respect to labour input we have:

$$E_L = \frac{\partial Q}{\partial L} \frac{L}{Q} = f_L \frac{L}{Q} = \left(\alpha \frac{Q}{L}\right) \frac{L}{Q} = \alpha \qquad (10.79)$$

that is, the elasticity of production with respect to labour is given by the α coefficient associated with that input in the production function. We could similarly show that $E_K = \beta$.

> **Student activity 10.9**
> Show that $E_K = \beta$.

Following from this we then face the question: if all inputs are changed in the same proportion what will be the proportionate change in production? Clearly, it will fall into one of three categories: the change in production could be (proportionately) larger than, smaller than or equal to the simultaneous change in inputs. Let us assume that we change both L and K by some proportion which we denote as λ. We then have:

$$A(\lambda L)^{\alpha}(\lambda K)^{\beta} \qquad (10.80)$$

which can be rewritten as:

$$\lambda^{\alpha+\beta}(AL^{\alpha}K^{\beta}) = \lambda^{\alpha+\beta}(Q) \qquad (10.81)$$

that is, a change in both inputs of λ gives rise to a change in production of $\lambda^{\alpha+\beta}$. Since, by definition, both α and β are between 0 and 1 then we face three possibilities.

Case 1 $\alpha + \beta < 1$ The proportionate change in output will be less than the proportionate change in both inputs. Clearly we would classify this as decreasing returns to scale.

Case 2 $\alpha + \beta = 1$ The proportionate change in output will be the same as the proportionate change in both inputs. This would represent constant returns to scale.

Case 3 $\alpha + \beta > 1$ The proportionate change in output will be greater than the proportionate change in both inputs. This would represent increasing returns to scale. In general such a function is said to be *homogeneous of degree n* if changing L and K by some proportion λ leads to a proportionate change in Q of λ^n.

10.11   Utility functions

Our final area of application in this chapter brings us to *utility functions*. Economic theory relating to consumer behaviour is based on the assumption that a rational consumer will seek to maximize the satisfaction they obtain from goods (and services) that they consume. Naturally, such satisfaction will be limited—or constrained—primarily by their available income and we shall be exploring the principles of such *constrained maximization* in Chapter 12. Here we can explore some of the principles behind such consumer behaviour using the principles of calculus. We can represent consumer behaviour with a utility function of the form:

$$U = u(X_1, X_2, \ldots, X_n)$$

where $X_1, X_2, \ldots, X_n$ represent the quantities of the various goods available consumed by the consumer. You may appreciate, from your studies of economics, that this approach has a major inherent problem. Unlike, say, a production function we cannot actually measure utility. While we can ask a firm what its total production was given certain inputs of labour and capital, we cannot ask a consumer how much satisfaction they derived from, say, spending their income on a holiday. However, it is still worth assuming that such measurement could be carried out since we can then explore general principles of consumer behaviour.

Let us assume a simplified case where the consumer faces a choice between two goods, X_a and X_b. The utility function will then be:

$$U = u(X_a, X_b)$$

If we apply the principles of partial differentiation to such a function we would derive

$$\frac{\partial U}{\partial X_a} \quad \text{and} \quad \frac{\partial U}{\partial X_b}$$

as the two relevant partial derivatives. In an economics context it is evident that the two partial derivatives will actually represent *marginal utility*. That is, $\partial U / \partial X_a$ will represent the marginal utility obtained by the consumer derived from marginal consumption of good a when the consumption of good b remains unchanged. Similarly, $\partial U / \partial X_b$ represents the marginal utility obtained by the consumer derived from marginal consumption of good b when the consumption of good a remains unchanged. Without proof, although the logic is fairly self-evident, we state a number of important principles relating to such utility functions:

- The law of diminishing marginal utility indicates that as consumption of one good increases then, *ceteris paribus*, the marginal utility of that good will eventually decrease.
- A consumer will maximize satisfaction associated with a utility function when each good is consumed up to the point where the marginal utility derived from one good relative to the price of the good is the same for all goods.

Consider the function:

$$U = 5A^{0.3}B^{0.2}$$

where A and B are the quantities of good A and good B that are consumed. The two marginal utilities will then be:

$$MU_A = 1.5A^{-0.7}B^{0.2}$$
$$MU_B = A^{0.3}B^{-0.8}$$

On inspection of the two partial derivatives we see that in the case of MU_A as A increases then MU_A decreases and similarly for MU_B as B increases MU_B decreases. Clearly, there will come a time when extra consumption of a good, *ceteris paribus*, leads to a decrease in the extra satisfaction derived from it. Let us further assume that the consumer has an available income of £100 and that the price of good A, P_A, is £2 and the price of good B, P_B, is £10. Can we derive the combination of the two goods that will maximize consumer satisfaction? From the second principle that was stated we have:

$$\frac{MU_A}{P_A} = \frac{MU_B}{P_B} \tag{10.82}$$

at the point where the consumer maximizes satisfaction from available income. Effectively, this implies that the last pound spent on each good produces the same extra utility as the last pound spent on any other good. Substituting the appropriate values in Eq. (10.82) gives:

$$\frac{1.5A^{-0.7}B^{0.2}}{2} = \frac{A^{0.3}B^{-0.8}}{10}$$

Rearranging this then gives:

$$15A^{-0.7}B^{0.2} = 2A^{0.3}B^{-0.8}$$

Dividing through by $B^{0.2}$ then gives:

$$15A^{-0.7} = 2A^{0.3}B^{-1}$$

while dividing through by $A^{0.3}$ gives:

$$15A^{-1} = 2B^{-1}$$

which gives:

$$15B = 2A$$

or $A = 7.5B$

From the prices of the two goods and the consumer's available income we derive a budget constraint such that:

$$Y = P_A A + P_B B \tag{10.83}$$

where Y is available consumer income. Note we assume that the consumer will spend all available income on the two available goods. If we wished to introduce the concept of saving part of income we could actually denote savings as an additional 'good' generating additional satisfaction. Equation (10.83) then becomes:

$$100 = 2A + 10B$$

and substituting $A = 7.5B$ gives:

$$100 = 15B + 10B$$

which solves as $B = 4$. Substituting back into the budget constraint we solve for A as 30. Thus, the combination of the two goods that will maximize consumer utility is $A = 30$ and $B = 4$.

In the case of a utility function involving only two goods we can also represent a utility function through the *indifference map*. If we assume some fixed value for the utility function, U_1, then all the combinations of the two goods which generate this utility can be determined and the relationship between the two goods revealed. This is illustrated in Fig. 10.3. For the indifference curve U_1 this links together all possible combinations of A and B which generate the same total utility, U_1. Thus, at point X the combination of A_1 and B_1 generates the same utility as the combination of A_2 and B_2 at point Y. Literally, given the assumption of the consumer wishing to maximize total utility, the consumer will be indifferent as to where on this particular line he or she will be.

A number of points emerge from the indifference map. The first is that we could derive a whole series of such curves each representing a different total utility, U_n. While the consumer may be indifferent as to where on any particular indifference curve he or she actually is, the consumer will have a preference for moving between curves. U_2 would be preferable to U_1 since it represents a higher level of total utility (which can be achieved only through consumption of additional units of A and/or B). Similarly, U_3 would be preferred to U_2 and so on. What will prevent the consumer moving from one curve to another higher curve will be his or her budget line. Effectively, the consumer's fixed income or the current prices of the two goods will act as a restraint.

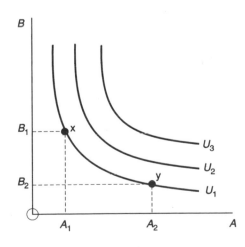

Figure 10.3 Indifference map

A second implication emerges from the shape of the curves which are downward sloping. This implies that if consumption of B decreases then to maintain the same total utility the consumption of A must increase to compensate. However, the curve is clearly non-linear, further implying that this rate of substitution of one good for another in order to maintain total utility is not constant, as we would expect given the concept of diminishing marginal utility. At point X, for example, a relatively small decrease in A must be compensated for by a relatively large increase in B. We can explain this by the fact that at point X consumption of A is relatively low, so the opportunity cost of reducing consumption of A will be relatively high. In comparison, consumption of B at this point is relatively high, so the marginal utility associated with additional consumption will be relatively low. In comparison, at point Y a small decrease in A would require only a relatively small increase in B to maintain total utility. In fact, this relationship between A and B can be referred to as the *marginal rate of substitution* (MRS). The MRS will be the slope of the indifference curve and where we have good B on the vertical axis the slope will be given by dB/dA. Hence:

$$MRS = \frac{dB}{dA}$$

Since the slope is negative it is common to represent MRS as

$$MRS = -\frac{dB}{dA}$$

to give a substitution rate which is positive (e.g. 3 units of A for 1 unit of B). However, in Section 10.6 we examined the use of implicit functions where the function was set to equal some constant value. Clearly, this is the case here with the indifference curves and from Eq. (10.37) we had:

$$\frac{dY}{dX} = \frac{-f_X}{f_Y}$$

In our case this would be:

$$MRS = \frac{-dB}{dA} = \frac{f_A}{f_B}$$

But $f_A = \partial U / \partial_A$ and $f_B = \partial U / \partial_B$, hence we have:

$$MRS = \frac{MU_A}{MU_B}$$

that is, the marginal rate of substitution is the ratio of the marginal utility of good A to the marginal utility of good B. In the context of our numerical example we have:

$$MU_A = 1.5A^{-0.7}B^{0.2}$$
$$MU_B = A^{0.3}B^{-0.8}$$

giving

$$\text{MRS} = \frac{1.5A^{-0.7}B^{0.2}}{A^{0.3}B^{-0.8}}$$

which simplifies to:

$$\text{MRS} = 1.5\frac{B}{A}$$

If, for example, $B = 10$ and $A = 20$ then $\text{MRS} = 0.75$, implying that a one unit decrease in A must be compensated for by a 0.75 unit increase in B in order to maintain total utility at its current value.

10.12   Summary

In this chapter we have extended the application of calculus to functions involving more than two variables. The principles of this are generally extensions of the principles we had already developed using more cumbersome approaches. You should ensure, however, that you have an adequate understanding of the concepts of partial derivatives, differentials and the total derivative.

Worked example

We have a national income model with both a government sector and foreign trade such that:

$$Y = C + I + G + X - M$$
$$C = 100 + 0.7Y_\text{d}$$
$$M = 0.1Y_\text{d}$$
$$Y_\text{d} = (1 - t)Y$$

with $t = 0.25$; $G = 500$; $I = 250$; $X = 200$.

The finance minister has been told that the government in this situation currently has a budget surplus and is under increasing public criticism for having such a surplus. Naively, the minister suggests that the government should increase its own spending, G, by the exact amount of the surplus so as to generate neither a budget deficit nor a budget surplus.

We have been asked to provide confirmation that such a policy of spending the exact amount of the current surplus will not lead to a balanced government budget.

Solution

First, we should confirm the current equilibrium position. For this type of model we derived equilibrium income in Sec. 3.12 with Eq. (3.49) to be:

$$Y_\text{e} = \frac{a + I + G + X}{1 - (1 - t)(b - m)}$$

Substituting the relevant numerical values, we derive:

$$Y_e = \frac{1150}{0.55} = 2090.91$$

and

$$T = tY = 522.73$$

Given that G is 500, this implies a government budget surplus of 22.73.

We know from our examination of national income models and the multiplier effect that an increase in G of 22.73 will lead to an increase in Y_e (and we can calculate this through the appropriate multiplier). However, such an increase in Y_e will by default also lead to a further increase in T (since $T = tY_e$). Hence although the increase in G will cause a (temporary) budget balance, once the economy reaches its new equilibrium income position then $T > G$ once again. Using the relevant partial derivative we would identify the G multiplier as

$$\frac{\partial Y}{\partial G} = \frac{1}{1 - (1-t)(b-m)} = \frac{1}{0.55} = 1.8182$$

So an increase in G of 22.73 would cause equilibrium income to rise by 41.33 and T to rise by 10.33 (0.25×41.33). Hence the government budget would soon move back to a surplus position. As an additional exercise you may wish to consider how you would put the economy into a balanced budget position.

Exercises

10.1 Assume a production function of the form:

$$Q = 10L^{0.75}K^{0.25}$$

(i)   Find the partial derivatives of labour and capital.
(ii) Find all the second-order partial derivatives.
(iii) Find the total differential.
(iv) For each of your answers explain the meaning of each and provide an economic interpretation.
(v) Calculate from first principles the elasticity of production with respect to labour and then to capital.

10.2 Assume a function:

$$Y = -100 + 80A - 0.1A^2 + 100B - 0.2B^2$$

where Y = profit
      A = output of product A
      B = output of product B

(i) Find the two first-order partial derivatives.
(ii) Find all the second-order partial derivatives.

(iii) Find the total differential.

(iv) Explain what each of your answers means in an economic context.

10.3 Assume a function:

$$S = f(Y, i)$$

where S = savings

Y = national income

i = rate of interest

(i) Comment on the economic logic of this function.

(ii) Find an expression for the partial derivatives with respect to Y and i.

(iii) Interpret each of these.

(iv) Find the total differential.

10.4 A production function is given as:

$$Q - f(L, K)$$

but where $L = g(t)$

$K = h(t)$

where t represents time. Find the total derivative with respect to time and interpret.

10.5 A consumer's utility function is given as:

$$U = f(A, B) = 10A + 30B - A^2 - B^2 + 5AB$$

where U represents total utility

A represents units of product A consumed

B represents units of product B consumed

(i) Comment on the economic logic of this function.

(ii) Find the first-order partial derivatives.

(iii) Find the second-order partial derivatives.

(iv) Find the total differential.

(v) Explain and comment upon each of your answers in an economic context.

10.6 Assume a demand function for product X where:

$$Q_x = 500 - 20P_x P_y + 5P_y Y$$

where P_x = price of product X

P_y = price of product Y

Y = income

(i) Find a general expression for the direct price elasticity, the cross-price elasticity and the income elasticity.

(ii) If $Y = 500$, $P_x = 10$ and $P_y = 20$, calculate each of these elasticities.

(iii) Interpret the results to (ii).

10.7 Find all the partial derivatives for each of the following functions:

(i) $Z = 4X^2 + 5Y^3$

(ii) $Z = 3X^2 + Y^4 - 4XY^2$

(iii) $Z = (X - 10Y)(4X + 2Y^2)$

(iv) $Z = (X^2 + 3XY + Y^2)^3$

(v) $Z = Y/X^2 - 2X^3 + 4Y^2X$

10.8 Return to the numerical model used in Sec. 10.11. Assume the consumer's income rises to 150. Derive the new utility-maximizing combination of the two goods.

11 Unconstrained optimization

It may be evident that so far in our examination of differential calculus as applied to multi-variable functions we have not considered the principles of optimization. When we were examining calculus principles for the simpler functions we saw that we could readily determine a maximum/minimum position for the function. Clearly, we require the same for the multivariable functions that we are now considering. In this chapter we shall introduce the relevant principles and, again, consider their use in economics. In the next chapter we shall examine a new type of optimization problem—that where we impose certain restrictions, or constraints, on the optimum that must be attained.

Learning objectives

By the end of this chapter you should be able to:

- Formulate optimization problems
- Find the solution to an unconstrained optimization problem
- Confirm whether the solution represents a maximum or minimum point
- Apply the principles of unconstrained optimization to a number of common economic models

11.1 General principles

You will recollect that for a simple function of the form:

$$Y = f(X)$$

we can find the stationary point(s) on such a function (if one exists) by taking the first derivative and setting it to zero:

$$f'(X) = 0$$

(where we referred to this as the first-order condition) and then using the second derivative to determine whether this stationary point represents a (local) maximum or a minimum value:

If $f''(X) > 0$ we have a minimum

If $f''(X) < 0$ we have a maximum

(which we referred to as a second-order condition). However, if we now have a function of the form:

$$Y = f(X_1, X_2) \tag{11.1}$$

we clearly seek the combination of X_1 and X_2 that will generate a maximum/minimum value for Y. Fortunately we can use the principles of partial derivatives in much the same way. Let us illustrate the principles by reference to the function we introduced in the previous chapter:

$$Y = -5 + 30X_1 - 3X_1^2 + 25X_2 - 5X_2^2 + X_1X_2 \tag{11.2}$$

which represents a firm's profit (Y) obtained from the production of two products (X_1 and X_2). In this context the firm seeks the combination of the two production levels that will maximize profit. Figure 11.1 shows the generalized situation that we face for the function.

We see that this function takes the shape of a dome in three-dimensional space. Point A—at the top of the dome—is clearly the point we seek. At this point Y will be at its maximum and, somehow, we need to be able to determine the values of X_1 and X_2 that will generate this maximum point. Clearly not all functions will give this type of three-dimensional picture. We may face the reverse situation—an inverted dome shape as in Fig. 11.2 where we would now be

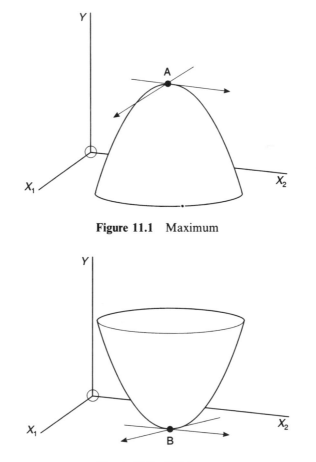

Figure 11.1   Maximum

Figure 11.2   Minimum

seeking a minimum Y value. Clearly there are two basic questions we need to resolve for multivariable functions:

1 How can we determine the relevant X_1 and X_2 values that correspond to such a point?
2 How can we establish whether such a point represents a maximum or a minimum position?

It will be instructive to consider the approach we adopted when introducing partial derivatives in the previous chapter. Assume, for example, that we fixed the value of X_2, say at 4. The relationship between Y and the other variable, X_1, could then be graphed as shown in Fig. 11.3.

It is evident that, under such an assumption, we could find the first derivative with respect to X_1 in order to find the stationary point and then use the second derivative to determine that we had obtained a maximum Y value. However, it is also evident that this optimum will relate only when $X_2 = 4$ and that, in fact, we face a whole series of such points for each possible value of X_2. Equally, of course, we would adopt the same approach with X_2. If we fixed X_1 at, say, 5, then we would face the situation shown in Fig. 11.4 and could follow the same approach as before. By combining these approaches, however, we can recognize intuitively how we can proceed. Clearly, if we hold X_2 constant to find the stationary point with respect to X_1 then this is the equivalent of finding the partial derivative with respect to X_1. With respect to X_1 we require:

$$f_{X_1} = 0$$

with 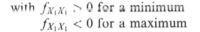 $f_{X_1 X_1} > 0$ for a minimum
$f_{X_1 X_1} < 0$ for a maximum

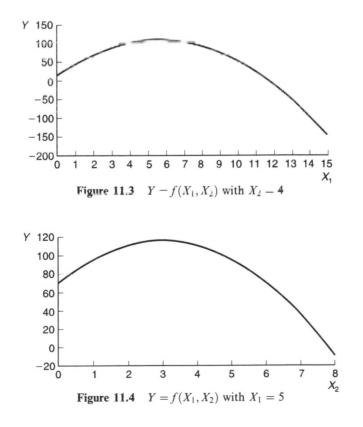

Figure 11.3 $Y - f(X_1, X_2)$ with $X_2 - 4$

Figure 11.4 $Y = f(X_1, X_2)$ with $X_1 = 5$

and with respect to X_2:

$$f_{X_2} = 0$$

with $f_{X_2 X_2} > 0$ for a minimum
$\quad f_{X_2 X_2} < 0$ for a maximum

Let us return to our numerical example to illustrate this. Obtaining the relevant partial derivatives we have:

$$f_{X_1} = 30 - 6X_1 + X_2 \qquad\qquad (11.3)$$
$$f_{X_2} = 25 - 10X_2 + X_1 \qquad\qquad (11.4)$$

Setting the two first partial derivatives to zero and solving simultaneously gives $X_1 = 5.5085$ and $X_2 = 3.050\,85$. It should be apparent why we require both partial derivatives to be zero at the same time. Clearly we cannot be at, say, a maximum if we can increase the value of Y by changing either of the variables, the other being held constant. However, how can we determine whether this point represents a maximum or a minimum position? Intuitively we might consider confirming that both second-order derivatives are negative, i.e.:

$$f_{X_1 X_1} < 0 \qquad \text{and} \qquad f_{X_2 X_2} < 0$$

However, this is in fact not sufficient by itself. We state without proof that for a maximum or minimum we also require:

$$f_{X_1 X_1} f_{X_2 X_2} > (f_{X_1 X_2})^2 \qquad\qquad (11.5)$$

(For readers who may be interested in the proof of this you are referred to one of the advanced mathematical texts that are available.) For our example we have:

$$f_{X_1 X_1} = -6$$
$$f_{X_2 X_2} = -10$$
and $\qquad\qquad\qquad f_{X_1 X_2} = 1$

(Note that $f_{X_1 X_2} = f_{X_2 X_1}$ so that the order of differentiation is irrelevant.) This gives:

$$f_{X_1 X_1} f_{X_2 X_2} > (f_{X_1 X_2})^2$$
$$(-6)(-10) > 1$$

confirming that the point we have found does represent a maximum. Therefore profit is maximized when X_1 takes a value 5.5085 and X_2 a value of 3.050 85.

> ### Student activity 11.1
> Calculate the value of Y for the given values of X_1 and X_2. Assume X_2 is fixed at 3.050 85. Calculate the new profit if $X_1 = 5.6$ and again if it is 5.5. Comment on the results. Now assume X_1 is fixed at 5.5085. Repeat the analysis for $X_2 = 3.0$ and 3.1.
> (Solution on p. 349.)

To summarize, therefore, we have the following conditions:

First-order conditions for a maximum or minimum:

$$f_{X_1} = 0$$
$$f_{X_2} = 0$$

Second-order conditions:

For a maximum:

$$f_{X_1 X_1} < 0$$
$$f_{X_2 X_2} < 0$$
$$f_{X_1 X_1} f_{X_2 X_2} > (f_{X_1 X_2})^2$$

For a minimum:

$$f_{X_1 X_1} > 0$$
$$f_{X_2 X_2} > 0$$
$$f_{X_1 X_1} f_{X_2 X_2} > (f_{X_1 X_2})^2$$

Note that the condition that $f_{X_1 X_1} f_{X_2 X_2} > (f_{X_1 X_2})^2$ is the same for both maximum and minimum points. This raises the interesting point of what happens if this last condition is not met? Suppose that we actually have:

$$f_{X_1 X_1} f_{X_2 X_2} < (f_{X_1 X_2})^2$$

On reflection it can be seen that this could occur if $f_{X_1 X_1}$ and $f_{X_2 X_2}$ were of opposite signs (i.e. one positive and one negative). This would indicate that we had a position where the function takes a maximum with respect to one variable but a minimum with respect to the other! This may be difficult to grasp but consider Fig. 11.5, which shows such a situation (known as a saddle point). We see that when viewed against X_1, Y is at a maximum but when viewed against X_2, Y takes a minimum. At point A we see that if we move along the X_1 axis the value of Y will actually increase while if we move along the X_2 axis the value of Y decreases.

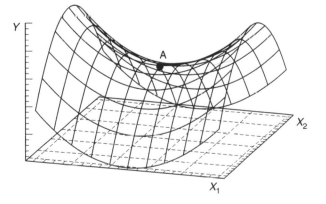

Figure 11.5 Saddle point

Student activity 11.2

For the following equations determine their optimum position and determine whether this is a maximum or a minimum:

(i) $Z = 10 - 5X + 3X^2 - 8Y + 2Y^2 - XY$
(ii) $Z = 50 + 50X - 5X^2 + 30Y - 3Y^2 - 5XY$
(iii) $Z = 2Y^2 - 3X^2 + 100$

(Solution on p. 350.)

11.2   Profit maximization

Using these principles let us examine some of the simple models we have developed thus far. Let us return to a firm producing two products and its desire to maximize profit. Assume that we have:

$$\text{TR} = P_1 X_1 + P_2 X_2 \tag{11.6}$$

$$\text{TC} = c(X_1, X_2) \tag{11.7}$$

that is while we do not specify the form of the cost function faced by the firm it is evident from the TR function that the firm operates under conditions of perfect competition (since the prices are fixed). Clearly we then have:

$$\pi = \text{TR} - \text{TC} = (P_1 X_1 + P_2 X_2) - c(X_1, X_2) \tag{11.8}$$

We require to determine the output levels that will maximize this function. Let us first digress to consider the partial derivatives of the TC function. We can obtain:

$$\frac{\partial(\text{TC})}{\partial X_1} \quad \text{and} \quad \frac{\partial(\text{TC})}{\partial X_2}$$

and it becomes apparent that these two derivatives actually refer to the two marginal costs; that is, $\partial(\text{TC})/\partial X_1$ will be the marginal cost of product 1 (assuming that the output of product 2 remains constant) while $\partial(\text{TC})/\partial X_2$ will be the marginal cost of product 2 (on the assumption that the output of product 1 is now fixed). Equally, by applying the same principles to the TR function, we have:

$$\frac{\partial(\text{TR})}{\partial X_1} = P_1 \quad \text{and} \quad \frac{\partial(\text{TR})}{\partial X_2} = P_2$$

which represent the marginal revenues of products 1 and 2 respectively. (Note that we have additional confirmation that the firm operates under perfect competition since, for both products, $P = \text{MR}$.) We now have the necessary first-order conditions for the profit function as:

$$\frac{\partial \pi}{\partial X_1} = \frac{\partial(\text{TR})}{\partial X_1} - \frac{\partial(\text{TC})}{\partial X_1} = \text{MR}_1 - \text{MC}_1 = 0 \tag{11.9}$$

$$\frac{\partial \pi}{\partial X_2} = \frac{\partial(\text{TR})}{\partial X_2} - \frac{\partial(\text{TC})}{\partial X_2} = \text{MR}_2 - \text{MC}_2 = 0 \tag{11.10}$$

that is, we require the marginal revenue of each product to be equal to its marginal cost.

Student activity 11.3
Assume the following TC function:

$$TC = 20 + 3X^2 + 2Y^2 - 0.5XY$$

where X and Y represent the output of two products. If the firm faces perfect competition with market prices of 10 for X and 5 for Y, determine the profit-maximizing combination of output.
(Solution on p. 350.)

11.3 Price discrimination

A further related example can be illustrated with regard to price discrimination. Consider a monopoly firm producing some single product. The product can then be sold in the domestic market or can be exported. Clearly, the firm will wish to determine the balance between the two markets in terms of the prices to be charged and the total profit to be maximized. Denoting output sold domestically as Q_1 and abroad as Q_2 we then have:

$$Q = Q_1 + Q_2 \tag{11.11}$$
$$TR - d(Q_1) + x(Q_2) \tag{11.12}$$

where $d(Q_1)$ represents the revenue function for the domestic market and $x(Q_2)$ that for the export market. We also have:

$$TC = c(Q) \tag{11.13}$$

The latter follows since we assume a single production plant. It also follows that the marginal cost of the product for each market must be the same. The profit function will then be:

$$\pi = TR - TC = d(Q_1) + x(Q_2) - c(Q) \tag{11.14}$$

We will then have:

$$MR_1 = \frac{\partial(TR)}{\partial Q_1} = d'(Q_1) \tag{11.15}$$

$$MR_2 = \frac{\partial(TR)}{\partial Q_2} = x'(Q_2) \tag{11.16}$$

while for marginal cost we have (through the chain rule):

$$MC_1 = \frac{\partial C}{\partial Q_1} = c'(Q)\frac{\partial Q}{\partial Q_1} = c'(Q) \qquad \text{(since } \partial Q/\partial Q_1 = 1 \text{ from Eq. 11.11)}$$

$$MC_2 = \frac{\partial C}{\partial Q_2} = c'(Q)\frac{\partial Q}{\partial Q_2} = c'(Q) \qquad \text{(since } \partial Q/\partial Q_2 = 1)$$

which indicates that $MC_1 = MC_2$. The first-order conditions will then be that:

$$\frac{\partial(\pi)}{\partial Q_1} = \frac{\partial(\pi)}{\partial Q_2} = 0$$

$$MR_1 - MC_1 = 0$$

$$MR_2 - MC_2 = 0$$

or

$$MR_1 = MR_2 = MC$$

that is, the output levels in each market must be such that the marginal revenue in each market is the same as the marginal cost of total output.

> *Student activity 11.4*
> Explain what would happen if the two marginal revenues were not the same.

We can now examine the implications for pricing policy. We know that $TR = PQ$; hence we have:

$$TR_1 = P_1Q_1 \qquad \text{and} \qquad TR_2 = P_2Q_2$$

Therefore:

$$MR_1 = \frac{\partial(TR)}{\partial Q_1} = P_1\frac{dQ_1}{dQ_1} + Q_1\frac{dP_1}{dQ_1}$$

$$= P_1\left(1 + \frac{dP_1}{dQ_1}\frac{Q_1}{P_1}\right) \tag{11.17}$$

and by the same logic we have:

$$MR_2 = P_2\left(1 + \frac{dP_2}{dQ_2}\frac{Q_2}{P_2}\right) \tag{11.18}$$

However:

$$E_{D_1} = \frac{dQ_1}{dP_1}\frac{P_1}{Q_1} \tag{11.19}$$

Hence:

$$1/E_{D_1} = \frac{dP_1}{dQ_1}\frac{Q_1}{P_1}$$

and

$$MR_1 = P_1\left(1 + \frac{1}{E_{D_1}}\right) \tag{11.20}$$

and

$$MR_2 = P_2\left(1 + \frac{1}{E_{D_2}}\right) \tag{11.21}$$

However, we know that E_D will take a negative value. Hence by inspection we see that if, for example, E_{D_1} is inelastic (taking values $< |1|$) then MR_1 must take a negative value. Similarly, if $|E_{D_1}| = 1$ then $MR_1 = 0$ while if $|E_{D_1}| > 1$ then $MR_1 > 0$. However, we also know that MC must be positive; hence $MR_1 > 0$ also. It therefore follows that the optimum level of sales in each market must be such that the corresponding elasticity of demand is greater than 1. Given that we required $MR_1 = MR_2$ then we now have:

$$P_1 \left(1 + \frac{1}{E_{D_1}}\right) = P_2 \left(1 + \frac{1}{E_{D_2}}\right) \qquad (11.22)$$

Clearly, $P_1 = P_2$ only when the elasticity of demand in each market is the same. If these elasticities differ then the firm must charge different prices in the two markets in order to maximize total profit. We can also infer that, *ceteris paribus*, the lower the elasticity in one market then the higher the price to be charged in that market, relative to the other available market. Let us examine the following simple example:

$$TC = f(Q) = 500 + 10Q$$
$$Q = X + Y$$
$$P_x = 110 - 10X$$
$$P_y = 80 - 5Y$$

We then have a profit function:

$$\pi = 100X - 10X^2 + 70Y - 5Y^2 - 500$$
where : $\qquad f_x = 100 - 20X$
and : $\qquad f_y = 70 - 10Y$

Setting both these to zero and solving gives $X = 5$ and $Y = 7$ as the profit-maximizing combination of output for the two products.

> **Student activity 11.5**
> Calculate the elasticity of demand for each product at these levels of output. Confirm that the lower elasticity product has the higher price. Explain why this should be the case. (Solution on p. 351.)

11.4 Profit maximization revisited

It will also be instructive to examine the profit-maximizing problem from a slightly different perspective. We have seen on a number of occasions that costs are related to the firm's production function. Consider the production function:

$$Q = q(L, K)$$

relating output to inputs of labour and capital. Assume that we represent the price charged per unit sold as p, and w and i represent the prices of the labour and capital inputs respectively. We then have:

$$\text{TR} = pQ \tag{11.23}$$

$$\text{TC} = wL + iK \tag{11.24}$$

and

$$\pi = \text{TR} - \text{TC} = pQ - (wL + iK) \tag{11.25}$$

which, on substituting the production function, gives:

$$\pi = pq(L, K) - (wL + iK) \tag{11.26}$$

which expresses profit purely in terms of the inputs of labour and capital. Let us assume further that w and i are fixed (perhaps because we are considering the short term or a firm under perfect competition). Clearly, we can now examine the problem as one to determine the combination of L and K that will maximize the firm's profit. We then have:

$$\frac{\partial \pi}{\partial L} = p\frac{\partial Q}{\partial L} - w \tag{11.27}$$

$$\frac{\partial \pi}{\partial K} = p\frac{\partial Q}{\partial K} - i \tag{11.28}$$

Since both are required to be zero we then have:

$$\frac{\partial Q}{\partial L} = \frac{w}{p} \quad \text{and} \quad \frac{\partial Q}{\partial K} = \frac{i}{p} \tag{11.29}$$

that is, the marginal product of labour must equal the factor input price divided by the product's selling price (what we can refer to as the real input price). We can view this ratio as the selling price expressed in terms of the production that it would buy, which must be equal to the marginal product. A similar interpretation can be given to capital.

A simple numerical example might be informative at this stage. If we assume that $p = £2$ and $w = £10$ then, under the first-order conditions, $\text{MP}_L = 5$; that is, the extra unit of labour (for which we are paying £10) must produce 5 units of extra output to be worthwhile (given that we sell this output at £2 per unit). Let us now consider the second-order conditions for a maximum:

$$\frac{\partial^2 \pi}{\partial L^2} = p\frac{\partial^2 Q}{\partial L^2} < 0 \quad (\text{i.e. } \partial^2 Q/\partial L^2 < 0) \tag{11.30}$$

$$\frac{\partial^2 \pi}{\partial K^2} = p\frac{\partial^2 Q}{\partial K^2} < 0 \quad (\text{i.e. } \partial^2 Q/\partial K^2 < 0) \tag{11.31}$$

$$\frac{\partial^2 \pi}{\partial L^2}\frac{\partial^2 \pi}{\partial K^2} > \left[\frac{\partial^2 \pi}{\partial K\, \partial L}\right]^2 \tag{11.32}$$

Let us consider these restrictions. Since the first partial derivative with respect to labour represents the marginal product, the second derivative shows the change in marginal product.

We are being told that, at profit-maximization levels of output, an extra unit of labour input will lead to a change in output smaller than that of the previous level of labour input (with the same logic applying to capital). Since the marginal product of labour must (through the first-order condition) be equal to the real wage rate, then the marginal product of this extra labour unit will be less than the real wage rate. Hence extra labour at this point will reduce profit. Clearly the second-order conditions imply that diminishing marginal products for both inputs are necessary for profit maximization. Let us consider the following numerical example. We have a production function:

$$Q = f(L, K) = 5L^{0.25}K^{0.5}$$

and a total cost function:

$$TC = 10L + 5K$$

that is, labour costs are £10 and capital costs are £5 per unit. If the product sells for £4 we then have a profit function:

$$\pi = 20L^{0.25}K^{0.5} - 10L - 5K$$

Taking the first-order derivatives we require:

$$\pi_L = 5L^{-0.75}K^{0.5} - 10 = 0 \qquad (11.33)$$
$$\pi_K = 10L^{0.25}K^{-0.5} - 5 = 0 \qquad (11.34)$$

We then require values for K and L that satisfy Eqs (11.33) and (11.34). If we rewrite these we have:

$$\frac{5K^{0.5}}{L^{0.75}} = 10$$

and

$$\frac{10L^{0.25}}{K^{0.5}} = 5$$

If we divide the first of these by the second and rearrange, we have:

$$\frac{5K^{0.5}K^{0.5}}{10L^{0.75}L^{0.25}} = \frac{10}{5}$$

giving:

$$\frac{5K}{10L} = 2$$
$$5K = 20L$$
$$K = 4L$$

We can now substitute $K = 4L$ into either of Eq. (11.33) or (11.34) and solve numerically for L and then for K. This turns out to be straightforward (if somewhat tedious) and gives $L = 1$ and

$K = 4$ as the optimal combination of inputs. You may wish to check for yourself that the relevant first- and second-order conditions set out earlier are satisfied with this solution.

11.5 Summary

We have examined how we can determine the optimal solution to some problem where there are no additional restrictions placed on the solution—an unconstrained optimization problem. We have seen that the principles involved are similar to those where we looked at two variable functions. Although we have examined only a limited number of economic applications, it should be evident that these principles are readily extended to a considerable variety of other multivariable economic models.

Worked example

An enterprising economics student was impressed by the concept of consumer utility detailed in the previous chapter. The student has derived a personal utility function such that:

$$U = 100W + 150L + 0.78WL - 2.5W^2 - 0.708L^2$$

where W refers to the hours per week the student spends in part-time paid work in order to raise income for course fees and L refers to the number of hours per week spent in 'leisure', where L is effectively non-paid work (comprising time spent on all other activities during the week). The student is keen to determine the appropriate number of hours spent in paid work each week in order to maximize utility (U). Unfortunately, the student has been too busy earning money to understand the principles of optimization and has asked for help.

Solution

We have:

$$f_W = 100 + 0.78L - 5W$$
$$f_L = 150 + 0.78W - 1.416L$$

and solving gives $W = 40$ and $L = 128$ as the optimal combination (fortunately with the number of hours worked being considerably less than those classed as 'leisure').

We can confirm that this combination generates maximum utility since:

$$f_{WW} = -5$$
$$f_{LL} = -1.416$$

and

$$f_{WL} = 0.78$$

and hence

$$f_{WW} < 0$$
$$f_{LL} < 0$$
$$f_{WW} f_{LL} > (f_{WL})^2$$

confirming a maximum utility value.

Exercises

11.1 Return to the function in Exercise 10.2 where we had:

$$Y = -100 + 80A - 0.1A^2 + 100B - 0.2B^2$$

where: y = profit
A = output of product A
B = output of product B

Determine the profit-maximizing combination of output.

11.2 Assume a utility function:

$$U = f(A, B) = 50A + 200B - 0.05A^2 - 0.25B^2$$

where U represents total utility
A represents units of product A consumed
B represents units of product B consumed

Determine the combination of the two products that will maximize total utility. Examine the change in utility that will occur if we keep one of these optimal values constant but increase the other.

11.3 Assume a production function:

$$Q = 10L^{0.5} K^{0.25}$$

With a selling price for the product of 10 and factor prices of 5 for L and 4 for K, determine the firm's profit-maximizing levels of inputs. Determine the level of output that this will produce. Determine the corresponding values for TC, TR and profit.

11.4 Return to the problem in activity 11.3. Assume the market prices now change to 12 and 7. Calculate the new solution.

11.5 Return to the problem that formed the basis for activity 11.5. Assume the cost function now changes to:

$$TC = f(Q) = 500 + 15Q$$

Calculate the new solution to the problem. Calculate the new elasticities. Explain why the solution has changed in the way that it has.

11.6 Assume a situation where:

$$P_x = 20 - 2X$$
$$P_y = 25 - 4Y$$
$$TC = 1000 + 10X + 5Y$$

Calculate the profit-maximizing combination of outputs for X and Y. Determine the relevant prices and elasticities at this combination.

12 Constrained optimization

So far all our investigations into optimization have been in terms of unconstrained problems. Simply, we have some function and we wish to find its maximum/minimum value. In economic analysis, however, we do not always face such a straightforward problem. We may well have some function that we wish to optimize but, at the same time, we face certain constraints that limit the options we have available. A firm may wish to maximize profit, for example, but face a constraint in terms of maximum production levels that can be attained with current levels of capital. A consumer may wish to maximize utility but faces a constraint imposed by a fixed budget or income. It will be apparent that this type of problem lies at the heart of most economic analysis. It implies that there are restrictions imposed on the economic decision we can make and that we must make choices between the alternatives that are available. Clearly, if we can approach such decision making rationally through the use of relevant mathematics it will make our task of deciding what to do that much easier. It is to this type of *constrained optimization* problem that we now turn.

Learning objectives

By the end of this chapter you should be able to:

- Formulate constrained optimization problems
- Use Lagrange multipliers to find the solution to a constrained optimization problem
- Interpret the meaning of a Lagrange multiplier in an economic context
- Apply Lagrange multipliers to a number of common economic models

12.1 Constrained optimization

Consider the problem:

$$\pi = -100 + 80A - 0.1A^2 + 100B - 0.2B^2 \tag{12.1}$$

which relates to the profit function for some firm and where A and B represent the levels of output of two products produced by the firm. This is the type of problem that we have examined thus far and, applying the principles we have developed, we can readily determine the profit-maximizing level of output. Taking the relevant partial derivatives we have:

$$f_A = 80 - 0.2A \tag{12.2}$$
$$f_B = 100 - 0.4B \tag{12.3}$$
$$f_{AA} = -0.2$$
$$f_{BB} = -0.4$$
$$f_{AB} = 0$$

Setting Eqs (12.2) and (12.3) to zero and solving gives $A = 400$ and $B = 250$. We see that both second derivatives are negative and we can confirm that this output combination does represent a maximum through:

$$f_{AA} f_{BB} > (f_{AB})^2$$
$$(-0.2)(-0.4) > 0$$

and we calculate that the firm attains a profit of 28 400. However, let us assume that this output combination is actually unattainable, given the current level of capital investment in the firm. Let us further assume that the firm knows its maximum combined feasible production to be 325—perhaps because of fixed labour or capital availability; that is, we face the constraint such that:

$$A + B = 325 \tag{12.4}$$

Clearly, our original solution is now unattainable. Somehow we must seek an optimum value for the profit function but still satisfy the constraint that we face. In general we could face a number of such constraints and they must all be satisfied simultaneously while we seek an optimum value for what we refer to as the objective function. It will be instructive to consider the graphical representation of the problem that we face. Figure 12.1 shows a series of objective function lines for different levels of profit. Each line indicates, for a given and fixed level of profit, the different combinations of output that will achieve this profit. For example, a profit of £20 000 can be achieved with a combination of (approximately) $A = 250$, $B = 75$ or $A = 150$, $B = 150$ or $A = 110$, $B = 250$ or indeed any of the specific combinations that occur on this line. Similarly any of the combinations falling on the second line will generate a profit of £22 500. Such a series of lines are generally referred to as *iso* lines (here we would refer to iso-profit lines)

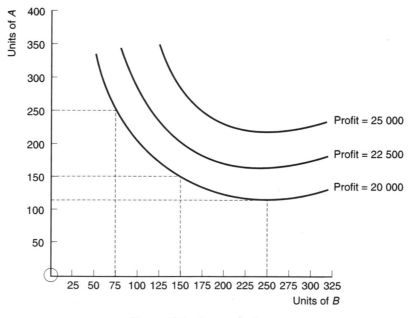

Figure 12.1 Iso-profit lines

and each represents a constant and fixed value for the objective function. It is evident on inspection that the further the line moves outward and away from the origin, the higher the profit it represents. Turning to Fig. 12.2, this shows the same iso-profit lines together with the line representing the constraint (Eq. (12.4)). This line shows the various combinations of the two outputs that match the constraint specification. Any point on this line represents a combined output of 325. On examining Fig. 12.2 the general principles of what we are seeking to achieve become evident. In terms of the objective function we require the highest possible iso-profit line (since we seek to maximize profit, the objective function). However, it is also evident that, given the constraint, we must remain on the constraint line. Given the shape of the iso-profit lines it is also evident that we seek the point illustrated in Fig. 12.3. We seek to attain the highest possible

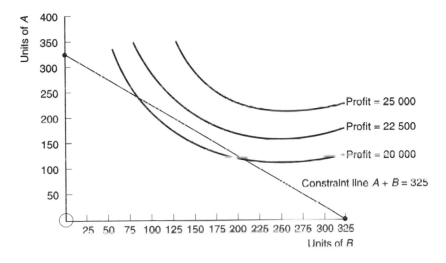

Figure 12.2 Iso-profit lines and constraint lines

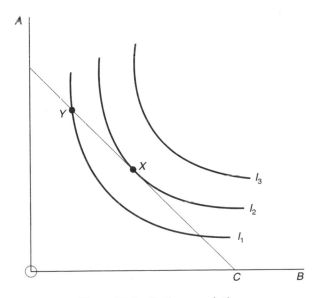

Figure 12.3 Optimum solution

iso line (and here we have $I_1 < I_2 < I_3$) but must also remain on the constraint line (line C). It is evident that all our solutions must occur on the constraint line. Point Y represents one possible solution since it falls on the line, as does point X. It will be evident that the highest iso line attainable will be that which is tangential to the constraint line, as at point X, which will, therefore, represent the optimum solution to the constrained problem. It is also worth recollecting that the objective function is actually three-dimensional (in our example; in general it would be n-dimensional). We would therefore require the gradient of the relevant surface with respect to A to be the same as that of the constraint line and the gradient with respect to B to be the same also. The issue remains unresolved, however, as to how we can find such a position (other than the usual cumbersome and tedious graphical approach).

12.2 Lagrange multipliers

The method we introduce utilizes what are known as *Lagrange multipliers* and offers considerable benefits to economic analysis. It is clear from Fig. 12.3 that at the point we are seeking the gradient of the relevant iso line will be equal to the gradient of the constraint line. Clearly, differential calculus is potentially a solution method that we can consider. We shall introduce the method of Lagrange multipliers through the numerical example we are currently examining and then we shall attempt to understand its justification. Let us denote the objective function as:

$$Z = -100 + 80X - 0.1X^2 + 100Y - 0.2Y^2 \tag{12.5}$$

with our constraint:

$$X + Y = 325 \tag{12.6}$$

The constraint is easily transformed into an implicit function:

$$X + Y - 325 = 0 \tag{12.7}$$

and we can create a new function—known as a Lagrange function—such that:

$$F = (-100 + 80X - 0.1X^2 + 100Y - 0.2Y^2) - \lambda(X + Y - 325) \tag{12.8}$$

where λ (pronounced 'lamb-da') is a new variable known as a Lagrange multiplier. The Lagrange multiplier method now proceeds as follows. We seek to establish the values of X, Y and λ that will maximize/minimize the Lagrange function. If we do this then the X and Y values we thereby determine will also prove to be the values that maximize/minimize the original function, Z, subject to the constraint imposed. A formal mathematical proof of this is beyond our current capabilities but we can consider the logic of the method. In solving for F we seek values for X and Y that satisfy the imposed constraint (Eq. (12.7)). However, from Eq. (12.7) such values for X and Y will cause the Lagrange function to become:

$$F = (-100 + 80X - 0.1X^2 + 100Y - 0.2Y^2) - \lambda(0) = Z \tag{12.9}$$

that is, the value taken by the Lagrange function will be the same value as taken by the original objective function, Z. But if F and Z are identical then the values of X and Y that maximize/

minimize F must simultaneously maximize/minimize Z. Therefore, maximizing/minimizing F must be the same as maximizing/minimizing Z subject to the imposed constraint since it is only when this imposed constraint is satisfied that we find a value for F in the first place. However, we can now use the standard approach to finding the optimum value for Eq. (12.8). We require the relevant partial derivatives:

$$F_X = 80 - 0.2X - \lambda \tag{12.10}$$

$$F_Y = 100 - 0.4Y - \lambda \tag{12.11}$$

$$F_\lambda - (X \mid Y \quad 325) \tag{12.12}$$

and we require all three partial derivatives to be zero simultaneously. Solving this as a straightforward set of simultaneous equations gives:

$$X = 183.3$$
$$Y = 141.7$$
$$\lambda = 43.3$$
and
$$F = 21\,358.3$$

which, through our logic earlier, must also be the value for Z, that is, $Z = F = 21\,358.3$. We also confirm that these values for X and Y satisfy the constraint equation. (Note that the solution with the constraint imposed generates a smaller profit than the unconstrained problem for which we found the solution originally.) The Lagrange multiplier method, therefore, can be used to determine the solution to a constrained optimization problem. However, it may have been noticed that we have not established a method for determining whether this solution represents a maximum or a minimum position. Once again, we have to state that the proof of how we can derive the relevant second-order conditions is beyond our present scope. All that we can do is to state that, for the typical type of economic problems we are considering, the method generates a maximum point for a maximization problem and a minimum point for a minimization problem. There are rigorous methods available for determining the type of optimal point but the mathematics is beyond our present capabilities (and indeed interests).

> *Student activity 12.1*
> Assume that the constraint equation changes to:
>
> $$X + Y = 400$$
>
> Find the new solution.
> (Solution on p. 351.)

12.3   Interpretation of the Lagrange multiplier

It will be instructive at this stage to examine the interpretation of the Lagrange multiplier itself, as this goes some way to illustrating why it is productive to get to grips with Lagrange functions in the first place. For the numerical example we have been considering we derived a value for λ of 43.3.

Student activity 12.2
Assume the constraint equation alters to:

$$X + Y = 326$$

How would this affect the relevant graph? Find the new solution and the extra profit that has been attained.

Finding the new solution as before (in fact only F_λ alters) we have:

$$X = 184$$
$$Y = 142$$
$$\text{Profit} = 21\,401.6$$

and we determine that the increase in profit brought about by increasing the constraint restriction by 1 unit has been 43.3—exactly the same as the value for λ that we derived in the original formulation. Clearly, this is not simply coincidence. In fact if we denote the constraining equation in general as:

$$c(X, Y) = k$$

where k is some constant value (such as 325 or 326) then:

$$\lambda = \frac{\partial Z}{\partial k} \tag{12.13}$$

that is, λ, the Lagrange multiplier, shows the change that occurs in the optimal Z value given some (marginal) change in the constraint constant, k. The potential importance of this use of λ is self-evident. In the context of our example, λ indicates the opportunity cost of this constraint. We are being told that if we could reduce the constraint restriction (i.e. increase k) then production and hence profit will increase as a result. Clearly, to the economic decision maker such information on opportunity costs is of considerable benefit. If we can increase production capacity to 326 at an extra cost of less than 43.3 then it will be beneficial to do so, given the resulting increase in profit. In the context of this problem, we might consider acquiring extra supplies of labour or capital to increase productive capacity. These extra resources have an opportunity cost of 43.3. You will no doubt be aware of the economic importance of such opportunity cost information.

To see how we arrive at Eq. (12.13) let us generalize the problem we hve examined so that we require:

$$\text{Maximize } Z = f(X, Y)$$
$$\text{subject to : } c(X, Y) = k$$

We then have a Lagrange function, F:

$$F = f(X, Y) - \lambda[c(X, Y) - k]$$

The two partial derivatives of F with respect to X and Y will then be:

$$\frac{\partial F}{\partial X} = \frac{\partial f}{\partial x} - \frac{\lambda \partial c}{\partial X}$$

and

$$\frac{\partial F}{\partial Y} = \frac{\partial f}{\partial Y} - \frac{\lambda \partial c}{\partial Y}$$

and the optimal values for X and Y will occur when the two partial derivatives are zero, hence:

$$\frac{\partial F}{\partial X} = \frac{\partial F}{\partial Y}$$

But this can be rewritten as:

$$\frac{\partial f}{\partial X} - \frac{\lambda \partial c}{\partial X} = \frac{\partial f}{\partial Y} - \frac{\lambda \partial c}{\partial Y}$$

and rearranging then gives:

$$\frac{\partial f / \partial X}{\partial c / \partial X} - \lambda = \frac{\partial f / \partial Y}{\partial c / \partial Y} - \lambda$$

and with the two λs cancelling we then have:

$$\frac{\partial f / \partial X}{\partial c / \partial X} = \frac{\partial f / \partial Y}{\partial c / \partial Y}$$

We shall use this result shortly. We require dZ/dk where dZ and dk are total differentials. Taking the total differential of $Z = f(X, Y)$ we then have:

$$dZ = \frac{\partial f}{\partial X} \, dX + \frac{\partial f}{\partial Y} \, dY$$

and taking the total differential of $c(X, Y) = k$ we have:

$$dk = \frac{\partial c}{\partial X} \, dX + \frac{\partial c}{\partial Y} \, dY$$

However, let us multiply dk through by the expression derived earlier $(\partial f / \partial X)/(\partial c / \partial X)$:

$$\frac{\partial f / \partial X}{\partial c / \partial X} \, dk = \frac{\partial f / \partial X}{\partial c / \partial X} \frac{\partial c}{\partial X} \, dX + \frac{\partial f / \partial Y}{\partial c / \partial Y} \frac{\partial c}{\partial Y} \, dY$$

This simplifies to:

$$\frac{\partial f/\partial X}{\partial c/\partial X}\,\mathrm{d}k = \frac{\partial f}{\partial X}\,\mathrm{d}X + \frac{\partial f}{\partial Y}\,\mathrm{d}Y$$

But the RHS of this expression is identical to that we had for $\mathrm{d}Z$, hence:

$$\frac{\partial f/\partial X}{\partial c/\partial X}\,\mathrm{d}k = \mathrm{d}Z$$

But from the earlier partial derivatives we had:

$$\frac{\partial F}{\partial X} = \frac{\partial f}{\partial X} - \frac{\lambda \partial c}{\partial X} = 0$$

and hence:

$$\lambda = \frac{\partial f/\partial X}{\partial c/\partial X}$$

Hence:

$$\frac{\partial f/\partial X}{\partial c/\partial X}\,\mathrm{d}k = \mathrm{d}Z$$

which can be written as:

$$\lambda \mathrm{d}k = \mathrm{d}Z$$

and therefore

$$\frac{\mathrm{d}Z}{\mathrm{d}k} = \lambda$$

proving Eq. (12.13), that λ, the Lagrange multiplier, is the change in the optimal Z value given a marginal change in the constraint value, k.

It should be noted that our investigation of Lagrange multipliers only scratches the surface of their applications. We have only examined the application of a single constraint and might wish to extend the problem to involve several constraints. Equally, the constraints have taken the form of strict equations ($=$), while we may wish to impose minimum/maximum conditions on the constraints through the use of inequality signs ($<$, $>$). Such considerations are beyond our examination of the topic, although they do involve relatively little new material to allow their inclusion. As with other topics, you are directed to one of the more advanced texts if you wish to pursue this further. Let us now turn to examine some of the economic applications of these principles. It is worth noting that we shall be considering only two key applications: the first relating to the theory of the firm and the second to consumer behaviour. The extent to which constrained optimization can be applied to economic analysis is particularly large and reading around the topic is to be strongly encouraged.

12.4 Output maximization subject to a cost constraint

Consider a firm facing a production function:

$$Q = q(L, K) \qquad (12.14)$$

and a cost function:

$$TC = wL + rK \qquad (12.15)$$

We may establish a cost constraint of the form:

$$TC = c$$

where c is some specified value, perhaps through a limit on the firm's maximum cost expenditure, and our problem then becomes one of choosing the levels of factor inputs that will maximize output subject to the cost constraint imposed; that is:

$$\text{Maximize } Q = q(K, L)$$
$$\text{subject to } . \ wL + rK = c \qquad (12.16)$$

Diagrammatically we face a situation as in Fig. 12.4. C represents the cost constraint while we face a series of iso lines with each representing a given value for Q. The point we seek is Y, where the level of factor inputs occurs both on the cost constraint line and the production function. It is worth noting that the slope of the production function can be expressed by implicitly differentiating Eq. (12.14) as:

$$\frac{\partial L}{\partial K} = -\frac{\partial q/\partial K}{\partial q/\partial L} \qquad (12.17)$$

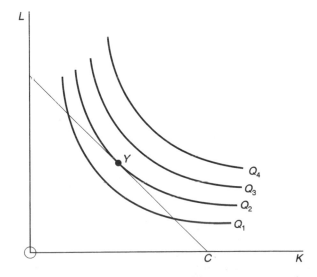

Figure 12.4 Optimizing output subject to cost constraint

which represents the marginal rate of technical substitution between the two factor inputs; that is, it measures the rate at which we can substitute one input for another and leave output unchanged. The Lagrange function is:

$$F = q(L, K) - \lambda(wL + rK - c) \tag{12.18}$$

and the relevant partial derivatives:

$$F_L = \frac{\partial q}{\partial L} - \lambda w = 0 \tag{12.19}$$

$$F_K = \frac{\partial q}{\partial K} - \lambda r = 0 \tag{12.20}$$

$$F_\lambda = -wL - rK + c = 0 \tag{12.21}$$

Multiplying Eq. (12.19) by r and Eq. (12.20) by w and subtracting the two results gives:

$$\left(r\frac{\partial q}{\partial L} - \lambda wr \right) - \left(w\frac{\partial q}{\partial K} - \lambda wr \right) = 0$$

giving

$$r\frac{\partial q}{\partial L} - w\frac{\partial q}{\partial K} = 0$$

and rearranging gives:

$$\frac{\partial q/\partial K}{\partial q/\partial L} = \frac{r}{w} \tag{12.22}$$

Since this is an optimality condition it implies that we must choose values for L and K so that the ratio of their two marginal products is equal to the ratio of their prices. Let us now consider the optimal value for λ. Directly from Eqs (12.19) and (12.20) we see that we require:

$$\lambda = \frac{\partial q/\partial L}{w}$$

$$\lambda = \frac{\partial q/\partial K}{r}$$

and hence:

$$\lambda = \frac{\partial q/\partial L}{w} = \frac{\partial q/\partial K}{r} \tag{12.23}$$

Recollect that λ represents the change in output (the objective function) that will arise from a unit change in the factor inputs. We conclude that, from the optimal position, the change in output will be the same regardless of whether we change L or K (although of course we may require different quantities of L and K to generate this extra output). These conclusions are hardly those we could have obtained without the use of the calculus techniques we have developed.

12.5 Cost minimization subject to an output constraint

Let us now examine the situation from a different perspective. Assume we now require:

$$\text{Minimize } C = wL + rK \tag{12.24}$$
$$\text{subject to: } q(L, K) = Q_0 \tag{12.25}$$

where we now wish to minimize total costs while satisfying some imposed level of production, Q_0. Figure 12.5 shows diagrammatically the situation we now face.

We now have the constraint represented by Q and are seeking the optimum C. The Lagrange function is now:

$$F = (wL + rK) - \lambda[q(L, K) - Q_0] \tag{12.26}$$

and the relevant partial derivatives:

$$F_L = w - \lambda \frac{\partial q}{\partial L} = 0 \tag{12.27}$$

$$F_K = r - \lambda \frac{\partial q}{\partial K} = 0 \tag{12.28}$$

$$F_\lambda = q(L, K) + Q_0 = 0 \tag{12.29}$$

> *Student activity 12.3*
> Using the same principles as before obtain an expression from Eqs (12.27) and (12.28) showing the optimal requirement. Obtain a comparable expression for λ.

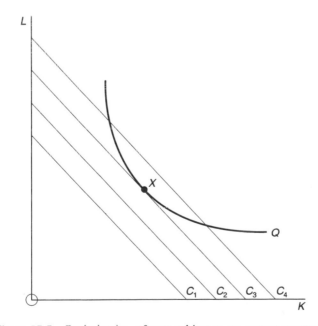

Figure 12.5 Optimization of cost subject to an output constraint

We can derive an expression such that:

$$\frac{\partial q / \partial K}{\partial q / \partial L} = \frac{r}{w} \qquad (12.30)$$

which is identical to Eq. (12.22) that we derived from the output-maximization model. Equally, the value of the Lagrange multiplier in this cost-minimization model is seen to be:

$$\lambda = \frac{r}{\partial q / \partial K} = \frac{w}{\partial q / \partial L} \qquad (12.31)$$

which indicates that, at the optimal solution, the change in costs results from a unit change in Q_0; that is, λ represents marginal costs and we see that, from the cost-minimizing position, the marginal cost will be the same no matter whether we obtain extra output from employing more labour or from more capital. It is evident that our two models are effectively mirror images of each other, and it is instructive to merge Figs 12.4 and 12.5 to examine the complete picture that we face.

Figure 12.6 shows both a series of iso-costs and iso-quants and it is evident that if the firm is able to vary both its production *and* its total costs (as opposed to one of these being a fixed constraint) then we have a series of tangent points, marked as $X_1, \ldots, X_5$ in Fig. 12.6, which we can refer to as an expansion path, as it indicates a path through all the cost/production combinations. The firm seeking to maximize production/minimize costs will select a labour/capital combination that lies on this path.

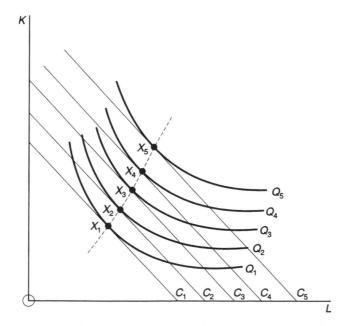

Figure 12.6   Iso-quants and iso-costs

12.6   Maximizing consumer utility subject to a budget constraint

Finally, we turn to examine an aspect of consumer behaviour: utility. Consider a consumer who faces a function such that:

$$U = u(X, Y) \tag{12.32}$$

where X and Y represent the quantities of products X and Y consumed and U the total utility derived from such consumption. The graph of these iso curves would take the usual form with the curves more generally referred to as *indifference curves* in this context. Given that on any one curve the consumer attains a constant level of utility he or she will literally be indifferent as to where on this curve he or she will be. The slope of such an indifference curve will be given by:

$$\frac{\partial X}{\partial Y} = -\frac{\partial U/\partial Y}{\partial U/\partial X} \tag{12.33}$$

which we can refer to as the marginal rate of substitution of one good for the other. What will matter to the consumer will be the total utility obtained that we will seek to maximize. Clearly, the typical consumer does not face unlimited consumption of either good but rather will be constrained by the available income or budget. We thus have a problem where:

Maximize: $U = u(X, Y)$
subject to: $P_x X + P_y Y = B$ \hfill (12.34)

where P represents the price for each good and B the consumer's available budget. The Lagrange function is then:

$$F - u(X, Y) - \lambda(P_x X + P_y Y - B) \tag{12.35}$$

and

$$F_X = \frac{\partial u}{\partial X} - \lambda P_x = 0 \tag{12.36}$$

$$F_Y = \frac{\partial u}{\partial Y} - \lambda P_y = 0 \tag{12.37}$$

$$F_\lambda = -P_x X - P_y Y + B \tag{12.38}$$

Eliminating λ from Eqs (12.36) and (12.37) and rearranging gives an optimality condition:

$$\frac{\partial u/\partial X}{\partial u/\partial Y} = \frac{P_x}{P_y} \tag{12.39}$$

which indicates that, to maximize utility, the consumer should ensure that the ratio of the marginal rate of substitution of one good for the other is the same as the ratio of their prices.
    Equation (12.39) can be rearranged into:

$$\frac{\partial u/\partial X}{P_X} = \frac{\partial u/\partial Y}{P_Y}$$

indicating that when utility is maximized given a budget constraint then the ratio of marginal utility to price is the same for all goods consumed. This further implies that if the price of a good altered then so would the optimal solution, *ceteris paribus*, since this equality requirement would no longer hold. Equally, we can derive an expression for λ such that:

$$\lambda = \frac{\partial u/\partial X}{P_x} = \frac{\partial u/\partial Y}{P_y} \tag{12.40}$$

As before, the Lagrange multiplier indicates, at the optimum position, the change in utility that will occur with a unit change in the constraint limitation. Here λ will show the change in utility as income changes; hence we can refer to λ as the marginal utility of income.

12.7 Summary

In this chapter we have been able to extend our analysis of optimization by considering constrained problems. We have seen how these can be solved through the use of the Lagrange multiplier and we have also seen that the multiplier has a particularly important meaning in the context of economics. The approach can readily be extended to include more than two variables and, indeed, more than one constraint (inwhich case we would have a separate Lagrange multiplier for each constraint). The calculation of such problems, however, quickly becomes tedious for manual solution. The exercises that follow will allow you to gain further practice in constrained optimization. You may wish to return to the unconstrained problems we have examined in earlier chapters and impose a sensible constraint on these to apply the Lagrange multiplier approach.

Worked example

A firm produces two goods, 1 and 2, each of which faces a demand function:

$$P_1 = 100 - 2Q_1 + Q_2$$
$$P_2 = 75 + 2Q_1 - Q_2$$

where Q denotes the quantity of each good and P its price. The firm's total costs are given by:

$$\text{TC} = 1000 + 20Q_1 + 10Q_2 + 2Q_1Q_2$$

The firm wishes to determine profit-maximizing levels of production of the two goods but knows that its maximum combined production with its existing labour supply is 50.

Solution

We first need to derive a profit function:

$$\pi = \text{TR}_1 + \text{TR}_2 - \text{TC}$$
$$\text{TR}_1 = 100Q_1 - 2Q_1^2 + Q_1Q_2$$
$$\text{TR}_2 = 75Q_2 + 2Q_1Q_2 - Q_2^2$$

giving

$$\pi = -1000 + 80Q_1 - 2Q_1^2 + Q_1Q_2 + 65Q_2 - Q_2^2$$

and we then have:

Maximize $\pi = -1000 + 80Q_1 - 2Q_1^2 + Q_1Q_2 + 65Q_2 - Q_2^2$
subject to: $Q_1 + Q_2 = 50$

The Lagrangian function is then:

$$Z = -1000 + 80Q_1 - 2Q_1^2 + Q_1Q_2 + 65Q_2 - Q_2^2 - \lambda(Q_1 + Q_2 - 50)$$

We then have:

$$F_{Q1} = 80 - 4Q_1 + Q_2 - \lambda = 0$$
$$F_{Q2} = Q_1 + 65 - 2Q_2 - \lambda = 0$$
$$F_\lambda = -Q_1 - Q_2 + 50 = 0$$

Setting $Q_1 = 50 - Q_2$ and substituting into F_{Q1} and F_{Q2} we derive:

$$Q_1 = 20.625$$
$$Q_2 = 29.375$$
$$\lambda = 26.875$$

as the optimal values.

We can go one stage further, however. We are told that the production constraint arises because of a fixed supply of labour. The value of the Lagrange multiplier, 26.875, implies that profit will increase by this amount if we can improve the production constraint (i.e. to 51 or above). The value of the multiplier provides a maximum cost the firm should be willing to incur in order to allow the production to increase by an extra unit.

Exercises

In addition to the exercises detailed below you should return to any of the previous optimization problems we have examined. Impose a (sensible) constraint of your own and see what effect this has on the optimal solution.

12.1 Explain in terms of economics the logic of Eq. (12.40).

12.2 Assume a profit function:

$$\pi = -100 + 80A - 0.1A^2 + 100B - 0.2B^2$$

relating to the output of two products. If total production is limited to 500 find the solution that will maximize profit. Interpret the Lagrange multiplier obtained.

12.3 Assume a utility function:

$$U = 50A + 200B - 0.05A^2 - 0.25B^2$$

If the price of good A is £10 per unit and that of B is £5 then determine the optimal combination of the two goods if the consumer has an income of:

(i) £5000
(ii) £6000
(iii) £7000
(iv) How do you explain the change in the combination as income rises?

12.4 Assume a utility function:

$$U = 4X^{0.5}Y^{0.25}$$

If the price of X is £2.50 and that of Y is £4, calculate the optimal combination for an income of £50. What interpretation can be given to the Lagrange multiplier?

12.5 Return to the production function used in Exercise 11.3. Assume that the firm has a fixed budget for its labour and capital costs. For each of the budgets shown below calculate the optimal level of inputs. Interpret the value of the Lagrange multiplier in each case.

(i) £38 000
(ii) £40 000
(iii) £45 000

12.6 Assume that the firm now wishes to minimize costs subject to an output constraint of 8000 units. Determine the optimal solution and interpret the Lagrange multiplier.

13 Integration

We now turn our attention away from differential calculus towards another branch: that concerned with integral calculus. Integration of a function can be seen, as we will shortly discover, as the reverse of the differentiation process. However, the use of integral calculus opens up areas of economic analysis that until now have been closed.

Learning objectives

By the end of this chapter you should be able to:

- Use notation appropriate for integral calculus
- Use common rules of integrating
- Calculate definite integrals
- Calculate the area under a curve using integral calculus
- Apply integral calculus to common economic models

13.1 Notation and terminology

Assume we have a marginal cost function:

$$MC = 25 - 0.08Q \tag{13.1}$$

and that we require to obtain the corresponding total cost function. Based on our knowledge of differential calculus we know that:

$$TC = f(Q)$$
$$MC = f'(Q)$$

that is, that the derivative of the TC function is MC. It seems logical that as we now know MC we ought to be able to 'rediscover' the TC function from which it was obtained. Integration is primarily concerned with this type of task and we state that we wish to integrate the MC function. From our knowledge of differential calculus we know that:

$$f'(25Q) = 25$$
$$f'(-0.04Q^2) = -0.08Q$$

and hence we can infer that if MC $= 25 - 0.08Q$ then:

$$TC = 25Q - 0.04Q^2 \tag{13.2}$$

However, from both our knowledge of calculus and our understanding of the TC function in economics it is evident that Eq. (13.2) may well be incomplete. There is no value for the fixed cost element in the TC function and we realize that the derivative of such a constant term would be zero and hence there is no clue in the MC function as to what this constant value might have been. In other words, we have to specify the function as:

$$TC = 25Q - 0.04Q^2 + c \tag{13.3}$$

where c refers to an unknown constant, the value of which we can only obtain with additional information that may have been provided. The notation that we adopt to indicate this process of integration is:

$$TC = \int (25 - 0.08Q)\mathrm{d}Q = 25Q - 0.04Q^2 + c \tag{13.4}$$

or in general:

$$Y = \int f'(X)\mathrm{d}X = f(X) \tag{13.5}$$

The symbol $\int$ is known as an integral sign, $f(X)$ is known as the integrand and the $\mathrm{d}X$ symbol indicates that the integral operation is being undertaken with respect to the X variable (which may not be the only variable in more complex equations). While the process of integration is frequently a trial-and-error activity, there are a number of useful rules that we might be able to apply depending on the type of problem faced.

13.2 Rules of integration

Many of the rules can be obtained simply by reversing the process of differentiation. These are stated briefly below, with a short explanation where necessary. It is recommended that you complete the student activity immediately following before proceeding with the rest of the material in this chapter. It is also useful to get into the habit of checking your solution by differentiating your answer (which should, of course, give you the original expression).

The power rule

If $Y = f(X)$ and $f'(X) = aX^b$, then

$$\int aX^b \mathrm{d}X = \frac{a}{b+1} X^{b+1} + c \tag{13.6}$$

For example, if $f'(X) = 2X^3$, then:

$$\int 2X^3 \mathrm{d}X = \frac{2}{3+1} X^{3+1} + c = 0.5X^4 + c$$

The log rule

If $f'(X) = 1/x$, then:

$$\int \frac{1}{X} dX = \ln X + c \qquad \text{for} X > 0 \tag{13.7}$$

Integral of a constant times a function

If the function we wish to integrate is made up of some constant, k, and some function of X such as $kf(X)$, then:

$$\int kf(X) dX = k \int f(X) dX \tag{13.8}$$

where k is some constant.

Integral of a sum or difference

If the function we wish to integrate is made up of two separable functions of X: $f(X) \pm g(X)$, then:

$$\int [f(X) \pm g(X)] dX = \int f(X) dX \pm g(X) dX$$
$$= \int f(X) dX \pm \int g(X) dX \tag{13.9}$$

The substitution rule

Consider the function:

$$f(X) = 12X^2(X^3 - 10)^5 \tag{13.10}$$

for which we seek the integral. The rules we have developed thus far are not readily applicable to such a complex function. However, under certain conditions, we can apply the substitution rule. Let:

$$u = X^3 - 10$$

Then $du/dX = 3X^2$ and therefore $dX = du/3X^2$. We require $\int 12X^2(X^3 - 10)^5 dX$ or, in general, $\int f(X) dX$. The rule is that:

$$\int f(X) dX = \int \left(u \frac{du}{dX} \right) dX \tag{13.11}$$

We require $\int 12X^2(X^3 - 10)^5 dX$, but substituting for u and dX we have:

$$\int 12X^2 u^5 \frac{du}{3X^2}$$

which simplifies to:

$$\int \frac{12X^2}{3X^2} u^5 du = \int 4u^5 du = 4\int u^5 du$$

However:

$$4\int u^5 du = 4(\tfrac{1}{6}u^6) + c$$
$$= \tfrac{2}{3}(X^3 - 10)^6 + c$$

which is therefore the integral of the original function. It is important to realize that this rule can only be applied if we can express the required integral in the form of Eq. (13.11). For example, if we required:

$$\int 12X^2(X^4 - 10)dX$$

the rule cannot be applied as $du/dX = 4X^3$ is not a multiple of $12X^2$, which must be the case for the rule to be applicable.

> **Student activity 13.1**
> Find the integrals for the following functions. Confirm your solution by differentiating your solution to confirm that the original function expression is obtained.
>
> (i) X^6
> (ii) $X^{-0.3}$
> (iii) $X^3 - X^2$
> (iv) $5X^4$
> (v) $1/X$
> (vi) $9X^2(X^3 + 10)^3$
>
> (Solution on p. 351.)

13.3 Definite integrals

If this were the only aspect to integral calculus then you would probably be justified in the view that it was not really worth the effort. However, the type of integrals we have examined thus far are known as indefinite integrals. We now turn our attention to the definite integral. Consider the integral:

$$\int (10X + 5)dX = 5X^2 + 5X + c = f(X)$$

This is simply another example of the indefinite integral that we have examined. However, suppose we had instead:

$$\int_3^4 (10X + 5)dX \tag{13.12}$$

What does this type of integral represent? In fact this is an example of a *definite* integral and is used to represent a situation where we require the value of the integral expression between the stated numerical limits—here between 4 and 3. That is, we require to evaluate the integral for $X = 4$ and again for $X = 3$. The definite integral is then the result of the difference between these two values; that is, we require:

$$f(X = 4) - f(X = 3)$$

Naturally in this simple example this is easily obtained. We have:

$$f(X) = 5X^2 + 5X + c$$
$$f(X = 4) = 5(4)^2 + 5(4) + c = 80 + 20 + c = 100 + c$$
$$f(X = 3) = 5(3)^2 + 5(3) + c = 45 + 15 + c = 60 + c$$
$$\int_3^4 (10X + 5)dX = (100 + c) - (60 + c) = 40$$

that is, the value of the integral between the stated limits is 40. Note that the c term in the integral is cancelled out in the process, which will always be the case. In fact the standard notation for definite integrals takes the form:

$$\int_3^4 (10X + 5)dX = \left[\frac{10X^2}{2} + 5X\right]_3^4 \tag{13.13}$$

or in general:

$$\int_b^a f(X)dX = \left[F(X)\right]_b^a = F(a) - F(b) \tag{13.14}$$

where a represents the upper limit and b the lower limit of the integral.

Student activity 13.2
Calculate the value of the definite integral for $(10X + 5)$ between the following values:

(i) $X = 0$ to 3
(ii) $X = 0$ to 4

(Solution on p. 352.)

13.4 Definite integrals and areas under curves

Consider Figs 13.1 and 13.2 which show the integral function (Eq. (13.12)). Figure 13.1 relates to the upper limit of the integral we have just calculated, $X = 4$ (at which point $(10X + 5) = 45$). The total area under the curve to this point (i.e. for $X = 0$ to $X = 4$) has been divided into two to allow for easier calculation. Area A represents a triangle and its area is readily found:

$$\frac{\text{Height} \times \text{width}}{2} = \frac{(45 - 5) \times (4)}{2} = \frac{160}{2} = 80$$

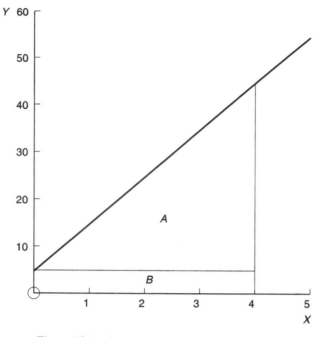

Figure 13.1 Area under $Y = 10X + 5$: $X = 4$

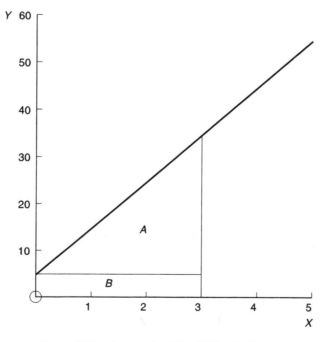

Figure 13.2 Area under $Y = 10X + 5$: $X = 3$

while B is a rectangle with area equal to height times width which here gives $5 \times 4 = 20$. Compare the values for the two areas with the values we had when evaluating the upper limit value for the integral expression. Clearly they are the same and we would denote $A + B$ as the area under this line between $X = 0$ and $X = 4$ ($= 100$). Figure 13.2 repeats this process for $X = 3$. Area A is now:

$$\frac{(35 - 5) \times (3)}{2} = \frac{90}{2} = 45$$

and B is $(5 \times 3) = 15$, giving an area under the line from $X = 0$ to $X = 3$ of 60. If, as we now did for the definite integral, we find the difference between these two values we have:

(Area from $X = 0$ to $X = 4$) $-$ (area from $X = 0$ to $X = 3$) $= 100 - 60 = 40$

which must represent the area under the line between $X = 3$ and $X = 4$, as shown in Fig. 13.3. Clearly, therefore, when we are evaluating a definite integral we are actually finding the equivalent area under the curve between the upper and lower limits of the integral specified.

In fact this holds for non-linear functions also. For example, consider Fig. 13.4, showing some non-linear function. Finding the definite integral between points a and b will be the equivalent of finding the area under the curve between these two values for X. One further point is worth noting. It is possible to obtain negative values when evaluating a definite integral. This would represent an area below the X axis, as shown between points c and d in Fig. 13.4. This can lead to possible difficulties. Consider that we required the integral between c and e. Clearly, evaluating the integral over this range will not produce the appropriate solution since the cd area will be negative and the de area positive, and there will be a cancelling effect. It is

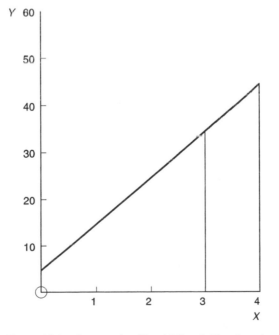

Figure 13.3 Area under $Y = 10X + 5$: $X = 3$ to 4

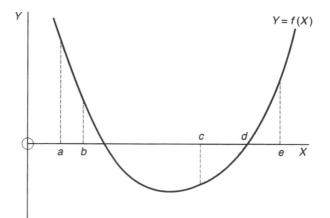

Figure 13.4   Non-linear function

necessary, therefore, to evaluate the two parts of the area separately and then add them together—with an effective dividing point where the function crosses the X axis.

> ***Student activity 13.3***
> For each of the integrals in activity 13.1 calculate the value of the definite integral between $X = 2$ and $X = 2.5$.
> (Solution on p. 352.)

13.5   Consumer's surplus

Let us now consider the application of these principles to the area of consumer's surplus. It is evident that with a downward-sloping demand curve some consumers would have been willing to pay a higher price for the product than the prevailing market price. The gap between the market price and the price that a consumer would have been willing to pay can be regarded as a measure of the consumer's surplus satisfaction and is accordingly known as consumer's surplus. Consider the situation shown in Fig. 13.5.

P_e represents the prevailing market price and the consumer is able to purchase some quantity Q_e. Naturally the consumer pays the same price for each of the units comprising this total quantity even though, as we see from the downward-sloping curve, he or she would have been willing to pay a higher per unit price to begin with. The area shaded in Fig. 13.5 ($0-P_0-E-Q_e$) represents the amount the consumer would have been willing to pay in total for this quantity. The consumer's surplus is the difference between this total area and the area representing actual expenditure ($0-P_e-2E-Q_e$) and is clearly suitable for analysis through the definite integral approach we have just examined. Consider the function:

$$P = 100 - 5Q$$

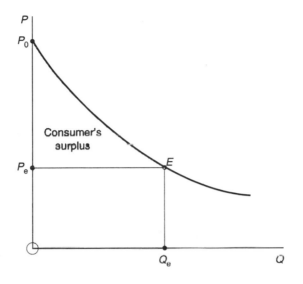

Figure 13.5 Consumer's surplus

with a current market price of 50 and hence a quantity of 10. We then require:

$$\int_0^{10} (100 - 5Q)\mathrm{d}Q - \text{actual expenditure}$$

$$\int_0^{10} (100 - 5Q)\mathrm{d}Q \quad (50 \times 10)$$

$$\left[100Q - 2.5Q^2 \right]_0^{10} - 500 = (750 - 0) - 500 = 250$$

as the size of the consumer's surplus.

13.6 Producer's surplus

The comparable situation applies to the firm and its supply function. The firm receives a uniform price per unit sold whereas the firm would have been willing to sell some units for less than this. If we have a supply function such that:

$$P = 5Q$$

and a current market price as before of 50, then Q will again be 10. The producer's surplus will be:

$$\text{Actual revenue} - \int_0^{10} (5Q)\mathrm{d}Q = 500 - \left[2.5Q^2 \right]_0^{10}$$

$$= 500 - (250 - 0) = 250$$

The principle is illustrated in Fig. 13.6.

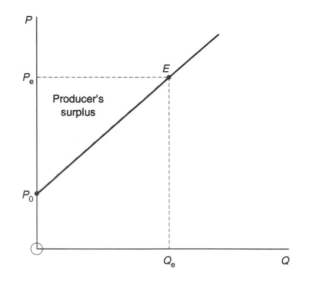

Figure 13.6 Producer's surplus

Total revenue will be given by the area $0-P_e-E-Q_e$. However, the price the producer would have been willing to accept at lower levels for Q is given the supply function line. Hence the producer's surplus revenue is that shown shaded in the diagram: P_0-P_e-E.

13.7 Capital stock formation

Over a period of time we would expect the capital stock of an economy, K, to change. In fact we can define net investment, I, in the economy as:

$$I = \frac{dK}{dt}$$

where t is a time variable. While K represents total capital stock at time t, I represents the net flow of investment at time t. If the net investment function is known then we can apply the principles of integration to derive capital stock formation in general or over a specified period of time. This would be given by:

$$\int_{t1}^{t2} I_t dt$$

For example, assume we have an investment function such that:

$$I_t = 4000t^{-0.5}$$

and we require the capital formation between years 4 and 5:

$$\int_{4}^{5} 4000t^{-0.5} dt$$

Integrating the function gives:

$$K = 2000t^{0.5}$$

and for $t = 5$ we derive $K = 4472$ while for $t = 4$ $K = 4000$. Hence between years 4 and 5 the capital stock increased by 472.

13.8 Summary

The principles of integration are straightforward but the derivation of integrals in practice can be difficult. As with many of the topics we have covered, the only way forward is to practise the principles of integration on as many different functions as possible. Equally, we have examined only three specific areas of definite integrals in economics. It will be evident that these principles can be applied where we require the area under some function. For example, if we wished to calculate total cost, or total revenue, between specific levels of output, we can readily do so by obtaining the definite integral between those values. The exercises illustrate a number of these applications.

Worked example

A firm's marginal cost is given as:

$$MC = 150 - 10Q + 0.2Q^2$$

where Q is output. The firm wishes to estimate the increase in total costs as output increases from 30 to 32 units.

Solution

Clearly, the firm requires the change in total cost as output changes. Using the principles of integration we can derive TC as:

$$TC = \int MC \, dQ = \int (150 - 10Q + 0.2Q^2) \, dQ = 150Q - 5Q^2 + \frac{0.2Q^3}{3} + c$$

The TC function is incomplete since we have no information on fixed costs (the c term in this case). However, if we evaluate the definite integral of MC between $Q = 30$ and $Q = 32$ then we will effectively evaluate the change in TC over this range. When $Q = 30$ the value of the definite integral is evaluated at 2300 and when $Q = 32$ as 2364.533. Therefore the increase in TC as Q increases from 30 to 232 will be 364.533. The principle is illustrated in Fig. 13.7 where the shaded area under the MC function equates to the value we have determined for the change in TC.

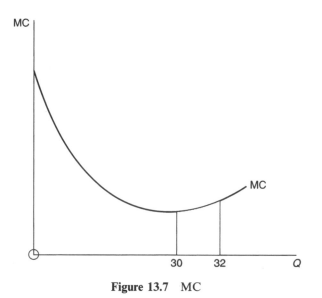

Figure 13.7   MC

Exercises

In addition to the specific exercises below you should return to all the functions for which we obtained a derivative in Chapters 6, 7 and 8. Taking the derivative obtain the integral expression to check your ability to perform the relevant manipulations.

13.1 A firm faces the following marginal revenue function:

$$MR = 125 - 2Q$$

(i) Find the TR function.
(ii) Calculate the change in TR as Q changes from:

$$Q = 50 \text{ to } Q = 60$$
$$Q = 60 \text{ to } Q = 70$$
$$Q = 70 \text{ to } Q = 80$$
$$Q = 80 \text{ to } Q = 90$$

You may find it useful to plot the TR function to check your solutions.

13.2 A firm faces the following supply and demand functions:

$$Q_d = 500 - 9P$$
$$Q_s = -100 + 6P$$

Find the consumer's and producer's surpluses at equilibrium.

13.3 We define the rate of investment (I) as the rate of capital formation dK/dt, where K is the total capital stock and t is time. If:

$$I = 3t^{0.8}$$

then find the total capital formation between periods $t = 10$ and $t = 15$.

13.4 A monopolist faces the following:

$$P = 25 - 4Q$$
$$\text{ATC} = \frac{200}{Q} + 0.2Q + 10$$

Examine how both the consumer's and producer's surpluses are affected if the monopolist decides to maximize revenue rather than profit.

14 Series, exponential functions and financial mathematics

So far in the text we have examined the usefulness of mathematics in economic analysis and economic models. This chapter extends the use of mathematics to cover the financial analysis typically undertaken in a business organization. The concepts of interest, and arithmetic and geometric series are introduced together with those of discounting and present value. The chapter also examines the use of exponential functions in economics. You will need to use logarithms in this chapter and access to a spreadsheet for the student activities will be helpful.

Learning objectives

By the end of this chapter you should be able to:

- Perform a variety of interest calculations
- Evaluate an arithmetic and a geometric series
- Calculate the discounted values of a stream of financial data
- Calculate present value
- Use the exponential function in a number of common economic models

14.1 Financial mathematics

The necessity to be able to deal with, and understand, a variety of financial calculations in the world of business and economics is self-evident. Businesses—and the people who manage them—are primarily concerned with finance in one form or another. Businesses generate profits and have to determine where those profits should be invested for maximum return. Finance needs to be arranged to support investment plans and the cheapest sources of finance must be located. Equally, at a macroeconomic level an understanding of financial mathematics—relating to capital stock formation, investment decisions, government taxation—is important. Underpinning most of the financial mathematics covered in the text is the concept of interest and this is the focus of much of this chapter.

14.2 Time preference

The principles of financial mathematics are based on a simple and obvious feature of behaviour. If you were offered the choice of receiving £100 today or £100 in 12 months' time you would choose the £100 now. You would rationalize your decision on the grounds that—even ignoring inflation—£100 now has more value to you than £100 in 12 months' time. This preference for payment in the present rather than payment in the future is known as 'time preference'. Given that businesses and individuals frequently wish to borrow finance it follows that they have to find someone willing to lend that finance. Following on from the time preference concept it is apparent that the person wishing to borrow money will have to offer the person lending the money some inducement or incentive for the sacrifice they are making. This incentive is the rate of interest.

14.3 Arithmetic and geometric series

To understand properly the principles and methods of calculation involved in financial mathematics it is necessary to examine two general mathematical principles: that of an arithmetic series and that of a geometric series.

Arithmetic series

Consider a sequence of numbers starting with the value a and progressing in the form:

$$a$$
$$a + d$$
$$a + 2d$$
$$a + 3d$$
$$a + 4d$$

and so on, where d is a fixed term added (or subtracted) to the previous value. Such a sequence is known as an arithmetic series. Without proof we state two general formulae for use with such a series:

1 To find the nth term in such a series

$$a + (n - 1)d \tag{14.1}$$

2 To find the sum of the first n terms

$$\frac{n}{a}(2a + (n - 1)d) \tag{14.2}$$

Let us illustrate with a simple problem. An individual is trying to plan for retirement. An investment broker has recommended a scheme whereby the individual pays a lump sum of money to the investment company and, in return, receives a guaranteed monthly income of £100. Moreover, the monthly income will increase by £10 per month. The individual wants to know what monthly income he will be receiving in 5 years' time. Here $a = 100$ and $d = 10$. Using Eq. (14.1) we have:

$$a + (n - 1)d$$
$$100 + (59)10 = £690$$

with $n = 60$ (5 years $\times$ 12 months). That is, in 5 years' time the individual will be receiving a monthly income of £690. The individual also wants to know what his total income from the scheme would be over the first 5 years. Here we use Eq. (14.2).

$$\frac{n}{2}(2a + (n-1)d)$$

$$\frac{60}{2}(2(100) + (59)10) = 30(200 + 590) = £23\,700$$

That is, the individual will receive total payments of £23 700 over the five-year period.

Geometric series

Not all series we may be interested in will be arithmetic, however. Some will be geometric. This occurs where we have:

$$a$$
$$ar$$
$$ar^2$$
$$ar^3$$
$$ar^4$$

and so on where a is the initial sum and r is a common ratio (rather than difference as before). Again, without proof, we state three formulae:

1 To find the nth term in such a series

$$ar^{(n-1)} \tag{14.3}$$

2 To find the sum of the first n terms

$$\frac{a(r^n - 1)}{r - 1} \tag{14.4}$$

3 To find the sum of all terms (to infinity) *provided $r < 1$*

$$\frac{a}{1 - r} \tag{14.5}$$

Note that in the case of Eq. (14.5) it is necessary to specify that $r < 1$. In such a case as n increases the value of r^n approaches zero. To illustrate the use of such a series let us return to the individual contemplating his retirement. A second investment broker has found a scheme whereby, for the same lump-sum investment, a guaranteed monthly income of £100 is provided together with an increase in each month's income of 4%. Here $a = £100$ and $r = 1.04$ (expressed as a decimal). The individual again wishes to know his monthly income from the scheme in 5 years' time. Using Eq. (14.3) we have:

$$ar^{(n-1)}$$

$$100(1.04^{59}) = £1011.50$$

Similarly, the total income up to this time would be given using Eq. (14.4):

$$\frac{a(r^n - 1)}{r - 1}$$
$$\frac{100(1.04^{60} - 1)}{1.04 - 1} = \frac{100(10.51962741 - 1)}{0.04} = £23\,799.07$$

It is clear that, in this example, we cannot apply Eq. (14.5) as $r > 1$.

14.4 Simple and compound interest

Assume that you have the sum of £100 in a bank account, attracting an interest rate of 5 per cent per year (per annum). The initial sum deposited—your £100—is known as the *principal* and it is this amount on which interest will be paid at a rate of 5 per cent per annum. At the end of the first year your account would be credited with a further £5 representing the interest. Assume that you left the money (the principal plus first-year interest) in the account for a further year. What interest would you be entitled to at the end of the second year? You would not expect the interest to be £5 again. This amount would reflect interest paid on the principal. But you have had no reward for leaving your first year's interest untouched in the account. You would expect this sum to attract interest also. The appropriate interest credited at the end of year 2 should be:

£5 which is 5 per cent of the principal

plus £0.25 which is 5 per cent of the interest from year 1

The interest paid should be £5.25. The same process can be applied to years 3, 4, 5 and so on. Table 14.1 shows the relevant calculations.

The table shows the initial principal sum and the interest earned at the end of each year which is then added to the account for the following year. You should ensure that you understand the timings implicit in the table as they are critical for such interest calculations. At the end of the five-year period (which is the same as the start of year 6) the original sum of £100 will have increased to £127.63. This method of interest calculation—where the interest from one period itself earns interest—is known as *compound interest*. If interest is based only on the original principal and not subsequent interest payments as well it is known as *simple interest*. From such

TABLE 14.1   Interest calculations: principal of £100, interest rate of 5 per cent per annum

	Principal at start of year (£)	Interest on principal at end of year (£)
Year 1	100	5
Year 2	105	5.25
Year 3	110.25	5.51
Year 4	115.76	5.79
Year 5	121.55	6.08
Year 6	127.63	

principles of compound interest we can determine a number of useful formulae. We can express the calculations in Table 14.1 as a series:

$$\text{Value at end of period} = P(1+i)^t \qquad (14.6)$$

where P = the original principal sum
   i = the rate of interest expressed as a decimal per period
   t = the appropriate number of periods.

(You will see the similarity here to the geometric series.) Hence, for the example in Table 14.1 we could have calculated the value of our original sum (£100) at the end of the 5-year period as:

$$\text{Value} = 100(1 + 0.05)^5$$
$$= 100(1.05)^5 = 100(1.2763) = £127.63$$

This formula allows us to calculate the future value that a principal sum invested at a given rate of interest will have grown to by a specific period. At the end of, say, a 10-year period the equivalent calculation would show that the original investment would increase to £259.37. The basic formula can be presented in a different way to perform other related calculations. Let us suppose that we wish to invest a sum now, at a rate of interest of 5 per cent per annum, such that it will be worth £127.63 in 5 years' time. What sum should we invest (i.e. what principal amount)? Of course, we already know the answer from the example, but the formula would also confirm. Rewriting the original formula we have:

$$P = \frac{V}{(1+i)^t} \qquad (14.7)$$

Similarly, the formula could be expressed as:

$$i = \sqrt[t]{\frac{V}{P}} - 1 \qquad (14.8)$$

to determine the rate of interest that will turn a given principal into a known value after a specified number of periods. Thus the basic formula linking the variables (P, V, i) can be used to find any of the variables once we know the others.

Student activity 14.1

(i) In four years' time you will require £10 000 as a deposit on a house purchase. The rate of interest is currently 8 per cent. How much should you invest now?

(ii) You have decided that you cannot afford to invest the amount determined in (i) and have only £6000 to invest. What annual rate of return do you require on your investment?

(Solution on p. 352.)

14.5 Nominal and effective interest rates

The formula derived earlier for compound interest can, as we have seen, be used for any combination of P, i and t. In the example used we assumed for simplicity that interest was added to the account at the end of each year. This will not necessarily be the case. Interest may be credited semi-annually, quarterly, monthly, even daily. The same formula can still be used but in such cases we need to distinguish between the nominal and effective rate. Assume that, instead of paying interest annually, an account credits the accrued interest to your account on a monthly basis. You decide to invest the principal of £100 and leave the principal and accruing interest untouched for 5 years. What would the final value of your account be if the annual rate of interest is 10 per cent?

$$P = £100$$
$$i = 0.8333\% \text{ per period } (10\%/12) \quad (\text{or} \quad 0.008333 \text{ as a decimal})$$
$$t = 60 \ (12 \text{ months for 5 years})$$

giving

$$V = 100(1.008333)^{60} = £164.53$$

If we had calculated the accrued amount in an account adding interest only once a year the amount would be £161.05 (you should confirm this yourself from the formula in the previous section). The difference, understandably, is that interest in the first case is being added to the account more frequently and this interest will in turn attract interest for the rest of the 5-year period. The quoted rate of 10 per cent per annum is known as the *nominal* rate. The rate actually earned is known as the *effective* rate or as the *annual* percentage rate (APR). You may well see the APR figure quoted in advertisements exhorting people to borrow money or take out credit to finance their consumer purchases. The APR can be calculated using the formula:

$$\text{APR} = \left(1 + \frac{i}{t}\right)^t - 1 \tag{14.9}$$

where $t = 60$
$i = 0.10$ (10% as a decimal)

$$\text{APR} = \left(1 + \frac{0.1}{60}\right)^{60} - 1$$
$$\text{APR} = (1 + 0.001666667)^{60} - 1$$
$$= 1.1051 - 1 = 0.1051 \text{ or } 10.51\%$$

The effective or annual rate of interest is, therefore, 10.51 per cent.

Student activity 14.2
A credit card company publicizes that it charges only 2 per cent per month interest on any outstanding debt. What is the company's APR?
(Solution on p. 352.)

14.6 Depreciation

Depreciation can be regarded as the gradual reduction in the value of capital assets of an organization or an economy. Typically, if a firm buys, say, a computer for use in the office, then over time the value of this item will reduce. Allowance has to be made in the value for wear and tear, usage, obsolescence, etc. It is standard accounting practice to allow for such depreciation in financial analysis and we shall examine two of the common methods of determining depreciation.

Straight-line depreciation

This is the simplest method where the value of the asset is averaged equally over the time period in which it is used. Let us suppose that a firm has purchased a new computer-based desktop publishing system for use within the accounts department. The system has cost £20 000 and is expected to have a useful life of 4 years, after which it will be obsolete and will need to be replaced by an up-to-date, state-of-the-art system. At that time the system will have a scrap value of £1000. Using this method the annual depreciation is simply calculated as:

$$\frac{\text{(Current value} - \text{value at end of period)}}{\text{Number of periods}}$$

Here:
Current value is £20 000
Value at end of period = £1000
Number of periods is 4

$$\text{Annual depreciation} = \frac{20\,000 - 1000}{4} = \text{£4750}$$

(You will be aware that it is referred to as the 'straight-line' method because we are assuming a linear function for depreciation. A graph showing the current value and the final value would be joined by a straight line and the slope of the line would give the rate of depreciation.)

The reducing-balance method

This second method assumes that the value of the asset is reducing not by a constant amount as in the straight-line method but rather by a constant percentage or proportion. The relevant formula is given by:

$$D = V(1 - r)^t \tag{14.10}$$

where D is the depreciated value at the end of a particular time period, V is the initial value of the asset, r is the rate of depreciation and t is the number of time periods. By rearranging the formula (as with the compound interest formula) we can determine any of the variables in the set:

$$V = \frac{D}{(1 - r)t} \tag{14.11}$$

and

$$r = 1 - \sqrt[t]{D/B} \qquad\qquad (14.12)$$

To illustrate let us assume, in the example above, that the firm has decided to depreciate the computer at the rate of 40 per cent a year. At the end of the first year the depreciated value will be:

End year 1   £20 000 − 0.40(20 000) = £12 000

That is, for year 2, the asset is seen as having a value of £12 000. At the end of year 2 the depreciated value will be:

End year 2   £12 000 − 0.040(12 000) = £7200

Subsequent calculations are shown below:

Depreciated value

End of year 1	£12 000
End of year 2	£7200
End of year 3	£4320
End of year 4	£2592
End of year 5	£1555.2
and so on	

The depreciated values are, of course, easily found using the formula. With such a geometric series the value of the asset will technically never reach zero. Assume instead that we wished to find the rate of depreciation to be used over a 4-year period. Here we would use the formula:

$$r = 1 - \sqrt[t]{D/B}$$
$$r = 1 - \sqrt[4]{\frac{1000}{20\,000}}$$
$$r = 1 - \sqrt[4]{0.05} = 1 - 0.4729 = 0.5271$$

i.e. $r = 52.71\%$.

14.7 Present value

Typically, in an assessment of financial alternatives we wish to compare different projects or investments with a view to deciding which is 'best'. The problem frequently arises that such projects generate cash flows at different periods of time so direct comparison and evaluation is not possible. Accordingly we determine the *present value* of the cash flows—literally its current worth—in order to facilitate such comparisons. An extension to such present value is to examine the internal rate of return on a project. We have already established the principle of time preference. That is, *ceteris paribus*, we would prefer a sum of money now (i.e. in the present) to the same sum of money at some stage in the future. Given the choice of £100 now or £100 in a year's time we would choose the £100 now. But suppose, instead, the choice were £100 now or £110 in a year's time. Would we still choose the £100 now? To answer such a question we need to assess the present value of the future sum of money. Literally, the present value is an indication of what some future sum is worth to us now. Let us assume a rate of interest of 8 per cent. The present value (PV) of £110 in one year's time is given by:

$$PV = \frac{V}{(1+i)^t} \qquad (14.13)$$

where PV is the calculated present value

V is the value at some time in the future (here £110)
i is the rate of interest (here 0.08)
t is the number of periods into the future we are examining (here 1)

so the PV is given as:

$$PV = \frac{110}{(1+0.08)^1} = \frac{110}{1.08} = £101.85$$

This means that—for our purposes—the amount of £101.85 now and the amount of £110 in one year's time are identical and equal. Given a free choice between receiving £101.85 now and £110 in one year's time we would be indifferent. Effectively, both are worth the same. It is apparent that—from the compound interest formula introduced earlier—we could invest the principal of £101.85 at 8 per cent per annum interest and in one year's time it will have increased to £110. Returning to the original alternatives, we were offered £100 now or £110 in one year's time. Which should we take? The answer is evident. We should choose the £110 in one year's time because its present value (£101.85) is more than the alternative present value of £100 now. Such a decision, naturally, is only based on the financial information available. Under normal business circumstances a number of other factors would also be considered before reaching a decision: the risk involved in the alternatives, the rate of interest to be used, whether the rate of interest will remain the same over the entire period, and so on. The principles involved in present value remain the same, however.

14.8 Simple investment appraisal

Let us examine the use of such present value calculations with a simple illustration. A firm is considering investing in a new machine which will save on labour costs. The machine will cost £10 000 to purchase and install and will have a useful life of 5 years. It is estimated that the machine will reduce labour costs by £3000 each year. The current cost of capital to the group is 10 per cent. What advice can we give on the viability of the investment? First, in Table 14.2 let us examine the relevant cash flows (we ignore aspects of the decision relating to depreciation and tax).

At first sight the project looks viable, generating a net cash flow of +£5000. However, this takes no account of the fact that the cash outflow takes place at the start of the project while the cash inflow (in the form of savings in labour costs) occur throughout the life of the project. To

TABLE 14.2   Project cash flows

Year	Cash inflow (£)	Cash outflow (£)	Net cash flow (£)
0	0	10 000	−10 000
1	3000	0	3 000
2	3000	0	3 000
3	3000	0	3 000
4	3000	0	3 000
5	3000	0	3 000
Total	15 000	10 000	5 000

determine whether the project is worth while we must determine its present value: the value of the future stream of cash flows now. We can determine in Table 14.3 the PV of each year's cash flow using the PV formula in Eq. (14.13).

The second column in the table shows the net cash flows as in Table 14.2. The third column shows the discount factor $(1/(1+i)^t)$. This is taken from the PV formula and represents the rate at which we have to discount a future value to determine its present value. The final column shows the present value of each year's net cash flow determined by multiplying the net cash flow by the discount factor. So, for example, £3000 in one year's time has a present value of £2727.30.

There are two points to be noted about these present values. First, the present value for year 0 is the same as the net cash flow. This is not surprising as this cash flow is already taking place in the present. Second, the present value of £3000 decreases the further into the future we go. Again, this is not surprising. The longer we have to wait to receive a given cash flow, the less it is worth to us compared with the present. The total present value (known as net present value, or NPV, as it deals with net cash flows) is £1372.10. What does this mean? It means that the present value of the net cash flows shown is equal to this amount. If you like, this is the present net worth of the cash flows generated by this project. If we were given the choice of a net cash flow now of £1372.10 or a net cash flow spread over the next 5 years of £5000 we would have no particular preference. The NPV is positive and this indicates that, *ceteris paribus*, the project is worth while in that the NPV of the cash inflows is greater than the NPV of the cash outflows. Had the NPV figure been negative it would indicate the reverse: the PV of the outflows was greater than that of the inflows. Similarly, an NPV = 0 would indicate that the PVs of the inflows and outflows were exactly the same. Such NPVs all take account of the timing of the various flows.

TABLE 14.3   Present value of cash flows

Year	Net cash flow (£)	Discount factor $1/(1+i)^t$	Present value Cash flow * DF
0	−10 000	1.0000	−10 000
1	3 000	0.9091	2 727.30
2	3 000	0.8264	2 479.20
3	3 000	0.7513	2 253.90
4	3 000	0.6830	2 049.00
5	3 000	0.6209	1 862.70
Total	5 000		1 372.10

Student activity 14.3
For the project in Table 14.2 assume the cost of capital rises to 12 per cent. How does this affect the NPV? How do you explain this effect?
(Solution on p. 352.)

14.9 Internal rate of return

Partly because of the fact that the NPV will change if the rate of interest/cost of capital changes it is frequently useful to calculate the internal rate of return (IRR). By definition, the IRR is simply the discount rate which yields an NPV of zero for a project, that is, a discount factor that gives an NPV which is neither negative or positive. This IRR can then be compared to the actual cost of capital to determine at what rate of interest/cost of capital the project would cease to be profitable. By way of illustration let us return to the example of a firm buying a labour-saving machine for £10 000. Earlier we used a discount rate of 10 per cent. Let us use, instead, a rate of 15.24 per cent (we shall see why shortly). The relevant calculations are shown in Table 14.4.

Allowing for arithmetic rounding (the discount factors are to only four decimal places) gives an NPV effectively equal to zero. This means that, at a rate of discount of 15.24 per cent, this stream of cash flows has a zero present value: the present value of the inflows is exactly the same as that of the outflows. More useful, however, is the following evaluation. At 10 per cent the project had a positive NPV; at 15.24 per cent a zero NPV. It is apparent that at a rate above 15.24 per cent the NPV will be negative (the present value of the outflows greater than that of the inflows). Accordingly, if the cost of capital to fund this project is more than 15.24 per cent the project is not worth while. At rates of interest/cost of capital less than this, however, the project is viable. At exactly 15.24 per cent the project is at breakeven (in present value terms that is not in terms of costs and revenues). Similarly, the IRR of two or more projects can be compared to determine which is 'better'.

The question arises, however: how is the IRR determined? How did we know that the IRR of the project above was 15.24 per cent? The brief answer is: use a computer package! It is possible, however, to estimate the IRR by manual methods. There are two such methods available: one graphical, one mathematical. Both require the NPV of a project at two different discount rates to generate a positive NPV and a negative NPV and we shall illustrate the mathematical method.

TABLE 14.4   Discount rate 15.24 per cent

Year	Net cash flow (£)	Discount factor	Present value
0	−10 000	1.0000	−10 000
1	3 000	0.8678	2 603.40
2	3 000	0.7530	2 259.00
3	3 000	0.6534	1 960.20
4	3 000	0.5670	1 701.00
5	3 000	0.4920	1 476.00
Total	5 000		−£0.40

TABLE 14.5   Present value of cash flows with two discount rates

Year	Net cash flow (£)	Present value DF 10%	Present value DF 16%
0	−10 000	−10 000	−10 000
1	3 000	2 727.30	2 586.21
2	3 000	2 479.20	2 229.49
3	3 000	2 253.90	1 921.97
4	3 000	2 049.00	1 656.87
5	3 000	1 862.70	1 428.34
Total	5 000	1 372.10	−£177.12

In Table 14.5 the NPV for the project has been evaluated with a discount rate of 10 per cent and again with a rate of 16 per cent. The IRR can now be estimated using a mathematical formula:

$$\text{IRR} = R_1 + (R_2 - R_1)\frac{|\text{NPV}_1|}{(|\text{NPV}_1| + |\text{NPV}_2|)} \tag{14.14}$$

where R_1 is the discount rate used for the first NPV

R_2 is the discount rate used for the second NPV

$|\text{NPV}_1|$ is the absolute value for the first NPV

$|\text{NPV}_2|$ is the absolute value for the second NPV

Here:

$$\text{IRR} = 10\% + (16\% - 10\%)\frac{1372.1}{(1372.1 + 177.12)}$$

$$= 10\% + 6(0.88567) = 15.3\%$$

This method should be seen as a linear approximation only to the true value of the IRR. In fact, the relationship between NPV and the discount rate is non-linear so the approximation methods used here are valid only over small parts of the function. Figure 14.1 illustrates a range of NPV and discount rate values for this problem and the non-linear pattern is clearly evident. Accordingly, the IRR value should be treated as an approximation only and used with caution.

14.10 Annuities

An annuity is a term for a series of fixed equal payments or receipts made at specified periods of time. Such annuities (although they are rarely called this) occur frequently: payments of wages or salaries, repayments of loans, consumer credit repayments, repayments on mortgages, payments of insurance premiums and so on are all common examples. Calculations involving annuities are based around formulae already introduced:

1 Value of future amount $= P(1 + i)^t$

2 Sum of terms in a geometric progression $= \dfrac{a(r^n - 1)}{r - 1}$

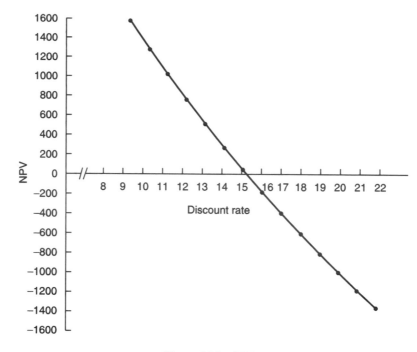

Figure 14.1 IRR

3 Present value $= \dfrac{V}{(1+i)^t}$

We shall examine a number of typical applications of annuities. Before doing so, however, it is necessary to be aware of a number of differing features of annuities:

1 The term of an annuity may be defined as:
  • Certain. It starts and ends on given fixed dates
  • Contingent. It depends on some event that cannot be fixed in time (e.g. insuring against a person's death)
2 The annuities may be paid/received:
  • On an ordinary basis. They are paid/received at the end of the payment intervals
  • On a due basis. They are paid/received at the beginning of payment periods.
3 An annuity may also carry on indefinitely: this is known as a perpetual annuity.

It is particularly important to establish exactly which type of annuity is applicable to a given problem. To begin with, we shall concentrate on annuities which are due and certain.

14.11 Value of an annuity

Let us suppose that a firm offers its employees the opportunity to invest part of their wages and salaries in an investment scheme. At the start of each year, for 5 years, an employee will pay the scheme £1000. This will be invested on his or her behalf and is expected to earn 8 per cent per annum. The employee wishes to know what the investment is worth on an annual basis. You should see that, although this is similar to a compound interest problem, the difference is that the principal sum does not remain constant. However, the basic calculation is straightforward. We are dealing here with an annuity which is certain and due. The first payment—invested at the start of year 1—will attract interest for the first year at 8 per cent per annum. This gives:

$$£1000(1.08) = £1080.00$$

Similarly, the second premium of £1000 will be added to this amount at the start of year 2. All this will now attract interest of 8 per cent during year 2 to give:

$$£2080(1.08) = £2246.40$$

We could progress in the same way through the remainder of the period to produce the results shown in Table 14.6.

At the end of 5 years, therefore, the fund contains £6335.93. In the same way we could use the geometric progression approach. The first payment will attract interest for the full 5 years:

$$£1000(1.08)^5$$

The second for 4 years: $£1000(1.08)^4$
The third for 3 years: $£1000(1.08)^3$
The fourth for 2 years: $£1000(1.08)^2$
The last for one year: $£1000(1.08)$

Collecting these together we have:

$$£1000[1.08 + 1.08^2 + 1.08^3 + 1.08^4 + 1.08^5]$$

where the term in the square brackets is evidently a geometric progression with a at 1.08 and r at 1.08. Using the formula to find the sum of a geometric series we have:

$$\text{Sum} = \frac{1.08(1.08)^5 - 1)}{1.08 \quad 1} = 6.33593$$

giving $£1000(6.33593) = £6335.93$.

TABLE 14.6

Year	Premium (£)	Total in fund at start of year (£)	Interest (8%) (£)	Total in fund at end of year (t)
1	1000	1000.00	80.00	1080.00
2	1000	2080.00	166.40	2246.40
3	1000	3246.40	259.71	3506.11
4	1000	4506.11	360.49	4866.60
5	1000	5866.60	469.33	6335.93

Sum of an ordinary annuity

The appropriate formula for the sum of an ordinary annuity can be derived in the same way. Remember that ordinary annuities are paid/received at the end of the period, not at the beginning, like the due annuity. The relevant formula is:

$$\text{Sum} = \text{Payment}\left[\frac{(1+i)^t - 1}{i}\right]$$

For example, assume that you are investing in an annuity for 5 years of £1000 at a rate of 10 per cent, the sum to be invested at the end of each year. The corresponding sum will be:

$$\text{Sum} = 1000\left[\frac{(1.1)^5 - 1}{0.1}\right] = 1000(6.1051) = £6105.10$$

14.12 NPV of an annuity

Frequently we wish to determine the present value of an annuity (often in the form of income receipts). Assume that an employee who has retired from the firm has certain pension rights. These rights involve receipt of an annual income of £2000 a year for the next 10 years. Assume that the employee receives the payments at the start of the periods. We wish to determine the PV of this due, certain annuity. Let us assume a discount rate of 10 per cent. It is apparent that the series of income receipts could be discounted individually:

	Receipt	*PV*
Start	£2000	£2000
Year 2	£2000	$\dfrac{£2000}{1.10}$
Year 3	£2000	$\dfrac{£2000}{1.1^2}$
Year 4	£2000	$\dfrac{£2000}{1.1^3}$

and so on through the series. This could be presented as:

$$\text{Sum of PV} = £2000\left(1 + \frac{1}{1.1} + \frac{1}{1.1^2} + \frac{1}{1.1^3}\cdots\right)$$

It is also apparent that we have a geometric series in the PV calculations with $a = 1$ and $r = 0.9091$.

To calculate the sum of such a series we have:

$$\text{Sum} = \frac{1(0.9091^{10} - 1)}{0.9091 - 1} = 6.759$$

$$\text{Sum of PV} = £2000(6.759) = £13\,518$$

The interpretation of this result is the same as for any present value calculation. This sum represents the value now of the stream of annuity income over the next 10 years.

Present value of an ordinary annuity

Similarly, the formula for the PV of an ordinary annuity is given as:

$$PV = P \left[\frac{1 - \frac{1}{(1+i)^t}}{i} \right]$$

and the present value is interpreted in the same way as before.

14.13 Repayment annuity

Annuity calculations are often applied to repayment of debt. For a sum of money borrowed for a fixed period of time a certain and due annuity can be used to repay both capital and interest. Such a series of repayments is sometimes known as an amortization annuity. Typically, the problem faced relates to determining the periodic payment in order to repay the sum borrowed plus related interest in a stated number of periods. Assume that a firm offers its employees a mortgage facility whereby the employee can borrow money to purchase a house. One individual has borrowed £20 000. The rate of interest is 10 per cent and the loan (and interest) is to be repaid over the next 10 years. To calculate the annual payment needed to pay off the debt we can use the following approach.

If we denote the repayments as V, r as the rate of interest and the amount initially borrowed as P then we can relate P to the present value of the future stream of repayments:

$$P = \frac{V}{(1+i)} + \frac{V}{(1+i)^2} + \frac{V}{(1+i)^3} + \cdots + \frac{V}{(1+i)^t}$$

This can be rewritten as:

$$P = V \left[\frac{1}{(1+i)} + \frac{1}{(1+i)^2} + \frac{1}{(1+i)^3} + \cdots + \frac{1}{(1+i)^{10}} \right]$$

and the term in square brackets is seen to be a geometric series with a and r both equal to $1/(1+i)$. So here, with rate of interest at 0.10, we have $1/(1+i) = 0.9091$ to give:

$$\frac{0.9091(0.9091^{10} - 1)}{0.9091 - 1} = 6.144567105$$

TABLE 14.7

Year	Debt	Interest	Debt + interest	Payment made	Amount owing	Principal repaid
1	20 000.00	2 000.00	22 000.00	3 254.91	18 745.09	1 254.91
2	18 745.09	1 874.51	20 619.60	3 254.91	17 364.69	1 380.40
3	17 364.69	1 736.47	19 101.16	3 254.91	15 846.25	1 518.44
4	15 846.25	1 584.63	17 430.88	3 254.91	14 175.97	1 670.28
5	14 175.97	1 417.60	15 593.57	3 254.91	12 338.66	1 837.31
6	12 339.66	1 233.97	13 572.53	3 254.91	10 317.62	2 020.94
7	10 317.62	1 031.76	11 349.38	3 254.91	8 094.47	2 223.15
8	8 094.47	809.45	8 903.92	3 254.91	5 649.01	2 445.46
9	5 649.01	564.90	6 213.91	3 254.91	2 959.00	2 690.01
10	2 959.00	295.90	3 254.90	3 254.91	−0.01	2 959.01
Total		12 549.19		32 549.10		19 999.91

So with

$$P = V\left[\frac{1}{(1+i)} + \frac{1}{(1+i)^2} + \frac{1}{(1+i)^3} + \ldots + \frac{1}{(1+i)^{10}}\right]$$

we have £20 000 = V(6.144567105) to give V = £3254.91. That is, £3254.91 must be paid each year for 10 years to repay both the principal sum borrowed and the interest on the amount outstanding.

Frequently, it is necessary and useful to draw up a period repayment schedule to confirm the detailed payments as in Table 14.7. Allowing for arithmetic rounding, it can be seen that the annual payment of £3254.91 repays the principal sum and the interest charged on the loan.

14.14 Sinking funds

A sinking fund is another common method of debt repayment. If a sum of money is borrowed at a given rate of interest for a fixed period then the total amount owing at the end of the period is easily calculated. An annuity can then be arranged with regular payments such that the value of the annuity at the end of the fixed time period is just sufficient to repay the debt. Such a scheme is known as a sinking fund. For example, let us consider an individual who takes out a mortgage of £20 000 over 10 years at a rate of interest of 10 per cent. She wishes to invest regularly in an investment scheme paying a rate of 12 per cent per annum in order to use the proceeds from the scheme to repay the mortgage loan with a lump sum at the end of the period. How much per year should she invest in the scheme? At the end of 10 years the person will owe the following amount in relation to the mortgage debt (principal plus interest):

$$20 000(1 + 0.10)^{10} = £51 874.85$$

The proceeds from the investment scheme must equal this sum. It is clear that the investment scheme (the sinking fund) represents a geometric series. Using the appropriate formula to find the sum of such a series we have:

$$\text{Sum} = \frac{1.12(1.12^{10} - 1)}{1.12 - 1} = 19.65458328$$

Here $V = P(19.65458328)$ where V must equal £51 874.85 in 10 years' time. This gives a value for P of £2639.33. This is the annual amount to be invested in the sinking fund to generate the amount needed to repay the loan in 10 years' time.

14.5 The mathematical constant e

At the very beginning of this text we introduced the concept of a function. One of the types of function that we briefly examined was the general exponential function together with a specific type of exponential function involving the mathematical constant e. We return to this type of function to examine its general principles and consider its use in economics in general and financial mathematics in particular. You will recollect from Chapter 2 that the general form of an exponential function is given by:

$$Y = a^X \tag{14.15}$$

where $a > 1$. We also saw that one specific type of exponential function involved the mathematical constant e and took the form:

$$Y - ae^{bX} \tag{14.16}$$

where a and b are the relevant numerical parameters. We shall now examine this latter function in more detail.

We saw earlier that the mathematical constant e is given the value of approximately 2.718 28. We did not at the time try to justify how this value had arisen. While we cannot provide a definitive mathematical proof we can illustrate the basic concepts and this is likely to prove instructive. Consider a function:

$$Y = f(X) = \left(1 + \frac{1}{X}\right)^X \tag{14.17}$$

Let us examine what happens as the value of X increases.

X	Function	Y
1	$\left(1 + \frac{1}{1}\right)^1$	2
2	$\left(1 + \frac{1}{2}\right)^2$	2.25
3	$\left(1 + \frac{1}{3}\right)^3$	2.370 37

10	$\left(1 + \dfrac{1}{10}\right)^{10}$	2.593 74
100	$\left(1 + \dfrac{1}{100}\right)^{100}$	2.704 81
1000	$\left(1 + \dfrac{1}{1000}\right)^{1000}$	2.716 92
10 000	$\left(1 + \dfrac{1}{10\,000}\right)^{10\,000}$	2.718 15

It can be seen that as we take increasingly larger values of X then the Y values increase, but at a decreasing rate. In fact as X increases indefinitely Y will converge to the number 2.718 28 ... which, for convenience, we denote as e, the exponential constant. The principle behind this is visible in Fig. 14.2, which shows Y for successively larger values of X. In fact the value for $(1 + 1/X)^X$ will converge to e for any initial value for X.

Student activity 14.4

(i) Take the initial value of X as 13.6. Calculate the value for Y using Eq (14.17). Gradually increase X by a factor of 10 and find Y. Confirm that Y converges to e as X increases.

(ii) Choose your own initial value for X. Increase this in whatever size steps you wish and confirm that Y converges to e.

A spreadsheet is recommended for this activity.

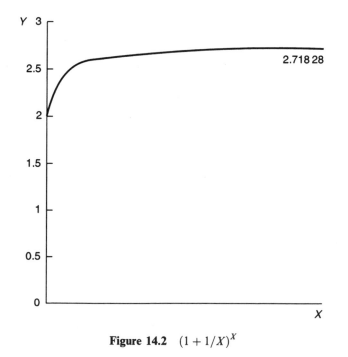

Figure 14.2 $(1 + 1/X)^X$

In general, therefore, we can define e as:

$$e = \lim_{X \to \infty} \left(1 + \frac{1}{X}\right)^{X} \simeq 2.718\,28 \tag{14.18}$$

indicating that as X approaches infinity the value of the function approximates to $2.718\,28$ no matter what the value of X. It will be worth considering a simple application of the use of e in economics. Consider that we have invested a sum of money, say £100, in a bank account which pays interest of 10 per cent annum. After 1 year the investment will be worth:

$$100 + 100(10\%) = 100(1 + 0.1) = £110$$

that is, the sum will have increased by 10 per cent. If we left this amount invested then after a further year its value would be:

$$100 + 110(10\%) = 110(1 + 0.1) = £121$$

and we could clearly carry on calculating the value of the investment for further future time periods. However, let us begin to generalize. If we denote the initial investment as V_0 and the rate of interest as i (denoted as a decimal or fraction), then we have:

$$V_1 = V_0(1 + i) \tag{14.19}$$
$$V_2 = V_1(1 + i) \tag{14.20}$$

However, substituting Eq. (14.19) into Eq. (14.20) we have:

$$V_2 = [V_0(1 + i)](1 + i) = V_0(1 + i)^2$$

or in general:

$$V_t = V_0(1 + i)^t \tag{14.21}$$

where Eq. (14.21) allows us to work out the value in any period t of some initial investment V_0 at a given rate of interest.

However, how does this relate back to e, given that we may not be specifically interested in evaluating how an initial sum of money invested increases over time given some rate of interest? It will be evident, however, that this general principle is readily applied to any economic variable where we wish to be able to calculate the rate of growth. If, for example, we knew that investment in the economy was growing by 3 per cent per year, then we can readily calculate the effect on total investment in, say, 5 years' time. We have made the assumption thus far, however, that in our monetary example the interest earned is added to the amount invested once each year; that is, the growth in the variable occurs at one specific moment in time. Figure 14.3 illustrates the general principles.

We see that once each year the value of the variable takes a step upwards (the size of the step, of course, determined by i). Consider the effect if interest on the investment were added not once each year but twice: say at six-monthly intervals. Equation (14.21) would now have to be amended to:

$$V_t = V_0\left(1 + \frac{i}{2}\right)^{2t}$$

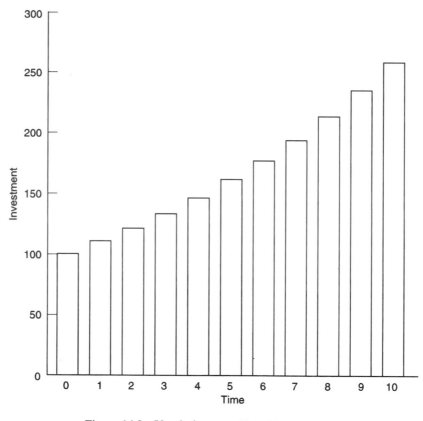

Figure 14.3   Yearly interest: $V_0 = 100$ $i = 0.1$

Note that we divide the interest rate, i, by two. In our example, the initial investment of £100 will earn interest of £5 for the first 6 months (i.e. half of 10 per cent) and then 5 per cent on £105 (=£110.25) at the end of the next 6 months and so on through time (hence the term $2t$). The general effect on the growth of the variable will be as shown in Fig. 14.4. The steps upward in the value of the variable now occur at twice the frequency but, naturally, the size of each step is smaller than before. Continuing the logical process if we consider that interest is now added quarterly the relevant equation becomes:

$$V_t = V_0 \left(1 + \frac{i}{4}\right)^{4t}$$

and the growth of the variables is as shown in Fig. 14.5. In general, therefore, we can calculate such changes with:

$$V_t = V_0 \left(1 + \frac{i}{n}\right)^{nt} \tag{14.22}$$

where n refers to the number of times per year interest is added to the investment. It will be evident from the three figures we have examined that as n gets larger (i.e. as we add interest

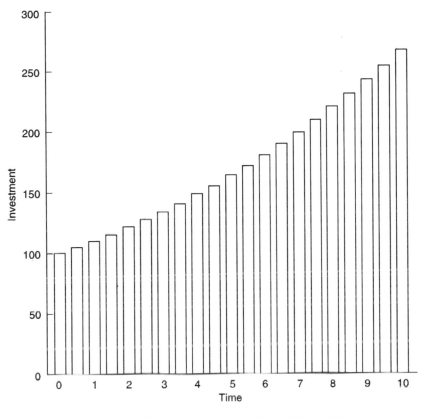

Figure 14.4 Semi annual interest. $V_0 - 100$ $I = 0.1$

more frequently to the investment) the step changes in the variable get closer and closer together. If we allow n to tend to infinity, then the growth path of the variable will effectively become smooth and we can regard the value of the investment as changing *continuously* over time (rather than at discrete periods as we have up to now). We can also transform Eq. (14.22):

$$V_t = V_0 \left(1 + \frac{i}{n}\right)^{nt}$$

$$= V_0 \left[\left(1 + \frac{i}{n}\right)^{n/i}\right]^{it}$$

and letting $m = n/i$ gives:

$$V_t = V_0 \left[\left(1 + \frac{1}{m}\right)^{m}\right]^{it}$$

However, if we allow $n \to \infty$ then $m \to \infty$ and we then have, through Eq. (14.18):

$$V_t = V_0 e^{it} \tag{14.23}$$

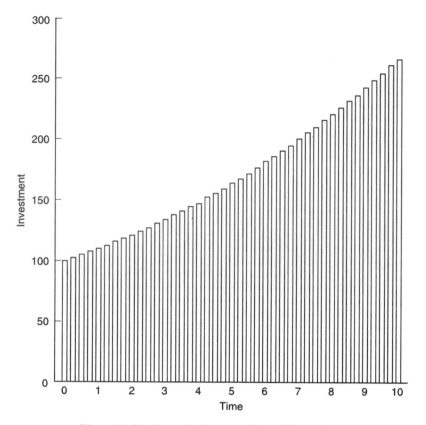

Figure 14.5   Quarterly interest: $V_0 = 100$ $i = 0.1$

or in general:

$$Y = A\, e^{it} \qquad\qquad (14.24)$$

This indicates that if a variable has an initial value of A and grows continuously at a rate of i per year then its value after t years will be given by Y in Eq. (14.24).

While the compound interest formula (and its derivatives) are useful for financial mathematics applications the continuous rate formula in Eq. (14.24) is useful in many economic models where the assumption that a variable changes continuously over time is an important one.

Student activity 14.5
Assume that investment in the economy is currently £250 billion and is estimated to grow at 3 per cent per annum over the next 5 years on a continuous basis. Determine the total investment at the end of each of the next 5 years and hence derive the change in investment that has taken place each year.
(Solution on p. 353.)

14.6 Calculus and e

It will be instructive to consider the application of both differential and integral calculus to the exponential function we have introduced. In general we have the function:

$$Y = A\, e^{ix}$$

Let us begin with a simple example of

$$Y = e^{X}$$

This implies that $X = \ln Y$ (since $\ln e = 1$) and recollect the derivative rule we introduced in Chapter 6 that:

$$\text{If } Z = f(W) = \ln W$$
$$\text{then } f'(W) = 1/W$$

In the case of our example we have $X = \ln Y$; hence $dX/dY = 1/Y$. Let us now consider the derivative of the exponential function $Y = e^{X}$:

$$\frac{dY}{dX} = \frac{1}{dX/dY} = \frac{1}{1/Y} = e^{X}$$

that is, the derivative of the exponential function is the exponential function! This turns out to be a useful property. If we now have:

$$Y = A\, e^{X}$$

then

$$f'(X) = A\, e^{X} \tag{14.25}$$

and if we have:

$$Y = A\, e^{iX}$$

then if we let $u(X) = iX$ we have:

$$Y = A\, e^{u}$$

and via the chain rule and Eq. (14.25) we have:

$$\frac{dY}{dX} = \frac{dY}{du}\frac{du}{dX} = A\, e^{u}\, i = iA\, e^{iX} \tag{14.26}$$

It is now a simple task to consider the integration of exponential functions: Since:

$$f'(e^{X}) = e^{X} \quad \text{then} \quad \int e^{X}\, dX = e^{X} + c \tag{14.27}$$

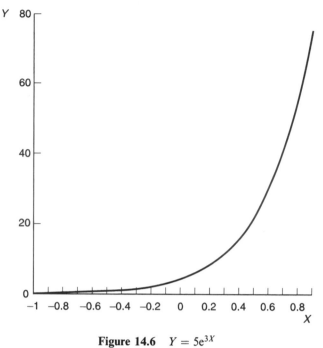

Figure 14.6 $Y = 5e^{3X}$

where, as usual, we have to allow for a constant, c, in the integration process. These principles allow us to sketch exponential functions fairly readily. Consider the function which we can sketch as shown in Fig. 14.6:

$$Y = f(X) = 5e^{3X}$$

Then:

$$f'(X) = 15e^{3X}$$

and
$$f''(X) = 45e^{3X}$$

We know that the intercept of this function will be 5 ($= A$ when $X = 0$). Equally, we see that as X increases ($\to \infty$) then Y will increase also but that when X takes larger negative values ($\to \infty$) then Y will tend to zero. Looking at the first derivative (showing the slope of the function) we see that this must be positive for all values of X while the second derivative indicates that the rate of change of the slope is positive for all values of X also. This implies that the slope (i.e. the first derivative) is increasing with X. Logically, therefore, this must give us the sketch that we have in Fig. 14.6.

14.17 Rates of growth

One of the main areas of application of such functions to economic analysis is through models involving growth or change of some kind. We have already seen how the basic exponential formula can be used to calculate the future value of some variable, given its current level and a rate of growth. Let us consider the following. We have some economic variable, Y, such that:

$$Y_t = Y_0 \, e^{it}$$

The variable in question could relate, for example, to the labour supply, the capital stock or any variable that we would expect to change over time. It will be instructive to consider r, the rate of change. We see that:

$$\frac{dY_t}{dt} = r Y_0 \, e^{rt} = r(Y_t) \tag{14.28}$$

where dY_t/dt is the rate of change in the Y variable over time. However, we can define the proportional rate of change as:

$$\frac{dY_t/dt}{Y_t}$$

which can be expressed as:

$$\frac{1}{Y_t} \frac{dY_t}{dt}$$

and, therefore, for any given period of time t the proportional rate of growth in Y is given as:

$$\frac{1}{Y_t} \frac{dY_t}{dt} = \frac{r Y_t}{Y_t} = r \tag{14.29}$$

and we see that Y grows at a constant, proportional rate over time. We can go one stage further and use the exponential relationship to quantify the (continuous) rate of change that has occurred in some variable over time. Consider the following.

We observe that the capital stock now is £300 billion. Four years previously the capital stock was £250 billion. Assuming a continuous rate of change, what has been the rate of growth in the capital stock per year over this period? We have:

$$Y = A \, e^{rt}$$

Hence

$$300 = 250 e^{4r}$$

and rearranging to solve for r gives a general expression of:

$$r = \frac{\ln(Y/A)}{t} = \frac{\ln(300/250)}{4} = 0.0456$$

This gives a rate of change of 4.56 per cent per year over this period.

As a final example let us consider the following situation. We have:

$$Z = f(X, Y)$$

and that:

$$X = g(t)$$
$$Y = g(t)$$

and that both X and Y grow exponentially at a rate of r for X and s for Y; that is:

$$X = X_0 \, e^{rt}$$
and
$$Y = Y_0 \, e^{st}$$

We then have:

$$dZ = \frac{\partial Z}{\partial X} \, dX + \frac{\partial Z}{\partial Y} \, dY$$

and hence we can express the rate of change in Z over time as:

$$\frac{dZ}{dt} = \frac{\partial Z}{\partial X} \frac{dX}{dt} + \frac{\partial Z}{\partial Y} \frac{dY}{dt} \tag{14.30}$$

However, we know from the exponential growth functions for X and Y that:

$$r = \frac{1}{X} \frac{dX}{dt} \qquad \text{and hence} \qquad \frac{dX}{dt} = rX$$

$$s = \frac{1}{Y} \frac{dY}{dt} \qquad \text{and hence} \qquad \frac{dY}{dt} = sY$$

From Eq. (14.30) we then have:

$$\frac{dZ}{dt} = \frac{\partial Z}{\partial X} rX + \frac{dZ}{dY} sY$$

If we now require the proportionate rate of growth in Z we seek:

$$\frac{dZ/dt}{Z}$$

which gives:

$$\frac{1}{Z} \frac{dZ}{dt} = \frac{1}{Z} \frac{\partial Z}{\partial X} rX + \frac{1}{Z} \frac{\partial Z}{\partial Y} sY \tag{14.31}$$

Let us examine the term:

$$\frac{1}{Z} \frac{\partial Z}{\partial X} rX$$

and rearrange to:

$$r\frac{\partial Z}{\partial X}\frac{X}{Z}$$

On reflection the term following r can be understood as the elasticity of Z with respect to X (given that we are considering proportionate changes in both Z and X) and the equivalent expression for Y as the elasticity of Z with respect to Y. In general, therefore, we have:

$$\frac{1}{Z}\frac{dZ}{dt} = rE_x + sE_y \qquad (14.32)$$

From this we conclude that if X and Y are growing at their respective exponential rates and if the elasticities remain constant over time then Z will grow exponentially at the rate indicated in Eq. (14.32). Let us now consider an economic application.

Assume a Cobb–Douglas production function:

$$Q = AL^\alpha K^\beta$$

and you will recollect that α and β represent the elasticities of output respectively of labour and capital. If we now assume that labour and capital are growing exponentially at rates r and s respectively, we now know that output will be growing at a rate of:

$$\alpha r + \beta s$$

Further, if we assumed that $r = s$ (that both labour and capital were changing at the same rate) and that the production function operated under constant returns to scale ($\alpha + \beta = 1$) then output would be growing at the same exponential rate as labour and capital:

$$(\alpha + \beta)r = r$$

14.18 Summary

In this chapter we have developed the use of mathematics into the area of financial analysis and decision making. The principles of interest calculations, depreciation and present value relate directly to many microeconomic decisions. Equally, at the macroeconomic level policy decisions on interest rate changes, government borrowing and taxation and investment are directly influenced by the issues introduced in this chapter.

Worked example

You have inherited a government security as part of a relative's will. The security is a £1000 government stock at 7 per cent per annum which is redeemable in 6 years' time. Effectively, what this means is that in 6 years' time the government will buy back the security for a price of

£1000. Until then, at the end of the each year, it will pay the security owner £70 interest. If the current market rate of interest is 10 per cent for how much would you be prepared to sell the security now?

You also have heard a rumour that the central bank may be about to cut interest rates. How would this affect your decision on an acceptable price?

Solution

Clearly, we have a security which will generate a stream of income over the next 6 years and we wish to ascertain its present value: what sum of money we would be prepared to accept now in exchange for the income stream in the future generated by the security. At a current interest rate of 10 per cent the relevant calculations are shown in Table 14.8.

At the end of each year you would receive £70 interest and additionally at the end of year 6 the government will buy back the security for £1000. In total, your income stream would be £1420. However, this is over a 6-year period. By discounting (using the discount factors shown, at 10 per cent) we can derive the discounted income stream as shown. This totals £869.34. This is the present value of the income stream from the security and would represent the minimum price you should be prepared to accept in exchange for the security (unless you are hugely in debt and require cash quickly, which will negate the usual 'rational' decision-making assumption used in economics).

If you believe the general interest rate is likely to fall then this will affect your view as to what is a 'fair' price for the security now. With a reduction in interest rates (bearing in mind that your income stream is fixed at £70 per year) then you would require a higher price, *ceteris paribus*, since you will need a larger amount in the present in order to generate the income stream shown.

TABLE 14.8

End of year	Income	Discounted income	Discount factor
1	70	63.64	0.909090
2	70	57.85	0.826446
3	70	52.59	0.751314
4	70	47.81	0.683013
5	70	43.46	0.620921
6	1070	603.99	0.564473

Exercises

14.1 The sum of £3100 is invested now. At a rate of interest of 12 per cent per annum calculate the value of the investment in 10 years' time if interest is compounded:

  (i) Annually
  (ii) Quarterly
  (iii) Monthly
  (iv) Daily
  (v) Continuously

14.2 You know that an investment made now will mature in 5 years' time with a value of £750. If the current interest rate is 10 per cent what must you invest now to produce this maturity value? What assumptions have you made?

14.3 You are offered one of the following:

(i) £100 now
(ii) £120 in 2 years' time
(iii) £150 in 4 years' time

Which would you take and why? What assumptions have you made?

14.4 A firm is considering replacing part of their computer network with the latest equipment. Two suppliers have been asked to tender for the project. The relevant costs of the project and the corresponding savings (in terms of reduced labour costs, increased efficiency, etc.) are shown in Table 14.9.
(i) If the current rate of interest is 12 per cent which supplier would you recommend should be given the contract?
(ii) What other factors would you wish to take into account before reaching a decision?
(iii) If the rate of interest were to fall how do you think this would affect your recommendation?
(iv) For both suppliers calculate the IRR.
(v) How could you use this information?

14.5 A company is considering purchasing a labour-saving piece of equipment which will cost £40 000 and have a useful life of 4 years from now. Current cost of capital is 7.5 per cent. Purchasing the machine will allow the company to cut its workforce by 1 person. At present average annual labour costs are £10 000 per person per year and are expected to increase by 5 per cent per annum over the next few years.

(i) Advise the company as to whether it should purchase the machine.
(ii) At what cost of capital (per cent) would you change your mind about the recommendation made?

14.6 You invest in an annuity paying a rate of 5 per cent per annum. If you invest £500 per year determine:

(i) The value after 5 years if the annuity is due
(ii) The value after 5 years if the annuity is ordinary
(iii) The PV after 5 years if the annuity is due
(iv) The PV after 5 years if the annuity is ordinary

TABLE 14.9

Year	Supplier A		Supplier B	
	Cost	Savings	Cost	Savings
	£		£	
Now	100 000	0	75 000	0
1	0	20 000	25 000	0
2	0	30 000	0	60 000
3	0	40 000	0	40 000
4	0	50 000	0	35 000
5	0	20 000	0	25 000

14.7 You have borrowed £10 000 from the bank at a rate of interest of 12 per cent, the loan to be repaid over 10 years.

    (i) Determine the annual repayments.
    (ii) Draw up a repayment schedule.
    (iii) You wish to repay the loan via a sinking fund paying interest at 15 per cent.
    (iv) Draw up a schedule of the sinking fund payments.

14.8 You will be aware that the price of shares and securities on the Stock Exchange is inversely linked to the general rate of interest in the economy. Using the principles of interest and present value, explain why this is the case.

15 An introduction to dynamics

As we saw in the previous chapter, a number of interesting avenues of economic analysis begin to appear once we consider economic models over time rather than in a static position as we have largely done up to now. Our analysis thus far, on market equilibrium, for example, or macroeconomic equilibrium, has focused upon determining the change in equilibrium that occurs when the model we are examining changes. Thus, for example, if the intercept of the demand function alters how will this affect equilibrium price and quantity? However, there is another related aspect to this examination. This is to ask the question: *how* do we move from one equilibrium position to another over time? Given that we may have an equilibrium now and some change in the model structure occurs, how do we reach the future new equilibrium position? It is this type of question that the area of economic dynamics tries to answer. In this chapter we shall introduce the basics of dealing with dynamic situations, although it must be stressed that this is simply a general introduction since the area of economic dynamics is a particularly complex one.

Learning objectives

By the time you have completed this chapter you should be able to:

- Find the solution to a difference equation
- Determine the stability of an economic model
- Solve common dynamic economic models

15.1 Difference equations

Let us examine the simplest macroeconomic model with no government sector, no foreign trade and a simple equilibrium determined by:

$$Y = C + I \tag{15.1}$$

It will be more appropriate, however, since we are concerned with changes over time, to ensure that we can identify the time period relevant to each variable. Hence we can rewrite Eq. (15.1) as:

$$Y_t = C_t + I_t \tag{15.2}$$

and we make the usual assumption that I_t is exogenous. Let us further define a consumption function such that:

$$C_t = a + bY_{t-1} \qquad (15.3)$$

This is different from the functions we have used before. We are now saying that consumption in the current period t is made up of some autonomous element, a, and an element that is determined from the income in the previous period $t - 1$. This is not unrealistic as we can logically argue that from the perspective of the individual consumer consumption spending will be influenced by past income since present income may not yet be known. Substituting Eq. (15.3) into (15.2) we then have:

$$Y_t = a + bY_{t-1} + I_t \qquad (15.4)$$

Equation (15.4) is referred to as a difference equation (since the equation relates to two (or more) periods of time). Equation (15.4) is technically known as a *first-order* difference equation since there is a difference of one period between the various elements of the equation. If, for example, we had specified a consumption function of the form:

$$C_t = a + bY_{t-1} + cY_{t-2}$$

we would have a second-order equation. We also have a linear difference equation (for the obvious reason) in Eq. (15.4). It will be instructive to consider a numerical example of this model to examine its behaviour over time. Let us assume that I is fixed at 500, that a is 1000 and that b (the marginal propensity to consume) is 0.7. We then have:

$$Y_t = 1500 + 0.7Y_{t-1} \qquad (15.5)$$

If we wish to calculate Y_t, then clearly we require a value for Y_{t-1}. Let us assume an initial value, Y_0, of 3000. We then have:

$$Y_1 = 1500 + 0.7(3000) = 3600$$

Having obtained Y_1 we can proceed to calculate $Y_2, Y_3, \ldots, Y_{t-n}$. Shown below are the relevant results for the first few values of t:

Y_0	3000
Y_1	3600
Y_2	4020
Y_3	4312
Y_4	4520
Y_5	4664
$\vdots$	
Y_{20}	4999.72
$\vdots$	
Y_{30}	4999.94

and it is apparent that over time the value for Y is approaching 5000—that is, as $t \to \infty$ then $Y_t \to 5000$. Figures 15.1 and 15.2 show the movement of the variable over the first 30 periods. Figure 15.1 shows the value for Y in each period while Fig. 15.2 shows the change between successive periods. It is apparent that by period 20 successive values of Y are changing only in terms of their last few decimal places. (It will be apparent from the analysis we undertook earlier in the text into the multiplier process how and why this is occurring.) It is clear, however, that we cannot rely on such a clumsy calculation approach to examine the behaviour of the model over time. We evidently require a suitable mathematical approach comparable to that we examined in the previous chapter when re-examining exponential functions.

15.2   The equilibrium position

If an equilibrium position for Y exists then we can assume that once attained in a particular period the equilibrium will be repeated in successive periods (assuming no further changes are introduced in any of the model parameters or exogenous values). In other words, once the model has reached an equilibrium we assume this to be a stable position, *ceteris paribus*. If we denote the equilibrium as Y^* then we have:

$$Y_t = Y^* = Y_{t-1}$$

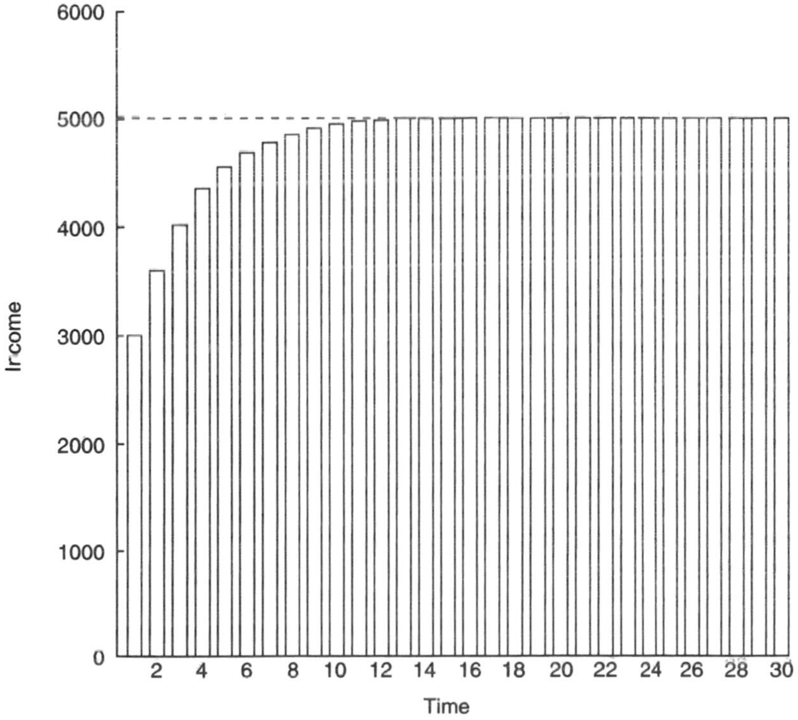

Figure 15.1   Income

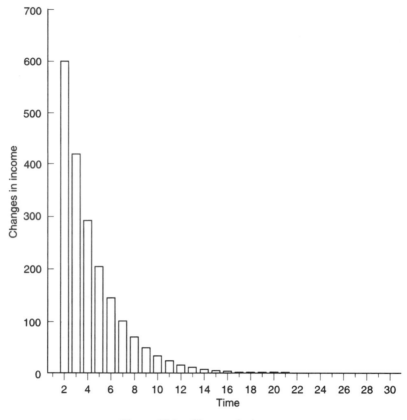

Figure 15.2 Changes in income

and hence:

$$Y_t = Y_{t-1}$$

We then have:

$$Y^* = 1500 + 0.7Y^*$$

which can be solved in the usual way to give $Y^* = 5000$. In general, if we have a difference equation of the form:

$$Y_t = \alpha + \beta Y_{t-1} \tag{15.6}$$

then such a solution (if it exists) can be found from:

$$Y^* = \frac{\alpha}{1 - \beta} \tag{15.7}$$

This confirms for our illustrative model that a solution exists but still does not answer the question of determining how Y approaches this equilibrium over time. Clearly what we require is a function of the form:

$$Y_t = f(t)$$

and not in the current form $Y_t = f(Y_{t-1})$; that is, we wish to be able to relate Y to t directly rather than indirectly through earlier values of Y. This will enable us more readily to examine the behaviour of Y over time.

15.3 The solution to a difference equation

The derivation of such a solution equation is approached by identifying what is known as a *particular* solution and a *complementary* solution. We then state:

General solution = particular solution + complementary solution

The particular solution is in fact what we found in the previous section: the solution that provides the equilibrium position—here at 5000. The complementary solution is found by removing the constant from the difference equation, giving:

$$Y_t = 0.7 Y_{t-1} \qquad (15.8)$$

Since we require a solution of the form $Y_t = f(t)$, let us consider the general exponential type of function:

$$Y_t = f(t) = km^t \qquad (15.9)$$

and we wish to determine suitable values for the parameters in Eq. (15.9).
    Since $Y_t = f(Y_{t-1})$ then via Eq. (15.8):

$$km^t = km^{t-1}$$

and
$$km^t = 0.7km^{t-1}$$

and dividing through by km^{t-1} gives:

$$\frac{km^t}{km^{t-1}} = 0.7\frac{km^{t-1}}{km^{t-1}}$$

which gives $m = 0.7$. Hence we now have:

$$Y_t = k(0.7)^t$$

Therefore the general solution is given as:

$$Y_t = 5000 + k(0.7)^t$$

However, we know the initial value of Y, Y_0 (at 3000), so we now have:

$$Y_0 = 3000 = 5000 + k(0.7)^0$$

Therefore:

$$3000 = 5000 + k$$

Hence $k = -2000$, giving the general solution as:

$$Y_t = 5000 - 2000(0.7)^t \tag{15.10}$$

Equation (15.10) thus provides a general solution for finding Y_t for any particular time period in which we have an interest. The solution provides us with a method for tracking the period-by-period changes in the model as it moves towards equilibrium.

> ***Student activity 15.1***
> Using Eq. (15.10) confirm the values we calculated earlier for Y_t when $t = 0, 1, 2, 3, 4, 5$.

It will be worth reviewing what we have accomplished. We started with a first-order difference equation expressed in general as:

$$Y_t = \alpha + \beta Y_{t-1}$$

and we have derived a related function where we relate Y_t only to t. In general such a solution can be derived as:

$$Y_t = \frac{\alpha}{1 - \beta} + \left(Y_0 - \frac{\alpha}{1 - \beta} \right) \beta^t \tag{15.11}$$

providing that $\beta \neq 1$, which for convenience we can express as:

$$Y_t = a + k\beta^t \tag{15.12}$$

where:

$$a = \frac{\alpha}{1 - \beta}$$

and

$$k = \left(Y_0 - \frac{\alpha}{1 - \beta} \right)$$

where Y_0 is taken as an initial value in the model.

> ***Student activity 15.2***
> For the equation
>
> $$Y_t = 1500 + 0.8 Y_{t-1}$$
>
> Derive a function in the form of Eq. (15.12) with $Y_0 = 5000$.
> (Solution on p. 353.)

It is important to realize that the exact form of the difference equation we derive will, in part, depend on the Y_0 value that we use. Effectively, Y_0 indicates the initial starting point of the model and since the new equilibrium will remain the same then we require an equation for tracing the movement of Y from a given value of Y_0 to the new equilibrium position. A different value for Y_0 in Student activity 15.1 would generate a different difference equation.

15.4 Stability of the model

In the example that we have examined we see that the simple model we have is stable over time; that is, it converges towards some equilibrium position and once attained will remain at that equilibrium, *ceteris paribus*. There is, however, no guarantee that a particular model will necessarily exhibit such stability over time. Let us consider the general model:

$$Y_t = a + kb^t$$

where a and b take the form shown earlier. We have already noted that the a term indicates the particular solution while the kb^t term represents the complementary solution. On reflection we can interpret the particular solution as representing an equilibrium level for Y over time. The complementary solution can then be interpreted as showing deviations from that equilibrium over time. We can determine, therefore, whether a particular model will be dynamically stable (i.e. will tend to the equilibrium over time) by determining whether:

$$kb^t \rightarrow 0 \qquad \text{as } t \rightarrow \infty$$

It is also clear that it is primarily the b^t term that will determine whether this convergence occurs and we can naturally consider the effect on stability of different values for b.

Case 1 $0 < b < 1$ Assume a simple system such that:

$$Y_t = 1000 + 100(0.8)^t \tag{15.13}$$

We note that b lies between 0 and 1 and we can calculate as before the period-by-period values for Y. Figures 15.3 and 15.4 show this system over a 30-period time scale.

Figure 15.3 shows the movement in the Y variable over time and it is evident that the Y value gradually converges towards the a term in the general expression (here $a = 1000$). We see the logic of this since if b is positive but less than 1 then raising b to successively higher powers will cause it to tend to zero. This is also illustrated in Fig. 15.4, which shows the period-by-period change in Y which clearly converges to zero. It may also be evident that the smaller the value of b between these limits then the faster the system will approach equilibrium.

Case 2 $b > 1$ Now consider the equation:

$$Y_t = 1000 + 100(1.1)^t \tag{15.14}$$

(Note that we keep the a term and the k term constant in this and subsequent equations so we can more easily assess the effect of changing b). In this case b is now greater than 1 and Figs 15.5 and 15.6 show the patterns for Y and changes in Y over time respectively. We now see that for

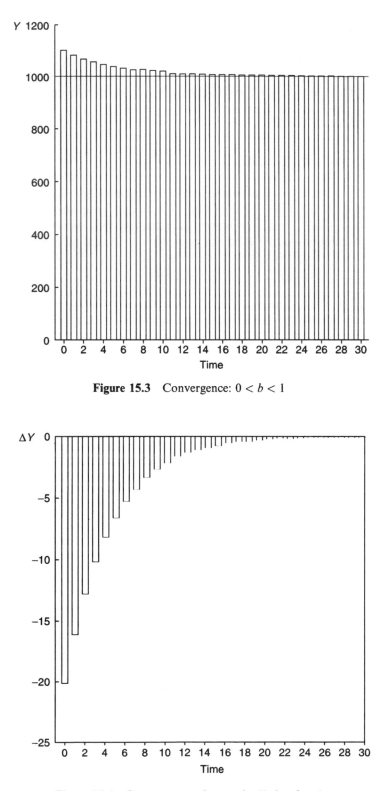

Figure 15.3 Convergence: $0 < b < 1$

Figure 15.4 Convergence: changes in Y: $0 < b < 1$

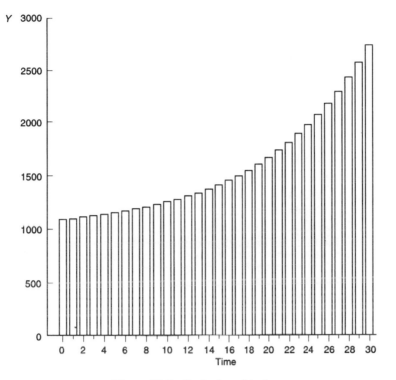

Figure 15.5 Explosion: $b > 1$

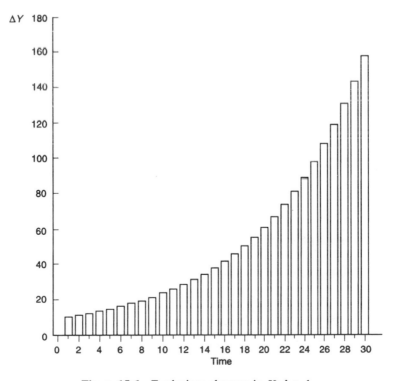

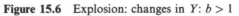

Figure 15.6 Explosion: changes in Y: $b > 1$

this value of b the Y variable 'explodes' over time, with Y moving further and further away from equilibrium. Once again we recognize that the larger the value for b, then the faster the system explodes.

Case 3 $0 > b > -1$ Now consider the following equation:

$$Y_t = 1000 + 100(-0.8)^t \tag{15.15}$$

where b takes a negative value between 0 and -1. Clearly we have $b^t \to 0$, which implies that Y will tend to equilibrium. The system is clearly stable. However, since b is negative the b^t term will take negative values when t is an odd value and positive values when t is even. The deviations for the equilibrium, therefore, will oscillate from period to period. The situation is shown in Figs 15.7 and 15.8. Y can be seen to fluctuate around the equilibrium value over time although these fluctuations gradually diminish. Such a system is said to exhibit *damped oscillations*.

Case 4 $-1 > b$ We now have a model where the b term is negative but exceeds -1:

$$Y_t = 1000 + 100(-1.1)^t \tag{15.16}$$

Here as $t \to \infty$ then $b^t \to \infty$ also, that is the model explodes. However, as with the previous model, the system will also exhibit oscillations as $b^t \to \pm\infty$. The situation is shown in Figs 15.9 and 15.10. Again, we see that the system is unstable and will move further away from equilibrium over time, alternating between positive and negative deviations, exhibiting an explosive oscillations pattern.

Finally, let us consider the other element of the complementary solution, the k term. In general this could be positive (as it has been in all our examples in this section) or negative (as it was in the original macroeconomic model). Since the term kb_t represents deviations from the equilibrium then effectively k indicates whether these deviations will be positive or negative. If we compare Figs 15.2 and 15.4, for example, we see that they are effectively mirror images of each other. Recollect that in the model for Fig. 15.2 the k term was negative while for Fig. 15.4 it was positive. Finally we should note that the a term in the system will determine the vertical intercept on the graph.

15.5   A macro model with a government sector

Let us consider a slightly more complex macro model introducing a government sector. We now have:

$$Y_t = C_t + I_t + G_t \tag{15.17}$$
$$\text{YD}_t = Y_t - xY_t \tag{15.18}$$
$$C_t = c + d[\text{YD}_{t-1}] \tag{15.19}$$
$$\text{TX}_t = xY_t \tag{15.20}$$

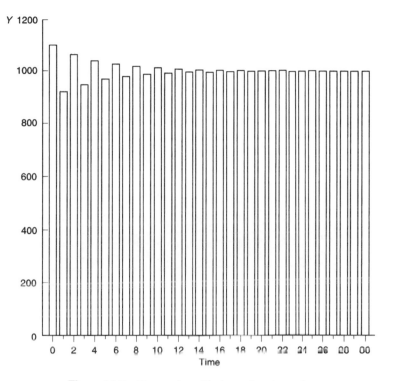

Figure 15.7   Damped oscillations: $0 > b > -1$

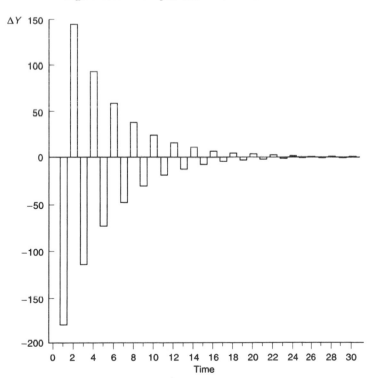

Figure 15.8   Damped oscillations: changes in Y: $0 > b > -1$

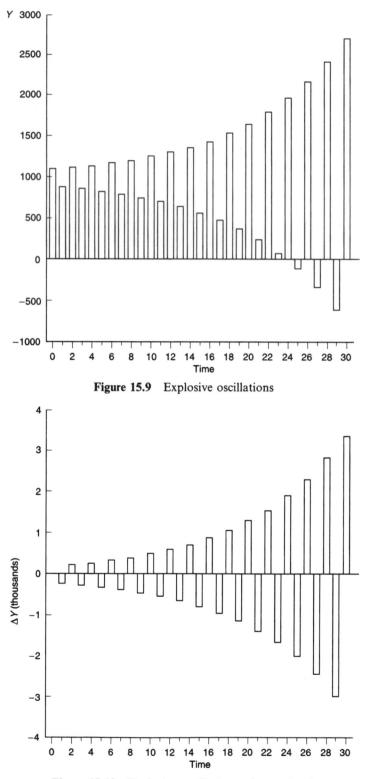

Figure 15.9   Explosive oscillations

Figure 15.10   Explosive oscillations: changes in Y

where x represents the tax rate imposed, d the marginal propensity to consume, YD is disposable income, TX the total tax collected and I and G are exogenous. We then have:

$$\begin{aligned} Y_t &= c + d[\text{YD}_{t-1}] + I + G \\ &= c + d(Y_{t-1} - xY_{t-1}) + I + G \\ &= c + d(1 - x)(Y_{t-1}) + I + G \end{aligned} \tag{15.21}$$

which collecting the exogenous terms together gives:

$$Y_t = (c + I + G) + d(1 - x)Y_{t-1} \tag{15.22}$$

which can be expressed in the standard difference equation form as:

$$Y_t = \alpha + \beta Y_{t-1}$$

where $\alpha = c + I + G$ and $\beta = d(1 - x)$.
The general solution can be derived as:

$$\begin{aligned} Y_t &= \frac{\alpha}{1 - \beta} + \frac{(Y_0 - \alpha)\beta^t}{1 - \beta} \\ &= \frac{c + I + G}{1 - d(1 - x)} + \frac{Y_0 - (c + I + G)}{1 - d(1 - x)}[d(1 - x)]^t \end{aligned} \tag{15.23}$$

Let us focus on the β^t term, $d(1 - x)^t$. Recollecting what we know about the stability of such a system we would require $d(1 - x)$ to be both positive and less than 1 for the system to be stable. This is entirely consistent with the usual economic assumptions of such a model, where we would expect both d and x (the marginal propensity to consume and the rate of tax) to be positive and < 1. Hence the β term will generate a stable system. Note also that this model— with a government sector—will converge at a faster rate than the model without the government sector. If x were zero, the β term would collapse to c, which must be larger than $c(1 - d)$. Recollect that the smaller the β term (when $0 < \beta < 1$) the faster the convergence process.

> **Student activity 15.3**
> Assume a marginal propensity to consume of 0.7 and a tax rate of 0.25. Let $c = 100$, $I = 500$ and $\bar{G} = 250$, $Y_0 = 800$. Analyse the model in terms of its movement over time.
> (Solution on p. 353.)

15.6 Harrod–Domar growth model

Let us consider a simple macroeconomic growth model known as the Harrod–Domar model. We assume that:

$$S_t = sY_t \tag{15.24}$$

$$I_t = p(Y_t - Y_{t-1}) \tag{15.25}$$

Savings in period t, S_t, are some proportion, s, of income. Investment in period t, I_t, is some proportion, p, of the change in income since the last period. If we require $S_t = I_t$ for equilibrium, then we have:

$$sY_t = p(Y_t - Y_{t-1})$$

which on rearranging gives:

$$Y_t = \frac{p}{p-s} Y_{t-1} \qquad (15.26)$$

and a general solution of:

$$Y_t = k\left(\frac{p}{p-s}\right)^t \qquad (15.27)$$

but k will then be:

$$Y_0 = k\left(\frac{p}{p-s}\right)^0 = k$$

giving a solution of:

$$Y_t = Y_0\left(\frac{p}{p-s}\right)^t \qquad (15.28)$$

We recognize that both p and s will be positive but less than 1; hence the term $[p/(p-s)]$ will be greater than 1, indicating that the system is explosive. Income will expand indefinitely unless there is some change in the parameters of the model over time (if, for example, the propensity to save altered). In order to assess whether the system oscillated we would need to assess which of p and s was the larger. If $s > p$ then the term $[p/(p-s)]$ becomes negative and the system oscillates.

> **Student activity 15.4**
> Assume that $s = 0.1$, $p = 0.25$ and $Y_0 = 1000$. Draw a graph of the value of Y_t over the first 10 periods.
> (Solution on p. 353.)

15.7 Market equilibrium

Finally, let us examine a microeconomic application of difference equations. Consider the market model:

$$D_t = a + bP_t \qquad (15.29)$$
$$S_t = c + dP_{t-1} \qquad (15.30)$$

where we see that quantity demanded in the time period t (D_t) is a function of the price in that period, while the quantity supplied in the period t (S_t) is a function of the price in the previous period. This is not an unreasonable assumption since firms may well take time to react to price changes and their output decisions may well lag behind the market price. Naturally, we could also apply the usual numerical restrictions to the equation parameters. If we assume there is an equilibrium price, P^*, then:

$$P_t = P^* = P_{t-1} \tag{15.31}$$

and we have:

$$a + bP^* = c + dP^*$$

which gives:

$$P^* = \frac{a - c}{d - b} \tag{15.32}$$

The difference equation can also be obtained. We require:

$$a + bP_t = c + dP_{t-1}$$

which on rearranging gives:

$$P_t = \frac{c - a}{b} + \frac{dP_{t-1}}{b} \tag{15.33}$$

fitting into our general form:

$$Y_t = \alpha + \beta Y_{t-1}$$

This will then give a general solution (which you may want to confirm through your own calculations):

$$P_t = \frac{(c - a)/b}{1 - d/b} + \left[P_0 - \frac{(c - a)/b}{1 - d/b} \right] \left(\frac{d}{b} \right)^t \tag{15.34}$$

and it is evident that the expression $(d/b)^t$ will control the stability of the system. It is evident first of all that the d/b term will be negative (since we usually require b, the slope of the demand function, to be negative). The system therefore will oscillate over time. Will the system converge to equilibrium or will it explode? Clearly, we require:

$$0 < d/b < -1$$

for a convergent system. If this condition were not met then the system would not converge to an equilibrium price/quantity combination. This value is simply the ratio of the slopes of the two functions. To illustrate consider the model:

$$D_t = 90 - 0.8P_t$$
$$S_t = -10 + 0.2P_{t-1}$$

We have:

$$P_t = \frac{(-10-90)/-0.8}{1-(0.2/-0.8)} + \left[P_0 - \frac{(-10-90)/-0.8}{1-(0.2/-0.8)} \right] \frac{(0.2)^t}{-0.8}$$
$$= 100 + (P_0 - 100)(-0.25)^t$$

We see that the d/b term is negative but does not exceed -1; hence the system will converge to an equilibrium which we confirm to be:

$$P^* = \frac{90-(-10)}{0.2-(-0.8)} = 100$$

Student activity 15.5
If $P_0 = 80$ calculate the period-by-period change in P.
(Solution on p. 354.)

However, consider the model:

$$D_t = 90 - 0.4P_t$$
$$S_t = -10 + 0.5P_{t-1}$$

We see that the ratio d/b is now $0.5/-0.4 = -1.25$, which would lead to an explosive oscillation. The price would never reach an equilibrium position, with quantity demanded and supplied getting further and further away from balance over time. These models are often referred to as *cobweb* models because of the weblike pattern that emerges if we were to plot the period-by-period movement in P on a graph (Fig. 15.11).

The movement in P over the first five periods for this model, with an initial price of 100, would be:

t	P_t
0	100
1	124.975
2	138.85
3	152.725
4	166.6
5	180.475

and it can be seen from Fig. 15.11 that D and S continue to move further and further apart over time.

15.8 Summary

In this, the final chapter, we have introduced some of the basic concepts that relate to the application of mathematics to dynamic economic models. It must be stressed that we have

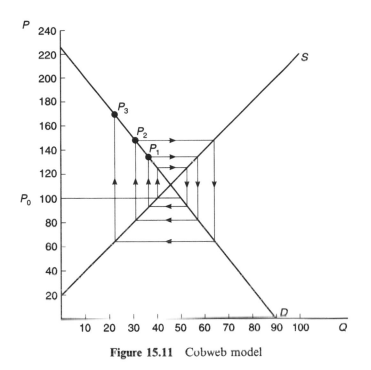

Figure 15.11 Cobweb model

examined only some of the more fundamental and simpler economic models in this context. We have looked at the principles of simple linear first-order difference equations. It is evident on reflection that many of the more complex models will involve difference equations of higher order and will need to include non-linear relationships. However, the mathematical principles required to deal with such are only an extension of those we have developed.

Worked example

Assume a simple national income model:

$$Y_t = C_t + I_t$$
$$C_t = 500 + 0.8Y_{t-1}$$

The economy is currently in equilibrium with I, exogenous, at 200.

I now increases to 250. Derive the level of national income five periods after this increase. How many periods will it take for the model to reach its new equilibrium position?

Solution

We can derive a suitable equation:

$$Y_t = C_t + I_t$$
$$C_t = 500 + 0.8Y_{t-1}$$

Hence with $I = 200$

$$Y_t = 500 + 0.8 Y_{t-1} + I_t$$
$$Y_t = 700 + 0.8 Y_{t-1}$$

and giving an equilibrium income of 3500. However, with the increase in I this becomes:

$$Y_t = 750 + 0.8 Y_{t-1}$$

and we can quickly confirm that the new equilibrium would be 3750 (with a multiplier in this simple model of 5). This then allows us, using Eq. (15.11), to develop a difference equation such that:

$$Y_t = 3750 - 250(0.8^t)$$

With $t = 5$ we then have:

$$Y_t = 3668.08$$

as the income level in this period. However, we are also asked to determine how long it will be before the economy reaches its new equilibrium position. We have:

$$Y_t = 3750 - 250(0.8^t)$$

and we require to solve for t. In general, this would be:

$$Y_t - 3750 = -250(0.8^t)$$
$$\frac{Y_t - 3750}{-250} = 0.8^t$$

If we then took logarithms we would have:

$$\log \frac{(Y_t - 3750)}{-250} = t \log(0.8)$$

and rearranging to give:

$$t = \frac{\log(Y_t - 3750)}{-250} \times \frac{1}{\log(0.8)}$$

Initially we might set Y_t to 3750 since we know this will be the new equilibrium. However, this will require finding the log of 0. Instead we can set Y_t to a non-zero value as close to the equilibrium as we require, say $Y_t = 3749$. Substituting this then gives:

$$t = \frac{\log(3749 - 3750)}{-250} \times \frac{1}{\log(0.8)} = \frac{-2.39794}{-0.09691} = 24.7$$

Effectively then the economy will have reached its new equilibrium position when $t = 25$. You may wish to use a spreadsheet to show that the period-by-period changes using the difference equation are the same as those to be derived using the simple multiplier approach and calculating period-by-period changes for Y and C.

Exercises

15.1 Return to the macro model with a government sector that we introduced in this chapter. Assume that G is no longer exogenous but takes the form:

$$G_t = gY_{t-1}$$

Assess the effect this will have on both the stability of the model and the time taken to converge to equilibrium.

15.2 For the model in Sec. 15.7 we had a market system:

$$D_t = 90 - 0.4P_t$$
$$S_t = -10 + 0.5P_{t-1}$$

If $P_0 = 100$, examine the behaviour of this model over time. Plot the movement in P and Q on a graph showing both functions. Comment on the behaviour you observe and on how it could arise.

15.3 Assume the following model:

$$D_t = 200 - 5P$$
$$S_t = -50 + 3P_{t-1}$$

Assume $P_0 = 25$. Assess the behaviour of the model over time. Plot the movement in P and Q on a supply and demand graph. How would this behaviour change if:

(i) The slope of the demand function changed?
(ii) The intercept of the supply function changed?

15.4 Assume a national income model as in Sec. 15.5 involving a government sector where I and G are exogenous and the consumption function is a first-order difference equation with m.p.c. $= 0.8$. Assume $I = 100$, $G = 50$ with a tax rate of 10 per cent. If the autonomous level of consumption is 100 and $Y_0 = 750$, examine the behaviour of the model.

(i) Plot the change in Y over time.
(ii) If the tax rate changes to 20 per cent, what effect will this have?
(iii) If G increases to 75, what effect will this have?
(iv) If I changes to 75, what effect will this have?

15.5 From Exercise 15.4 derive a suitable savings function if we now assume that:

$$I_t = 0.05(Y_t - Y_{t-1})$$

Re-examine the models in Exercise 15.4.

Postscript

We have now reached the end of our examination of the use of mathematics in economics. The first thing to say is 'Congratulations' on working your way through the text. Hopefully you have found it both a rewarding and an interesting experience and as a result have seen your mathematical knowledge and your mathematical confidence increase.

Having successfully covered this introductory material you are now in a position to proceed further in terms of extending both the mathematical rigour and the coverage of the application of mathematics to economics. You will probably find it useful as a next stage in the development of your mathematical skills to examine a number of other texts:

Burrows, P. and Hitiris, T.: *Macroeconomic Theory: A Mathematical Introduction*, Wiley, New York, 1974.

Chiang, A.C.: *Fundamental Methods of Mathematical Economics*, 3rd edition, McGraw-Hill, New York, 1987.

Henderson, J.M. and Quandt, R.E.: *Microeconomic Theory: A Mathematical Approach*, 3rd edition, McGraw-Hill, New York, 1980.

Silberberg, E.: *The Structure of Economics: A Mathematical Analysis*, McGraw-Hill, New York, 1978.

Smith, A.: *A Mathematical Introduction to Economics*, Blackwell, Oxford, 1982.

Appendix 1 Solutions to student activities

Note that not all activities have a solution shown here. In some cases the solution is self-evident and in others the solution appears immediately after the activity in the text itself.

2.2
Using Fig. 2.4 we see that at a price of £6 Q will be 70 units and at a price of £3 will be 85 units. Similarly, with $Q = 40$ then we see P would be £12.

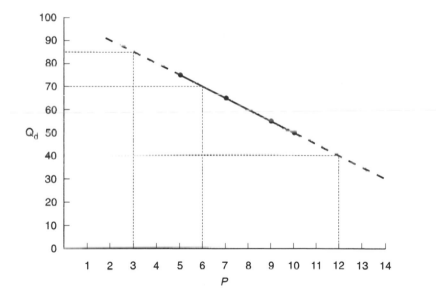

Figure 2.4 Price and quantity line

2.4
Q is set as the independent variable in this equation because it is logical to assume that TC will be 'caused' by Q. That is, the level of Q will determine the total costs incurred.

There are a variety of other independent variables that we might include in such a function, in part depending on the type of good under consideration. Wages and salaries, transport costs, foreign exchange rates, tax levels are a few.

2.5

(i) The new equation will be:

$$TC = 150 + 5Q$$

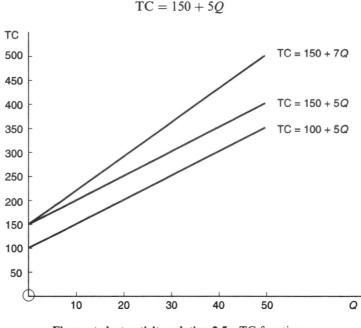

Figure student activity solution 2.5 TC functions

with the a term increasing by 50 to 150. The b term remains unchanged. On Fig. student activity solution 2.5, we see that this has the effect of moving the line upwards for every value for Q by 50. That is, the new line and the original are parallel but TCi is 50 higher than TC for any given value for Q.

(ii) If variable costs now also increase by £2 this gives a new equation:

$$TC = 150 + 7Q$$

with the ii term increasing by 2. The new TC line, $TCii$, intercepts the y axis at the same point but has a steeper slope.

2.6

From Fig. student activity solution 2.6 we begin to see the impact of the numerical parameters on the shape of the function. Y_i intercepts the Y axis at 100 which is the same as the first numerical parameter. Y_{iii} intercepts at the same point and has the same parameter value while Y_{ii} has a different parameter, 500, and has an intercept also at 500.

It is also evident on inspection that Y_i and Y_{ii} have the same parameters except for the first. On the graph we see that they are parallel—effectively, they are identical except for the Y intercept. Y_{iii}, on the other hand, is the same as Y_i except that the sign of the third parameter is reversed, negative for Y_i and positive for Y_{iii}. On the graph we see that the two lines are different: Y_i clearly follows the quadratic pattern shown in Fig. 2.11(a) while Y_{iii} follows that in Fig. 2.11(b). It appears that this third parameter effectively controls which of these two general types the quadratic function will follow. We shall explore this in more detail in a later chapter.

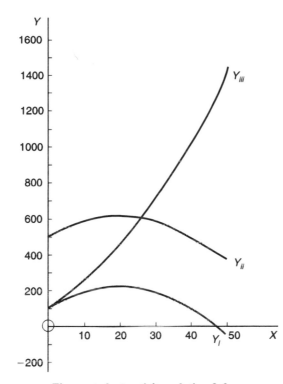

Figure student activity solution 2.6

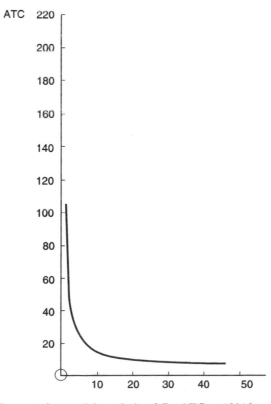

Figure student activity solution 2.7   ATC $= 100/Q + 5$

2.7

Graphing the TC function is straightforward. Graphing the ATC function is more difficult. When $X = 0$ the value for Y is technically infinite. To be able to graph values for Y when X is low (say, less than 5) we have to use a number of smaller steps (a range of X values, say 0.25, 0.5, 1, 2, 3, 4, 5) in order to assess the shape of the function over this range. We see that for low values of X ATC takes very high values but this quickly falls as X increases. In terms of economics the logic is simple. ATC is the average cost. Given that TC is made up of a fixed cost element (100) and a variable cost element ($5Q$) the fixed cost element is being shared over ever larger levels of output as Q increases. The impact of the fixed cost on each unit produced is particularly high at low levels of output and less so once output has reached relatively high levels.

2.8

(i) Rule 1: 8^9
(ii) Rule 2: 7^6
(iii) Rule 3: 8^3
(iv) Rule 3: 8^{-3}
     Rule 4: $1/8^3$
(v) Rule 6: $1/\sqrt[3]{5}$
(vi) Addition does not relate to any of the rules developed so there is no simplification possible (other than actually working out the numerical result).
(vii) Rule 1: $(10^8)^2/10^4$
     Rule 2: $10^{16}/10^4$
     Rule 3: 10^{12}

2.9

(i) $173 \times 56.2 = 9722.6$
     Rule 1: $\log(173) + \log(56.2) = 2.238046103 + 1.749736316 = 3.987782419$
     Antilog $= 9722.6$
     $\ln(173) + \ln(56.2) = 5.153291594 + 4.028916757 = 9.182208351$
     Antilog $= 9722.6$
(ii) $173/56.2 = 3.078291815$
     Rule 2: $\log(173) - \log(56.2) = 2.238046103 - 1.749736316 = 0.488309787$
     Antilog $= 3.078291815$
     $\ln(173) - \ln(56.2) = 5.153291594 - 4.028916757 = 1.124374838$
     Antilog $= 3.078291815$
(iii) $173^5 = 154963892093$
     (You may have needed pen and paper to get this!)
     Rule 3: $5\log(173) = 5 \times 2.238046103 = 11.19023052$
     Antilog $= 154963891900$
     (note the rounding effect depending on the number of decimal places your calculator/ spreadsheet can handle)
     $5\ln(173) = 5 \times 5.153291594 = 25.76645797$
     Antilog $= 154963892000$
(iv) There is not really an easy way of calculating this using 'ordinary' arithmetic.
     Rule 4: $\log(173)/3 = 2.238046103/3 = 0.746015367$
     Antilog $= 5.572054655$
     (A quick check can be made by cubing the result to see if it gives 173.)
     $\ln(173)/3 = 5.153291594/3 = 1.717763865$
     Antilog $= 5.572054655$

2.10
The relevant values for Y and Log Y are:

	Y	Log Y
1	100.0	2.0000
2	110.0	2.0414
3	121.0	2.0828
4	133.1	2.1242
5	146.4	2.1656
6	161.1	2.2070
7	177.2	2.2484
8	194.9	2.2897
9	214.4	2.3311
10	235.8	2.3725

with Y increasing by 10 per cent of its previous value. The graphs of the two series against time
are shown in Figs student activity solution 2.10(a) and 2.10(b).

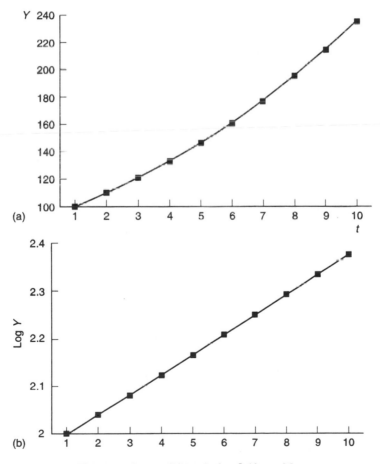

Figure student activity solution 2.10a and b

The Y value can be seen to be exponential—each period increase is larger in absolute terms than the previous increase. For the log function, however, we see a linear relationship—in log terms the rate of increase is constant. This becomes evident if we show:

$$\text{Period 1} \quad Y = 100 \times 1.1$$
$$\text{Period 2} \quad Y = (100 \times 1.1) \times 1.1 = 100 \times 1.1^2$$
$$\text{Period 3} \quad Y = (100 \times 1.1^2) \times 1.1 = 100 \times 1.1^3$$

and so on. This generalizes into:

$$Y = 100 \times 1.1^t$$

We then have:

$$\text{Log } Y = 2 + 0.0414t$$

which we see is a linear function.

3.1
The sketch for each pair of equations is shown in Fig. student activity solution 3.1.

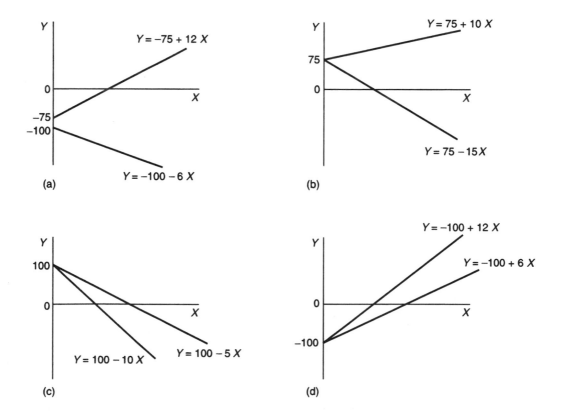

Figure student activity solution 3.1

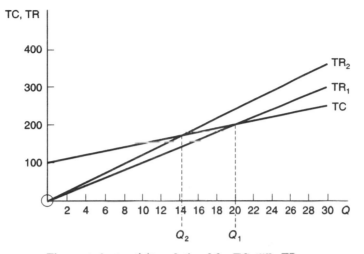

Figure student activity solution 3.2   TC, TR, TR$_2$

3.2

The graph showing the original relationships and the new TR function is shown in Fig. student activity solution 3.2. Using Eq. (3.6) we have:

$$Q = \frac{a}{p - b}$$

with $a = 100$, $p = 10$, $b = 12$. This gives:

$$Q = \frac{a}{p - b} = \frac{100}{12 - 5} = 14.3$$

The breakeven level of output has decreased to 14.3 units. Logically, since the price charged per unit has increased the firm needs to sell fewer units to achieve the same total revenue. Since TC has not changed it then follows that breakeven output must fall.

3.3

Using the general solution:

$$X = \frac{a_1 - a_2}{b_2 - b_1} \quad \text{and} \quad Y = \frac{a_1 b_2 - a_2 b_1}{b_2 - b_1}$$

we can solve for each pair in turn. Note that we must be especially careful since we shall be subtracting negative values when using the formulae. It will be helpful to use brackets around the negative a and b values to ensure we get the arithmetic right. It is also worth checking your solutions by substituting the X value found back into one of the two equations in each pair.

(i) $a_1 = 100$, $a_2 = -75$, $b_1 = -18$, $b_2 = 17$

$$X = \frac{100 - (-75)}{17 - (-18)} = \frac{175}{35} = 5$$

$$Y = \frac{100(17) - (-75)(-18)}{35} = \frac{1700 - 1350}{35} = \frac{350}{35} = 10$$

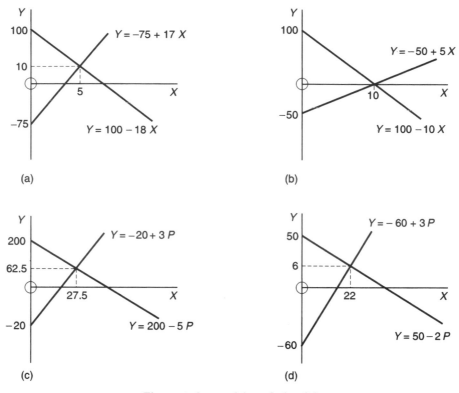

Figure student activity solution 3.3

The two equations intersect when $X = 5$ and $Y = 10$.

(ii) $a_1 = 100, b_1 = -10$
$a_2 = -50, b_2 = 5$

$$X = \frac{100 - (-50)}{5 - (-10)} = \frac{150}{15} = 10$$

$$Y = \frac{100(5) - (-50)(-10)}{15} = \frac{500 - 500}{15} = 0$$

The two equations intersect when $X = 10$ and $Y = 0$. In this case the two functions actually intersect on the X axis (where $Y = 0$).

(iii) $a_1 = -20, a_2 = 200, b_1 = 3, b_2 = -5$

$$X = \frac{(-20) - 200}{(-5) - 3} = \frac{-220}{-8} = 27.5$$

$$Y = \frac{(-20)(-5) - (200)(3)}{-8} = \frac{100 - 600}{-8} = \frac{-500}{-8} = 62.5$$

The two equations intersect when $X = 27.5$ and $Y = 62.5$.

(iv) $a_1 = -60, a_2 = 50, b_1 = 3, b_2 = -2$

$$X = \frac{(-60) - 50}{(-2) - 3} = \frac{-110}{-5} = 22$$

$$Y = \frac{(-60)(-2) - 50(3)}{-5} = \frac{120 - 150}{-5} = \frac{-30}{-5} = 6$$

The two equations intersect when $X = 22$ and $Y = 6$.

3.7
We require:

$$a_1 > 0, a_2 < 0$$
$$b_1 < 0, b_2 > 0$$
$$\text{and } a_1 b_2 > a_2 b_1$$

(i) The requirements in terms of a and b are met and we have:

$$a_1 b_2 > a_2 b_1$$
$$(100)(17) > (-18)(-75)$$
$$1700 > 1350$$

This set of equations does meet the criteria, as we can confirm from the simultaneous equations solution that we worked out in a previous activity.

(ii) The individual parameters meet the restrictions but we have $a_1 b_2 > a_2 b_1$ as $100(5) > (-50)$ (-10) or $500 > 500$, which is clearly not true. We see from Fig. student activity solution 3.3(b) that $Q(Y)$ takes a zero value at equilibrium which would not be 'sensible' in an economics context.

(iii) The individual parameters meet the restrictions and we have $a_1 b_2 > a_2 b_1$ as $200(3) > (-5)$ (-20) or $600 > 100$ confirming that Q takes a positive value at equilibrium.

(iv) Again we have a 'sensible' solution since $50(3) > (-60)(-2)$ or $150 > 120$

3.8
Here we observed an increase in price of 1 per cent. While this has the effect of reducing Q_d it did so by less than the increase in price—a reduction in Q_d of only 0.67 per cent. Since TR is the product of both P and Q_d the net effect on TR is an increase since the fall in Q_d is more than compensated by the rise in P.

3.9
(i) We have $E_d = bP/Q$, with $P = 8$, $Q_d = 20$, giving

$$E_d = \frac{(-10)8}{20} = -4$$

(ii) $P = 2$, $Q_d = 80$

$$E_d = \frac{(-10)2}{80} = -0.25$$

Hence for (i) we have a highly elastic situation when $P = 8$. When $P = 2$ we have an inelastic situation. The implication for the firm, in terms of its TR, is that in case (i) a relatively small increase in price will have a much larger effect on Q_d, hence TR would fall even though the price increased. For case (ii) the opposite is true. A relatively large increase in P will bring about a smaller decrease in Q_d, hence TR will actually rise.

3.10

With $a > 0$ and $0 < b < 1$ then Y_e must be positive since $(a + I)$ must be positive and $(1 - b)$ must also be positive and less than 1. For C_e, $(a + bI)$ must always be positive as must $(1 - b)$ so C_e must always be positive also. We can also conclude, however, that $C_e < Y_e$. Since $b < 1$ then $bI < I$ and the numerator for Y_e must be larger than that for C_e.

3.11

(i) We have:

$$\begin{aligned} Y &= C + I \\ &= (1000 + 0.8\,Y) + 250 \\ &= 1250 + 0.8\,Y \end{aligned}$$

Rearranging gives:

$$\begin{aligned} 0.2\,Y &= 1250 \\ Y &= 1250/0.2 = 6250 \end{aligned}$$

as the equilibrium level of income.

(ii) $k = \dfrac{1}{1 - 0.8} = \dfrac{1}{0.2} = 5$

(iii) With mpc $= 0.75$ the solution in (i) becomes:

$$Y = 1250/0.25 = 5000$$

The equilibrium income has fallen as a result of the fall in mpc. Since, by definition, income which is not spent must be saved this is the equivalent of saying that the marginal propensity to save has increased. Since savings are a 'leakage' out of the model then equilibrium income must fall.

3.12

The relevant calculations are shown below for the first 20 periods:

Period start	Y	C	I	New Y	Change in Y
1	6250.00	6000.00	260	6260.00	10.00
2	6260.00	6008.00	260	6268.00	8.00
3	6268.00	6014.40	260	6274.40	6.40
4	6274.40	6019.52	260	6279.52	5.12
5	6279.52	6023.62	260	6283.62	4.10
6	6283.62	6026.89	260	6286.89	3.28
7	6286.89	6029.51	260	6289.51	2.62
8	6289.51	6031.61	260	6291.61	2.10
9	6291.61	6033.29	260	6293.29	1.68
10	6293.29	6034.63	260	6294.63	1.34
11	6294.63	6035.71	260	6295.71	1.07
12	6295.71	6036.56	260	6296.56	0.86
13	6296.56	6037.25	260	6297.25	0.69
14	6297.25	6037.80	260	6297.80	0.55
15	6297.80	6038.24	260	6298.24	0.44
16	6298.24	6038.59	260	6298.59	0.35
17	6298.59	6038.87	260	6298.87	0.28
18	6298.87	6039.10	260	6299.10	0.23
19	6299.10	6039.28	260	6299.28	0.18
20	6299.28	6039.42	260	6299.42	0.14

We start with Y_e at 6250, C_e at 6000. I then changes to 260 and $Y = C + I$ to $6000 + 260$ or 6260 (with a change in Y of 10, equal to the change in I). However, this new level of income leads to an increase in C and so the cycle continues. Notice that in the last column the successive changes diminish and it is evident that if we continued then the individual change would approach zero. It is also evident that Y_e (in the second column) would approach 6300, which would be the new equilibrium income.

3.14

For T we have: $T = tY$ and substituting Eq. (3.40) for Y we have:

$$T = t\frac{(a + I + G)}{1 - b(1 - t)}$$

Given the parameter restrictions then if G increases $(a + I + G)$ must be positive. t is positive by definition of the model so $(1 - t)$ will be positive but less than 1. $b(1 - t)$ must also be positive and less than one, hence $1 - b(1 - t)$ must be positive. So the whole expression must be positive, implying a positive change in G must lead to a positive change in T.

3.15

The denominator in the k expression is positive but less than 1, giving $k > 1$. If t increases then the denominator increases also and k will decrease. Since t is a leakage out of the system the net effect on income of an increase in G will be smaller, the larger is t.

4.1

Only $D + E$ and $E + D$ are possible given the matrix dimensions and, in fact, $D + E = E + D$ using Eq. (4.2). We then have:

$$\begin{bmatrix} 15+10 & 7+5 & 11+4 \\ 6-3 & 4+6 & 7+1 \\ 4+11 & 3+9 & 2+2 \end{bmatrix} = \begin{bmatrix} 25 & 12 & 15 \\ 3 & 10 & 8 \\ 15 & 12 & 4 \end{bmatrix}$$

4.4

(i) We have

$$p = \begin{bmatrix} 8 \\ 11 \\ 15 \end{bmatrix}$$

(ii) We have

$$\begin{bmatrix} 1000 & 500 & 750 \\ 750 & 400 & 600 \\ 100 & 50 & 80 \end{bmatrix} \begin{bmatrix} 8 \\ 11 \\ 15 \end{bmatrix}$$

$$= \begin{bmatrix} (1000 \times 8) & + & (500 \times 11) & + & (750 \times 15) \\ (750 \times 8) & + & (400 \times 11) & + & (600 \times 15) \\ (100 \times 8) & + & (50 \times 11) & + & (80 \times 15) \end{bmatrix} = \begin{bmatrix} 25\,750 \\ 19\,400 \\ 2550 \end{bmatrix} = c$$

(iii) Profit $= r - c$

$$\text{Profit} = \begin{bmatrix} 29\,500 \\ 23\,100 \\ 3040 \end{bmatrix} - \begin{bmatrix} 24\,750 \\ 19\,400 \\ 2550 \end{bmatrix} = \begin{bmatrix} 4750 \\ 3700 \\ 490 \end{bmatrix}$$

(iv) We have a matrix where the columns represent the three products and the rows represent, respectively, price, cost and profit:

$$\begin{bmatrix} 10 & 12 & 18 \\ 8 & 11 & 15 \\ 2 & 1 & 3 \end{bmatrix}$$

4.5

For **DE** we have:

$$\begin{bmatrix} 250 & 216 & 89 \\ 125 & 117 & 42 \\ 53 & 56 & 23 \end{bmatrix}$$

and for **ED**:

$$\begin{bmatrix} 196 & 102 & 153 \\ -5 & 6 & 11 \\ 227 & 119 & 188 \end{bmatrix}$$

If your answers differ check your arithmetic for that cell carefully. For **DE**, for example, a_{23} is found by:

$$(6 \times 4) + (4 \times 1) + (7 \times 2) = 24 + 4 + 14 = 42$$

4.6

(i) Y and C are endogenous, I is exogenous so we rearrange to give:

$$Y - C = I$$
$$-bY + C = a$$

and this gives

$$\begin{bmatrix} 1 & -1 \\ -b & 1 \end{bmatrix} \begin{bmatrix} Y \\ C \end{bmatrix} = \begin{bmatrix} I \\ a \end{bmatrix}$$

(ii) We now have Y, C and T as endogenous and I and G as exogenous. However, we also have a term Y_d which needs to be removed from the model. This gives an equation system:

$$Y = C + I + G$$
$$C = a + b(Y - T)$$
$$T = tY$$

to give:

$$Y - C = I + G$$
$$-bY + C - bT = a$$
$$-tY + T = 0$$

giving:

$$\begin{bmatrix} 1 & -1 & 0 \\ -b & 1 & -b \\ -t & 0 & 1 \end{bmatrix} \begin{bmatrix} Y \\ C \\ T \end{bmatrix} = \begin{bmatrix} I + G \\ a \\ 0 \end{bmatrix}$$

4.7

(i) You should have confirmed that the resulting vector is the same as **r**. If not, check your arithmetic for the incorrect cells.

(ii) If the **r** vector changes then we have:

$$\begin{bmatrix} 0.016 & -0.02 & 0 \\ 0 & 0.04 & -0.3 \\ -0.02 & 0 & 0.2 \end{bmatrix} \begin{bmatrix} 35\,000 \\ 27\,400 \\ 3595 \end{bmatrix}$$

to give

$$\mathbf{p} = \begin{bmatrix} 12 \\ 17.5 \\ 19 \end{bmatrix}$$

as the new price vector.

4.8

The inverse of **D** and **E** is, respectively:

Inverse of **D**

$$\begin{bmatrix} 15 & 7 & 11 & 1 & 0 & 0 \\ 6 & 4 & 7 & 0 & 1 & 0 \\ 4 & 3 & 2 & 0 & 0 & 1 \end{bmatrix} \quad \text{Original}$$

$$\begin{bmatrix} 1 & 0.466667 & 0.733333 & 0.066667 & 0 & 0 \\ 0 & 1.2 & 2.6 & -0.4 & 1 & 0 \\ 0 & 1.133333 & -0.93333 & -0.26667 & 0 & 1 \end{bmatrix} \quad \text{Row 1}$$

$$\begin{bmatrix} 1 & 0 & -0.27778 & 0.222222 & -0.38889 & 0 \\ 0 & 1 & 2.166667 & -0.33333 & 0.833333 & 0 \\ 0 & 0 & -3.38889 & 0.111111 & -0.94444 & 1 \end{bmatrix} \quad \text{Row 2}$$

$$\begin{bmatrix} 1 & 0 & 0 & 0.213115 & -0.31148 & -0.08197 \\ 0 & 1 & 0 & -0.2623 & 0.229508 & 0.639344 \\ 0 & 0 & 1 & -0.03279 & 0.278689 & -0.29508 \end{bmatrix} \quad \text{Row 3}$$

giving $\mathbf{D}^{-1}$ as:

$$\begin{bmatrix} 0.213115 & -0.31148 & -0.08197 \\ -0.2623 & 0.229508 & 0.639344 \\ -0.03279 & 0.278689 & -0.29508 \end{bmatrix}$$

For **E** we have:

$$\begin{bmatrix} 10 & 5 & 4 & 1 & 0 & 0 \\ -3 & 6 & 1 & 0 & 1 & 0 \\ 11 & 9 & 2 & 0 & 0 & 1 \end{bmatrix} \quad \text{Original}$$

$$\begin{bmatrix} 1 & 0.5 & 0.4 & 0.1 & 0 & 0 \\ 0 & 7.5 & 2.2 & 0.3 & 1 & 0 \\ 0 & 3.5 & -2.4 & -1.1 & 0 & 1 \end{bmatrix} \quad \text{Row 1}$$

$$\begin{bmatrix} 1 & 0 & 0.253333 & 0.08 & -0.06667 & 0 \\ 0 & 1 & 0.293333 & 0.04 & 0.133333 & 0 \\ 0 & 0 & -3.42667 & -1.24 & -0.46667 & 1 \end{bmatrix} \quad \text{Row 2}$$

$$\begin{bmatrix} 1 & 0 & 0 & -0.01167 & -0.10117 & 0.07393 \\ 0 & 1 & 0 & -0.06615 & 0.093385 & 0.085603 \\ 0 & 0 & 1 & 0.361868 & 0.136187 & -0.29183 \end{bmatrix} \quad \text{Row 3}$$

and an inverse $\mathbf{E}^{-1}$:

$$\begin{bmatrix} -0.01167 & -0.10117 & 0.07393 \\ -0.06615 & 0.093385 & 0.085603 \\ 0.361868 & 0.136187 & -0.29183 \end{bmatrix}$$

4.9

For **D** we have (using row 1)

$$15\begin{vmatrix} 4 & 7 \\ 3 & 2 \end{vmatrix} - 7\begin{vmatrix} 6 & 7 \\ 4 & 2 \end{vmatrix} + 11\begin{vmatrix} 6 & 4 \\ 4 & 3 \end{vmatrix}$$

$$15(8 - 21) - 7(12 - 28) + 11(18 \quad 16) = -91$$

For **E** we have (using row 1):

$$10\begin{vmatrix} 6 & 1 \\ 9 & 2 \end{vmatrix} - 5\begin{vmatrix} -3 & 1 \\ 11 & 2 \end{vmatrix} + 4\begin{vmatrix} -3 & 6 \\ 11 & 9 \end{vmatrix}$$

$$10(12 - 9) - 5(-6 - 11) + 4(-27 - 66) = -257$$

4.12

Expanding across the first row we have:

$$4\begin{vmatrix} 1 & 3 \\ 3 & 1 \end{vmatrix} - 3\begin{vmatrix} 3 & 3 \\ -1 & 1 \end{vmatrix} + 5\begin{vmatrix} 3 & 1 \\ -1 & 3 \end{vmatrix}$$

$$4(1 - 9) - 3(3 + 3) + 5(9 + 1) = 0$$

confirming that there is no unique solution to this set of equations, something that would not have been apparent simply on inspecting the equation system.

6.1

The TR function is linear and of the form

$$\text{TR} = pQ = 260Q$$

where p is price. This implies that the price remains the same no matter what quantity is demanded. In such circumstances, the firm must face a perfectly competitive market situation where it is a price taker—that is, the price remains constant at any level of demand the firm faces.

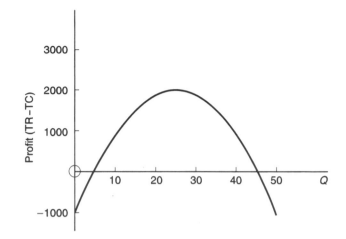

Figure student activity solution 6.2 $Y = -1125 + 250Q - 5Q^2$

6.2

The corresponding graph has been plotted in Fig. Student activity solution 6.2. In fact this function will represent the Profit function for this firm (since, by definition, Profit = TR − TC). The points where the function crosses the X axis will denote breakeven levels of output and it is evident from the graph that Profit will be maximized when $X = 25$. Note also that the function has a negative intercept: at low levels of output profit will be negative (the firm is making a loss, in other words, with TC > TR).

6.4

We require an equilibrium where $Q_d = Q_s$ or:

$$100 - 2P = -100 + 10P + 10P^2$$
$$0 = -200 + 12P + 10P^2$$

Using the roots formula to solve we have:

$$a = -200$$
$$b = 12$$
$$c = 10$$

to give

$$Q = \frac{-12 \pm \sqrt{12^2 - 4(-200)(10)}}{2(10)}$$
$$= \frac{-12 \pm 90.244}{20}$$

which gives $P_1 = 3.9122$ and $P_2 = -5.1122$. See Fig. Student activity solution 6.4.

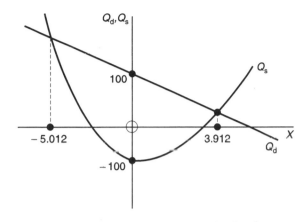

Figure student activity solution 6.4 Q_d, Q_s

6.6

The relevant calculations are shown below. We see that as x approaches 10 (and as Δx approaches zero) then the quotient value (the slope) gets increasingly closer to 150. We can infer that as we approach 10 then this would be the slope of the function at that point.

Q	Profit	Δx	Δy	Quotient
11	1020.0000	1	145	145
10.9	1005.9500	0.9	130.95	145.5
10.75	984.6875	0.75	109.6875	146.25
10.5	948.7500	0.5	73.75	147.5
10.1	889.9500	0.1	14.95	149.5
10.05	882.4875	0.05	7.4875	149.75
10.01	876.4995	0.01	1.4995	149.95
10.001	875.1500	0.001	0.149995	149.995
10	875.0000			

6.8

For $Q = 9.99$ we have Profit $= 873.4995$ and for $Q = 10$ Profit $= 875$. The difference quotient is then:

$$\frac{873.4995 - 875}{9.99 - 10} = \frac{-1.5005}{-0.01} = 150.05$$

There is a slight difference between this result and that obtained using the derivative:

$$f'(9.99) = 150.01$$

The reason is that the quotient calculation still relates to the line joining the two Q points together while the derivative calculation is technically accurate only at the specific point on the function when $Q = 9.99$. The derivative is therefore more accurate than the quotient. We can use the derivative to find the slope at different points on the function:

$$f'(15) = 100$$
$$f'(25) = 0$$
$$f'(35) = -100$$

If we refer back to Fig. 6.2 we see that when $Q = 15$ the slope of the profit function is positive (implying that an increase in output will lead to an increase in profit). When $Q = 35$ the slope is negative (implying an increase in output will lead to a decrease in profit). When $Q = 25$ (the turning point we derived earlier) the slope is zero.

6.9

Using the same approach we have:

$$\frac{\Delta Y}{\Delta X} = \frac{Y_1 - Y_0}{X_1 - X_0} = \frac{Y_1 - Y_0}{k}$$

where $x_1 = x_0 + k$. We then have:

$$\frac{\Delta Y}{\Delta X} = \frac{50 - 10(x_0 + k) + (x_0 + k)^2 - (50 - 10x_0 + x_0^2)}{k}$$

$$= \frac{50 - 10x_0 - 10k + x_0^2 + k^2 + 2x_0 k - 50 - 10x_0 + x_0^2}{k}$$

$$= \frac{-10k + k^2 + 2x_0 k}{k} = -10 + k + 2x_0$$

which, as k approaches zero, becomes:

$$\frac{dY}{dX} = -10 + 2X$$

From the derivative (which is linear) we can obtain the X value which will equate the derivative to zero as $X = 5$. From the original MC function we can deduce that this point will be where MC takes its minimum value (since the c term in the quadratic indicates the function takes the U shape).

We cannot in fact derive the roots of this MC function. This implies that the function does not intercept the X axis but remains above it at all values for X. We do not need to draw the graph but can sketch it from the information we have derived. This is shown in Fig. student activity solution 6.9. The sketch confirms that we have the familiar MC curve from economics: MC

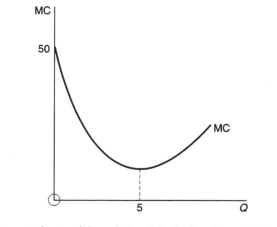

Figure student activity solution 6.9 $MC = 50 - 10Q + Q^2$

initially falls as Q increases (arising from economies of scale taking place), reaches a minimum value and then begins to increase (due to the diseconomies of scale effect).

6.10
We have:

(i) $f'(X) = 1.8X^2$ $\qquad$ $f''(X) = 3.6X$

(ii) $f'(X) = 72X^5$ $\qquad$ $f''(X) = 360X^4$

(iii) $f'(X) = \dfrac{7X^{-2/3}}{3}$ $\qquad$ $f''(X) = \dfrac{-14X^{-5/3}}{9}$

(iv) $f'(X) = -1/9X^{-4/3}$ $\qquad$ $f''(X) = 4/27X^{-7/3}$

Graphs are shown in Fig. student activity solution 6.10. You should study these carefully to ensure you appreciate why the first derivative curve follows the pattern it does, given the original function.

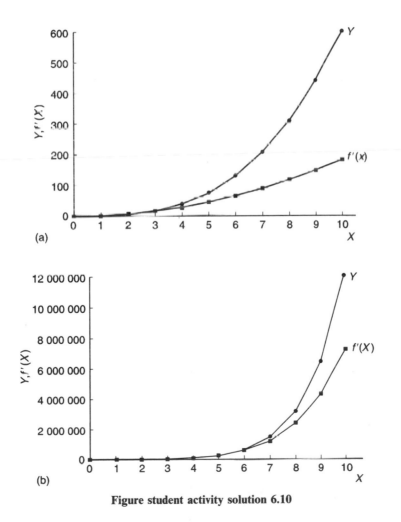

Figure student activity solution 6.10

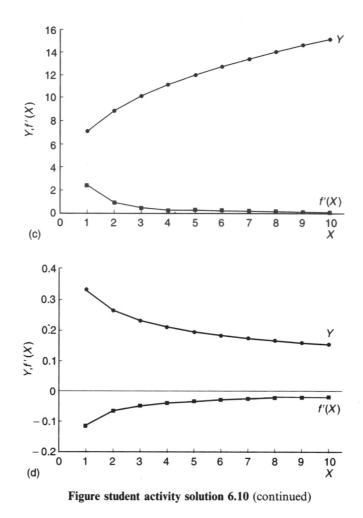

Figure student activity solution 6.10 (continued)

6.11

(i) We have:

$$f'(Q) = 50 - 10Q + Q^2$$

(ii) In terms of economics this derivative indicates the change in TC for a change in Q. In other words, this derivative function is a marginal cost function in economics.

(iii) The derivative is a quadratic and we could calculate the roots to find the minimum Q value. However, since we know that this function represents MC and that in economics MC will always be positive (i.e. the function will not intersect the X axis) then we must use the derivative approach instead. If we treat the derivative as a function in its own right we have

$$MC = 50 - 10Q + Q^2$$

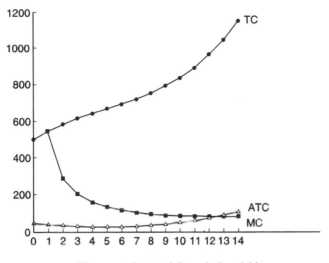

Figure student activity solution 6.11

This function is a U-shaped quadratic and at the minimum point will have a zero slope. The slope of the MC function is then the derivative of MC (technically the second derivative of TC):

$$f'(\text{MC}) = f''(\text{TC}) = -10 + 2Q$$

and the minimum point (where the slope is zero) will be found when $Q = 5$.

(iv) ATC will, by definition, be TC/Q:

$$\text{ATC} = \frac{500}{Q} + 50 \quad 5Q + 1/3Q^2$$

The graph showing TC, MC and ATC is shown in Fig. Student activity solution 6.11.

6.13

With $g(X) = 2X^4 - 10$ and $h(X) = 6X^2 + 5X$ we have:

$$f'(X) = \frac{8X^3(6X^2 + 5X) - (12X + 5)(2X^4 - 10)}{(6X^2 + 5X)^2}$$

$$= \frac{24X^5 + 30X^4 + 120X - 50}{(6X^2 + 5X)^2}$$

6.15

The graph is shown in Fig. student activity solution 6.15. It is evident from the graph that the function is non-differentiable, following the form of the function in Fig. 6.9.

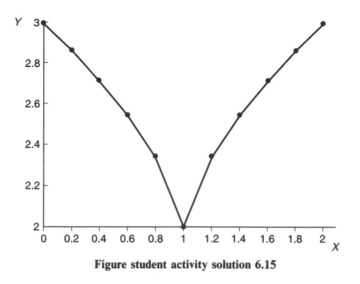

Figure student activity solution 6.15

7.1

The logic is similar to the example in the text. First we restrict $W \geq 0$. We then see D must always be positive and that D will take larger values as W decreases and smaller values as W increases. We also note that the function has no a value, hence will not intercept the Y axis. The first derivative, $f'(D) = -800/W^3$, indicates that with the parameter restriction on W the slope must always be negative and again the value of the slope decreases as W increases. This is confirmed through the second derivative, $f''(D) = 2400/W^4$, which indicates the rate of change of the slope which must decrease with W. Putting this together we obtain a sketch of D as in Fig. Student activity solution 7.1.

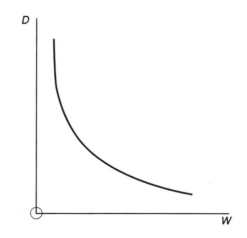

Figure student activity solution 7.1   Sketch of $D = 400/W^2$

7.3

We have $E_d = -10P/Q$ and we require $E_d = -1$. This then gives:

$$-10P/Q = -1$$

but since $Q = 250 - 10P$ this becomes:

$$\frac{-10P}{250 - 10P} = -1$$

or $-10P = -250 + 10P$, giving $250 = 20P$ or $P = 12.5$ as the price which will equate to an elasticity of 1.

7.4
We have:

$$Q_d = f(P) = aP^{-b}$$
$$f'(P) = -baP^{-b-1}$$

and

$$E_d = -baP^{-b-1}\frac{P}{Q} = \frac{-baP^{-b}}{Q}$$

But $Q - aP^{-b}$, hence:

$$E_d = \frac{-baP^{-b}}{aP^{-b}} - -b$$

Using the logic from activity 7.1 we deduce a sketch of the demand function as shown in Fig. student activity solution 7.4.

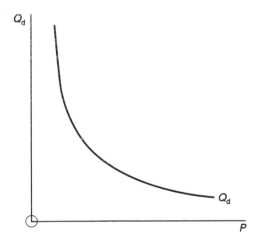

Figure student activity solution 7.4 $Q_d = Q/P_b$

7.5
(i) We have:

$$E_s = \frac{5(15)}{15} = 1.67$$

That is, at this price level a change in price will lead to a 1.67 times change in quantity supplied: supply is relatively responsive to a change in price at this point on the supply function.

(ii) We have:

$$E_Y = \frac{-3(10)}{170} = -0.18$$

Note that as the price of Y increases, quantity demanded of X decreases. This implies that X is complementary to good Y, for example X might relate to burger buns and Y to burgers. As the price of burgers increases, *ceteris paribus*, the quantity demanded of burger buns will decrease also, although at this price level cross-elasticity is inelastic.

(iii) Here we have:

$$E_Y = \frac{3(10)}{230} = 0.13$$

In this case the two goods are direct substitutes since an increase in the price of Y leads to an increase in the quantity demanded of X.

7.6
For $P = 5$, $Q_d = 500$:

$$E_d = \frac{-25(5)}{500} = -0.25$$
$$MR = 25 - 0.08Q = -15$$

but also $MR = P(1 + 1/E_d) = 5(1 - 4) = -15$, indicating that at this price level an increase in price is associated with a negative MR, implying that TR will fall if the price is increased.

When $P = 15$ we have:

$$Q_d = 250$$
$$E_d = \frac{-25(15)}{250} = -1.5$$
$$MR = 25 - 0.08Q = 5$$

but also $MR = P(1 + 1/E_d) = 15(1 - 0.67) = 5$, indicating that at this price level an increase in price is associated with a positive MR, implying that TR will increase if the price is increased.

8.1
We have:

$$Y = X^3 - 20X^2 + 13X - 50$$

and

$$f'(Y) = 3X^2 - 40X + 13$$
$$f''(Y) = 6X - 40$$

From $f'(Y)$, setting to zero and solving we find $X = 13$ and $X = 1/3$ as the two turning points. Substituting $X = 13$ into $f''(Y)$ we obtain 38, indicating that when $X = 13$ the turning point represents a minimum value for Y. Similarly, for $X = 1/3$ we find $f''(Y) = -38$, indicating that Y reaches a maximum when $X = 1/3$.

9.1

The various functions (and their interrelationships) are shown in Fig. Student activity solution 9.1. The profit-maximizing level of output occurs when MR = MC:

$$30 = 20 - 10Q + 1.5Q^2$$

and solving gives two solutions: $Q = -0.88$ and $Q = 7.55$. From the graph and from economics (as well as the second derivative of the profit function) $Q = -0.88$ is not a feasible solution so we are left with $Q = 7.55$ as the profit-mazimizing level of output. The second-order conditions are

$$r''(Q) < c''(Q) \qquad \text{or}$$
$$0 < -10 + 3Q < 12.65$$

and are satisfied.

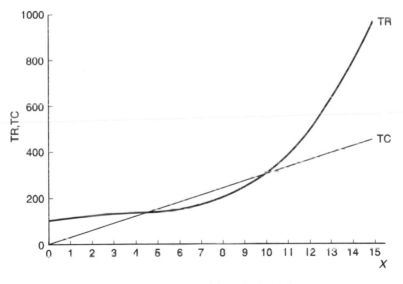

Figure student activity solution 9.1

We also see that when $Q = 7.55$ MC = MR. When $Q = 7.54$ we have MR = 30, MC = 29.8774 (i.e. MC < MR and the firm will have an incentive to increase marginal production). When $Q = 7.56$ we have MR = 30, MC = 30.1304 (i.e. MC > MR and the firm has an incentive to reduce marginal production).

9.3

The profit before tax is 14.21231 and that after tax is 2.5 less.

9.4

The new profit will be 40% of the original: 5.685.

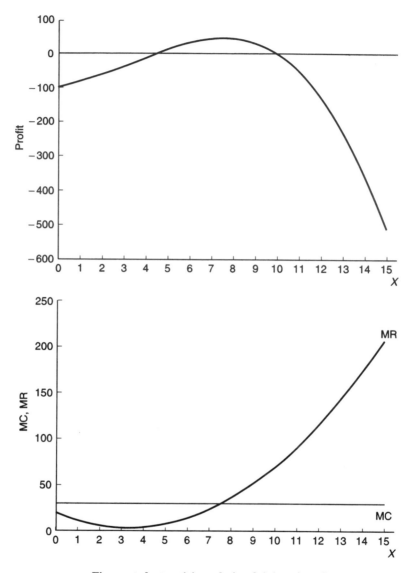

Figure student activity solution 9.1 (continued)

9.5
We have:

$$TR = 125Q - Q^2$$
$$TC = 500 + 5Q + 0.5Q^2$$
$$\pi = -500 + 120Q - 1.5Q^2$$
$$f'(\pi) = 120 - 3Q \text{ which gives } Q = 40$$

$f''(\pi) = -3$, confirming a maximum. From the TR function $(P = TR/Q)$ we derive $P = 85$. Tax maximization is when:

$$t = \frac{b_1 - b_2}{2} = \frac{125 - 5}{2} = 60$$

So the optimum tax amount is 60 per unit sold. This gives:

$$\pi = -500 + 120Q - 1.5Q^2 - 60Q = -500 + 60Q - 1.5Q^2$$
$$f'(\pi) = 60 - 3Q, \text{ which gives } Q = 20$$

$f''(\pi) = -3$, confirming a maximum. From the TR function $(P = TR/Q)$ we derive $P = 105$, confirming that the tax increases price and reduces quantity.

9.6

The original equilibrium is given when $P = 40$ and $Q = 140$. The new equilibrium is found when

$$P = \frac{a_1 - a_2}{b_2 - b_1} + \frac{b_2 t}{b_2 - b_1} = 40 + \frac{6(19.44)}{15} = 47.78$$

(indicating that the consumer will effectively pay £7.78 of the tax and the firm the remainder):

$$Q = \frac{a_1 b_2 - b_1 a_2}{b_2 - b_1} + \frac{b_1 b_2 t}{b_2 - b_1} = 140 + \frac{(-9)(6)(19.44)}{15} = 70.02$$

With this new equilibrium quantity tax income will be $tQ = £1361.19$. From Eq. (9.60) we have:

$$T = 140t - 3.6t^2$$
$$f'(T) = 140 - 7.2t, \text{ which gives } t = 19.44$$

$f''(T) = -7.2$, confirming that this is a maximum.

10.1

We shall illustrate the solution only for $X_1 = 0$ since the method is then replicated for the remaining X_1 values. When $X_1 = 0$ Eq. (10.2) becomes

$$Y = 5 + 25X_2 - 5X_2^2$$

and the derivative becomes:

$$\frac{dY}{dX_2} = 25 - 10X_2$$

which is identical to the partial derivative in Eq. (10.3). The partial derivative clearly defines a method of finding the derivative with respect to X_2 for any fixed value of X_1. The partial derivative of X_1 is:

$$\frac{\partial Y}{\partial X_1} = 30 - 6X_1 + X_2$$

10.2

When $X_1 = 5$ and $X_2 = 2$ then by substitution back into the original function $Y = f(X_1, X_2)$ we derive $Y = 110$. When $X_1 = 5.02$ and $X_2 = 2.02$ we derive $Y = 110.2372$, an increase of 0.2372 compared with the differential of 0.24.

For the second function we have:

$$f_{X_1} = -3 + 12X_1 - 3X_2$$

and

$$f_{X_2} = -5 - 20X_2 - 3X_1$$

giving

$$dY = (-3 + 12X_1 - 3X_2)dX_1 + (-5 - 20X_2 - 3X_1)dX_2$$

10.3
We have

$$f_X = 4X^{-0.6}Y^{0.5}$$
$$f_Y = 5X^{0.4}Y^{-0.5}$$
$$\frac{dY}{dX} = 1.6X$$

and

$$\frac{dZ}{dX} = (4X^{-0.6}Y^{0.5}) + (5X^{0.4}Y^{-0.5})1.6X$$
$$= (4X^{-0.6}Y^{0.5}) + 8X^{1.4}Y^{-0.5}$$

10.4
For a_2 we have

$$\frac{dP}{da_2} = -\frac{1}{b_2 - b_1}$$

Since the denominator is positive then the effect on P must be the opposite to the direction of change in a_2. That is, if a_2 increases then P_e will decrease. We also have

$$\frac{dQ}{da_2} = \frac{-b_1}{b_2 - b_1}$$

which again, given the model parameter restrictions, must be positive. An increase in a_2 leads to an increase in Q_e.

10.6
For I we have:

$$\frac{dY}{dI} = \frac{1}{1 - b(1 - t)}$$

and for a

$$\frac{dY}{da} = \frac{1}{1 - b(1 - t)}$$

Clearly, these partial derivatives will all be the same since G, I, a are all exogenous to the model.

10.7

For this combination of values we derive $Q_d = 60$, giving

$$E_{P_a} = -10 \, \frac{10}{60} = -1.67$$

$$E_{P_b} = 15 \, \frac{2}{60} = 0.5$$

$$E_Y = 0.3 \, \frac{100}{60} = 0.5$$

With the direct elasticity elastic, cross-price elasticity and income elasticity relatively inelastic.

10.8

Following the same logic as for f_{LL} we derive f_{KK} as:

$$f_K = \beta A L^\alpha K^{\beta-1}$$
$$f_{KK} = (\beta - 1)\beta A L^\alpha K^{\beta-2}$$
$$= (\beta - 1)\beta \frac{Q}{K^2}$$

and f_{KL} as:

$$f_{KL} = \alpha\beta \frac{Q}{LK}$$

and we note that $f_{KL} = f_{LK}$.

11.1

Substituting for X_1 and X_2 we derive $Y = 115.7627$. Keeping X_2 fixed when $X_1 = 5.6$ $Y = 115.7375$ and when $X_1 = 5.5$, $Y = 115.7624$. We see that for X_1 values less than 5.5085 and for values greater than 5.5085 the value of Y decreases, implying a maximum at this point. Similarly, when we fix X_1 and allow X_2 to vary we also confirm a maximum for Y when $X_2 = 3.05085$.

11.2

(i) We have:

$$f_X = -5 + 6X - Y$$
$$f_Y = -8 + 4Y - X$$

and solving gives $Y = 2.304$ and $X = 1.216$. We also have:

$$f_{XX} = 6$$
$$f_{YY} = 4$$

and

$$f_{XY} = -1$$

confirming that the solution represents a maximum.

(ii) We have:

$$f_X = 50 - 10X - 5Y$$
$$f_Y = 30 - 9Y - 5X$$

and solving gives $Y = 0.7692$ and $X = 4.6154$. We also have:

$$f_{XX} = -10$$
$$f_{YY} = -9$$

and

$$f_{XY} = -5$$

confirming that the solution represents a minimum.

(iii) We have:

$$f_X = -6X$$
$$f_Y = 4Y$$

and solving gives $Y = 0$ and $X = 0$. We also have:

$$f_{XX} = -6$$
$$f_{YY} = 4$$

and

$$f_{XY} = 0$$

confirming that the solution represents a saddle point.

11.3

We have $MR_X = 10$ and $MR_Y = 5$:

$$MC_X = 6X - 0.5$$
$$MC_Y = 4Y - 0.5X$$

Setting $MC_X = MR_X$ and $MC_Y = MR_Y$ and solving as a pair of simultaneous equations gives $X = 1.789474$ and $Y = 1.473684$ as the profit-maximizing level of output.

11.5

For X we have an elasticity of

$$E_X = -0.1\frac{60}{5} = -1.2$$

and for Y

$$E_Y = -0.2\frac{45}{7} = -0.1286$$

confirming that the lower elasticity is associated with the higher price. You may wish to confirm the validity of Eq. (11.22) also (with both expressions equal to 10).

12.1

In fact only F_λ changes:

$$F_\lambda = -(X + Y - 400)$$

Setting to zero and rearranging gives:

$$Y = 400 - X$$

Substituting back into F_Y gives:

$$F_Y = -60 + 0.4X - \lambda$$

and we can then solve for X using F_X and the derived F_Y expression to give $X = 233.33$. From F_λ, $Y - 166.67$ and from either F_X or F_Y, $\lambda - 33.33$.

13.1

(i) $f(X) = \dfrac{X^7}{7} + c$

(ii) $f(X) = \dfrac{X^{0.7}}{0.7} + c$

(iii) $f(X) - \dfrac{X^4}{4} - \dfrac{X^3}{3} + c$

(iv) $f(X) = X^5 + c$

(v) $f(X) = \ln X + c$

(vi) $f(X) = 0.75(X^3 + 10)^4 + c$

13.2

$$f(X = 3) = 60 + c$$
$$f(X = 0) = c$$

Hence the value of the integral between these values equals 60. Similarly, between the values of 0 and 4 the integral takes a value of 100.

13.3

Using the solution from activity 13.1 we have

(i) $X = 2.5$ 87.1931
    $X = 2$ 18.2857
    Area = 68.9074

(ii) $X = 2.5$ 2.7131
    $X = 2$ 2.3207
    Area = 0.3924

(iii) $X = 2.5$ 4.5573
    $X = 2$ 1.3333
    Area = 3.224

(iv) $X = 2.5$ 97.6562
     $X = 2$ 32
     Area $= 65.6562$

(v) $X = 2.5$ 0.9163
     $X = 2$ 0.6931
     Area $= 0.2232$

(vi) $X = 2.5$ 323382
     $X = 2$ 78732
     Area $= 244650$

14.1

(i) Using Eq. (14.7) with $V = 10\,000$ and $i = 0.08$ we derive $P = 10\,000/(1.08)^4 = £7350$ as the sum that must be invested now at 8 per cent per annum to increase to £10 000 in four years' time.

(ii) Using Eq. (14.8) with $P = 6000$ and $V = 1000$ we have:

$$i = \sqrt[4]{10\,000/6000} - 1 = 0.136 \text{ or } 13.6 \text{ per cent}$$

14.2

Using Eq. (14.9) with the nominal annual rate at 24 per cent the APR is then derived as

$$\text{APR} = (1 + 0.02)^{12} - 1 = 0.268 \text{ or } 26.8 \text{ per cent}$$

14.3

With a cost of capital of 12 per cent, the NPV will be £814.33. The reason why the NPV has decreased as i increases is that a smaller value in the present is now needed to produce a fixed value at some stage in the future.

14.5

Using Eq. (14.24) we have:

	I
1	257.6136
2	265.4591
3	273.5435
4	281.8742
5	290.4585

15.2

From Eq. (15.11) we have

$$a = 1500/0.2 = 7500$$

and

$$b = (5000 - 7500) = -2500$$

giving $Y_t = 7500 - 2500(0.8)^t$. So for illustration, in period $t = 5$ we have:

$$Y_5 = 7500 - 2500(0.8)^5 = 6680.8$$

It is important to appreciate what the result means. From an initial position of $Y = 5000$ (Y_0) by period $5Y$ has moved to a value of 6680.8 (on its way to a final equilibrium position of 7500).

15.3

Using Eq. (15.23) we have

$$Y_t = \frac{850}{1 - 0.7(0.75)} + \frac{800 - 850}{1 - 0.7(0.75)}(0.70)(0.75)^t$$

which gives

$$Y_t = 1789.5 - 105.3(0.525)^t$$

as the appropriate equation. We see that the model is stable since $0 < b < 1$. Calculations will show that the model moves very quickly towards its equilibrium position.

15.4

We derive an equation:

$$Y_t = 1000(1.67)^t$$

with Fig. student activity solution 15.4 showing the results for the first 10 periods. We confirm that the model is explosive.

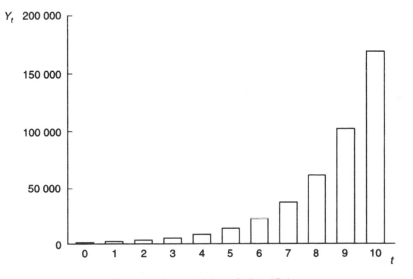

Figure student activity solution 15.4

15.5

The results from the model for the first 10 time periods are:

t	P_t
0	80
1	95
2	98.75
3	99.6875
4	99.92187
5	99.98046
6	99.99511
7	99.99877
8	99.99969
9	99.99992
10	99.99998

Appendix 2   Revision of basic algebra

This appendix provides a revision of a number of basic algebraic principles. As you may already have realized (and perhaps this was the reason for you to turn to this appendix), economics in general and mathematical economics in particular make considerable use of algebra to support and develop economic theory. It may be some time since you last had to use algebra so this appendix is intended to refresh your memory. It does not provide a detailed explanation of algebraic principles. If this is what you require you should turn to one of the many business mathematics texts. The material that follows should be sufficient to allow you gradually to develop your own algebraic skills as we move through the text. However, if you find yourself unable to follow some of the algebraic manipulations that take place in the text then return to the appropriate part of this appendix to help you.

One of the purposes of using algebra in economics is to enable us to develop general economic conclusions without having to resort to specific numerical values. For example, we may wish to determine the general implications of a downward-sloping demand curve without having to worry about the precise numerical values associated with any one specific demand function. Algebra allows us to do this, and although some algebraic procedures may at first seem more like black magic than reasoned economic logic you will find with practice that such manipulations begin to make sense.

Algebraic notation

Let us begin by seeing how algebra can be used to denote a simple economic situation. An individual consumer can represent his or her disposable income in algebraic form (after first describing that situation verbally). A consumer would 'define' disposable income as that income left for consumption after any deductions (such as tax) had been taken from the gross income. If we use Y to refer to disposable income, S to refer to the gross income (or salary) and D to refer to all deductions then algebraically we would have:

$$Y = S - D \tag{A2.1}$$

that is, disposable income, Y, is simply gross income, S, less deductions, D. Even with such a simple algebraic expression it is evident that we can derive two related expressions:

$$D = S - Y \tag{A2.2}$$
$$S = Y + D \tag{A2.3}$$

Equation (A2.2) indicates that deductions, D, are simply the difference between gross income, S, and disposable income, Y, and Eq. (A2.3) that gross income is equal to disposable income plus deductions. While Eqs (A2.2) and (A2.3) are easily derived using some simple logic it will be worth exploring the algebraic manipulations that we can use to derive them also. These principles will be useful when we come to look at more complex expressions.

From Eq. (A2.1) we wish to derive an expression where D equals some combination of the other two variables. We can rearrange Eq. (A2.1) (or indeed any other algebraic expression) by understanding that if we alter one side of an algebraic expression then we keep the algebraic relationship exactly the same *as long as* we alter the other side of the expression in exactly the same way. So from Eq (A2.1) we have

$$Y = S - D$$

The algebraic expression remains unchanged in terms of the underlying relationships (although it looks different) if we alter both sides of the expression in the same way. If we add D to each side we have:

$$D + Y = S - D + D = S \quad \text{(since the terms } -D \text{ and } +D \text{ cancel)}$$

We can then subtract Y from both sides to give:

$$D + Y - Y = S - Y$$

or

$$D = S - Y$$

Student activity A2.1
Rearrange each of the following expressions so that you derive an expression in the form
$Y =:$
  (i) $A - C = Y + 10 - B$
  (ii) $6A = 4Y - 5C$
  (iii) $0.2X - 0.75Z = 0.3Y + 1512$

Taking each in turn we have:

(i) $A - C = Y + 10 - B$

Adding B to both sides:

$$A - C + B = Y + 10$$

Subtracting 10:

$$A - C + B - 10 = Y$$

and simply changing over the left- and right-hand sides gives

$$Y = A - C + B - 10$$

(ii) $6A = 4Y - 5C$
  Adding $5C$:

$$6A + 5C = 4Y$$

To obtain an expression for Y (as opposed to $4Y$) we divide both sides by 4:

$$\frac{6A}{4} + \frac{5C}{4} = \frac{4Y}{4} = Y \qquad (\text{since } 4/4 = 1)$$

Simplifying and switching both sides gives:

$$Y = 1.5A + 1.25C$$

(iii) $0.2X - 0.75Z = 0.3Y + 1512$
Subtracting 1512:

$$0.2X - 0.75Z - 1512 = 0.3Y$$

Dividing through by 0.3:

$$\frac{0.2X}{0.3} - \frac{0.75Z}{0.3} - \frac{1512}{0.3} = Y$$

Rearranging and simplifying gives

$$Y = 0.67X - 2.5Z - 5040$$

Brackets

In fact in the last part of activity A2.1 we could have derived an alternative (but identical) expression:

$$Y = 1/0.3(0.2X - 0.75Z - 1512)$$

where we have a common factor (here $1/0.3$) which will be applied to each term in the bracket expression. The use of brackets in algebra is quite common and extracting common factors as above can be particularly productive.

Let us return to Eq. (A2.1) where we had:

$$Y = S - D$$

Let us now define D, deductions, as

$$D = f + tS \tag{A2.4}$$

where f is a fixed amount deducted from each person's gross income while t is a proportionate tax (expressed as a decimal) deducted from gross income S. For example, if income tax is set at 25 per cent of gross income then t would be 0.25, implying that deductions would be a fixed sum regardless of actual income plus 25 per cent of gross income earned. We can now substitute Eq. (A2.4) into Eq. (A2.1):

$$Y = S - D$$
$$Y = S - (f + tS) \tag{A2.5}$$

It is evident that Eq. (A2.5) could be simplified by removing the brackets and rearranging the expression. We must remember that we cannot simply remove the brackets from the expression to give:

$$Y = S - f + tS$$

You should be able to see what is wrong with this expression. We should really subtract *both f* and *tS* and not just *f*. This gives a simple rule that if we wish to remove brackets from an expression then all the terms within the brackets must have the same arithmetical operation performed on them. In this case from Eq. (A2.5) we must multiply each term within the brackets by a negative sign (since this is the mathematical operator immediately before the bracket expression). This would then give:

$$Y = S - f - tS$$

We could then rearrange this to collect all the S terms together (something we will frequently want to do in economics):

$$Y = S - tS - f$$
$$Y = S(1 - t) - f \tag{A2.6}$$

It may seem odd that we want to remove brackets first and then reintroduce them but what we have been able to do from Eq. (A2.5) is derive an expression where similar terms appear together to aid interpretation and evaluation of the expression. We can generalize the approach by saying that:

$$a(b + c) = ab + ac$$

where we multiply out the bracket (in our example a was actually -1). We could just as well have had three, four or more terms inside the brackets and the same approach would be appropriate. Similarly, we could have had more than one term, a, before the bracket. For example:

$$(a + b)(c + d)$$

would give:

$$ac + bc + ad + bd$$

and you can see that we have multiplied each term within the first set of brackets by each term in turn within the second set of brackets.

Note that the order in which we multiply through does not matter. The principle is readily extended to more than two sets of brackets or to brackets containing more than two expressions.

> ***Student activity A2.2***
> For each of the following expressions multiply out the brackets and, where relevant, simplify the expressions.
>   (i) $10x(3a - c)$
>   (ii) $(5x - 3y)(2x + 4y)$
>   (iii) $3(x + y - z) - (4y + 2)x$

Taking each in turn we have:

(i) $30ax - 10cx$
(ii) $10x^2 - 6xy + 20xy - 12y^2$ (ensure that you have the last term negative) or $10x^2 + 14xy - 12y^2$.
(iii) $3x + 3y - 3z - 4xy - 2x$ (ensure that you have the last term negative) or $x + 3y - 3z - 4xy$.

We have seen how we can multiply our brackets in an expression. There are times when we have multiple brackets. For example:

$$3x(4 - y(15 - x))$$

We multiply this out in much the same way but ensuring that we start with the inside set of brackets—those around $15 - x$—and gradually work outwards. So multiplying out the inside set first we would have:

$$3x(4 - 15y + xy) \qquad \text{(since we are multiplying through by } -y)$$

and then

$$12x - 45xy + 3x^2y$$

Expressions involving compound brackets can readily be simplified using this approach.

> **Student activity A2.3**
> Simplify each of the following expressions:
> (i) $15x(3x - 2y(y - x))$
> (ii) $(4x - 3y(4x + 3y)(5x))$
> (iii) $(2x - 3y + 4z(2x + 3(15y)))$

For (i) we have:

$$15x(3x - 2y(y - x)) - 15x(3x - 2y^2 + 2xy)$$

(multiplying the $(y - x)$ term by $2y$ and remembering the change in sign when we have two negatives multiplied). This then becomes:

$$15x(3x - 2y^2 + 2xy) = 45x^2 - 30xy^2 + 30x^2y$$

Note that we cannot simplify further: the last two terms are not identical.
(ii) $(4x - 3y(4x + 3y)(5x))$
Multiplying together the two bracket terms inside the outside bracket, $(4x + 3y)$ and $(5x)$, we have

$$(4x - 3y(20x^2 + 15xy))$$

Multiplying through by $-3y$:

$$4x - 60x^2y + 45xy^2$$

(iii) $(2x - 3y + 4z(2x + 3(15y)))$

Multiplying through the two terms on the right of the expression:

$$(2x - 3y + 4z(2x + 45y))$$

Multiplying through by $4z$:

$$2x - 3y + 8xz + 180yz$$

Inequalities

So far we have explored algebraic expressions in the form of equations, where an expression is set equal to some other expression. Occasionally we will wish to explore relationships which are expressed in the form of an inequality. For example, we may have

$$x > y$$

where $>$ implies that x must take values greater than y at all times. Similarly, we may have:

$x < y$ x takes values less than y
$x \geq y$ x takes values which are greater than or equal to y (i.e. x values cannot be less than y)
$x \leq y$ x takes values which are less than or equal to y (i.e. x values cannot be greater than y)

Consider Eq. (A2.4) where we had

$$D = f + tS$$

where t is a tax imposed on gross income, S. If we express the tax as a decimal (e.g. a tax which took 25 per cent of income would be shown as 0.25) then we would have:

$t \geq 0$ i.e. the tax rate could not be negative
$t < 1$ the tax rate must be less than 1 (or less than 100 per cent)

The first inequality could be rewritten as:

$$0 \leq t$$

so we could merge the two inequalities together to give

$$0 \leq t < 1$$

that is, t must lie within a range between 0 but less than 1.

    It will also be worth exploring how inequalities are affected if we manipulate them using the principles developed earlier. We have already seen that we can manipulate equations in any way we wish as long as we alter both sides of the equation in the same way. Let us see if the same principle applies to inequalities. Consider:

$$x < y \quad \text{where } x = 2 \quad \text{and} \quad y = 10$$

Then:

$$2 < 10$$

which is clearly correct. Suppose we add 4 to both sides:

$$2 + 4 < 10 + 4$$
$$6 < 14$$

which is still correct. Suppose we now subtract 20 from both sides:

$$6 - 20 < 14 - 20$$
$$-14 < -6$$

which is still correct (although you may have to think about this one: -14 is lower (less) on the negative scale than -6 so the inequality holds true).

So addition and subtraction do not affect the inequality. What about multiplication and division? We had

$$2 < 10$$

If we multiply both sides by 5:

$$2 \times 5 < 10 \times 5$$
$$10 < 50$$

which is correct. Suppose we now multiply by -2:

$$10 \times -2 < 50 \times -2$$
$$-20 < -100$$

which is clearly incorrect since -100 is a larger negative number and is less than -20. This leads us to a simple manipulation rule when dealing with inequalities: *if both sides of an inequality are multiplied/divided by a negative number the direction of the inequality is reversed.*

So if we had

$$x < y$$

and multiplied through by $-n$ we would then have

$$-nx > -ny$$

Student activity A2.4
Simplify the following expressions by collecting all variable terms on one side and all numerical values on the other:
  (i) $4x + 7 < 3x - 5$
  (ii) $4x - 3 > 6x + 2$
  (iii) $-4x + 5 \geq 6 - 3x$

For (i) we have

$$4x + 7 < 3x - 5$$

Subtracting 7 gives:

$$4x < 3x - 5 - 7 < 3x - 12$$

Subtracting $3x$:

$$4x - 3x < -12$$
$$x < -12$$

that is, x must always take values which are less than -12.

(ii) $4x - 3 > 6x + 2$
Add 3 to give

$$4x > 6x + 5$$

Subtract $6x$:

$$4x - 6x > 5$$
$$-2x > 5$$

Divide through by -2:

$$x < -2.5$$

(remembering that as we divide through by a negative value we must reverse the inequality sign).

(iii) $-4x + 5 \geq 6 - 3x$
Adding $3x$:

$$-4x + 3x + 5 \geq 6$$
$$-x + 5 \geq 6$$

Subtracting 5:

$$-x \geq 6 - 5 \geq 1$$

Dividing through by -1:

$$x \leq -1$$

again remembering to reverse the direction of the inequality.

Fractions

We now turn to look at the use of fractions in algebra. You will already be familiar with numerical fractions such as

$$\frac{2}{3} \quad \frac{1}{10} \quad \frac{72}{100}$$

You may also remember that the number on the top of the fraction expression is referred to as the numerator and the one on the bottom as the denominator. In algebra we may have fractions such as

$$\frac{a}{b} \quad \frac{a^2 - 3b}{2a - b^2} \quad \frac{15 - b}{3a^2 - 2ab}$$

The rules for manipulation of algebraic fractions are virtually the same as those for numerical fractions.

Multiplication

To multiply two (or more) fractions we multiply the numerator terms together and then we multiply the denominator terms together. For example:

$$\frac{a}{b} \times \frac{c}{d} = \frac{a \times c}{b \times d} = \frac{ac}{bd}$$

Division

To divide one fraction by another we invert (turn upside-down) the fraction we are dividing by and then multiply the two fractions:

$$\frac{a}{b} \Big/ \frac{c}{d} = \frac{a}{b} \times \frac{d}{c} = \frac{ad}{bc}$$

Addition/subtraction

To add or subtract two fractions we put them over a common denominator and add/subtract the numerators. We will illustrate this with a numerical example first. We require

$$\frac{3}{4} + \frac{1}{2}$$

A common denominator is some number of which 4 and 2 (the two original denominators) are exact multiples. In this case one common denominator would be 4 since the denominator 4 goes into this exactly once and the other denominator 2 goes into this exactly twice. We then use these multiples to multiply the respective numerators. That is:

$$\frac{3}{4} + \frac{1}{2} = \frac{(1 \times 3) + (2 \times 1)}{4} = \frac{3 + 2}{4} = \frac{5}{4}$$

Note that we have multiplied the first numerator, 3, by 1 since its denominator (4) goes into the common denominator exactly once. We have multiplied the second numerator (1) by 2 since its denominator goes into the common denominator exactly twice.

Choosing a common denominator

Frequently when we are trying to decide on a common denominator to use it is evident that some obvious number will be exactly divisible by each of the two fraction denominators. There are times, however, when such a value is not immediately obvious. In such a case an easy approach is simply to use a common denominator which is the product of multiplying the two fraction denominators together. For example:

$$\frac{3}{7} + \frac{2}{3}$$

There is no obvious common denominator that springs to mind so we choose to use 21 (7×3). The arithmetic would then be

$$\frac{(3 \times 3) + (2 \times 7)}{21} = \frac{9 + 14}{21} = \frac{23}{21}$$

Student activity A2.5
Simplify each of the following:
  (i) 3/5 + 8/4
 (ii) 2/6 + 3/7
(iii) 4/5 + 2/3 + 6/8

For (i) we use a common denominator of 20 (5×4) to give

$$\frac{(3 \times 4) + (8 \times 5)}{20} = \frac{12 + 40}{20} = \frac{52}{20}$$

Note that while we can leave the result as 52/20 we can simplify further since both the numerator and denominator can be divided through by a common factor. For example, dividing both through by 2 (and since we are applying the same arithmetic to top and bottom it will leave the expression unchanged):

$$\frac{52}{20} = \frac{26}{10}$$

26/10 can be further simplified, again dividing by 2 to give

$$\frac{26}{10} = \frac{13}{5}$$

Of course, if we had realized, we could have divided the top and bottom of 52/20 through by 4 straightaway. This type of simplification is quite common in economics although it can take some getting used to, particularly with algebraic rather than arithmetic examples.

(ii) $2/6 + 3/7$

We have a common denominator of 42 (6×7) giving

$$\frac{(2 \times 7) + (3 \times 6)}{42} = \frac{14 + 18}{42} = \frac{32}{42}$$

This again can be simplified by:

$$\frac{32}{42} = \frac{16}{21} \text{ (dividing through by 2)}$$

(iii) $4/5 + 2/3 + 6/8$

Although we have not explicitly looked at three fractions being added together, we can simply add the first two and then add this product to the third (although with practice we might be able to perform the arithmetic in one step rather than two). We have:

$$\frac{(4 \times 3) + (2 \times 5)}{15} = \frac{22}{15}$$

and then:

$$\frac{22}{15} + \frac{6}{8} = \frac{(22 \times 8) + (6 \times 15)}{120} = \frac{176 + 90}{120} = \frac{266}{120}$$

Simplifying gives

$$\frac{266}{120} = \frac{133}{60} \text{ (dividing through by 2)}$$

We could have performed the arithmetic in one step as:

$$\frac{4}{5} + \frac{2}{3} + \frac{6}{8}$$

$$\frac{4(3 \times 8) + 2(5 \times 8) + 6(5 \times 3)}{(5 \times 3 \times 8)} = \frac{96 + 80 + 90}{120} = \frac{266}{120}$$

Subtraction

Although we have only looked at addition of fractions exactly the same approach applies to subtraction. For example:

$$\frac{3}{5} - \frac{2}{3} = \frac{(3 \times 3) - (2 \times 5)}{15} = \frac{9 - 10}{15} = \frac{-1}{15}$$

Student activity A2.6

Simplify each of the following expressions:

(i) $3/4 - 2/3$

(ii) $2/5 - 1/9$

(iii) $2/5 - 4/7 + 1/8$

For (i) we have

$$\frac{3}{4} - \frac{2}{3} = \frac{(3 \times 3) - (2 \times 4)}{4 \times 3} = \frac{9 - 8}{12} = \frac{1}{12}$$

For (ii):

$$\frac{2}{5} - \frac{1}{9} = \frac{(2 \times 9) - (1 \times 5)}{45} = \frac{18 - 5}{45} = \frac{13}{45}$$

For (iii):

$$\frac{2}{5} - \frac{4}{7} + \frac{1}{8}$$

$$\frac{2(7 \times 8) - 4(5 \times 8) + 1(5 \times 7)}{5 \times 7 \times 8} = \frac{112 - 80 + 35}{280} = \frac{67}{280}$$

Fractions with algebraic expressions

The same principles apply to algebraic expressions.

> ***Student activity A2.7***
> Simplify each of the following expressions:
> (i) $x/(x + 2) \times 3x/2x^2$
> (ii) $(3x - 6)/x^2/5x/3x^2$
> (iii) $5x/4x^2 + 3x^3/5x$
> (iv) $7x/4x^2 - 8x/2x^3$

Taking each in turn:
(i)

$$\frac{x}{x + 2} \times \frac{3x}{2x^2}$$

Multiplying the two numerators and then the two denominators gives

$$\frac{3x^2}{2x^3 + 4x^2}$$

However, if we divide both the numerator and denominator by x^2 we have

$$\frac{3}{2x + 4}$$

Note that when we are cancelling terms out in an algebraic expression we must be careful to ensure that the term being used appears in all parts of the expression as in this case.
For (ii) we have:

$$\frac{(3x - 6)}{x^2} \bigg/ \frac{5x}{3x^2}$$

Recollecting that we invert the second term and then multiply we have

$$\frac{(3x-6)}{x^2} \times \frac{3x^2}{5x}$$

Note that we can cancel the x^2 term on both top and bottom to give

$$\frac{(3x-6)}{1} \times \frac{3}{5x} = \frac{9x-18}{5x}$$

We cannot cancel the x terms since they do not appear in each part of the final expression (the -18 term does not have an x attached to it).

For (iii):

$$\frac{5x}{4x^2} + \frac{3x^3}{5x}$$

We have a common denominator of $(4x^2)(5x)$ or $20x^3$:

$$\frac{5x(5x) + 3x^3(4x^2)}{20x^3} = \frac{25x^2 + 12x^5}{20x^3}$$

If we wished we could simplify further as:

$$\frac{25 + 12x^3}{20x}$$

One useful way of checking whether we can simplify by cancelling a common term is to break the fraction into its component parts:

$$\frac{25x^2 + 12x^5}{20x^3} = \frac{25x^2}{20x^3} + \frac{12x^5}{20x^3}$$

It will then be apparent that both parts of the expression have a common term which can be cancelled (x^2 in this case).

For (iv):

$$\frac{7x}{4x^2} - \frac{8x}{2x^3}$$

We have a common denominator of $(4x^2)(2x^3)$ or $(8x^5)$ giving

$$\frac{7x(2x^3) - 8x(4x^2)}{8x^5} = \frac{14x^4 - 32x^3}{8x^5}$$

Cancelling through by $2x^3$ we have

$$\frac{7x - 16}{4x^2}$$

Transposing an expression

The last aspect of algebra that we shall examine relates to the transposition of an expression (basically, rearranging it into another form). For example, consider the expression

$$-ax = bx - cy + d \tag{A2.7}$$

We wish to rearrange this (using the principles introduced in this appendix) into an expression such that

$$x = \text{an expression involving all other terms}$$

The first step is to collect x terms together. From Eq. (A2.7) we can subtract bx from both sides to give

$$-ax - bx = -cy + d$$

The two terms on the left-hand side have an x term in common, so we have

$$x(-a - b) = cy + d$$

Dividing both sides through by $(-a - b)$ then gives:

$$x = \frac{cy + d}{-a - b}$$

Student activity A2.8
From Eq. (A2.7) derive an expression for y.

We have

$$-ax = bx - cy + d$$

Subtracting bx gives

$$-ax - bx = -cy + d$$

Subtracting d:

$$-ax - bx - d = -cy$$

Multiplying through by -1:

$$ax + bx + d = cy$$

Dividing through by c:

$$y = \frac{ax + bx + d}{c}$$

We may also apply these principles to a more complex expression. Suppose we wish to derive an expression for x from

$$y = \frac{x+2}{x-4}$$

Multiplying through by $(x-4)$:

$$y(x-4) = x + 2$$

Multiplying out the left-hand side:

$$yx - 4y = x + 2$$

Adding $4y$ to both sides:

$$yx = x + 2 - 4y$$

Subtracting x:

$$yx - x = 2 - 4y$$

The left-hand side terms have x in common, so:

$$x(y-1) = 2 - 4y$$

and dividing through by $(y-1)$:

$$x = \frac{2-4y}{y-1}$$

Although you might despair at the thought of trying to reach this solution it is actually only a matter of practice and applying a few basic rules. Use the algebraic principles we have developed to:

- Remove any fractions by cross-multiplication
- Multiply out any brackets
- Collect x terms on one side
- Find any factors/multiples of x
- Divide through by the x coefficient

If you're in any doubt as to whether you've done it right then choose a couple of numerical values for x and solve for y using the original expression. Then use these y values in your transposed result and see whether you get the same x values (which, of course, you will if you've not made a mistake anywhere).

Student activity A2.9
Find an expression for x from:

(i) $y = \dfrac{x-5}{x+3}$

(ii) $y = \dfrac{3x+3}{2x-5}$

For (i), using the steps above:

$$y(x+3) = x - 5$$
$$yx + 3y = x - 5$$
$$yx - x = -3y - 5$$
$$x(y-1) = -3y - 5$$
$$x = \frac{-3y-5}{y-1}$$

For (ii):

$$y = \frac{3x+3}{2x-5}$$
$$y(2x-5) = 3x + 3$$
$$2yx - 5y = 3x + 3$$
$$2yx - 3x = 5y + 3$$
$$x(2y-3) = 5y + 3$$
$$x = \frac{5y+3}{2y-3}$$

This brings us to the end of this revision of basic algebra. If, at any stage in the text, you are having difficulty following the algebraic manipulations then come back to the relevant part of this appendix and reread that section.

Index